Boeing 707
Group

Boeing 707
Group

A History

Graham M Simons

Pen & Sword
AVIATION
An imprint of
Pen & Sword Books Ltd
Yorkshire - Philadelphia

First published in Great Britain in 2018 by
PEN & SWORD AVIATION
An imprint of
Pen & Sword Books Ltd
Yorkshire - Philadelphia

Typeset in 10/11 Times
by GMS Enterprises

Printed and bound in India by Replika Press Pvt. Ltd.

Pen & Sword Books Ltd incorporates the Imprints of Aviation, Atlas,
Family History, Fiction, Maritime, Military, Discovery, Politics, History,
Archaeology, Select, Wharncliffe Local History, Wharncliffe True Crime,
Military Classics, Wharncliffe Transport, Leo Cooper, The Praetorian Press,
Remember When, Seaforth Publishing and Frontline Publishing.

For a complete list of Pen & Sword titles please contact

PEN & SWORD BOOKS LTD
47 Church Street, Barnsley, South Yorkshire, S70 2AS, England
E-mail: enquiries@pen-and-sword.co.uk Website: www.pen-and-sword.co.uk

Or

PEN AND SWORD BOOKS
1950 Lawrence Rd, Havertown, PA 19083, USA
E-mail: Uspen-and-sword@casematepublishers.com

Contents

Acknowledgements

A book of this nature would not have been possible without the help of many people and organisations. Thanks are offered to the many representatives of tens of airlines past and present I have contacted over the years, including everyone at Pan American Airways, Trans World Airlines, QANTAS, British Midland Airways, SABENA, Air France, Olympic Airways, the British Airways Archive and KLM, but especially to the late Peter M Bowers and Lance Kuhn at Boeing, Gudrun Gorner, Corporate Communications Executive UK & Ireland Lufthansa German Airlines and to Kerstin Roßkopp, Deutsche Lufthansa AG for digging deep in their files.

Thanks and a big salute should go to the Public Affairs and Community Relations Officers of the many military units who have provided help and assistance, especially to Jim Robinson, Media and Communications Officer RAF Coningsby, all on 8 Squadron RAF, especially their SENGO for granting me access, Dennis Cole and all at the 927 ARW, McDill AFB and the 100 ARW, RAF Mildenhall, Jeff Duford and Roger Deere at the National Museum of the US Air Force and all at the Smithsonian National Air and Space Museum.

My thanks also go to the staff of Dan-Air Services, Dan Air Engineering and the Dan-Air Staff Association, many of whom freely provided information, advice and photographs.

Thanks are also offered to John Hunt of Ian Allen Travel, Mr F E F Newman, CBE, MC, Michael Newman, Captain Keith Moody, Captain Yvonne Sintes, Captain Bryn Wayt, Captain Roger Cooper, Captain Arthur Larkman, John Stride, Bill Armstrong, David Lee, John Hamlin, Vince Hemmings, Brian Cocks, Michelle Millar, Mike Ramsden, Mick Oakey, Ian Frimston, Warrant Officer Paddy Porter BEM. Finally, thanks also go to Laura Hirst, Matt Jones, Jon Wilkinson, and Charles Hewitt of Pen & Sword!

I am indebted to many people and organisations for providing photographs for this story, but in some cases it has not been possible to identify the original photographer and so credits are given in the appropriate places to the immediate supplier. If any of the pictures have not been correctly credited, please accept my apologies.

Introduction

It has been claimed by many that the Boeing Model 707 airliner and its derivatives marked the true beginning of the jet-transport age, and in the process totally revolutionised the nature of air transport.

Assessments of the impact of the Boeing 707 on world air transportation differs from one side of the Atlantic to the other, mainly reflecting parochial attitudes. Whereas in the United States the National Air and Space Museum of the Smithsonian Institution designated the Boeing 367-80 - the famous 'Dash 80' - prototype as being one of the twelve most significant aircraft designs of all time - those 'in the know' in the rest of the world see the story in a somewhat different light. Boeing and the Smithsonian also insist on calling the Model 367-80 the 707, which, as we shall see, it clearly is not.

Outwardly similar to the 707s that were to follow, the Dash 80 was, in fact, very different. It was shorter, lower, lighter and had both a narrower cross-section and smaller wingspan than any 707 built.

Boeing and its supporters take great delight in using phrases like '...*the world's first commercially successful airliner*' which they have bandied about over the years when talking about the 707 and its derivatives, conveniently forgetting that '*commercially successful*' is something subjective. In reality the 707 was in fact the fourth jet airliner to fly and was launched on the back of a huge military order for a structurally similar but dimensionally different design. This use of military funded design work and tooling considerably reduced development costs.

There had been earlier jet transports in the forms of the De Havilland DH.106 Comet, the Avro Jetliner, the Sud-Aviation SE.210 Caravelle and Tupolev Tu-104; but for various reasons these had failed to secure the technical and commercial lead eventually assumed by the Model 707. The Comet had first flown on 27 July 1949, but suffered from problems associated with the then little-known phenomena of fatigue failures of the fuselage. It was also designed as what would today been called a medium range aircraft to serve the British Empire routes to South Africa, India, the Far East and Australia. The Caravelle was tailored to the short/medium-haul regime of airline operations and the Tu-104 was a small-capacity airliner of prodigious performance whose operating costs made the type too costly for all but the Russians to sustain in regular service.

Another thing that grates with many is the selective memory syndrome from which Boeing and many of its supporters seem to suffer. When talking about the Comet they always mention the structural failure of a window in the fuselage - in fact it was not a 'window', it was an aperture holding a direction finding aerial - but completely fail to mention the poor design of the vertical fin of the B.307 that led to the deaths of all on board the prototype. It's the same thing when it comes to the multiple engine failures of the Boeing 377 that led to the phrase '*the greatest three engined airliner ever built*'.

Indeed, this poor vertical fin design and the infamous 'dutch roll' that continued with the 367-80, C/KC-135 and 707 designs resulted in the loss of many lives that took a lot of time, money and effort to fix; but that is seldom mentioned.

This selective memory of the supporters continues in other areas: they always say '...*the long-range 707...*', conveniently forgetting that the Boeing 707-120 was incapable of non-stop transatlantic operation and barely capable of going transcontinental with a full payload. There are a number of recorded incidents where these early -120s were forced to land at non-jet registered airports due to being low on fuel and were impounded due to the airports not having the correct insurance!

Trawling through the list of phrases heaped upon the Boeing 707, the KC-135 tanker and the Boeing company, it seems that according to some, the company and the airliner could do no wrong. After all, it was well known that the company gambled everything - by budgeting $16 million of their own money - on letting the design go ahead!

In the words of many, it seems that the Boeing 707 and the KC-135 tanker for the US Air Force was an immaculate conception borne of an idea from William M Allen, the company president - from that moment on, every other airliner had faults, seemingly almost deliberately so! The rhetoric created an image that all 'the opposition' were down on range, had poor economics, were technically flawed, could not carry as many, for as far - or as fast. The hype surrounding the aircraft and the company reached fever pitch with the slogan that just had to come from sharp suited advertising executives of Madison Avenue and is still quoted today: '*Tell your travel agent - if it's not Boeing, you're not going!*'

The truth is that accidents happen; when pushing

the boundaries of knowledge there is always the risk of discovering new areas of danger. Likewise, comparisons should only be made when comparing like for like, not sticks and stones. To make claims through what appears at best to be rose-coloured glasses does a disservice to the many thousands of people who designed, built, serviced and flew the designs, be they tankers or airliners.

Was all this 'American pride' justified, or was it merely the cynical manipulation of the facts by the public relations and marketing people? The only solution was to objectively look in detail at the history of the design, its evolution and use.

Then, in the process of research for this book I was sent a tatty old piece of paper with far too many thumb-tack holes in it. Clearly it had hung on many a crew room notice board, and from the words used, American crew rooms at that. It shed a whole different light on the subject:

An Ode to the Boeing 707
Those were the good ole days. Pilots back then were men that didn't want to be women or girlie men. Pilots all knew who Jimmy Doolittle was. Pilots drank coffee, whiskey, smoked cigars wearing their uniforms in airport lounges and didn't wear digital watches.

They carried their own suitcases and brain bags like the real men that they were. Pilots didn't bend over into the crash position multiple times each day in front of the passengers at security so that some Government agent could probe for tweezers or fingernail clippers or too much toothpaste.

Pilots didn't go through the terminal looking a caddy pulling a bunch of golf clubs, computers, guitars and feed bags full of tofu and granola on a sissy-trailer with no hat and granny glasses hanging on a pink string around their pencil neck while talking to their personal trainer on a cell phone!

Being an airline captain was as good as being the King in a Mel Brooks movie. All the Stewardesses were young, attractive, single women that were proud to be combatants in the sexual revolution. They didn't have to turn sideways, grease up and suck it in to get through the cockpit door. They would blush and say thank you when told that they looked good, instead of filing a sexual harassment claim. Junior Stewardesses shared a room and talked about men; with no thoughts of substitution. Passengers wore nice clothes and were polite; they could speak AND understand English. They didn't speak gibberish or listen to loud gangsta rap on their IPods. They bathed and didn't smell like a rotting pile of garbage in a jogging suit and flip-flops. Children didn't travel
alone, commuting between trailer parks. There were no Mongol hordes asking for a seatbelt extension or a Scotch and grapefruit juice cocktail with a twist.

If a captain wanted to throw some offensive, ranting jerk off the airplane, it was done without any worries of a lawsuit or getting fired.

Axial flow engines crackled with the sound of freedom and left an impressive black smoke trail like a locomotive burning soft coal. Jet fuel was cheap and once the throttles were pushed up they were left there, after all it was the jet age and the idea was to go fast. Economy cruise was something in the performance book, but no one knew why or where it was. When the clacker went off no one got all tight and scared because Boeing built it out of iron, nothing was going to fall off and that sound had the same effect on real pilots then as Viagra does now for these new age guys.

There was very little plastic and no composites on the airplanes or Stewardesses' pectoral regions. Airplanes and women had eye pleasing symmetrical curves, not a bunch of ugly vortex generators, ventral fins, winglets, flow diverters, tattoos, rings in their nose, tongues and eyebrows.

It took 185 pounds pressure on the rudder to hold a 707 straight with an outboard engine out. That was because the Boeing's engineers were afraid the pilots would break their aeroplane if they gave them enough hydraulic power to hold it.

Airlines were run by men like C.R. Smith and Juan Tripp who had built their companies virtually from scratch, knew most of their employees by name and were lifetime airline employees themselves...Not pseudo financiers and bean counters who flip from one occupation to another for a few bucks, a better parachute or a fancier title, while fervently believing that they are a class of beings unto themselves.

And so it was back then . . . and never will be again!

Clearly, it was a different time...
This then is the story.

Graham M Simons
Peterborough
April 2017

PS: For those questioning why no metric dimensions and sizes appear in this book, please remember that the Boeing Aircraft company used Imperial dimensions - that is feet and inches etc - when designing and building the 707. For me to convert these to metric, using an accuracy of four decimal points, makes the original figures look silly. Anyone wishing to convert, please remember that one inch equals 25.4 millimetres!

Chapter One

In The Beginning

The Boeing Company was founded by William E. 'Bill' Boeing, the son of a wealthy timber man. Boeing took up flying for his own amusement at the age of thirty-four. He became convinced that he could build a better aeroplane. He and Commander G. Conrad Westervelt, a Navy officer assigned to engineering work at a Seattle shipyard, Washington, decided to build a pair of seaplanes. By December 1915, an aircraft called the 'B & W Seaplane' was under construction in a hangar on the east shore of Lake Union, a large body of freshwater roughly two miles long and three-quarters of a mile wide in the heart of the city. Often referred to as a floating hangar, the building was constructed above water level on piling driven offshore at the foot of Roanoake Street on the eastern shore of the lake. The impression of floating was conveyed by the sloping seaplane ramp which hid the piling from view, and was reinforced by the prevalence of houseboats and other floating buildings in the immediate area. Although used originally to house a Martin seaplane that 'Bill' Boeing had bought following his decision to build aircraft in partnership with Westervelt, it was constructed with the manufacture of aircraft in mind. Bluebird – some sources say it was called Bluebill - the first B & W, was completed in early 1916, marking the modest beginning of aircraft production at the Boeing Company; it flew for the first time on 29 June.

Although work on the aircraft had been in progress since 1915, Commander Westervelt did not see the fruits of his labours, having been transferred to the east coast on Navy orders before the machine made its first flight in June 1916. With the original partnership dissolved by Westervelt's departure, and the B & W aircraft a success, corporate identity was not achieved until the Pacific Aero Products Company was incorporated on 15 July 1916 and a new airline subsidiary, Boeing Air Transport, was formed. On 26 April 1917 the name was changed to The Boeing Airplane Company - Boeing kept his office in the Hoge building in downtown Seattle, while his plant managers were at the shipyard.

The company attracted interest from the US Navy, which was becoming aware of the rapid growth of military aviation in Europe and the need for expansion of its own air arm. While the Navy did not buy either B & W, it did encourage the development of a new model designed specifically as a trainer that could be used in the anticipated expansion of the Navy flight-training programme.

Pacific Aero enlarged its engineering and manufacturing facilities and undertook the design of two new models, a seaplane that could be used for private flying as well as meeting the Navy requirements for a primary trainer and a landplane for Army requirements. After testing in Seattle, the second and third examples of the new seaplane were sent by rail to the Navy test facility at Hampton Roads, Virginia.

The lakeside hangar was not suitable, so Boeing expanded by setting up aircraft manufacturing facilities in the Heath Shipyard, a small yacht-building firm on the Duwamish River, south of Seattle, which had built the floats for the B & W, and was a company that Bill Boeing had acquired some years previously. Many of the

William E 'Bill' Boeing
(b. 1 October 1881 – d. 28 September 1956)

existing buildings and much of the equipment could be used to produce aircraft parts, but additional facilities were still required.

A large final assembly building was erected after the Navy asked Boeing to build 50 Curtiss HS-2L flying boats for the wartime programme. The Lake Union hangar was retained as a flight operations base until after the war, when it was sold.

Boeing – the Man.

William Edward Boeing (b. 1 October 1881 – d. 28 September 1956) was born in Detroit, Michigan to a wealthy German mining engineer, Wilhelm Böing and his wife Marie. His father, who arrived in the United States in 1868, was a descendant from an old and well-to-do family in Hagen-Hohenlimburg area of Germany, and had served in the German army. Wilhelm had emigrated to the USA at the age of 20, starting work as a farm labourer, but soon joined forces with Karl Ortmann, a lumberman and, ultimately, his father-in-law. Young Wilhelm bought timberland, with its mineral rights, in the Mesabi Range in northern Minnesota, built a large home, and became the director of Peoples Savings Bank, president of the Galvin Brass and Iron Works, and a shareholder in the Standard Life Insurance Company. He also bought land in Washington State in the area now known as Ocean Shores and timberland in the redwood forest in California.

When Wilhelm was logging in Minnesota he had difficulty running compass lines on his property, the reasons being he was logging over an iron-ore range. Fortunately, when he purchased timberlands he kept the mineral rights also. There was low-grade iron ore known as taconite near the surface, and below that lay veins of high-quality ore. Though Wilhelm did not live to see the development of those mining

rights, his widow received the benefits of the mineral rights later in her life. Wilhelm Boeing died of influenza in 1890 when he was only 42 years old.

Young William was sent to school in Vevey, Switzerland, leaving after a year, continuing his schooling in public and private schools in the United States. Between 1899 and 1902, he studied at the Sheffield Scientific School at Yale but did not graduate. Instead, in 1903 at age 22, William E. Boeing left college, went west, and started his new life in Grays Harbor, Washington, where he learned the logging business on his own, starting with lands he had inherited. Boeing bought more timberland, began to add to the wealth he had inherited from his family, and started to explore new frontiers by outfitting expeditions to Alaska.

He moved to Seattle in 1908 to establish the Greenwood Timber Co. His first home there was a genteel apartment-hotel on First Hill, but in 1909, he was elected a member of The Highlands, a brand-new, exclusive residential suburb in the Shoreline area north of town. In 1910, he bought the Heath Shipyard on the Duwamish River to build a yacht, named the Taconite.

Three years later Boeing asked the architecture firm of Bebb and Mendel to design his white-stucco, red-roofed mansion in The Highlands. While president of Greenwood Timber Company, Boeing, who had experimented with boat design, travelled to Seattle, where, during the Alaska-Yukon-Pacific Exposition in 1909, he saw a manned flying machine for the first time and became fascinated with aircraft. He soon purchased an aircraft from the Glenn L. Martin Company, and received flying lessons from Martin himself. Just as many pioneer flyers, Boeing soon crashed the aircraft. When he was told by Martin that replacement parts would not become

In 1909, Edward Heath built a shipyard on the Duwamish River in Seattle. Heath became insolvent, and Bill Boeing, for whom Heath was building a luxurious yacht, bought the shipyard and land for ten dollars during 1917, in exchange for Boeing's acceptance of Heath's debts. Building 105, also known as the Red Barn, was part of the package. The Boeing Company began producing aircraft from the simple barn-like structure.

available for months, Boeing blew up. He angrily told his US Navy friend Cdr. George Conrad Westervelt ' We could build a better plane ourselves and build it faster'. Westervelt agreed. They soon built and flew the B & W Seaplane, an amphibian biplane that had outstanding performance. Boeing decided to go into the aircraft business and bought an old boat works on the Duwamish River near Seattle for his factory.

In 1921, William Boeing married Bertha Marie Potter Paschall (1891-1977). She had previously been married to Nathaniel Paschall, a real estate broker with whom she bore two sons, Nathaniel 'Nat' Paschall Jr. and Cranston Paschall. These two sons became Boeing's stepsons. The couple had a son of their own, William E. Boeing Jr. The stepsons went into aviation manufacturing as a career. Nat Paschall was a sales manager for Douglas Aircraft and then McDonnell Douglas. William E. Boeing Jr. became a noted private pilot and industrial real estate developer. Bertha was the daughter of Howard Cranston Potter and Alice Kershaw Potter. Through her father, Bertha was a descendant of merchant bankers Alexander Brown of Baltimore, James Brown and Brown's son-in-law and partner Howard Potter of New York; and through her mother, the granddaughter of Charles James Kershaw and Mary Leavenworth Kershaw, a descendant of Henry Leavenworth, a famous American soldier active in the War of 1812 and early military expeditions against the Plains Indians.

In 1926 Boeing began contracting for Air Mail postal routes, a business that made Boeing a wealthy man. His company took control of a loose-knit group of air carriers, bringing these entities together as United Air Lines Transportation Company, another Boeing subsidiary, which came to dominate air mail routes. Boeing threatened to move his companies to Los Angeles unless the local government built him a new airport, and in 1928 King County International Airport - commonly called Boeing Field - opened on Seattle's south side.

Bill Boeing began investing most of his time into his horses in 1937. Between 1935 and 1944, William Boeing and his wife Bertha set aside a massive tract of land north of Seattle city limits for subdivision, including the future communities of Richmond Beach, Richmond Heights, Innis Arden, Blue Ridge and Shoreview.

Boeing retired from the aircraft industry. He then spent the remainder of his years in property development and thoroughbred horse breeding. In 1942 Boeing donated his Highlands Hills Mansion to the Children's Orthopaedic Hospital and moved to the 500-acre Aldarra Farm near Fall City. The mansion was subsequently sold to raise funds for the hospital, and in 1988 was placed on both the National and Washington State Registers of Historic Places.

On 15 May 1954, he and his wife Bertha returned to The Boeing Company again for the 367-80 rollout. This time Bertha was able to use real champagne, unlike the time she was asked to launch the first Model 40A mail plane during the era of Prohibition, when no champagne was allowed on Crissy Field in San Francisco. '*I christen thee the airplane of tomorrow, the Boeing Jet Stratoliner and Stratotanker,*' she proclaimed.

William Boeing died on 28 September 1956, just three days before his 75th birthday. He was pronounced dead on arrival at the Seattle Yacht Club, having had a heart attack aboard his yacht.

Peace breaks out – and making ends meet.
With the end of the war in November 1918, the Boeing Airplane Company, like many others building aircraft for the war effort, suffered rapid, catastrophic loss of contracts. Suddenly finding itself without work, it turned its hand to other things, making furniture, phonograph cases, and even fixtures for a corset company.

Business slowly recovered. The company started to show a profit from repairing military aircraft and building biplane fighters designed by other companies. By 1921, the company had re-established itself, and soon new Boeing designs appeared for both naval and civilian use.

The Post Office Department issued a specification for a Liberty-engine powered biplane to replace the De Havilland DH.4s then in use. The Boeing Model 40 was designed in April 1925 as Boeing entry into the competition and first flew on 7 July. The Post Office bought the single machine, but did not place a production order.

US air mail operations had began in August 1918, after starting in the United States Army Air Service in May, with pilots and aircraft belonging to the United States Post Office. For nine years, using mostly war-surplus De Havilland DH.4 biplanes, the Post Office built and flew a nationwide network. Subsidies for carrying mail exceeded the cost of the mail itself, and some carriers abused their contracts by flooding the system with junk mail at 100% profit or hauling heavy freight as airmail. Historian Oliver E. Allen, in his book *The Airline Builders,* estimated that airlines would have had to charge a 150-pound passenger $450 per ticket in lieu of carrying an equivalent amount of mail.

Then, early in 1927 Boeing decided to bid for the San Francisco – Chicago portion of the transcontinental airmail route that the US Post Office Department had sought to turn over to private enterprise. The Seattle factory redesigned their 1925 Model 40 to take the new Pratt and Whitney air-cooled Wasp engine and based their bid on the modified design with its increased capacity and could therefore add passenger revenue to mail payments. Competing bids were based on aircraft using the heavy Liberty engine and carrying no passengers, so were twice as high – the Boeing Airplane Company was awarded the route.

A total of eighty-two Model 40s were built. Their introduction signalled the beginning of regular commercial passenger service over long distances and served as the vehicle for the first regular passenger and night mail flights.

So began a new era for the company. Boeing Air Transport was formed as an airline to operate the service as a separate corporation, but Boeing Airplane executives made up the entire management structure. The original routes were expanded late in 1928 by the acquisition of Pacific Air Transport (PAT), a San Francisco to Seattle airline. The combined lines became known as 'The Boeing System'. Under Boeing ownership, PAT bought Boeing machines but continued to operate some of its original aircraft.

The first of four Model 80 tri-motor biplanes were delivered to Boeing Air Transport in August 1928, only two weeks after its first flight. Twelve passengers - and later, eighteen - were carried in a large cabin provided with hot and cold running water, a toilet, forced air ventilation, leather upholstered seats and individual reading lamps. The needs of a dozen or more passengers during long flights soon indicated the desirability of a full-time cabin attendant who could devote all his/her attention to their comfort. While some European airlines used male stewards, Boeing Air Transport hired female registered nurses who became the first of the now-universal stewardesses. The pilot and co-pilot were enclosed in a roomy cabin ahead of and separate to the passenger cabin.

The company expanded in other directions, too. In February 1929, Boeing acquired the Hamilton Metalplane Company of Milwaukee, Wisconsin, which continued to manufacture aeroplanes of its own design under its own name. That same year Boeing and the Hoffar-Breeching Shipyard of Vancouver, Canada, a yacht-building concern, formed Boeing Aircraft of Canada Ltd to build Seattle-designed aircraft. Their first products were a number of Model 204 flying boats, called the C204s to denote their Canadian manufacture.

The United Aircraft and Transport Corporation, with headquarters in Hartford, Connecticut was created as a holding company owning all of the capital stock of the Boeing Airplane Company and its Hamilton subsidiary, Boeing Air Transport, Inc. and its subsidiary PAT, the Chance Vought Corporation, a manufacturer of Navy fighter-observation aircraft, Hamilton Aero Manufacturing Company, a propeller manufacturer, and the Pratt & Whitney Aircraft Company, the well-known engine manufacturer. Each company continued to trade under its own name with its own product line that complemented, rather than competed with, the products of the other member companies. This association resulted in the standardization of Pratt & Whitney engines and Hamilton propellers on most subsequent Boeing aircraft unless specifically requested by the customer. Both the airline and manufacturing sides of United grew rapidly. The Sikorsky Aviation Corporation, a New England manufacturer of amphibians, was added, followed by the Stearman Aircraft Company of Wichita, Kansas, and the Standard Steel Propeller Company.

Stout Airlines, who operated the route from Chicago to Cleveland, was added to the Boeing/PAT routes, followed by National Air Transport (NAT) with routes from Dallas, Texas, to New York City by way of Chicago. Varney Air Lines, which ran from Reno, Nevada, to Pasco, Washington, via Boise, Idaho was also added. As a result of the increased airline activity United Air Lines, Inc., was formed as a management company to operate the lines, which like the manufacturing companies continued to function under their original names.

In addition to the offices he held in the Boeing Airplane Company and Boeing Air Transport, Bill Boeing became chairman of the board of United Aircraft and Transport Corp., with Frederick. B. Renschler from Pratt & Whitney as president.

When markets for new aircraft designs developed, Boeing was ready. It was the first American manufacturer to use welded steel tubing for fuselage structure, a feature that became standard throughout the industry until generally replaced by monocoque sheet-metal structures in the mid-1930s. Boeing again demonstrated its technological leadership by introducing this new construction, matched to aerodynamically advanced aircraft, in both commercial and military production with the Monomail, B-9 and 247 models of 1930-1933.

The all-metal Model 200 Monomail mail and cargo carrier first flew on 6 May 1930. Designed as a combination mail and passenger aircraft, its performance came from structural and aerodynamic refinements, not from the addition of brute horsepower. The traditional biplane design with drag-producing struts and wires was replaced by a single, smooth, all-metal low wing of clean cantilever construction. The wheels were retracted into the wing during flight and the drag of the air-cooled 'Hornet' engine was greatly reduced by enclosing it in a newly developed anti-drag cowling. Efficient use of its full performance range required a variable-pitch propeller and when one was eventually installed, the aircraft was already on the verge of being replaced by the newer, multi-engined designs it had inspired.

Boeing Models 214 and 215, which became the US Army Y1B-9 and YB-9, were logical military developments of the Monomail. Boeing embarked on the two B-9 projects as a private venture in the hope that they would produce the same performance advance in the area of heavy bombers as the Monomail had done in the commercial sector; but the type was not ordered in quantity. The B-9 did, however, prove a major advance in bomber design and it greatly influenced the Model 247, the first airliner produced in quantity by Boeing.

An unprecedented decision was made to re-equip the Boeing Air Transport System with the new twelve-seater machine and an order for sixty Model 247s was placed while the design was still in the mock-up stage. The Model 247 was the first all-metal, streamlined monoplane transport. It was powered by two supercharged Pratt and Whitney 550hp S1D1 Wasps (the first time superchargers had been used on a transport type) and featured a retractable landing gear, an enclosed cabin, autopilot, trim tabs and de-icing equipment.

A scandal strikes.

The formation of such a huge corporation like United was indicative that aviation and air transport had become big business in the late 1920s. However, the economic depression that followed the stock market crash of 1929 resulted in curtailment of economic support for both civil and military aeronautical activity and governmental investigation of big business of which United became a major target.

The scandal enveloped Boeing when what was called the Air Mail fiasco struck. This was the name that the American press gave to the political scandal resulting from a congressional investigation of a 1930 meeting between Postmaster General Walter Folger Brown and the executives of the top airlines. The parties of the conference effectively divided amongst themselves the airmail routes, resulting in a Senate investigation.

The Air Mail Act of 12 June 1934, drafted by Senator Black, regulated the air mail business, dissolved the holding companies that brought together airlines and aircraft manufacturers, and prevented companies that held the old contracts from getting new ones. The industry's response to this was simply to change names; for instance Northwest Airways became Northwest Airlines. United Aircraft and Transportation Company (UATC) appeared to be its particular target and broke up on 26 September

The Boeing 247 is often claimed - usually by Boeing - to be the first modern airliner, which first took to the air on 8 February 1933.

The first Model 247 is seen below, carrying the experimental registration X-13301 and the Boeing Air transport logo.

The interior of the 247 featured steps over the main wing spar which passed through the passenger cabin.
(via David Lee)

1934 into three companies: United Aircraft Manufacturing Company, United Air Lines Transportation Company, and Boeing Aircraft Company.

The most punitive measure was to ban all former airline executives from further contracts. United Airlines' president, Philip G. Johnson, for instance, chose to leave the USA and helped to form Trans-Canada Airlines. William Boeing resigned as UATC's chairman on 18 September 1934. The effect of the entire scandal was to guarantee that mail-carrying contracts remained unprofitable, and pushed the entire industry towards carrying passengers. With bidding for contracts more competitive and air mail revenue less attractive than before, the airlines placed a new emphasis on passenger transportation.

William Boeing divested himself of ownership as his holding company, UATC, broke into three separate entities: Pratt & Whitney, Vought, Sikorsky, and the now-merged Hamilton Standard Propeller Company became a new United Aircraft Corporation, while the airlines, National Air Transport, Boeing Air Transport, Pacific Air Transport, Varney, and BAT's subsidiary, the Boeing School of Aeronautics, became United Air Lines Transport Corporation. The Boeing Airplane Company, with western US manufacturing, which later became The Boeing Company.

For the military - with a commercial spin-off.
In the 1930s it was accepted that a formation of unescorted bombers could get through to their target if they were properly arranged and adequately armed. During air manoeuvres in 1933, fighter aircraft - known by the Americans as 'pursuits' - repeatedly failed to intercept the bombers and there was even talk of eliminating pursuits altogether. Funds for new aircraft were very limited and mostly it was manufacturers who funded new developments which in turn could possibly attract orders from the military.

Boeing's first bomber development, in 1934, was the Model 294, or the XBLR-l (experimental bomber, long range), which became the XB-15.

The Model 294 underwent protracted development. It was the largest and heaviest aircraft built in the United States at the time of its first flight on 15 October 1937, and featured many new innovations. Electrical power was supplied by two 110-volt A.C. generators driven by two auxiliary petrol engines, sleeping and cooking facilities were provided for the crew, and many of the mechanical duties previously allocated to the pilot and co-pilot were taken over by a flight engineer, who had a separate station in the cockpit. The structure was generally similar to earlier Boeing monoplanes from the Monomail on except that the wing from the main spar aft was fabric covered. The wing was so thick at the root that it was possible for a member of the crew to service the engine accessory sections in flight from a passageway behind the nacelles. Because of the high gross weight, two wheels were used on each main undercarriage truck.

The XB-15 was designed to use Allison V-3420 liquid-cooled engines, but the power plants were changed to 1,000 h.p. P & W R-1830 twin-row radials before completion, but even so, the aircraft remained under-powered. Two service test machines were supposed to be built as the YB-20 with slightly larger P & W R-2180 engines, but these were cancelled before metal was cut. However, all was not a total waste, for the wing design was used on the Model 314 flying boat.

1934 saw the Army Air Corps issue a specification for a 'multi-engined' bomber, but manufacturers would have to build prototypes at their own expense. Although the term 'multi-engined' was generally taken to mean two engines, Boeing had a four-engined machine in the design stage, so on 16 September 1934, Boeing decided boldly to invest $275,000 in the Model 299. The new design, which was to become famous in World War Two as the B-17, incorporated many lessons learned with the X-15, B-9 and Model 247. Powered by four 750hp Pratt and Whitney Hornet radials, it would carry all bombs internally and accommodate a crew of eight. Thirteen service-test YIB-17s went into service with the AAC and established many long-distance records.

One of Boeing's biggest pre-war customers, who would prove fundamental to the success of Boeing airliners for decades to come, was Pan American Airways, headed by Juan Terry Trippe.

Trippe was born in Sea Bright, New Jersey. Due to his Hispanic first name, people often assume that Trippe was of Spanish descent, but his family was actually Northern European in ancestry and settled in Maryland in 1664. He was, in fact, named after Juanita Terry, the Venezuelan wife of his great uncle. Trippe attended the Bovea School and graduated from the Hill School in 1917.

He enrolled at Yale University but left when the United States entered World War One to apply for flight training with the US Navy. After completing training in June 1918, he was designated as a Naval Aviator and was commissioned as an Ensign in the US Naval Reserve. However, the end of World War One precluded him from flying in combat. Demobilized from active duty, he returned to Yale University, graduating in 1921. While at Yale, he was a member of St. Anthony Hall and of the Skull and Bones society. Trippe was treasurer at the first-ever meet of the National Intercollegiate Flying Association in 1920.

After graduation from Yale, Trippe began working on Wall Street, but soon became bored. In 1922 he raised money from his old Yale classmates, selling them stock in his new airline, which he called Long Island Airways, an air-taxi service for the elite. Once again tapping his wealthy friends from Yale, Trippe invested in an airline named Colonial Air Transport, which was awarded a new route and an airmail contract on 7 October 1925. Interested in operating to the Caribbean, Trippe created the Aviation Corporation of the Americas. Based in Florida, the company would evolve into the unofficial US flag carrier, Pan American Airways, commonly known as Pan Am.

He then followed this with another merger in 1930, which led to Pan Am gaining lucrative contracts to carry air mail on his Fokker Tri-Motors and Sikorsky S-38 flying boats between the US and South America. In 1932 Pan American ordered its first four-engined flying boats and it took delivery of three Sikorsky S-42s and three Martin M.130s for forty-eight passengers. Soon, delivering air mail accounted for three-quarters of the company's revenues. In the mid-1930s Trippe expanded Pan Am's operations to include the Pacific. Pan American Airways was the first big carrier to fly regular long-distance flights and quickly became the world's largest passenger airline as well as airmail carrier.

In 1936 Trippe ordered twelve Boeing Model 314 flying boats. Each was capable of carrying seventy-four passengers and was fitted out with sleeping berths and dining areas.

The flying boat used the same wing and tail surfaces of the Boeing Model 294, a design developed from a study awarded by the US Army in 1934 to determine to feasibility of an extremely heavy bomber. Termed the XBLR-1 (Experimental Bomber, Long Range Model 1) the designation was changed to XB-15 while the machine was under construction.

All twelve flying boats were called 'Clippers' and

Left: Juan Terry Trippe, (b.June 27, 1899 – d.April 3, 1981) the head of Pan American Airways.

Below: The prototype Boeing Model 307 Stratoliner NX19901 is seen undergoing engine runs. (both author's collection.)

had romantic names such as *California Clipper* and *Pacific Clipper;* collectively they were known as 'China Clippers'. By the eve of World War Two Pan Am World Airways were flying to London via Newfoundland and Lisbon and Marseilles via the Azores. During the war, Pan Am became the largest civilian troop carrier and almost all its energy was directed to assisting the war effort. Post-war, Trippe invested heavily in new aircraft and soon they were flying to every continent.

By business school standards, Juan Trippe was not a model chief executive. He didn't delegate well. He often made big deals without telling his top managers. He almost single-handedly built Pan American into a world airline, and often acted as if he owned the world. As history was to show, Trippe, always committed to revolutionizing commercial aviation, would take every opportunity to invest in new aircraft and it was Boeing that would benefit most in the post-war years and beyond.

Meanwhile, in 1935 Boeing designed a four-engine airliner based on its B-17 heavy bomber then in development, calling it the Model 307 'Stratoliner'. The intention from the outset was to produce simultaniously military and commerial versions using the same wings, tail, rudder, landing gear, and engines from their production B-17C with a new, circular 138 inch diameter cross-section

Right: Howard Robart Hughes, head of Transcontinental and Western Air.

Below: A Transcontinental and Western Airlines (TWA) Boeing 307 Stratoliner with cabin attendants. (Trans World Airlines)

fuselage designed to allow pressurization.

The first order, for two 307s - named Stratoliners - was placed in 1937 by Juan Tripp's Pan American Airways; Pan Am soon increased this to six, and a second order for five from Transcontinental & Western Air, later to be re-named Trans World Airways (TWA), prompting Boeing to begin production on an initial batch of the airliner.

The maiden flight of the first Boeing 307 Stratoliner (not a prototype as such, as it was planned to be delivered to Pan Am following testing and certification), registration NX19901, took place from Boeing Field, Seattle on 31 December 1938. It crashed on 18 March 1939, while its performance with two engines inoperative on one wing was being demonstrated to representatives of the Dutch airline KLM. When the engines were shut down, the pilot

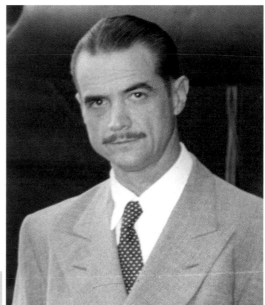

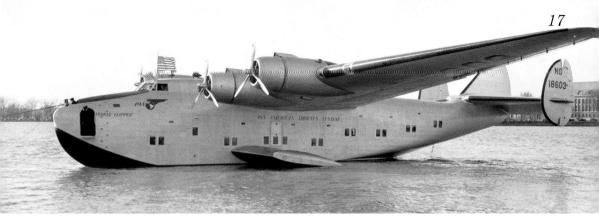

The Boeing 314 used the same wing and tail surfaces as the Boeing XB-15 bomber, developed from the US Army XBLR-1 design study. The picture shows NC18603 'Yankee Clipper' of Pan American Airways System. (author's collection.)

moved the rudder to maximum deflection to counter the resulting yaw. The Stratoliner then experienced rudder lock, where the control loads prevented the rudder from being re-centered. As a result, the 307 went into a spin and crashed. The ten people aboard, including KLM test pilot Albert von Baumhauer, Boeing test pilot Julius Barr, Boeing Chief Aerodynamicist Ralph Cram, Boeing Chief Engineer Earl Ferguson, and a TWA representative were killed. Subsequent wind tunnel testing showed that the addition of an extended dorsal fin ahead of and attached to the vertical tail prevented rudder lock. This was incorporated into the 307's rudder redesign, while also being incorporated in Boeing's rear fuselage redesign for their later models of B-17s.

The first delivery to a customer was to multi-millionaire Howard Hughes, who bought one Model 307 for a round-the-world flight, hoping to break his own record of 91 hours 14 minutes set from 10-14 July 1938 in a Lockheed 14. Hughes' Boeing Stratoliner was fitted with extra fuel tanks and was ready to set out on the first leg of the round-the-world attempt when Germany invaded Poland on 1 September 1939, causing the attempt to be abandoned. This 307 later had the extra fuel tanks removed, was fitted with much more powerful Wright R-2600 engines, and was transformed into a luxurious 'flying penthouse' for Hughes, although it was little used, eventually being sold to oil tycoon Glenn McCarthy in 1949.

Deliveries to Pan Am started in March 1940, with TWA receiving its first 307 in April. TWA's Stratoliners flew three-stop flights between Los Angeles and New York while Pan Am's flew from Miami to Latin America. Ten 307s were built, three being delivered to Pan-Am (*Clipper Flying Cloud, Clipper Comet,* and *Clipper Rainbow*) and five to TWA (*Comanche, Cherokee, Zuni, Navajo,* and

Apache) with one aircraft going to Hughes.

Hughes and Trippe were set to become bitter rivals - a battle that first came to the public attention when Senator Ralph Owen Brewster (*b.* February 22, 1888 – *d.* December 25, 1961) attempted to put Hughes before a special Senate Committe, of which he was the chairman, investigating defence procurement during World War Two. Brewster claimed concern that Hughes had received $40 million from the Defense Department without actually delivering the aircraft he had contracted to provide, but Brewster may have had an ulterior motive.

Hughes aggressively combatted the inquiring Brewster, alleging corruption on the part of Brewster. Memoirs by Hughes's right-hand man Noah Dietrich and syndicated newspaper columnist Jack Anderson each sketched Brewster as, in Dietrich's words, '*...an errand boy for Juan Trippe and Pan American World Airways,*' who pushed for legislation that would give Pan Am the single-carrier international air monopoly for the US Hughes spread rumors about Brewster's close association with Pan Am, alleging that he received free flights and hospitality in return for legislation such as his bill to withdraw government approval for TWA flights across the Atlantic.

In a Senate hearing that electrified the nation, Hughes repeated his accusations that Brewster had promised an end to the Senate inquiry if Hughes would agree to merging TWA with Pan Am. (Dietrich wrote that Hughes, in a bid to stall for time before the hearing, went so far as to launch negotiations with Trippe about such a merger.) In response, Brewster, stung by the allegations, stood aside from chairing the inquiry and became instead a witness before the committee – which also allowed Hughes to question Brewster directly. Brewster denied Hughes' allegations and made several counter-claims, but by

The 500th C-97 tanker-transport is rolled out at Renton for the USAF.

The Model 377 Stratocruiser was an airline development of the C-97 and fifty-six were built between 1947 and 1949, making much use of the design, structure and jigs of the military aircraft. Stratocruisers offered the last word in passenger comfort and a galley was located near the tail and men's and women's washrooms separated the forward compartments from the passenger cabin, where a spiral stairway led to a lower deck lounge behind the wing. When fitted out as a sleeper aircraft, the 377 was equipped with twenty-eight upper and lower berth units plus five seats.

Below: a line-up of Stratocruisers awaiting delivery, Northwest, BOAC and Pan Am.

the time the hearing ended Brewster's reputation had suffered greatly. Ironically, Hughes, for all his wealth, came across as what Dietrich described as the *'little guy who fought City Hall and won.'*

Postwar - the Stratocruisers
What Boeing had concieved pre-war with the Model 299/B-17 producing the Model 307 and major parts of the B-15 being used to produce the Model 314 flying boat seemed to be a sound business concept,

So came about the Boeing 377 Stratocruiser, a commercial derivative of the Boeing Model 367, known as the Boeing C-97 Stratofreighter, which first flew in late 1944 for the USAAF. The C-97 itself was an evolvement of the B-29 bomber that dropped the two atom bombs on Hiroshima and Nagasaki to end World War Two.

William Allen, who had become President of The Boeing Company in September 1945, sought to introduce a new civilian aircraft to replace greatly reduced military production after Second World War.

The Model 377 Stratocruiser was the only commercial product on Boeing's drawing board in 1945 and Bill Allen went ahead with production of fifty airframes. At the time, there were no orders, but it was the only way to save the company's civil aircraft business.

This has often been described as a gamble, but in truth, a lot of the development costs of the 377 had been borne by the Model 367 Stratofreighter.

On 29 November 1945 Pan American World Airways became the launch customer with the largest commercial aircraft order in history, a $24,500,000 order for twenty Stratocruisers. Earlier in 1945 a C-97 had flown from Seattle to Washington, D.C. nonstop in six hours and four minutes; with this knowledge, and with Pan Am President Juan Trippe's high regard for Boeing after their success with the Boeing 314 Clipper, Pan Am was confident in ordering the expensive airliner.

The 377 shared the distinctive design of the C-97, with a 'double-bubble' fuselage cross-section, resembling a figure-8, with 6,600 cubic feet of interior space, allowing for pressurization of a large cabin with two passenger decks. Outside diameter of the upper lobe was 132 inches, compared to 125 inches for the DC-6 and other Douglas types. The lower deck served as a lounge, seating fourteen.

The Model 377 had innovations such as higher cabin pressure and air conditioning; the superchargers on the four Pratt & Whitney R-4360 engines increased power at altitude and allowed consistent cabin pressure. The wing was the Boeing 117 airofoil, regarded as the 'fastest wing of its time'.

First flight of the Model 377 was on 8 July 1947, two years after the first commercial order. Supposedly, the flight test fleet of three 377s underwent 250,000 miles of flying to test its limits before certification.

As the launch customer, Pan Am was the first to begin scheduled service, from San Francisco to Honolulu in April 1949. By the end of that year, Pan Am, BOAC and American Overseas Airlines were flying Model 377s transatlantic, while Northwest Orient Airlines was flying in the United States; in January 1950 United began flights from San Francisco to Honolulu. By the fall of 1950, Northwest Orient was serving New York City, Chicago, Detroit, Minneapolis/St. Paul, Milwaukee and Spokane with the aircraft and was also operating the Stratocruiser nonstop between Seattle and Honolulu.

Despite a service record plagued by disasters arising from the Curtiss Electric propellers fitted to early production aircraft, the 377 was one of the most advanced and capable of the propeller-driven transports, and among the most luxurious. A total of 56 were built, one prototype (later reconditioned) and

N7301C, a 1049A Starliner of Trans World Airlines.

The ultimate in piston engined airliners as far as American Airlines was concerned, was the Douglas DC-7B. This is N303AA 'Flagship Missouri' delivered in February 1954. Its four Wright R-3350 turbo-compound engines allowed eight hour non-stop coast-to-coast operations in direct competition with TWA's Super Constellations.

55 production aircraft. Within six years of first delivery, the Stratocruiser had carried 3,199,219 passengers; it had completed 3,597 transcontinental flights, and 27,678 transatlantic crossings, and went between the United States and South America 822 times. It also lost the Boeing company $7 million.

In 1953, United's Chief Executive, Ray Ireland, went on record describing the Stratocruiser as unbeatable as a luxury attraction but totally uneconomic. Ireland said PAA's Stratocruiser competition to Hawaii induced United to buy the aircraft originally. In 1950 United's seven Model 377s averaged $2.46 direct operating cost per aircraft-mile, and that '...indirect costs are generally considered to be equal or greater than the direct costs.' So a 57-passenger Model 377 was unlikely to make money anyway.

Other rivals

By the end of the Second World War the Boeing Aircraft Company had established itself as the premier manufacturer of bomber aircraft in the USA. Boeing had developed the technology, skills and expertise to build large, multi-engined aircraft, but had lost touch with the airlines and the needs of the civilian market. In the immediate post-war years, Boeing saw their rivals for airliner manufacture as being Lockheed aircraft with their Constellations and Douglas with their Douglas Commercial range of airliners - and Boeing were definitely in third place, especially when one considers the numbers built. Both Lockheed and Douglas built many hundreds of their airliner designs, whereas Boeing only built fifty-six Stratocruisers. Boeing would have to sell itself as a company to the airlines, as much as it had to sell its products; and with a much less experienced sales force.

Douglas, with its long line of successful airliners from the DC-3 onwards, had a reputation of listening to what the airlines wanted. Lockheed meanwhile had developed their Constellation on the back of

government contracts and were the undisputed leaders in the commercial aircraft sphere.

Howard Hughes and TWA, Juan Trippe and Pan American were placing huge orders for the time, with their marketing men constantly pushing the holy trinity of speed, distance and luxury.

Douglas' DC-4, led to the DC-6 and the DC-7 whilst Lockheed's Model 049 Constellation evolved through several stages into the L-1049 series. Parallel to airframe development, engine advances struggled to keep pace. Both aircraft companies and Pratt & Witney developed multi-cylinder-row turbo-compound engines of ever-increasing complexity - thus demanding more and more maintenance time - employing a turbine to recover energy from the exhaust gases.

The turbine was usually mechanically connected to the crankshaft, such as on the Wright R-3350 Duplex-Cyclone engines fitted to Douglas DC-7B and Lockheed L-1049 Super Constellation airliners, but electric and hydraulic power recovery systems were investigated as well. Recovery turbines increased the output of the engine without increasing its fuel consumption, thus reducing the specific fuel consumption.

Reciprocating engines tended to be operated at higher levels of power output for longer periods of time, this increasing the risk of over-stressing and overheating. However, not only did the horsepower increase, but so did the mechanical complexity of the engines, which in turn led to a higher likelihood of mechanical failure.

Across the board, failures of reciprocating engines became more and more common and it was obvious that piston-engine development had reached its peak with further advances becoming self-defeating. Clearly it was time for a different, less complex style of powerplant, but the airliner manufacturers, engine makers and airlines were reticent.

Chapter Two

Playing catch-up

The sharp-suited copywiters and executives in the Madison Avenue advertising agencies would have the public believe that the Boeing 707 was an all-American jet airliner, designed by white-shirted pocket-protector wearing college graduates with flat-top crew cuts to revolutionalise air transport and powered by the latest engine technology. It was draped in Old Glory and as American as baseball, hot dogs, and Mom's apple pie. Nothing could be further from the truth.

In reality, America was late to enter the era of the jet engine – indeed, it were dismissive of it. In 1923, US physicist Edgar Buckingham of the US National Bureau of Standards published report No.159 expressing scepticism that jet engines would be economically competitive with propeller driven aircraft at the low altitudes and airspeeds: '...*there does not appear to be, at present, any prospect whatever that jet propulsion of the sort here considered will ever be of practical value, even for military purposes.*'

From this moment on, apart from a few visionaries, American officers, engineers scientists and industrialists failed to devote significant attention to aviation turbine engine research.

The jet age began in great secrecy on 27 August 1939, when the German Heinkel He 178 research aircraft, powered with a 1,100 pound thrust Heinkel He 53 gas-turbine - or jet engine - made its first flight in the hands of Erich Warsitz.

A young German physicist, Hans Joachim Pabst von Ohain, worked for Ernst Heinkel, specialising in advanced engines and pioneered this development work. von Ohain was born 14 December 1911, in Dessau, Germany. While pursuing doctorate work at the University of Gottingen, he forumulated his theory of jet propulsion in 1933. After receiving his degree in 1935, he became a junior assistant to Robert Wichard Pohl, director of the university's Physical Institute.

Granted a patent for his turbojet engine in 1936, Ohain joined the Heinkel Company in Rostock, Germany. By 1937 he had built a factory-tested demonstration engine and, by 1939, a fully operational jet aircraft, the He 178. Soon after, Ohain directed the construction of the He S.3B, the first fully operational centrifugal-flow turbojet engine. Ohain developed an improved engine, the He S.8A, which was first flown on 2 April 1941. This engine design, however, was less efficient than one designed by Anselm Franz, which powered the Me 262, the first operational jet fighter aircraft.

Ohain was one of hundreds of German scientists, academics and technicians who were 'sheep-dipped' under Operation Paperclip and moved to the United States in the immediate post-war years, becoming a research scientist in 1947 at Wright-Patterson Air Force Base, the Aerospace Research Laboratories, Wright's Aero Propulsion Laboratory, and the University of Dayton Research Institute.

This process of changing names and identities became common practice – the term 'sheep-dipping' was developed by those in the intelligence community and is more-or-less slang and not official terminology. It is commonly used in intelligence circles as a way of saying a person or item has been given an alternate identity.

This new form of propulsion met resistance on the part of German officialdom and, fortunately for the Allies, the operational debut of the jet fighter was delayed for nearly three years. Even then it was grossly mismanaged.

In the meantime, an entirely independent research programme was being conducted in England, where the first British jet, the Gloster E28/39, made its first flight on 14 May 1941. The development of this machine dates back to 1928, when RAF College Cranwell cadet Frank Whittle formally submitted his ideas for a turbo-jet to his superiors. On 16 January 1930, Whittle submitted his first patent (granted in 1932) that showed a two-stage axial compressor feeding a single-sided centrifugal compressor. Practical axial compressors were made possible by ideas from A.A. Griffith in a seminal paper in 1926

(*An Aerodynamic Theory of Turbine Design*).

Whittle would later concentrate on the simpler centrifugal compressor only, for a variety of practical reasons. Whittle had his first engine running in April 1937. It was liquid-fuelled, and included a self-contained fuel pump. Whittle's team experienced near-panic when the engine would not stop, accelerating even after the fuel was switched off. It turned out that fuel had leaked into the engine and accumulated in pools, so the engine would not stop until all the leaked fuel had burned off. Whittle was unable to interest the government in his invention, and development continued at a slow pace.

As soon as the merits of this new type of powerplant were acknowledged by the Royal Air Force, jet fighters were designed and put into production.

In America, there had been two exceptions to ignoring any development of the jet engine – in 1939 both Northrop Aircraft and the Lockheed Corporation both started work on turbine engines, Lockheed with their twin-spool, axial flow L-1000 turbojet that was expected to develop 5,000 pounds of thrust and Northrop with their Turbodyne axial-flow propeller-turbine which eventually developed 10,000 shaft horsepower but did not progress past the development stage.

Since the Lockheed design was never completed, and the only three Northrop prototype engines did not bench-run until 1947, the Americans had to rely on British assistance and the capabilities of its turbine manufacturers to get into the jet age.

It was not until 1941 that the powers that be decided to start work on their own concept designs for a jet aircraft that was something of a contest between Bell and Lockheed Aircraft.

Major General Henry H. 'Hap' Arnold became aware of the United Kingdom's jet programme when he attended a demonstration of the Gloster E.28/39 in April 1941. The subject had been mentioned to the Americans as part of the Tizard Mission the previous year. General Arnold requested, and was given, the plans for the aircraft's engine, Frank Whittle's Power Jets W.1, which he took back to the US

The Tizard Mission, officially the British Technical and Scientific Mission, was a delegation that visited the USA in order to obtain the industrial resources to exploit the military potential of the research and development work completed by the UK up to the beginning of World War Two, but which Britain itself could not exploit due to the immediate requirements of war-related production. It received its popular name from the program's instigator, Henry Tizard FRS (*b*.23 August 1885 – *d*.9 October 1959) - a British scientist and chairman of the Aeronautical Research Committee, which had propelled the development of radar.

The objective of the mission was to cooperate in science and technology with the US, which at that time was neutral and, in many quarters, unwilling to

The Northrop company-designed gas-turbine engine - named the Turbodyne on its test bed at Hawthorne, CA.

become involved in the war. The US had greater resources for development and production, which Britain desperately wanted to use. The information provided by the British delegation was subject to carefully vetted security procedures, and contained some of the greatest scientific advances made during the war. The shared technology included Radar (in particular the greatly improved cavity magnetron which the American historian James Phinney Baxter III later called '...*the most valuable cargo ever brought to our shores*'), the design for the 'Variable Time' or proximity fuse, details of Frank Whittle's jet engine and the Frisch-Peierls memorandum describing the feasibility of an atomic bomb. Though these may be considered the most significant, many other items were also transported, including designs for rockets, superchargers, gyroscopic gunsights, submarine detection devices, self-sealing fuel tanks and plastic explosives.

Tizard met with both Vannevar Bush, the chairman of National Defense Research Committee, and George W. Lewis of the National Advisory Committee for Aeronautics (NACA) and told them about jet propulsion, but he revealed very little except the seriousness of British efforts. Bush later recalled: '*The interesting parts of the subject, namely the*

explicit way in which the investigation was being carried out, were apparently not known to Tizard, and at least he did not give me any indication that he knew such details'.

It was not until later that Bush realised that the development of the Whittle engine was far ahead of the NACA project.

In July 1941 he wrote to General 'Hap' Arnold, commander of the USAAF, '*It becomes evident that the Whittle engine is a satisfactory development and that it is approaching production, although we yet do not know just how satisfactory it is. Certainly if it is now in such state that the British plans call for large production in five months, it is extraordinarily advanced and no time should be lost on the matter*'.

Bush recommended that arrangements should be made to produce the British engine in the United States by finding a suitable company.

The American political establishment had many proponents of neutrality - and even a fair number of isolationalists - for the USA and so there were barriers to co-operation. This was despite the fact that there were a large number of 'Special Observers' operating out of the American Embassy in London from as early as January 1939 whose duties included getting their hands on as much information regarding British new technology as possible. However, it seems that the information regarding British activities gained by the Special Observers had not yet percolated down to the level of the NACA.

Tizard decided that the most productive approach to circumvent any Congressional 'objections' would be simply to give the information and use America's productive capacity. Neither Winston Churchill nor the radar pioneer, Robert Watson-Watt, were initially in agreement with these tactics for the mission. Nevertheless, Tizard first arranged for Archibald Hill,

Above: Sir Henry Tizard FRS (b. 23 August 1885 – d. 9 October 1959)

Right: Air Commodore Sir Frank Whittle OM KBE CB FRS FRAeS (b.1 June 1907 – d. 9 August 1996)

Two views of the Whittle W1 X and its installation in a Bell YP-59. (author's collection)

another scientific member of the committee, to go to Washington to explore the possibilities.

As a result, the National Advisory Committee for Aeronautics set up a special Committee on Jet Propulsion, which in turn asked Allis Chalmers, General Electric and Westinghouse, the nations three leading turbine manufacturers to participate in the Committees investigations.

General Arnold arranged for an example of the engine, the Whittle W.1X turbojet, to be flown to the US in the bomb bay of a USAAC Consolidated B-24 Liberator, along with drawings for the more powerful W.2B/23 engine and a small team of Power Jets engineers.

On 4 September 1941 Hap Arnold offered the General Electric engine company a contract to 'build fifteen 'Type I superchargers' based on the Whittle W2D turbojet design. It is worthy of record to state that the letter 'I' designation was chosen to give the appearance that GE, which was then manufacturing turbo-superchargers for contemporary aircraft engines-such as the Type B fitted to the Wright R-1820 radials powering Boeing B-17s - would merely be working on an improved turbo-supercharger. The American version of the Whittle W2B engine, which subsequently became the General Electric I-A in order to disguise its origins.

On the following day, Arnold approached Lawrence Dale Bell, head of Bell Aircraft Corporation, to build a fighter to utilise it. Bell agreed and set to work on producing three prototypes. As a disinformation tactic, the USAAF gave the project the designation 'P-59A', to suggest it was a development of the unrelated Bell XP-59 fighter project that had been cancelled. The design was finalised on 9 January 1942, and construction began. In March, long before the prototypes were completed, an order for 13 'YP-59A' pre-production machines was added to the contract.

Bench-testing of the GE Type I started in Lynn, Massachusetts, on 18 April 1942 by a GE group under Dale Streid and a pair of Type I-A engines powered the Bell XP-59B on its first flight on 1 October. General Electric went on to develop uprated versions of the Type I -the I-14, I-16, and 1-20.

Thirteen service test YP-59As had a more powerful engine than its predecessor, the General Electric J31, but the improvement in performance was negligible with top speed increased by only 5 mph and a reduction in the time they could be used before an overhaul was needed. One of these aircraft, the third YP-59A (S/n: 42-22611) was supplied to the Royal Air Force (receiving British serial RG362/G), in exchange for the first production Gloster Meteor I, EE210/G. British pilots found that the aircraft compared very unfavorably with the jets that they were already flying. The YP-59A also compared unfavourably to the propeller-driven North American P-51 Mustang. Two YP-59A Airacomets (42-108778 and 42-100779) were also delivered to the US Navy where they were evaluated as the YF2L-1 but quickly found completely unsuitable for carrier operations.

The United States Army Air Force was not impressed by the P-59's performance and cancelled the contract when fewer than half of the aircraft ordered had been produced. Although no P-59s went into combat, it paved the way for another design generation of US turbojet-powered aircraft and was the first turbojet fighter to have its turbojet engine and air inlet nacelles integrated within the main fuselage.

The Lockheed XP-80 had a conventional all metal airframe, with a slim low wing and tricycle undercarriage and had straight wings like the previous propeller-driven machines. Concept work began on the XP-80 in 1943 with a design being built around the blueprint dimensions of a British Halford H-1B turbojet, manufactured by and later called the De Havilland Goblin, an engine to which the Lockheed design team did not initially have actual access. Lockheed's team, of twenty-eight engineers, was led by the legendary Clarence L. 'Kelly' Johnson. This teaming was an early product of Lockheed's Skunk Works.

Previously, Kelly Johnson had approached the War Department to build an experimental design, but was turned down, it is alleged because Johnson's design required an entirely new type of engine and the Air Forces were more eager to obtain multitudes of existing piston-engined aircraft than to experiment with new kinds of machines.

Then, on 17 June 1943 while at Eglin Field, Florida, Johnson met with Colonel M S Roth of the Materiel Command's Wright Field research and development division. Roth told him of the poor flight tests of the Bell P.59A. Roth is supposed to have asked Johnson *'Kelly, why can't you design a jet plane around that British engine?'*

With the Germans and British clearly far ahead in development, Lockheed was pressed to develop a comparable jet in as short a time as possible. Kelly Johnson submitted a design proposal in mid-June and promised that the prototype would be ready for testing in 180 days. The Skunk Works team, beginning 26 June 1943, produced the airframe in 143 days, delivering it to Muroc Army Air Base. This was the XP-80A. The project was so secret that only five of the more than 130 people working on it knew that they were developing a jet aircraft.

The arrival - and subsequent use - of some of the very few first jet engines by the Americans was something of a comedy of errors, as C Martin Sharp was later to describe in *'DH a history of de Havilland'*: *'Information was being passed to the Americans all along and on October 30 1943, when de Havilland had done about thirteen hours of test flying with the Vampire, they sent off one of their first few engines to the Lockheed Company of California, to be installed in their new X.P.80A [sic] aircraft, designed for jet propulsion. With it went one of the best DH development engineers, Bristow, who could ill be spared.*

That foggy Saturday the specially packed Goblin

Left: A De Havilland Gobin jet turbine of a type supplied to the Americans.

Below: Guy Bristow, chief test engineer for De Havillands (right) and tester Mr F Bench check over a Goblin on the test stands at Hatfield. Guy Bristow went over to the USA with two of the very early Gobins to get the American jet programme going. (both DH via BAE Hatfield)

left Welsh Harp, Hendon, on a lorry for Prestwick; by special concession the driver was allowed to use undimmed headlights. The case was loaded into a C-54 which left Prestwick on Sunday evening, transhipped at New York, and arrived (with the engineer) at Burbank, California, on Tuesday evening.

The use of 'undimmed headlights' was highly unusual as the UK was under strict wartime blackout restrictions. By the time Guy Bristow reached Burbank with his charge, he found one further obstacle in his way - he was detained by the police because Lockheed officials could not vouch for him!

Previously a well-finished mock-up had been flown across during June and used for the trial installation, so that by the time Guy Bristow arrived with the actual engine, it slipped into place in three and a half hours without any troubles.

However, during ground runs this engine was badly damaged by sucking in its own intake ducts, which were not strong enough, and so a hurredly despatched telegram asked for a second engine to be urgently sent from Hatfield.

Records show that this engine went north by train from Camden Town and was flown to America on Christmas Eve, accompanied again by Guy Bristow.

The first prototype (44-83020) was nicknamed *Lulu-Belle* (also known as the 'Green Hornet' because of its paint scheme). Powered by the replacement Halford H1 taken from the prototype de Havilland Vampire jet fighter, it first flew on 8 January 1944, with Lockheed test pilot Milo Burcham at the controls. Following this flight, Johnson said, '*It was a magnificent demonstration, our plane was a success – such a complete success that it had overcome the temporary advantage the Germans had gained from years of preliminary development on jet planes.*'

Clearly the donated British jet programme data and hardware had proved invaluable.

The second prototype was designed for the larger General Electric I-40 engine (an improved Rolls-Royce Derwent, later produced by Allison as the J.33). Two aircraft (44-83021 and 44-83022) were built. 44-83021 was nicknamed the *Gray Ghost* after its pearl gray paint scheme, while 44-83022, left unpainted for comparison of flight characteristics, became known as the *Silver Ghost*.

Two months before General Electric had begun to adapt the Whittle design to US specifications as the Type I, the three industrial turbine manufacturers which had been supporting research by the NACA Special Committee on Jet Propulsion were awarded development contracts. Navy contracts went to Allis Chalmers for the development of a ducted-fan engine and to Westinghouse for turbojets. An Army Air Forces contract went to General Electric for the design of a turboprop engine.

The Allis Chalmers ducted-fan engine did not pan out, and the General Electric TG100, which in May 1945 became the world's first turbine propeller engine to be bench tested, ended up powering only the Consolidated-Vultee XP-81 (the first turboprop-powered flight in the United States was made on 21 December 1945, just two months after the experimental Gloster Meteor-Trent had become the world's first turboprop aircraft to fly in England). More successful, the series of small diameter turbojets developed by Westinghouse resulted in the WE-19XB-2B powering the first USN carrier jet, the McDonnell XFD-1 Phantom, on its maiden hop on 2 January 1945. A development of the WE-19, the first American axial-flow turbojet, went on large-scale production as the J34 for naval fighters.

While working on improved models of the Whittle turbo-jet and on its TG100 turboprop, General Electric took an early lead in US turbojet development by incepting two turbojet designs. First bench tested in January 1944, the 1-40 centrifugal-flow turbojet powered the Lockheed XP-80A, the production prototype of the Shooting Star, on its first flight in June 1944. Redesignated J-35 and mostly built under license by Allison, the I-40 became the first American turbojet engine to be mass produced. Even more successful, the General Electric TG-180 axial-flow turbojet was built in large numbers as the I-35, mostly by licensees Allison and Chevrolet.

However, when the war ended, Allison, Pratt & Whitney and Wright were left to catch up with turbine technology. At first, Allison fared a bit better, as it had been selected as a licensee for General Electric J33 centrifugal-flow and I.35 axial-flow turbojets, but Pratt & Whitney and Wright had to turn to Britain to get into the turbojet engine business.

Pratt & Whitney started negotiating for manufacturing and sales rights for the Rolls-Royce Nene in April 1947, eight months after the original American licensee, the Taylor Turbine Corporation, had acquired initial rights in this centrifugal-flow turbojet. Wright, which initially favoured turboprop engines, was even slower to grasp the turbojet potential and only acquired the license rights for the Armstrong Siddeley Sapphire axial-flow turbojet after war had broken out in Korea.

The 1945 surrender of Germany revealed substantial wartime discoveries and inventions. General Electric and Pratt & Whitney, added German lessons to those of Whittle and other British designers. Early jet engines, such as those of the Me 262, gulped fuel rapidly. Thus, an initial challenge was posed: to build an engine that could provide high thrust with less fuel consumption.

Pratt & Whitney resolved the fuel consumption dilemma in 1948 by combining two engines into one. The engine included two compressors; each rotated independently, the inner one giving high compression for good performance. Each compressor drew power from its own turbine; hence there were two turbines, one behind the other. This led to the J-57 engine.

This two-spool turboprop was launched as the PT4, funded by the Air Force as the XT45. Components were made in late 1947, while parallel studies were made of the two-spool JT3-8 turbojet, which by March 1948 was supercharged by adding two stages at the front, giving 10,000 pounds of thrust. During 1948 Air Force interest hardened on a high-compression turbo- jet for long-range

A General Electric I-40 seen in a NACA facility on 9 March 1945. GE was repeatedly unable to deliver enough engines for Army and Navy demand, and production of the I-40 (now known as the J33) was also handed to Allison Engines in 1944. (NACA)

bombers, and the XT45 was terminated in September 1948. Instead the J57-P-1 specification was written, and the shops began building two actual engines, the X-176 (JT3-8) and X-184 (JT3-10). Even as they were being built, rig testing indicated poor performance, mainly because of the very small HP compressor blades, poor turbine disc design and excessive weight.

Mechanical design came under Andrew Willgoos and aerodynamic design under Perry W. Pratt. In February 1949 they worked out a scheme to re-design the JT3 in a wasp-waisted form, the rotor discs having a constant diameter but the casings tapering towards the HP end amidships, to give higher efficiency, better sealing and cut 600 pounds off the weight, besides improving the arrangement of accessories to give a more compact installation in fighters or in bomber pods. Pratt got the go-ahead to redesign in May 1949, but it was decided to complete both the barrel engines, the X-176 running on 28 June 1949 and the X-184 in February 1950. Both confirmed the poor performance. The wasp-waisted design threw up its own problems, notably with bearings and compressor-blade vibration, but with massive effort these were eliminated. The first redesigned JT3 ran on 21 January 1950, flew under a B-50 in March 1951, completed a 150-hour test in J57-3 production configuration in November 1951, powered the 8-jet YB-52 on 15 April 1952, and with afterburner took the YF-100A beyond Mach One on its first flight on 25 May 1953.

It initially gave 10,000 pounds dry thrust or 15,000 pounds with afterburner yet, because of its pressure-ration of 12.5, it set totally new standards in jet fuel economy.

Developments in aeronautics

Technological change during World War Two had proceeded at an almost frightening pace. Developments in aircraft design, propulsion, weapons, and electronics all contributed vitally to the outcome of events in the global conflict.

There were, however, a number of scientists, largely civilians, who initially invented and designed military equipment and then drove these developments forward to turn the tide of the war. After that came the might of production.

Among the scientists and thinkers was Hungarian aerodynamicist Dr. Theodore von Kármán. Since his arrival in the United States from Europe, and having obtained Guggenheim funding and hoping to avoid rising nationalism and Nazism, he had become acquainted with several high-ranking Army Air Force officers, including Henry 'Hap' Arnold.

Since their first meeting at the California Institute of Technology (CalTech) in the early 1930s, Arnold had witnessed the professor's skilled use of mathematical equations to solve complex aerodynamic problems.

Arnold's trust in Kármán grew as the CalTech programme continued to tackle the most difficult projects without hesitation. During the early part of 1943, the Experimental Engineering Division of the United States Army Air Forces Material Command forwarded to von Kármán reports from British intelligence sources describing German rockets capable of reaching more than 100 miles . In a letter dated 2 August 1943 von Kármán provided the Army with his analysis of and comments on the German programme.

Only after D-Day and the realization of several key elements in wartime operations did Arnold believe that Allied victory in Europe was a foregone conclusion. The air war had become a deadly routine and was becoming a mere numbers game - growing Allied air strength versus dwindling Axis air capability.

By now General Arnold had decided that the Army Air Force was in a position to capitalise on the many technological developments. Following the

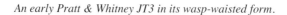

An early Pratt & Whitney JT3 in its wasp-waisted form.

29

shipment of several tons of captured German material back from France by US Intelligence not long after the start of Operation Overlord, Arnold realised that the United States and its Allies by no means led the world in military aeronautical development. He used his influence with Kármán at a super-secret meeting on the runway at La Guardia Airport, New York, convincing him to head a task force of scientists who would evaluate captured German aeronautical data and laboratories for the Army Air Force.

Kármán – who was recovering from recent abdominal surgery - was transported by Army Staff car to the end of the runway at La Guardia, where he met Arnold's recently arrived aircraft. Arnold dismissed Kármán's driver and then discussed his plans for Kármán and his desires for the exploitation project. Supposedly General Arnold spoke of his concerns for the future of American air power and wondered how jet propulsion, radar, rockets and other gizmos might affect the future. In response to the question as to what he wanted Kármán to do, Arnold told him that he wanted Kármán to go to the Pentagon, gather a group of scientists together and work out a blueprint for air research for the next fifty

years.

To accomplish his mission, Kármán officially became an AAF consultant on scientific matters on 23 October 1944. His first, unofficial AAF report was organisational in nature, naming as his deputy Dr. Hugh L. Dryden, longtime head of the National Bureau of Standards. November 1944 saw endless conferences and establishment of '...relations with the various agencies in the labyrinth of military and scientific aviation'. Arnold drafted official, written instructions on 7 November, solidifying the La Guardia Agreement, a four-page letter that set the boundaries for the report of Kármán's group. They were not very restrictive: '...*Except perhaps to review current techniques and research trends, I am asking you and your associates to divorce yourselves from the present war in order to investigate all the possibilities and desirabilities for postwar and future war's development as respects the AAF. Upon completion of your studies, please then give me a report or guide for recommended future AAF research and development programs.*'

Initially, Kármán's group was called the Army Air Force Consulting Board for Future Research, but

On 18 February 1963 President John F. Kennedy presented the National Medal of Science to Dr. Theodore von Kármán in the Rose Garden of the White House, Washington, DC. Left to right: Chairman of the President's Committee on the National Medal of Science, Frederick Seitz; Air Force Aide to the President, Brigadier General Godfrey T. McHugh; General Bernard Schriever; President John F. Kennedy; Judge Victor L. Anfuso of the New York State Supreme Court; Dr. von Kármán; Chief of Staff of the United States Air Force, General Curtis E. LeMay; Special Assistant to the President for Science and Technology, Dr. Jerome B. Wiesner; President of the California Institute of Technology, Dr. Lee A. DuBridge; unidentified; Director of Defense Research and Engineering, Dr. Harold Brown.

apparently AAFCBFR proved too long an acronym, even for the Army. Redesignated the Scientific Advisory Group (SAG) on 1 December 1944, it reported directly to General Arnold. In 1944 intelligence experts at Wright Field had developed lists of advanced aviation equipment they wanted to examine. The US Army Air Forces Intelligence Service sent teams to Europe hard on the heels of the invading armies to gain access to enemy aircraft, technical and scientific reports, research facilities, and weapons for study in the United States. The Air Technical Intelligence (ATI) teams, trained at the Technical Intelligence School at Wright Field, Ohio, collected enemy equipment to learn about Germany's technical developments. The ATI teams competed with thirty-two other allied technical intelligence groups to gain information and equipment recovered from crash sites.

One member of Von Karman's Scientific Advisory Group was Boeing's chief aerodynamicist, George S Schairer.

After working for Bendix Aviation, Schairer joined Consolidated Aircraft, where he led the aerodynamic design effort of the Consolidated XP4Y Corregidor and the Consolidated B-24 Liberator. In particular, he was one of the engineers responsible for the incorporation of the Davis wing in these designs. At Consolidated Aircraft, he also gained extensive experience in the design of controls for aircraft.

In 1939 Eddie Allen hired Schairer to be chief of the aerodynamics unit at Boeing, replacing Ralph Cram, who had been killed in the crash of the Boeing 307 prototype. In this position, he helped develop and test the Boeing 307 Stratoliner, the first pressurised airliner, including the redesign of the vertical tail in response to the 18 March 1939 crash of the prototype. He also was involved in the development of the Boeing B-17 Flying Fortress particularly the incorporation of aerodynamically balanced control surfaces on the B-17E, replacing spring tabs. During the design of the Boeing B-29 Superfortress he was responsible for the incorporation the Boeing 117 wing airofoil, previously designed for use on the Boeing XPBB Sea Ranger. Schairer helped defend the use of a much higher wing loading - 69 pounds per square foot - on the B-29 than had been used on previous designs. This was accomplished by the use of a powerful flap system that allowed good low-speed performance.

Boeing had started work on a jet bomber design in 1943, when an informal requirement for a jet-powered reconnaissance bomber drawn up by the US Army Air Forces was received. This 'requirement' was issued to prompt manufacturers to start research into jet bombers. Boeing was among several companies that responded to this request; its initial design, the Model 424, was basically a scaled-down version of the piston-engined B-29 Superfortress equipped with four jet engines.

In 1944 this had evolved into a formal request-for-proposal to design a new bomber with a maximum speed of 550 mph, a cruise speed of 450 mph, a range of 3,500 miles and a service ceiling of 45,000 feet. In December 1944, North American Aviation, the Convair Corp., Boeing and the Glenn Martin Company submitted proposals for the new long-range jet bomber. Wind tunnel testing had shown that the drag from the engine installation of the Model 424 was too high, so Boeing's entry was a revised design, the Model 432, with the four engines buried in the forward fuselage.

The USAAF awarded study contracts to all four companies, requiring that North American and Convair concentrate on four-engined designs (to become B-45 and XB-46), while Boeing and Martin were to build six-engined aircraft (the B-47 and XB-48). The powerplant was to be General Electric's new TG-180 turbojet engine.

When Schairer visited Germany at the end of the war, he was already aware of the controversial swept-wing theory of Robert T. 'Bob' Jones at Langley, Virginia. Jones' work there allowed the development of the delta wing, based on thin-aerofoil theory. Others were extremely skeptical until supersonic testing of models was done by Robert Gilruth and in April by Theodore von Karman. Jones' theory was not truly accepted until that summer, when Schairer found that German experts had been working on swept-wing designs for several years at the Völkenrode research centre, The discovery was backed up with test results showing the drag reduction offered by swept wings at transonic speeds. Jones thin-wing design ultimately proved superior to thick aerofoils developed by Alexander Lippisch in Germany. For his pioneering work, he was given the IAS Sylvanus Albert Reed Award in 1946.

Schairer is supposed to have wired home office '*Stop the Bomber Design*' and then on 10 May it is recorded that he wrote a seven-page letter to Boeing colleague Bob Withington that included a drawing of the swept wing and, in cramped handwriting, presented the key mathematical formulas. To avoid delay, Schairer wrote 'Censored' on the envelope and mailed it. Upon returning from Germany, Schairer led an effort to overhaul Boeing's design for what became the Boeing B-47 Stratojet by incorporating wings that were swept back 35 degrees. The swept wing proved to be crucial in Boeing's efforts to win the design competition to build the B-47. In addition, he is credited with the incorporation of the podded engine concept on the B-47.

NACA wind tunnel tests showed that the model under consideration for the Air Force suffered from excessive drag. Boeing engineers then tried a revised design, the Model 432, that had the four engines buried in the forward fuselage, but though the Model 432 had some structural advantages, changing the engine layout didn't really reduce drag very much. The Boeing engineers turned to the swept-wing data obtained from the Germans and promoted by Schairer. Further design work by Boeing aerodynamicist Vic Ganzer led to an optimum sweepback of 35 degrees.

Boeing then modified the Model 432 design with swept wings and tail, resulting in the Model 448, which was presented to the USAAF in September 1945. The Model 448 had the four TG-180s in the forward fuselage as had the Model 432, plus two TG-180s buried in the rear fuselage. The Boeing project manager, George Martin, had decided that the company's entry into the bomber competition needed greater range and performance, and that led to six engines rather than four.

The flush-mounted air intakes for the rear engines were inadequate, while the USAAF disliked the installation of engines within the fuselage, considering it a fire hazard.

The engines were moved out to pylon-mounted streamlined pods under the wings, leading to the next iteration, the Model 450, which featured two TG-180s in a twin pod mounted on a pylon about a third of the way outboard on each wing, plus another engine at each wingtip. The Army Air Force liked this new configuration, and so Boeing's team of engineers continued to refine it, with the outer engines being moved further inboard, to about three-quarter span.

By the time the mockup of the Boeing Model 450 was approved in April 1946, the B-47 had moved even further from the conventional configuration. A tandem 'bicycle' landing gear was adopted, and a retractable outrigger wheel was mounted in each inboard jet pod for lateral ground stability. Because of the location of the main wheels relative to the

The B-47 - to quote Boeing's publicity machine 'The Stratojet's revolutionary design and construction endow it with performance entirely new to aircraft of its dimensions'. (USAF)

In 1953, two B-47Bs were modified for testing the probe-and-drogue refueling system. The tanker was given the designation KB-47G and was known as 'Maw' by flightcrews, and was fitted with a British-built tanker kit. The refuelling test aircraft was given the designation YB-47F and was known as 'Paw', though other aircraft (including the YB-52 prototype) were also used as refueling targets. The program was cancelled in 1954; it turned out that the KB-47G simply could not carry enough fuel to make it a useful tanker. The idea of fielding B-47 tanker conversions came up again a few years later, but the economics did not make sense, and the notion was finally put to rest for good. (USAF)

centre of gravity, the B-47 sat on the ground in take-off attitude and took off and landed at the same angle without 'rotating' in the traditional manner of aircraft with conventional landing gear. Because of its high wing loading and the slow acceleration characteristics of the early turbojet engines, 18 JATO rocket units, developed during the war for 'jet-assisted takeoff', were built into the sides of the fuselage. On later models, these units were carried on a jettisonable external rack as a weight-saving measure. The heavy weight of these units also resulted in faster landing speeds and a severe braking problem, which was met by deployment of a ribbon-type parachute - another German wartime invention - from the tail just as the wheels touched the ground. On later models, this practice was modified to trail a small drogue parachute while in the landing pattern and deploy the main braking parachute just before the aircraft touched down. Wartime experience with stripped-down B-29Bs revealed that bombers with near-fighter speeds could be successfully intercepted only from the rear, so the only defensive armament of the B-47 was in the form of tail turret guns that could be aimed and fired remotely from the cockpit or automatically by radar.

The USAAF was very pleased with the refined Model 450 design, and in April 1946 the service ordered two prototypes, to be designated XB-47. Assembly began in June 1947.

The first XB-47 was rolled out on 12 September 1947, a few days before the USAAF became a separate service, the US Air Force, on 18 September 1947. The XB-47 prototype made its first flight on 17 December 1947 with test pilots Robert Robbins and Scott Osler at the controls. It flew from Boeing Field in Seattle to the Moses Lake Airfield in central Washington state, in a flight that lasted just 27 minutes, with no major problems. Robbins had to pull up the flaps with the 'emergency hot wire system', and the 'engine fire' warning indicators were falsely lit. Robbins reported that the flight characteristics of the aircraft were good.

In February 1949, Russ Schleeh and Joe Howell broke all coast-to-coast speed records flying from Moses Lake Air Force Base to Andrews Air Force Base. They averaged 607.8 miles per hour.

Although heavier than the heaviest bomber of World War ll -the B-29 -the B-47 was classed as a medium bomber. lt normally was operated by a three-man crew: pilot and copilot in tandem under a fighter-type canopy and a bombardier-navigator in the nose.

The total number of B-47s built was 2,032.

Chapter Three

The Journey From Paper To Metal

When Boeing began jet airliner development the air transportation industry in America - Boeing's main customers - was very different than it is today. The all-important trans-continental routes linking the East and West coasts were flown by unpressurised twin-engine Douglas DC-3s in sixteen to twenty hours, depending on the number of intermediate stops.

During 1946, the introduction of four-engine airliners, unpressurized Douglas DC-4s and pressurised Lockheed Constellations, enabled fiercely competing trunk carriers to operate transcontinentally with one intermediate stop and to fly the 2,500-mile routes in thirteen to fourteen hours with DC-4s and eleven hours with Constellations. An east-bound transcontinental service was not offered until October 1953, when TWA began 1049C Super Constellation service between Los Angeles and New York in less than eight hours. West-bound nonstop scheduled services began the next month when American Airlines introduced the Douglas DC-7, making the flight against prevailing winds in eight and a quarter hours.

The other route that played a significant part in determining the payload-range characteristics of the first generation of jet airliners as far as the Americans were concerned was that across the North Atlantic. Although a limited passenger service had been initiated with a Boeing 314 flying-boat first taking twenty-two passengers from New York to Marseilles, France, in June 1939, a sustained service only started after the war.

Critical legs were between either Shannon, Ireland, or Prestwick, Scotland, and Gander, Newfoundland. The Shannon-Gander leg was 1,715 nautical miles, uncorrected for prevailing winds from the west. Over the North Atlantic, new and more capable aircraft were introduced in January 1946 with use of the Lockheed Constellation and in June 1949 the Boeing Stratocruiser, both by Pan American,

North Atlantic operations still required at least one stop until November 1954, when Pan American began flying non-stop eastbound using Stratocruisers fitted with additional fuel tanks. Westbound nonstop

flights between London or Paris and New York became possible only with the introduction by TWA of the 1049G Super Constellation in November 1955, but even then, winter winds and/or heavy payload often still required a refueling stop.

All domestic and international US services were offered in a single class. Coach fares were introduced on some routes by the end of 1948 and were extended to transcontinental services a year later. On North Atlantic routes, tourist fares and economy fares were introduced in May 1952 and April 1958 respectively.

The impact of these lower fares was dramatic. The number of passengers carried by the nine airlines offering transAtlantic services - Air France, BOAC, KLM, Pan American, Sabena, Scandanavian Airline System, Swissair, Trans-Canada Airlines, and TWA - jumped from 329,656 in 1951 to 452,272 in 1952. Nevertheless, in 1952, only four out of ten North Atlantic passengers traveled by air. Five years later, with the availability of cheaper fares air transportation finally overtook sea transportation across the North Atlantic.

In 1958, the introduction of economy class and jet service resulted in yet another jump in air traffic over the North Atlantic, with the number of air passengers first exceeding the one million mark.

Credit for introducing turbine-powered aircraft into airline service goes to Great Britain. Both the De Havilland Comet and the Vickers Viscount resulted from the inspired work of the Brabazon Committee. Chaired by Lord Brabazon of Tara, this committee had been set up by the British Government in December 1942 to make recommendations for the postwar development of airliners.

Reporting between August 1943 and November 1945, the second Brabazon Committee came up with recommendations for five classes of airliners: The Type I called for the development of a 500,000 pound machine for nonstop operations between London and New York. This resulted in the Bristol Brabazon landplane and Saro Princess flying-boat, neither of which proceeded past the prototype stage.

The Type II was tailored to European operations.

*Right: The World's first jet
airliner, albiet in
experimental form - the
sole Rolls-Royce Nene-
powered Vickers Viking
which first flew as G-AJPH
in 1948.
(author's collection)*

It resulted in the design of three aircraft: the Airspeed Ambassador, which was built in limited number; the experimental Armstrong Whitworth Apollo powered by four turboprop engines; and the Vickers Viscount.

The Type III was aimed at airliners for operations on the Empire routes - those linking Britain with colonies in Africa, Asia, and the Pacific. It resulted in the Avro Tudor which, powered by four Rolls-Royce Merlins, and was intended as an interim aircraft pending availability of the jet-powered Avro 695.

The Type IV began as a specification for a relatively small jet-powered aircraft to transport mail over the North Atlantic. However, it ended up as the De Havilland Comet, the world's first jet airliner, which was initially built for operations over the Empire routes.

The Type V resulted in two types of feeder liners, the De Havilland Dove and the Miles Marathon.

Brabazon Committee members recognized that British turbine engine manufacturers had a substantial lead over their American competitors, that resulted in the turboprop-powered Vickers Viscount and turbojet-powered De Havilland Comet. With these two aircraft, Britain heralded a new era in air transportation.

Originally projected as a jet-powered North Atlantic twin-boom mailplane, the Brabazon Type IV evolved into the commercially more justified DH.l06. Adopting a remarkably clean layout with a pressurized fuselage and moderately swept wings with four de Havilland Ghost turbojet engines buried in their roots, De Havilland ended up designing an aircraft no longer meeting Brabazon Type IV requirements for a North Atlantic mailplane. Instead, the revised D.H. 106 to Specification 22/46 met Type IIIA requirements for a medium range turbine-powered airliner for use on the Empire routes. Two D.H. 106 prototypes were ordered by the Ministry of Supply in May 1946. Eight months later British Overseas Airways Corporation (BOAC) placed a preliminary order for eight aircraft on 21 January 1947, thus becoming the world's first airline to step into the jet age. The first prototype flew at Hatfield on 27 July 1949 and was first shown publicly at the Society of British Aerospace Companies (SBAC)

Show less than two months later. Although generating much interest, the Comet initially failed to attract additional orders, as airlines felt that the new jet airliner with first-class accommodation for up to 36 passengers would be too expensive to operate, making it difficult to turn in a profit or even to break-even. However, a series of record flights between London and European capitals at average speeds above 420 miles per hour soon demonstrated that the Comet was likely to have high passenger appeal. Before the first 36-set production aircraft was delivered to BOAC on 2 April 1951, export orders for eight Comet 1As were received from Canadian Pacific Airlines and two French carriers, UAT - Union Aéromaritime de Transport - and Air France. After setting records between London and European capitals, the Comet 1 was ready for commercial operations. Carrying 36 passengers, the first production Comet left London on 2 May 1952 bound for South Africa. After five intermediate stops, it landed in Johannesburg after covering 6,724 miles in 23 hours 34 minutes. First flown on 16 February 1952, the Avon-powered Comet 2 proved more attractive to prospective customers, and orders for this longer-ranged version were placed by Air France, BOAC, British Commonwealth Pacific Airlines, Canadian Pacific, Japan Airlines, Linea Aeropostal Venezolana, Panair do Brasil, and UAT. Unfortunately, before Comet 2s could be delivered to airlines and before the Comet 3 prototype flew on 19 July 1954, six of the pioneering Comet 1s had crashed or been destroyed, with the loss of 99 passengers and crew members.

The UK was not the only country to realise that the development of turbine-engined transports offered an opportunity to challenge the US hegemony. While most of the early aircraft in this table were jet-powered testbeds, the Avro Canada C.102 Jetliner was a genuine transport aircraft intended for one-stop service between Montreal and Vancouver. Conceived in Great Britain, but designed, built, and flown in Canada, the C.102 jet airliner was the recipient of a letter of intent issued in April 1946 from Trans-Canada Airlines. However, non-availability of the planned Rolls-Royce Avon

Left and below: The Rolls-Royce Tay-powered Vickers Viscount. Originally it was registered as G-AHRG but redesignated as a Type 663 to specification 4/49 and serialled VX217.

The wide-axled, double mainwheel undercarriage is shown to advantage. It was completed with two Tay jet engines instead of Darts and was used for research into control systems.

To all intents and purposes this was the British 737 - at least fifteen years before Boeing came out with a similar design! (Author's collection)

turbo-jets forced the manufacturer to substitute four less powerful and more fuel-thirsty Rolls-Royce Derwent turbo-jets. Performance fell below those for the projected twin-Avon version, and TCA lost interest before the first flight of the Derwent-powered airliner on 10 August 1949. More importantly, design of the SNCASE Caravelle had been initiated in France before Boeing and Douglas committed to building jet airliners. Stemming from a request for proposals issued in November 1951 by the French government, the twinjet Caravelle was intended for operations on European, Middle Eastern, and North African routes. Selected as one of the three finalists in March 1952, one month before the Boeing board authorized development of the 367-80 demonstrator, the Caravelle first flew on 27 May 1955.

While at first the French challenger was not taken seriously in the United States, the turbine-powered British designs elicited serious interests from several

US carriers. Capital Airlines, which was acquired by United Airlines in 1961, ordered the first three of an eventual fleet of seventy-five Vickers Viscount turbo-props in May 1954. It initiated Viscount service in the United States in July 1955, 3½ years before the Lockheed Electra became the next turboprop airliner in US service. Orders from Continental Airlines and Northeast Airlines eventually resulted in 147 of the 445 Viscounts built by Vickers being delivered to US airlines, a remarkable achievement for the British aircraft industry, particularly in the light of the fact that Lockheed only built 170 turboprop- powered Electras and never quite matched the Viscount in the home market (144 Electras were delivered to US carriers).

When BOAC inaugurated scheduled jet service on 2 May 1952, US airlines suddenly lost their apathy toward jet airliners. Four months later, Ronald E. Bishop, director and chief engineer for De Havilland,

In its production form, the turbo-prop Vickers Viscount made deep inroads into the American airliner market, even outselling Lockheed's Electra. Continental Airlines of Denver, CO. took fifteen. (Author's collection)

The Tupolev Tu-104 (NATO reporting name: Camel) was a twin-engined medium-range narrow-body turbojet-powered Soviet airliner. (author's collection)

The Avro C102 Jetliner was a prototype medium-range turbojet-powered jet airliner built by Avro Canada in 1949. It was beaten to the air by only 13 days by the De Havilland Comet, thereby becoming the second jet airliner in the world. (author's collection)

proclaimed during the SBAC Show, *"We feel we have a lead on the Americans of between four and five years on jet transport aircraft. They are now in the same position we were in 1946."*

Among those in attendance at the 1952 SBAC Show were George T Baker and Captain Edward V 'Eddie' Rickenbacker, presidents respectively of National and Eastern Airlines. As the payload/range performance of even the original Comet 1 were sufficient for operations on the New York-Miami routes on which their airlines competed fiercely, both airlines were ready to order Comets. Rickenbacker, after a trip in the Comet 2X development aircraft, was quoted as saying *'It was all I expected—plus.'* He planned an initial order for thirty-five to fifty Comets, provided that de Havilland would deliver these aircraft within two years from contract.

It was not surprising that BOAC's inaugural jet service should cause more than one American airline executive to sit up and start taking a keen interest in Comet affairs, although it is doubtful even then if any of them would have been prepared to back the comparatively uneconomical Series I in the way BOAC had done.

It was BOAC's announcement that they intended to put Series 2 Comets on their South Atlantic route in less than 18 months, that finally shocked the US into the realization that Britain had stolen a clear five-year lead over them in prestige travel. It was not long before Pan American and a number of other leading airlines placed orders for the Comet 3, a 'stretched' version of the Series 2, with still more powerful Rolls-Royce engines, a longer fuselage seating up to 78 passengers, and additional nacelle-like fuel tanks near the wing tips that increased the range by

something like sixty per cent as compared with the Series I.

The American press was generous in its tribute; as the influential Christian Science Monitor put it, *"A good competitor knows how to congratulate a winner as well as how to carry off trophies himself.'* The *New York Daily Mirror* was brief and to the point with the headline *''Britain Out-Jets Us'*

Finally, on 20 October 1952, De Havillands were able to announce the purchase of three Comet Series 3 jet airliners by Pan American World Airways. Thus for the first time in history a British main-line transport aircraft had been chosen by an American airline operator.

'The contract just signed calls for delivery of the three Comets in 1956 and includes an option on seven additional aircraft for delivery in 1957. The advanced delivery date was made possible because Sir Miles Thomas, Chairman of the British Overseas Airways Corporation, agreed to release three of the 11 Comets Series 3 which have been earmarked for BOAC.

The historic importance of this event to the British aircraft industry becomes apparent when it is realised that not for 20 years have American operators found it necessary to go beyond their own borders for equipment. It may be recalled that 95 per cent. of all the American production of aircraft for the 1914-18 war were to de Havilland design, and that American-built D.H.4s were used to carry United States mails in the years between 1919 and 1927. Thereafter, while British air transport developed under a policy of minimum subsidies and struggled to pay for itself with specialised aircraft, American civil aviation thrived in its naturally favourable circumstances and yielded in the early 'thirties the Douglas DC-2 and a succession of fine American airliners. Just when British manufacturers were beginning to see broader opportunities the war broke out in 1939, debarring the British industry from further civil developments. British wartime progress with jet engines opened the way for the Comet.

Now, with the advent of the Comet 3 and its forthcoming entry into the United States airline system, comes a fresh opportunity for Britain to become established in the airline markets of the world. With a payload capacity and a cruising range in tune with the expected requirements of the early 1960s and with a speed of travel and a degree of passenger comfort marking nothing less than a new era in world communications, the Comet Series 3, backed by many thousands of hours of route-operating experience with the Series 1 and 2, shows every promise of international success.

Pan American World Airways will now become the first American operator to put jet liners into service. Since before the war Juan Trippe, the President of Pan American, has been a leading advocate of the low-fare tourist- class air service. In 1948, alone among the world's airlines. Pan American instituted a tourist-class service between New York and Puerto Rico, but it was not until late in 1951 that the principle of the tourist fare was generally accepted, to go into effect internationally on May 1, 1952. Pan American's enthusiasm for tourist-class air travel emphasises the fact that the Series 1A and Series 2 Comets, seating 44 passengers, were not large enough for operation on their system; the Comet 3, with a capacity ranging from 58 to 78 seats, allows full scope for a service combining high-density traffic with high-speed operation. The Comet's ability, by reason of its speed, to cover more miles for a given rate of utilisation increases its work capacity far above that of piston aircraft of comparable seating capacity. In a statement issued by Pan American, Juan Trippe pointed out that the Series 3, capable of carrying a full payload of passengers, mail and cargo for about 2,700 miles against a headwind of 50 mph with adequate reserves, will be the first jet transport able to operate efficiently over the principal routes of the Pan American system. Plain business reasons brought about the American purchase of the Comet and it is to be hoped that plain technical satisfaction will bring about its airworthiness certification by the USA'.

That same month Trans World Airlines chief pilot, Paul S Fredrickson, and TWA Vice-President Robert W Rummel - acting on behalf of the secretive

The De Havilland Comet - in this case G-AYLP - is 'waved away' on the world's first jet airliner passenger service. The date? 2 May 1952. *(DH Hatfield)*

American billionaire Howard R Hughes - visited Hatfield and Frank Lloyd, the Commercial Sales Manager.

Here they were briefed on the programme about the Comet I and 1A, the building of the Mk II, work being done on engineering the Mk III and the plans for the Mk IV. Frank Lloyd told them that the Mk IV, powered by Rolls-Royce Conway engines, would be larger and fully competitive with anything that the American market would offer in eight to ten years time.

As with many comments from the Americans, Rummel was privately dismissive and disparaging about De Havilland's efforts: *'By American standards, De Havilland's production tooling seemed meager and rudimentary. Wings were being constructed in an inefficient horizontal position over pits rather than with the wing chord (the line between the leading and trailing edges) vertical, as was customary in the States. Production was very slow. Only nine Mark 1s had been delivered. De Havilland planned to establish additional production lines at Chester and Belfast rather than expand the Hatfield facility. Frank Lloyd explained that this would make use of existing factory facilities. It was necessary to move the work to the workman rather than the opposite because of the housing shortage and the extreme reluctance of workmen to move. He said, 'They refuse to leave their homes, which in many cases have been in the family for generations."*

Rummel also raised one other point - that of certification. United States certification of the Comet was considered a major problem, for the authorities were already putting obstacles in the path of the new airliner. Lloyd said De Havilland wanted complete reciprocity to permit automatic certification in the United States without need for the aircraft design to comply with US Civil Air Requirements (CAR).

While Britain and the United States had agreed to reciprocal certification during the 1944 Chicago Convention, which resulted in the formation of the International Civil Aviation Organization, the United States held the view that this was limited to piston engined powered aircraft only - because US turbine aircraft certification requirements had not been written then, and still had not been written by 1952.

Rummel expressed the view that the expectation of automatic certification was unrealistic, and that he thought it would be more constructive for De Havilland and the British authorities to assist the Americans in establishing appropriate US turbine-powered aircraft certification requirements that would have to be complied with.

'I considered the Comet program to be a superb pioneering venture that quite obviously required pressing the state of the art of airplane design in nearly all significant technology areas to achieve the barest minimum acceptable overall efficiency. In the earlier models this produced marginal structure, minimal operating weights, and borderline performance. For example, the thin fuselage skin of the Comet had been stretched during manufacturing

At one stage Boeing referred to the work done on the jet transport as the infamous 'Project X', as demonstrated by this extract from a geneological chart from late 1953 shows. (author's collection)

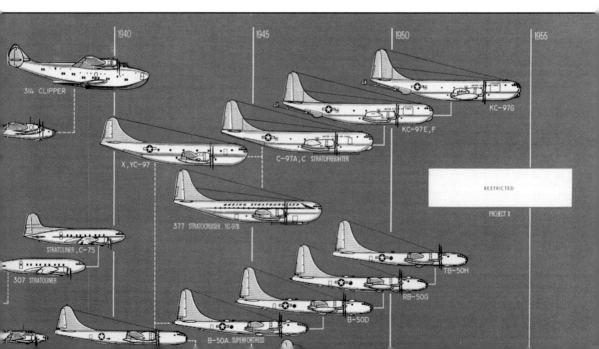

to increase strength at the expense of ductility; every pound of empty weight was critical re payload or range; higher-thrust engines were clearly needed. The limited range, sluggish takeoff at high rotation angles, and the ability to stop after landing on slippery runways were also important concerns.

Except for the lack of reverse thrust, I did not think any one of the marginal conditions ruled the airplane out, but the combination of them gave me serious pause. I thought it likely that the anticipated march of progress could lessen or erase these concerns in succeeding models, possibly in the Mark IV, which was years away.

I had evaluated potential TWA Comet operations several times and recommended each time to Hughes that none be procured because of borderline design and performance or because of program timing with respect to the clearly superior US jets. My early negative recommendations, which Howard accepted, generated considerable high-echelon TWA criticism after BOAC's initial operations proved the extreme popularity of the Comet. One TWA board member even commented, "Bob, you could have been a hero."

Clearly the USA were doing all that they could to forstall the introduction of foriegn jet-airliners into service on American soil until they were ready, a process that was unintentionally aided by a series of disasters that struck the Comet 1 and led to its grounding in April 1954.

De Havilland announced the development of a much heavier version of the Comet with greater range and increased payload. Powered by four 10,000 pounds thrust Rolls-Royce Avon turbojets instead of the 4,500 pounds thrust de Havilland Ghosts of the Comet 1, this Comet 3 was optimized to carry 50

passengers on single-stop service between London and New York. Consequently, to hedge its bet and be ready to compete with BOAC soon after the British flag carrier was expected to start Comet 3 service, Pan American ordered three of these aircraft on 20 October 1952. However, before the Comet 3 first flew, Comet 1s were withdrawn from use. By then the 367-80 was about to fly and Pan Am cancelled its Comet 3 order.

Only one other US carrier, Capital Airlines, showed sufficient interest in the pioneering British jet airliner to place an order for four Comet 4s and ten stretched Comet 4As in July 1956. Two years later, financial difficulties forced Capital to cancel its order.

American industry leaders still remained lukewarm toward the development of jet airliners, as greater benefit would be derived from developing turboprop-powered derivatives of their Super Constellation/Starliner and DC-6/DC-7 series.

In particular, after studying a 32- to 40-passenger CL-152 with three or four of its own L-1000 turbojets in 1946, Lockheed concentrated its efforts on turboprop-powered aircraft and on flying experimental Super Constellation models powered by Pratt & Whitney T34 Turbo-Wasps (four R7V-2s for the USN, with two becoming YC-121Fs for the USAF and one being re-engined with Allison 501 turboprops). Convair meanwhile, preferred turbine developments of its Model 240/540/440 series for operations over shorter routes. First flown on 29 December 1950 after being re-engined with a pair of Allison 501s, its Model 240 prototype became the first US airliner powered by turboprops. However, further turbine development of the 240/340/440 series did not materialize until ten years later.

The US Navy ordered four Super Connies modified with four Pratt & Whitney YT34-P12A turboprop engines, squared propellers and a shortened wing, being designated R7V-2. Lockheed leased one back from the Navy to use as a test aircraft for the upcoming L-188 Electra. The Air Force ordered their own pair of turbo Connies, designated as the YC-121F. only six were built and none entered airline service. (author's collection)

Dubbed 'Avitruc' by its manufacturer, the Chase Aircraft Company, the XC-123A conducted its maiden flight on 21 April 1951, so becoming the first jet-powered transport aircraft to successfully fly in the United States of America. (author's collection)

Douglas came close to launching a DC-7D powered by four Rolls-Royce Tyne turboprops but, reacting to customer preference for jet-powered aircraft, the Santa Monica manufacturer announced in August 1952 that it would launch a DC-8 jet airliner. This announcement preceded by one month that by Boeing concerning the 367-80. Douglas however lost the initiative as, unlike Boeing, it sought to wait for airline orders before proceeding with construction of a prototype.

Historically speaking, the honour of being the first American pure-jet transport aircraft fell to the little-known Chase XC-123A. While not a jet airliner, this testbed was the first US jet-powered aircraft with a transport-type airframe. Powered by four General Electric J47 turbojets in paired pods under the wing and utilizing the airframe of the second XCG-20 experimental cargo glider, this aircraft first flew on 21 April 1951. However, no further jet development of the C-123 was undertaken, and the type went into production for the USAF with two Pratt & Whitney R-2800 radials as the Fairchild C-123B Provider.

The Air Transport Association (ATA, later to become Airlines for America (A4A)), was and is an American trade association and lobbying group based in Washington, D.C. to which all American scheduled carriers belonged. They issued detailed jet transport design recommendations in October 1952. Recommendations included provision for carrying all fuel outside the fuselage, either in wings or pods or both; undercarriage wells designed to contain damage following tyre explosion; ability to operate in 40-miles per hour crosswinds; ability to manoeuver at low speeds despite failure of one engine in a two or three-engine aircraft or failure of two engines in a four or five-engine aircraft; 'fail safe' maintenance to preclude incorrect attachment of parts; improved fire warning and protection; 128-inch internal cabin width to make possible five-abreast coach accommodation; and sealed electrical system to eliminate all electrical booby traps.

The ATA favoured individual engine pods and expressed concerns over cabin pressurisation

problems. In the case of the powerplant, ATA considered it '...*imperative that the engine installation assure an advancement in the safety of the airplane with respect to fire over that provided in present transport airplanes. An engine fire should not jeopardize the airplane primary structure, adjacent engines, or airplane and engine controls.*'

Concerns over potential structural integrity was expressed by ATA as there was no previous experience in pressurising so large a volume as the cabin of a jet airliner flying at altitude of 40,000 feet.

ATA Jet Transport Specification

Cost per ton-mile:	Equal to DC-6
Cruise speed:	550 miles per hour
Range, domestic:	2,000 miles
Range, international:	3,200 miles
Runway length, domestic:	5,500 feet
Runway length, international:	7,500 feet
Fuselage width, inside diameter:	128 inches
Cabin aisle headroom:	80 inches
Passenger capacity, first class:	70-80

In the event, early Boeing 707s and Douglas DC-8s barely met ATA range specifications and completely failed to meet field-length requirements. However, they exceeded ATA requirements in terms of cabin width and seating, for ATA issued its specifications six years before economy class was introduced.

Boeing Gambles.
In the spring of 1947, four months after the undesignated layout mentioned at the beginning of this chapter had been prepared, Boeing initiated more comprehensive preliminary design studies for jet airliners under the Model 473 designation. The first of these studies, the 473-1, was a 27-seat, 48,430-pound gross weight aircraft with a tricycle undercarriage and four 6,000 pounds thrust Rolls-Royce Nene turbojets in underslung pods. With tanks for only 2,208 gallons of fuel, the 473-1 was optimized for domestic operations over flight sectors of less than 1,200 miles. It was not long before several other configurations were studied to increase

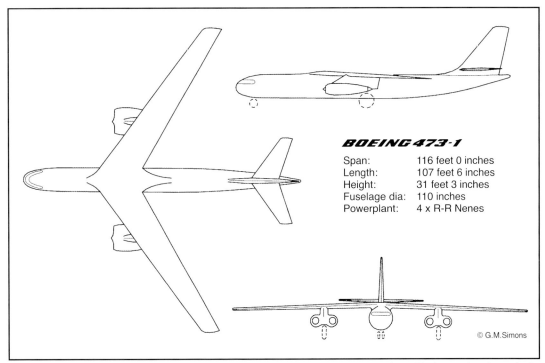

BOEING 473-1

Span:	116 feet 0 inches
Length:	107 feet 6 inches
Height:	31 feet 3 inches
Fuselage dia:	110 inches
Powerplant:	4 x R-R Nenes

© G.M.Simons

From December 1946 comes what is possibly the first three-view of the Boeing jet airliner. The layout that shows the B-47 influence with podded engines and shoulder-mounted wing.

range. Typical of these studies was the 473-11 which, still to be powered by a pair of Nenes, had its wing area increased from 790 to 1,000 square feet, carried 2,620 gallons of fuel, had a bicycle undercarriage, and range of up to 1,500 miles. These early 473 configurations had limited payload (with resulting very high seat-mile costs) and limited range that required one or two stops for transcontinental operations. It is not surprising therefore that they failed to attract airline interest. However, pending availability of more powerful and more fuel efficient turbojets, there was little that Boeing could do to increase payload and range.

Two years later, experience gained with the six-engined B-47 that was first flown in December 1947 and the eight-jet B-52 together with anticipated availability of civil derivatives of military turbojets in the 7,500- to 10,000-pound thrust class, enabled Boeing to scale up its proposed jet airliners. Typical of these configurations was the 473-25 detailed in May 1949. Bearing a strong family resemblance with the XB-52 but powered by six instead of eight J57 turbojets, the 285,000- pounds gross weight 473-25 was planned to carry 98 passengers non-stop across the North Atlantic. Internal and external tanks were to house 18,620 gallons of fuel and the 473-25 was expected to have a cruising speed of 530 miles per hour at 53,000 feet. This was a substantial

improvement over the performance of early Nene 473 configurations but still a long way from satisfying airline requirements. Notably, the use of shoulder-mounted wings and bicycle undercarriage resulted in the need to retract the four-wheel forward bogie into the fuselage, between the twenty-seat forward cabin and the main cabin. Only limited improvements resulted from the adoption of a double-lobe, inverted-eight, fuselage cross section for the 473-29, as housing the two bogies in the lower lobe limited space available for cargo, mail, and baggage. With the 473-47, Boeing returned to a Nene configuration for domestic operations in January 1950. Seating was provided for 32 first-class passengers and, with its engines fitted close beneath the low-mounted and moderately swept wings - an installation not unlike that adopted in the mid-sixties for the Boeing 737 - this configuration made possible the use of a conventional tricycle undercarriage.

Performance, though, left much to be desired. Because significant wing sweep was necessary to achieve the desired cruise performance, while at the same time the airlines were expressing a strong preference for low-mounted wings, configuration engineers were frustrated in their attempts to find a satisfactory housing for the main undercarriage units. On the 473-48, for example, the four-wheel main bogies were to retract into pods projecting forward

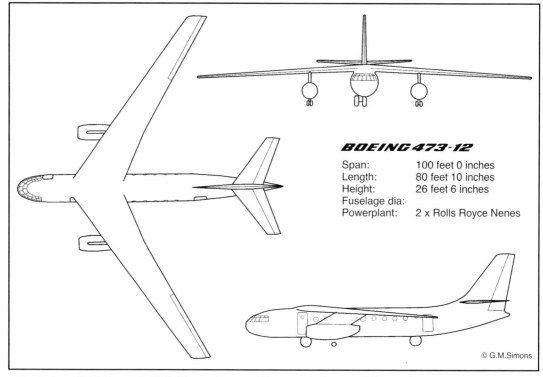

BOEING 473-12

Span:	100 feet 0 inches
Length:	80 feet 10 inches
Height:	26 feet 6 inches
Fuselage dia:	
Powerplant:	2 x Rolls Royce Nenes

© G.M.Simons

The Boeing 473-12, from July 1948. The machine would have carried a crew of three and twenty-seven passengers a range of 550 miles. The aircraft appears to have had a sideways retracting offset nosewheel.

of the leading edge, between the fuselage and the twin-engine pods. On the 473-49B, the main gear consisted of four separate legs, each with a large wheel and retracting forward with the wheel turning 90 degrees to lay flat in the underside of the wing. With a satisfactory solution still eluding the project team, the Model 473 came to an inconclusive end shortly after the 473-57 configuration with three J57 turbojets and accommodation for 50 passengers was elaborated in April 1950.

While one team at Boeing toiled to come up with a satisfactory Model 473 jet airliner configuration, another worked on continued developments of the Model 367 transport and tanker for the USAF. Combining the wings and Wright R-3350 radial engines of the B-29 Superfortress with a double-deck pressurized fuselage, the first of three XC-97 prototypes had flown on 9 November 1944. Subsequent developments, with more powerful Pratt & Whitney R-4360 radials and B-50 wings and tail surfaces, led to the production of 888 Model 367s as C-97s and KC-97s for the USAF and 56 Model 377 Stratocruisers for a small number of airlines. As a tanker, the Model 367 made its debut in 1950 when three C-97As were modified as KC-97A prototypes. Thereafter, no fewer than 811 of the 888 Model 367s

were completed as KC-97Es, KC-97Fs, and KC-97Cs. While these numbers reflected the Strategic Air Command's pressing need for tankers in the early Cold War years, they hid the fact that these piston engined aircraft proved only to be marginally satisfactory when refueling B-47 jet bombers. Substituting turboprops for the radial engines to improve C-97 performance was first contemplated as far back as April 1948 when a 367-15-23 configuration was proposed with Allison T38s, a lengthened fuselage of increased diameter, longer span wings, and a nose-loading ramp. Two months later, the dimensionally larger 367-18-28 configuration was studied with more powerful Allison T40s.

Although these design exercises did not result in production configurations, they provided a useful starting point for the 367-23-33 configuration proposed in June 1949 as a boom-equipped tanker with T40 turboprops. The Air Force it seems, was not overly concerned by the anticipated difficulties of refueling jet bombers with piston-engined tankers. Work on a turboprop-powered KC-97 was resumed in December 1950 when Boeing attempted to counter the Douglas YKC-124B with its Model 367-60-61 powered by four Pratt & Whitney T34 turboprops

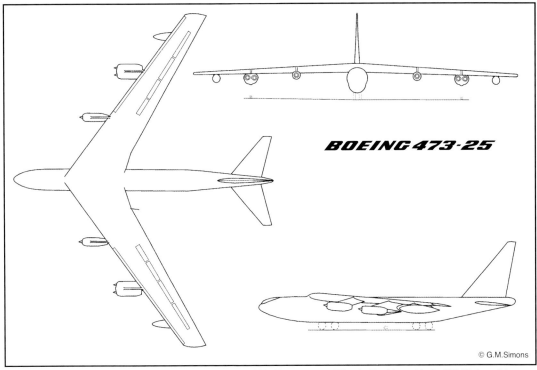

The Boeing 473-25 clearly demonstrates its Model 464-67 parentage. The similarities with the XB-52 is striking.

The Model 473-47 was almost a hark-back to earlier thinking.

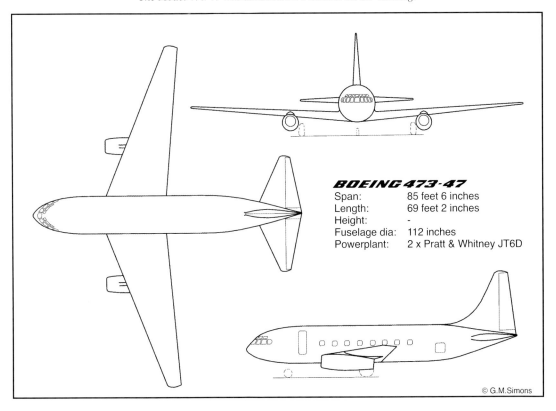

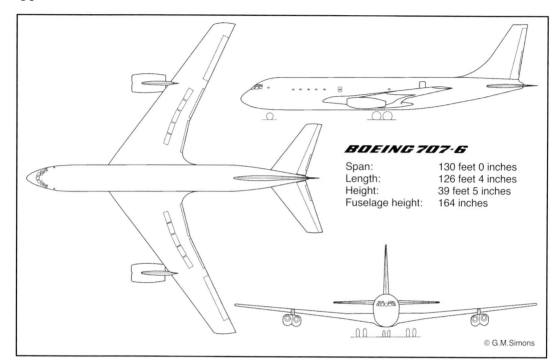

BOEING 707-6

Span:	130 feet 0 inches
Length:	126 feet 4 inches
Height:	39 feet 5 inches
Fuselage height:	164 inches

© G.M.Simons

and featuring gull wings with 25 degrees of sweep at the quarter chord. During the following month, the 367-64 was proposed with four Pratt 86 Whitney J57 turbojets as a Navy minelayer or Air Force tanker. Again, Boeing was unsuccessful, but the seed for a jet-powered development of the C-97 had been planted, promising significant performance improvements. In March 1951, initial B-47 refueling tests with a KC-97A had brought to light the performance shortcoming of piston- engined tankers. As by then Douglas was aggressively marketing its proposed turboprop-powered KC-124B to the Air Force, Boeing put new emphasis on designing turboprop- and turbojet- powered derivatives of its KC-97. These design efforts resulted in proposals for the 367-68 with four Bristol Olympus turbojets, the 367-69 with twin J57 pods, the 367-70 with swept wings and Olympus turbojets, the similarly configured 367-71 with 1575, and the 367-77 with four T34 turboprops. Unfortunately for the project team working on advanced developments of the Model 367, in 1951 the Air Force could not yet afford turbine-engined tankers. This may have been a blessing in disguise as, until funding for new tankers became likely to be budgeted, Boeing would again concentrate on jet airliner designs. Starting with a clean sheet of paper after earlier Model 473 configurations had failed to result in a satisfactory jet airliner design, Boeing launched Model 707 jet airliner preliminary design studies in September

1951. From the start, a solution was found for the previously frustrating problem of main undercarriage retraction. With the basic layout now calling for low-mounted wings with thirty-five degrees of sweep at the quarter chord, the main elements of the tricycle gear would be located close enough to the centre of gravity to facilitate rotation on take-off while being placed far enough aft to prevent the tail from coming in contact with the ground during aft loading. Using this arrangement, the 707-1 layout dated 16 November 1951 called for an aircraft providing accommodation for seventy-two first-class passengers in a 122-inch wide cabin and powered by four J57s in twin pods. In the months that followed, the design evolved only slightly, while wing area and fuselage cross section were enlarged. By the early spring of 1952, engineers finally felt that the 707-6 layout shown on the accompanying three-view drawing was close to what airlines wanted. Intended to be powered by four 9,500 pounds thrust civil derivatives of the Pratt & Whitney J57-P-1, the aircraft had wings with span of 130 feet, area of 2,510 square feet, and thirty-five degrees of sweep at the quarter chord. Its fuselage was 121 feet 3 inches long and had a 132-inch diameter to accommodate 76 first-class passengers in a four-abreast arrangement and to incorporate an eight-seat aft lounge. Performance promised to be substantially better than that of the De Havilland Comet 1 with which BOAC was about to start jet service.

Chapter Four

What's in a Name?

The Boeing jet transport prototype finally emerged through the C-97 development line although much use had been made of B-47 and B-52 design elements. By this time the basic Model 367 had reached the 80th study configuration and it bore no resemblance whatever to the original C-97/Stratofreighter airframe even though the original model number had been retained.

The design was not new, for it contained many of the aerodynamic, structural and engineering features introduced to Boeing practice by the B-47 and B-52, as well as the standards of passenger comfort established with the Model 377 Stratocruiser. It was a new model number that combined all the best features of Boeing's many years of experience with performance and passenger comfort, allied to a basic structure that was highly adaptable but easy to produce and thus economic in mass-production terms.

Popular books, television programmes, and even some specialized aviation publications have all fostered and propogated the myth that the Boeing 707 airliner and KC-135 tanker were the miraculous results of an 'immaculate conception' following a request from William M. Allen, the Boeing president. That was simply not the case.

As we have seen, Boeing had been conducting conceptual studies of jet airliners since 1946 while, from 1948 on, it also contemplated turbine-powered tanker versions of its Model 367. In the spring of 1952, the Board also had to consider the company's overall competitive position and financial health. On the civil side, activities had come to a grinding halt with the deliveries of the last Model 377 Stratocruiser to BOAC in May 1950. On the military side, the company had experienced a growing number of disappointments, especially when the turboprop-powered Model 495 had lost the Air Force 1951 medium transport competition to the Lockheed Model 082/YC-130, and the company suffered a string of failures in fighter competitions. However,

these disappointments were more than offset by numerous successes.

Notwithstanding Douglas' attempts to attract Air Force interest in its turboprop-powered KC-124B, Boeing was getting additional production contracts for piston-engined tankers, the final KC-97G contract being approved by the Air Force in June 1953. The first of 399 B-47B medium jet bombers were about to be delivered to the Strategic Air Command, and more contracts were expected. The XB-52 prototype was rolled out on 29 November 1951, nine-and-a-half months after a letter contract had been awarded to Boeing for thirteen pre-production B-52As, and confidence ran high that the B-52 would become a major production programme. Large-scale production of B-52s - which were known to require air-to-air refuelling in order to increase their range asnd endurance - would also mean that the Air Force would have to order tankers with compatible performance.

Another myth that also has been almost impossible to dispel is the notion that the KC-135A was somehow a military version of the Boeing 707 airliner. It was and is not. The KC-135A (or Boeing 717) preceded, and paved the way for the commercial machine which became so successful with the world`s civil carriers. Of course, both shared a common heritage in the vision of Boeing's engineers and finance people, and both are progeny of the private Model 367-80 prototype.

This one-of-a-kind aircraft was referred to by the press, and even by Boeing's own house organ, *Boeing News* as the Boeing 707, but it was not.

In external appearance the Model 367-80 was very similar in appearance to the Boeing 707 civil airliner and the KC-l35A tanker. As a private venture, a risk - the consequences of which could not have been predicted for certain - the Dash 80 turned out to be a bold and successful move by Boeing and a milestone in the history of aviation.

The Model 367-80, with the civil registration

A head-on shot of one of the B-52 prototypes - note the fighter-style tandem cockpit (USAF)

N70700, was rolled out on 14 May 1954 and soon embarked on an exhaustive, company-financed. proof-of-concept test programme.

To get the Dash 80 to this point is supposed to have required 432,000 direct design-engineer man-hours. The 707-120, the first true 707, was to require a further 772,000, demonstrating just how far from being a commercial airliner the 367-80 really was.

From then until its retirement to the Smithsonian Institution, one of the key roles of the basic Boeing design has been as a test aircraft - initially for the purpose of its own development and proving, and much later as the platform for a variety of experiments in advanced technology including 'Star Wars' research.

By October 1956, as a part of the Boeing test programme, the Dash 80 was retrofitted with a flying boom for mid-air tanker coupling trials, but the US Air Force shared Boeing's boldness and did not wait for proof that air-to-air refuelling by jet tanker was feasible. At the start of the 1955 fiscal year - 11 July 1954 - the Air Force placed an order for for 29 airframes in the KC-135A series, starting with aircraft 55-3118.

The K-135A flew eighteen months before the first genuine 707, however, and differed from it in several important respects, having a more narrow fuselage and entirely different cross-section, so that the two could not be produced on the same factory jigs.

In aerodynamic terms the 'Dash-80' - as the type was familiarly known by those concerned with the project - was similar to the B-47 and B-52 series, with characteristically shaped tail surfaces and a wing of 35° sweep. Consideration had been given to the mounting of the engines in twin pods, as had been used for the inner engines of the B-47 and for all the engines of the B-52, but safety considerations for a civil type persuaded the designers to adopt single-engine pods. The main problem with twin-engine pods lay in the fact that under certain circumstances, such as the disintegration of a compressor stage in one engine, both engines could be rendered inoperative.

Thus it was wise to separate the engines as far as was possible, and the use of four singly-podded engines also had benefits for the wing structure, where the cantilevering of the pods forward and below the wings on special pylons allowed the engines to be used as mass balances to prevent flutter. It also permitted the outer engines to be used to unload the outer panels of the wings, so that the roots would thus not be subject to such severe bending moments in flight. The fuselage and undercarriage were entirely new. The fuselage was designed to the fail-safe philosophy essential for pressurised airline operations, and featured provision only, in the 'Dash-80' austere prototype, for a large number of windows; a flight crew of three was carried in the nose section, which was comprehensively instrumented and provided with space for weather radar. The tandem type of undercarriage used on the company's jet bombers had been rejected as being impractical for commercial operations, so a more conventional arrangement was installed, with four-wheel main units retracting into the lower sides of the fuselage, and a twin wheel steerable nose unit retracting into the lower fuselage just aft of the flight deck. Fuel was accommodated in six main tanks, located three to a wing.

The Model 367-80 was intended solely as a prototype, the company designation Model 707 having been allocated for the production version, which was also given the name Jet Stratoliner.

As Maynard L Pennell, the 367-80 Chief Project Designer explained: '*In the case of the Boeing 707 jet tanker-transport design, the objective may be stated broadly as a desire to create a vehicle which could transport people or things more safely, more economically and faster than is possible by any other form of air transport today. As a result of preliminary studies, we convinced ourselves that improvements in safety and economy were achievable goals for a jet transport. Since this was contrary to the then common assumption that speed was the principal virtue of a jet transport and perhaps was achieved only at the expense of safety and economy, we scrutinized these preliminary studies carefully before proceeding. Today we are more than ever convinced that our conclusions were correct.*

Since it is perhaps the most controversial subject, let's look first at the economics of a jet transport. Can it compete on the basis of economy with the best of today's airplanes, carrying boxed goods or machinery, spare engines or spare fuel, combat troops, litter patients or commercial passengers as cheaply and as reliably as these jobs are being done today? The answer in our opinion is, emphatically, 'yes'.

The predicted direct operating cost of the 707 is below ten cents per ton mile, compared with commonly accepted operating costs of thirteen to fifteen cents for the most economical of the present-day transports.

How does one account for this remarkable improvement in economy, with all the signs pointing to further improvements in years to come? The answer is in the work capacity of this new type of airplane. It can carry more payload, at more miles per hour. The work capacity as expressed in ton-knots (the product of payload times block speed in knots) is three to four times that of current transports.

Another interesting aspect is the distribution of costs. For instance, fuel costs are found to be moderate, at least by today's standards. Other costs are consistently less than those of today's planes except for engine maintenance, which includes

Boeing constructed a full-scale wooden mock-up of the Model 367-80 in secrecy at Renton during 1952.

Two very important men in the KC-135 and 707 story are (left) Wellwood Edmeston Beall (b. 28.10 1906. d. 28.1.1978) Boeing's Vice-President, Engineering-Sales and Edward Curtiss 'Ed' Wells, (b. 26 August 1910 , d. July 1986) Boeing's Chief Engineer.
(both DGR Image Library)

spares and overhaul on a very conservative basis. Crew costs, although higher per hour in accordance with Air Line Pilots Association formulas, are divided by the larger work capacity of the new plane and show how much more can be accomplished with the same people.

In safety, the jet transport appears to offer definite improvements in such performance matters as climb after takeoff, en-route climb and terrain clearance. Approach and landing problems likewise appear to be easily solvable by available means. In fact, to the extent that the numerical approach can prove safety, the jet transport meets all available criteria.

On another aspect of safety, it seems obvious that the structure of a jet airplane can be made fully as safe as that of any other airplane. True, this involves the acquisition of knowledge concerning the behavior of thin, sweptwing structures which change shape and airload distribution under load, but such information or the means of obtaining it is available from earlier sweptwing bombers and fighters. It also

requires a carefully designed pressure structure for the body -one which will not allow failures even under adverse maintenance or operating conditions or after years of continuous service.

This might well appear to be an extremely difficult problem were it not for the fact that earlier Boeing airplanes, such as the B-29, B-50, C-97 and Stratocruiser, have been operated successfully for many years with a pressure differential of 6.5 pounds per square inch. Only slightly more - 7.5 to 8.5 - is desired for jet transport operation. Extra precautions against explosive decompression can and will be taken, but the problem is fully solvable.

Clearly from this statement Boeing were heavily relying on data flowing back from a number of military projects.

However, early in 1952 the construction of the prototype tanker-transport had not started, largely for lack of finance. In 1951 the company had tried to float the project with orders from the USAF, to which

'See more in '54!' Model Eddie Albright poses with a covered over model of the Dash 80 in late 1953. (via Peter M Bowers)

it had promoted the type as a jet-powered 'Advanced KC-97' tanker. The USAF readily conceded that such an aircraft was ideally suited to the support of the Strategic Air Command's B-47 fleet, offering exact compatibility with the bombers in terms of speed and altitude for rapid operational refuellings; but at the same time the service pleaded lack of finance in a period when burgeoning appropriations were being gobbled up by an expanding need for tactical aircraft demanded in the Korean arena, and for the new generation of strategic aircraft such as the B-52 already under final development.

Boeing rightly appreciated that few airlines would be prepared to put money into so ambitious but unproved a project, and also that such a method of financing would be unsuitable for its planned development of parallel military and civil aircraft.

In April 1952, William Allen distributed a questionnaire to five of his senior engineering and finance executives; Wellwood Beall, Fred Collins, Fred Laudan, Ed Wells, and John Yeasting, to elicit their comments regarding the feasibility and desirability of proceeding with the design, manufacturing, and testing of a jet tanker/ transport

Two views of the sole 367-80 in its assembly dock in Renton, Seattle. The aircraft is at the stage of having the vertical and horizontal stabilizers fitted, along with the two military-style cargo doors. (Boeing via Peter M Bowers)

demonstrator. Positive answers were received on 21 April and, with confidence boosted by the successful maiden flight of the YB-52 pre-production prototype of the Stratofortress strategic bomber six days earlier, William Allen recommended to the board of directors that the program be initiated. Reacting favourably, board members authorised a $16 million programme on 22 April 1952.

Ever since, much has been made of the risk taken by the Boeing directors. It is certainly true that $16 million in 1952 dollars represented two and a quarter times the profit realised by Boeing in the preceding year. However, when expressed in 2016 dollars that amount was $143 million or approximately 50% of the current quoted price of a single Boeing 787 Dreamliner - when looked in that way, it was a not so formidable sum!

Moreover, Boeing could expect to charge some of this expenditure to the US government as 'Independent Research and Development'. It did, in fact, do so when in 1957, under an Air Force contract, the XB-52 was modified by replacing the outboard pairs of J57s by single J75s to help in the development of the JT4A installation for Boeing 707 Models 220 and 320.

When the Boeing Board decided to proceed with the 367-80 demonstrator, it was with the intention that production military tankers and civil jetliners would be closely related and would therefore be built using similar if not identical tooling. This led to protracted negotiations between the Air Force and the manufacturer, as the government sought to recover some of the money seemingly spent for the benefit of commercial derivatives. In the end, however, the 707 and the KC-135 only had some 20% commonality as competitive pressures forced Boeing to adopt a wider fuselage cross-section and wings of greater span and area for production 707 models. Moreover, designed for a longer service life, the 707 used 2024 aluminum alloy instead of the lighter 7178

By March 1954 Boeing were prepared to release pictures of the Dash 80 under construction, along with the build team. (Boeing via Peter M Bowers)

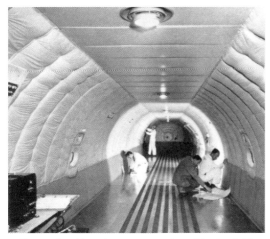

The insulated but almost empty cabin of the Dash 80. (Boeing via Peter M Bowers)

alloy adopted for 'shorter-lived' Air Force tankers. This was something which eventually proved to be a costly mistake, as KC-135s and derivatives remained in service long after the last 707s were cut by blowtorches of metal smelters.

Although the tanker/transport demonstrator was based on the 707-6 preliminary design layout, it was given the misleading 367-80 designation to make it to appear as being merely a jet derivative of the C/KC-97 series.

With the passing of time, one must now wonder how Boeing could seriously expect to succeed with this bit of disinformation - during the 1950s the Soviets were not the sole experts when it came to *disinformatsiya* - as aeronautical engineers freely moved from Boeing, to Douglas, and then to Lockheed, in search for better jobs. In the process, they took along knowledge of what was going on at Boeing. It is doubtful that their rivals were long fooled into believing that the 367-80 was a mere development of the KC-97 instead of being the all new design it was.

By the time the 367-80 was officially announced in September 1952, some three weeks after Douglas had announced its intent to develop their DC-8 jet airliner, Boeing had switched from twin-engine pods to single-engine pods to meet ATA recommendations. Detailed design also resulted in the adoption of multi-surface flight controls. For control at high speeds, the 367-80 was provided (as were its KC-135 and 707 derivatives) with inboard ailerons between inboard and outboard trailing-edge flaps and four-segment upper-surface spoilers. For control at low speeds, these surfaces were supplemented by outboard ailerons which were locked in neutral position when flaps were up. Quite surprisingly, the team led by Chief Design Engineer Maynard L. Pennell elected to dispense with servo-hydraulic boost for all primary flying controls in favour of aerodynamically balanced

The Dash 80 is readied for the rollout ceremony, and appears to be undergoing undercarriage retraction tests. One of the two cargo doors is also open. (Boeing via Peter M Bowers)

Mrs William E Boeing breaks a bottle of champagne over the nose of the Model 367-80 at Renton on 14 May 1954 while Boeing President William M Allen looks on. According to Boeing Magazine, she christened it Boeing Jet Stratotanker Stratoliner.

The aircraft started ground running tests four days later. (Boeing via Peter M Bowers)

and manually operated controls with spring tabs. Later, however, Boeing adopted powered rudder controls for the 707 and KC-135 and retrofitted the 367-80 with 707 powered-rudder controls in January 1958.

The overall project leader was Ed Wells; the aerodynamic design was the responsibility of a team led by the brilliant, yet demanding German engineer George S Schairer, himself mentor and taskmaster to draughtsman Jack Steiner, who turned theories into plans for the structural engineers, led by Meynard Pennel to turn into blueprints and then metal.

The all-important cabin design, including the doors and seating arrangements, were the responsibility of former systems engineer Milt Heinemann. He in turned hired Frank Del Guidice from the company Dorwin Teague to design the look of the interior.

Before manufacturing of the 367-80 - also known as the 707-7 - got much under way Boeing evaluated

alternative configurations and powerplant installations. A 707-7-27 configuration dated 17 August 1952 featured wingtip tanks and T34 turboprops mounted above and forward of the 35-degree swept wings. A few days later, a 707-7-39 configuration retained the wingtip tanks but was to be powered by six J57s in two twin pods and two single pods. Thereafter only minor configuration changes were made as the 367-80 slowly proceeded from concept to reality.

The 707's swept-back wings may have reduced drag, but they came with a high price in other directions - for they display an undesirable flying characteristic that is termed 'Dutch roll', an occurance that manifests itself as an alternating yawing and rolling motion. Boeing already had considerable experience with this on the B-47 and B-52, and had developed the yaw damper system on the B-47 that would be applied to later swept-wing configurations like the 707. However, many novice 707 pilots had no experience with this phenomenon, as they were transitioning from straight-wing propeller-driven aircraft such as the Douglas DC-7 and Lockheed Constellation.

On one customer-acceptance flight, where the yaw damper was turned off to familiarise the new pilots with flying techniques, a trainee pilot's actions violently exacerbated the Dutch roll motion and caused three of the four engines to be torn from the wings. The plane, a brand new 707-227, N7071, destined for Braniff, crash-landed on a river bed north of Seattle at Arlington, Washington, killing four of the eight occupants.

In his autobiography, *Tex Johnston: Jet-age Test Pilot* test pilot Johnston describes a Dutch roll incident he experienced as a passenger on an early commercial 707 flight. As the aircraft's movements did not cease and most of the passengers became

The Dash 80 is tugged slowly out of the factory onto the ramp on 14 May 1954. According to Boeing Magazine, 8,000 employees and 500 visiting community leaders crowded onto the ramp to watch the proceedings. (Boeing via Peter M Bowers)

ill, he suspected a mis-setting of the directional autopilot. He went to the cockpit and found the crew unable to understand and resolve the situation. He introduced himself and relieved the ashen-faced captain who immediately left the cockpit feeling ill. Johnston disconnected the faulty autopilot and manually stabilised the aircraft '...*with two slight control movements*'.

The first metal for the Dash-80 was cut in October 1952, with the intention that this aircraft would be an aerodynamic and structural prototype that would validate the anticipated performance of the type, but still be available as a company-owned aircraft for the large number of major and minor development programmes that would hopefully emerge as the type proved its worth as a civil and military transport. After steady progress on the Dash-80, the prototype was rolled out nineteen months later.

In March 1954 Boeing publically revealed that they were targeting the Dash 80 at three distinct 'customers'. The first was as a military tanker, designed for Strategic Air Command (SAC) of the USAF having dual duties for aerial refuelling and group movement transportation.

The second - also for the USAF - was as a military troop and cargo transport tailored to the needs of the Military Air Transport Service (MATS). The third, and mentioned almost as an afterthought, was as a long and medium range commercial airliner.

By the time the 367-80 flew in July 1954, all pretence had been dropped and the aircraft carried the 707 designation on its fin.

The Dash-80 emerged from the construction facility doors on 14 May 1954, complete in company livery of bare metal under surfaces, cream upper surfaces and chocolate brown trim along the fuselage sides, wing leading edges and engine pods. The specially chosen registration was N70700, picked out in brown on the vertical tail and along the upper surface of the starboard wing.

The Model 367-80 could be regarded as a combination of the fuselage capacity offered by the C/KC-97 series with the aerodynamics and structure of the B-47 and B-52, together with a conventional tricycle landing gear arrangement. The Dash-80 was powered by four Pratt & Whitney JT3C turbojets, the civil version of the J57 used in the B-52 bomber, and rated at a similar 10,000 pounds thrust. The tail unit was very closely modelled on that of the B-52 in design and basic structure, and so too was the wing, which was considerably more rigid, however, and provided with a pronounced dihedral angle slightly reduced from that of the tailplane. Field performance was improved by the provision of Fowler type flaps along the trailing edges of the wings between the roots and the ailerons, with a gap to the rear of the inboard nacelles to remove the possibility of interference with the exhausts of these two engines. Lateral control was ensured by two pairs of ailerons, a small inboard pair located between the flap sections being used at high speeds, and a larger outboard pair located in the conventional tip positions being used at low speeds, an interconnection with the flaps ensuring that these latter ailerons became operative only when the flaps were lowered. Extra roll control was added by upper-surface spoilers, which operated in concert as airbrakes or differentially as ailerons.

The fuselage was again a double-bubble (vertical figure 8) as used in the C/KC-97 series, but with the inward crease at the junction of the two lobes faired out to a superior aerodynamic profile. Also retained was the fuselage width of the C/KC-97, exactly 12 feet; the cabin area was 90 feet long. But as the Model 367-80 was intended solely for flight and experimental trials, the fuselage interior was bare to provide space for batteries of instrumentation, and though facilities were provided for galleys, lavatories and the like, these were not fitted; neither was the full row of windows along the sides of the fuselage. The use of the Dash-80 for experimental purposes was greatly facilitated by the fitting of two large cargo doors in the port side of the fuselage, one at each end of the cabin area. There was also provision of cargo tie-downs and aerial refuelling equipment.

The first flight of the Dash-80 was delayed by a near-disaster when the port main landing gear leg collapsed during taxying trials on 22 May. It was six weeks before the damage was repaired, and

Above: Tex Johnson signs for the Dash 80 from the projects flight engineer L A 'Bert' Binegar.

Below: Johnson and Loesch climb into their flight gear and prepare to board the aircraft. (both Boeing via Peter M Bowers)

Boeing President William M Allen poses for photographs with Tex Johnson and Dix Loesch before the first flight of the Dash 80.

Legend has it that Allen is supposed to have told them 'She's in your hands boys. Good luck and we'll be looking for you in a ltle while!' (Boeing via Peter M Bowers)

It flies! The Dash 80 climbs away from Renton. Alongside the runway are a number of KC-97 tankers and, lining the side of Interstate 5, literally hundreds of vehicles. (Robert Winans via Peter M Bowers)

examination of the broken unit revealed that the basic steel stock had been delivered with a flaw; Boeing thus altered its quality control procedures to involve closer examination of raw materials before the expensive machining process. All was ready on 15 July 1954.

At 2.14 pm Alvin M. 'Tex' Johnson, the chief of flight test, lined up the Dash 80 on the threshold of runway 13 and opened up the throttles; thirty seconds later he released the brakes for the take-off roll. With Interstate Five on his left, seventeen seconds and two thousands one hundred feet later the aircraft was airborne.

The first flight had been scheduled for 7am, but this being Seattle, the day dawned with a watery, low overcast Thursday morning. Daylight was diluted with gray mist. The weather bureau promised clearing by noon. The flight therefore was postponed until 2 pm. The gathered press grumbled and sat down to a five-gallon jug of hot coffee. Many of them had been up since 3:45 that morning to prepare for the 7 am flight.

By noon the weather was starting to clear. At 12:52 pm an aircraft tug was attached to the nose-wheel unit and the aircraft began a three-quarter-mile tow to the Renton field apron.

William M. Allen, president of the Boeing Airplane Company and the man most responsible for Boeing's entry into the jet transport field, was an early arriver at the airport. He waited until Johnston and co-pilot Richard L. 'Dix' Loesch had posed for cameras and answered reporters' questions before he caught Johnston's arm in a firm grip and checked on the progress.

Interestingly, nowhere in any of the contemporary reports or documentation relating to the early flights of the Dash 80 is there any mention of the third crewmember - the flight engineer being carried. This is somewhat surprising for the aircraft - along with its successors the KC-135/717 and the 707 - all had flightdecks arranged for three man operation, indeed, much of the aircraft's fuel system management could only be done from the flight engineer's station.

According to some sources, these early flights

A spectacular low-level head-on picture of the 367-80 taken during one of the early test flights.
(Vernon Manion via Peter M Bowers)

were flown without a flight engineer so as to keep the flight crew to a minimum - the reason? the aircraft had no escape hatches!

The occasion was definitely a media circus - white-overalled ground crew began asking the crowd to move back. Cars of other spectators lined the hills around and alongside Interstate 5 that ran along one side of the airport; some had been waiting more than eight hours.

Let us let a contemporary newsman pick up the story: *'Tex and Dix entered the plane and the hatch closed behind them.*

Engine No. 1 was started. The time was 1:58. The wind was west northwest 7 knots. A small plane came in just as Tex began to wheel out on the runway. He pulled the big transport to a stop and waited for the 'puddle-jumper' to get out of the way. Then the sound of jet engines echoed off the valley walls as the takeoff roll began.

The airplane gathered speed. Sunlight glinted on the bright yellow skin. Along the sidelines, it was time for the customary holding of breath. Spectators were as motionless as the new plane's older sisters, the KC-97 tankers which flanked the runway in two rows. Twenty-one hundred feet from the start of her run, the

plane lifted off the ground.

'She wanted to go up a little before that...' Tex was reported to have said later, '...but I held her down to slightly exceed minimum control speed'.

'Onlookers, expecting a gradual climb-out, were loudly surprised. For the new jet took to the air like a seal to water - with almost an eager leap. Her angle of climb was sharp'.

Aboard the aircraft, the two-man crew settled quickly into the routine of test flying. At 5000 feet Loesch climbed out of his seat and went down to- the lower cargo deck to make sure the landing gear was up and locked. At 195 knots, the undercarriage was retracted, taking twelve seconds for the mains, seven seconds for the nose.

To check control characteristics, Johnson turned the control wheel full over with one hand, then let go. The Dash 80 righted itself and levelled off quickly.

The first flight constituted a preliminary evaluation of the machine's flight characteristics. Its maximum speed during this flight was about 355 miles per hour. Most of the flying was done at 10,000 feet, but some at 18,500.

The tests included checking the aircraft's characteristics in roll, pitch and yaw.

To learn the landing characteristics of the machine, Johnston went through stall tests and established data used in computing best landing attitude and speed. The pilots were, in effect, writing an operator's manual on the prototype at the same time they flew the aircraft so that they could use the information for the landing. This first flight lasted one hour, twenty-four minutes.

A contemporary news report again: '*Newsmen, anticipating a landing at Boeing Field in Seattle, several miles away from Renton, again waited patiently. Across the runway's south end from them, the usual complement of first-flight fire trucks were stationed for possible emergency. A wind shift changed the plan to come in from the south. The first indication the newsmen had of the change was at 3:30 p.m., when they saw the fire-trucks turn and race for the other end of the runway. 'Where are they going?' asked a cameraman. 'The plane isn't in yet'*

'*That's too bad...' cracked an Air Force major without smiling. '...The fire department quits at 3 :30.''*

But there was time for everyone to catch up with the fire trucks at the north end before Tex and Dix brought the big ship in.

Throats still aching from the pre-takeoff tension were again swallowing dryly as a sweptwing shape settled on the horizon and began to get larger The plane touched down on the eight wheels of the main landing gear first and then settled to the two nose wheels. With light to moderate braking, she pulled up easily, turned and taxied off the 10,000-foot landing strip at the 5000-foot mark.

Bill Allen let his elbows relax against his sides, breathed deeply and wiped a drop of perspiration from the tip of his nose. The first flight was over and he could be proud. Boeing's new baby had performed gracefully.

Tex Johnston felt the same way, and summed his thoughts thus: "This is a very good airplane. So far it meets all of our expectations. I have always had great confidence in both Boeing engineering and Boeing manufacturing. This airplane has not only confirmed' that confidence—it has increased it."

In the course of this and another seven flights during the following week, the Dash-80 was in the air for a fraction under seventeen hours. Officially and publically, the aircraft had excellent performance in the parts of the flight envelope explored as well as

The Dash 80 is towed past a line-up of KC-97s for the US Air Force - the jet would be the forerunner to the design that replaced them. (Vernon Manion via Peter M Bowers)

impeccable handling characteristics. The longest flight lasted three hours fifty-five minutes.

Then the flight programme was again delayed by landing gear problems, when on 5 August 1954 the Dash-80 careered straight over the end of the runway and broke its nose leg when the pilot's, co-pilot's and emergency hydraulic braking systems all failed. It happened after Johnston had been heating up the brakes with a series of high-speed ground runs and stops, then taking off to see what happened in the cold temperatures aloft a process called 'cold soaking' by the engineers. What happened was an expansion of the hydraulic fluid on the ground and a contraction in the air. Johnston did not realise that the hydraulic system had responded by forming bubbles in the lines, which sensors interpreted as a broken brake line. Performing as designed, the sensors promptly shut off fluid flow to the brakes.

Johnston landed daintily, stepped on the brakes, then realised he had none. On one side of the field sat a row of private aircraft; on the other, a line of B-52s. Johnston had one place to go: a grassy median between the runway and taxiway. He hoped the soft earth would slow Dash 80 enough to let him swing the airplane around and roll to a stop. He recalls a sudden crunch. Contractors making runway repairs had left a big block of concrete exactly where Dash 80 would find it. It knocked the nose gear off and damaged the belly, but Boeing had Dash 80 flying again in about three days. A redesign of the braking system sensors solved the hydraulics problem and the Dash-80 returned to the trials process.

Not long after that, Dash 80 chalked up a midair landing gear explosion and fire when the new anti-skid brakes turned out to be spectacularly efficient heat reservoirs. Johnston had heated the brakes doing a series of ground runs, then had flown around with the wheels down for fifteen minutes to cool them. But as soon as the landing gear was retracted, there were several loud explosions accompanied by the smell of burning rubber. As Johnston was to recall: '*There was smoke everywhere, so I speeded up, put the gear down, and blew the fire out.*' He didn't need brakes to stop after landing: five of the ten tyres were flat!

Publicly, Tex Johnston praised the performance of the Dash 80. '*...Without going into specifics, 'this airplane* [was] *not likely to be outperformed by anything this side of the supersonic era*'.

In his flight test report to Boeing, however, he criticised the stability as 'marginal' in some flight regimes. Unfortunately, this finding was somewhat forgotten in the aftermath of the undercarriage collapse incident, and no corrective modifications were made until after several early 707 accidents.

Flight testing also showed that the Dash 80 could take off too soon at too high an angle of attack, resulting in an over-rotation and a much-increased take-off run. A small leading-edge flap cured this problem and was introduced into the early 707 production line. Fixed and moveable flaps were tested on the Dash 80 and a sudden application of the latter was found to convert a take-off roll to a climb of 700-800 feet per minute without application of elevator or trailing edge flaps.

The final thrill involving Dash 80's undercarriage occurred during a test of the thrust reversers. After a

General Albert Boyd in the left hand seat of the Dash 80, with Tex Johnston in the right. It seems that the early flights may have been done without a flight engineer, but by the time this mission was flown, someone was clearly in that role. The tubular-frame seats are a clear sign that this is indeed the Dah-80 airframe. (Boeing via Peter M Bowers)

Left: the forward end of the main cabin of the Dash 80, with flight test equipment and engineers.

Below: ground running. (both Boeing via Peter M Bowers)

series of landings, a hydraulic line let go and the flammable fluid leaked out onto a hot brake. The resulting blaze caused the crew to call for the fire truck and abandon ship. Boeing replaced the entire hydraulic system with one that used less flammable liquid. Flight testing resumed on 20 September.

Air Force interest.

So far the whole development and trials programme had netted Boeing precisely nothing. But the breakthrough of sorts came in August 1954. Boeing had extended every facility to the USAF for the examination of the Dash-80 on the ground and in the air, even allowing General Albert Boyd, commander of the Wright Air Development Center, to take a turn at the controls of the new Boeing jet tanker-transport in October 1954. Since General Boyd was one of the top Air Force pilots of the jet era, what he had to say after his flight was of particular interest to the company.

'*This airplane...*' said the general, '*...is one of the most important projects for the Air Force today. I am pleased with its simplicity and impressed with the rapid progress made in the short time the airplane has been flying. From a pilot's standpoint it is a simple, straightforward plane and very delightful to fly.*'

It seems that General Boyd was not the only one who was impressed. Other men in the Boeing flight crew who completed Phase I tests of the Dash 80 expressed similar reactions. Tex Johnston: '*On September 28 we flew the plane from Seattle to Portland in thirteen minutes. That was a distance of 138 air miles at the rate of 636 mph. At this speed it was entirely smooth riding.*

Boeing President William M Allen was aboard for this check-out flight, and so were E C Wells, vice-president engineering, and William G Reed, a Boeing director. I doubt that any airplane has had three more enthusiastic passengers, and it wasn't only the speed that impressed them. What they liked most were the quietness and smooth riding characteristics of the plane.

I remember Allen's words after the flight: 'I don't see why anyone would want to travel any other way.'

We made some outstanding discoveries about the '707' during these Phase I flight tests. In the first place, the plane had better lateral control at most speeds than any airplane of this size previously built.

One of the most unusual features of the Stratoliner-Stratotanker prototype is the air brake furnished by the spoilers. By raising the spoilers on both wings, the wing lift is decreased and the drag is increased. This feature makes possible a fast rate of descent if required.

As far as the crew is concerned, the '707' is very comfortable to fly and has excellent pilot vision. Cockpit controls are greatly simplified compared to the control and instrument arrangements of piston-engine transports. This is made possible, of course, by the greater simplicity of the jet engines, but it took some design skill to capitalize so thoroughly on the advantage

The four jet engines which power the '707' are JT3s, commercial adaptations of the J57 engine presently used in the Boeing B-52 Stratofortress and certain other military airplanes.

Checking the brake system - the knobbly tyres are 'interesting'! (Boeing via Peter M Bowers)

Engine performance during 100 hours of flight-testing provided essential date for later production. (Boeing via Peter M Bowers)

Soon others were checked out as first pilots on the Dash 80, including Loesch and Lt Col Guy M Townsend, Air Force representative at the Boeing Flight Test Center. Others serving as flight crew for the Phase I programme included L A Binegar, flight test project engineer; Bell Whitehead, lead test engineer; P L Clark and R R Larson, test engineers, and W B Mengel, lead ground operations engineer. In addition, several staff and project engineers were carried.

Instruments on the aircraft recorded all the pertinent data that was brought back to the flight centre and reduced to their most useful form by special equipment and specially trained employees, before being turned over to Boeing aerodynamicists for almost immediate evaluation.

The Dash 80's Phase I programme included tests of longitudinal stability and control, lateral and directional stability and control, stalls, airspeed calibration and vents, performance, power-plant and equipment function.

As many tests as possible were made on each flight - which did not stray more than 250 miles from Seattle. It was on this basis that the aircraft's loading and other factors were established.

All this hard work was rewarded with an announcement from Air Force Secretary Harold E Talbott, who stated that the Air Force intended to buy a 'limited number'of the Boeing jet tankers based on the Dash-80 and intended as cargo and tanker aircraft, primarily for use in support of the

The quintessential test pilot: basball cap, shades and headphones. Tex Johnston at the controls of the Dash 80. (Boeing via Peter M Bowers)

B-52 fleet of the Strategic Air Command. In making his announcement, Talbott declared that '...*aerial refueling of jet bombers with compatible jet tanker aircraft will vastly increase the range, flexibility and capability of the Air Force's bomber force.*'

Talbott gave no indication of how many Stratotankers were involved in the 'limited number' the Air Force had decided to order, nor of when production was expected to begin. He did say, however, that the tankers would be produced at Boeing's Renton, Washington, plant.

Neither the Air Force or Boeing revealed when deliveries of the jet tanker would start. The Boeing company did point out, though, that its building and flight experience with the Dash 80 would make possible a production model many months sooner than would otherwise be the case.

Meanwhile, according to Talbott, the Air Force would go ahead with a jet tanker design competition which it recently initiated among major aircraft manufacturers. The results of this competition, he said, would be used in connection with determination of total tanker requirements. Boeing was among the bidders entering designs.

The order for 29 KC-135A aircraft was placed on 5 October 1954, and marked the beginning of the Boeing design's great success story. As part of the validation programme for the KC-135A series, the Dash-80 was rapidly converted into an in flight-refuelling tanker configuration, a Boeing 'Flying Boom' system being added under the rear fuselage and hook-ups with a B-52 being made (though no fuel was transferred) before the contract was finally signed. The in flight-refuelling trials fully confirmed

the basic type's suitability for the tanker and transport roles demanded by the USAF, and paved the way for one of the most important USAF procurement programmes since the end of World War Two. This whole programme, centred round the airframe designated Model 717 by Boeing, is discussed in detail later.

Shake, rattle and Roll

Despite the tentative faith shown in the Dash 80 design by the USAF, there were ongoing problems with the design of Dash 80's tail. All three test pilots had been aware of them from the start of the test flights, and apparently they were noticeable to others as well.

Flutter is a vibration in the airframe that is induced at high speed in response to aerodynamic forces. It usually arises on an extremity, and, if left unchecked, it can intensify until it breaks up the strongest airframe. Dutch roll—so called because of its resemblance to the rolling side-to-side gait of ice-skating Dutchmen - occurs in all aircraft, but is harder to check in those with swept wings. As the machine yaws from side to side, one wing advances and develops additional lift, causing the airpcraft to roll to the opposite side, which results in a combined rolling and yawing motion. If this motion continues, it creates a cycle of alternating, increasing yaw angles that can result in uncontrollable roll.

The Dash 80's original tail fin was short compared with the fin of the B-52, and not much of a yaw inhibitor. Its size, coupled with the lack of a power boost for the rudder, may have contributed to

Left to right : Loesch, Johnston and Binegar aboard ground transportation. The forward cargo door of the Dash 80 doubled up as a crew door. (Boeing via Peter M Bowers)

its tendency to flutter. '*Flutter was a black science then...*' Dix Loesch is reported to have said.'...*When the flutter guys started talking to their bosses, everybody else just sort of looked at the ceiling.*'

Johnston hunted for flutter in Dash 80 early on, and he found it where it could be expectded - at near maximum speed. Even though the flight engineer's instrument panel was shaking so hard the mounting bolts broke, Johnston coolly reported, '*We're experiencing an appreciable vibration up here*'. Later Loesch encountered flutter during normal climb: '*I did the normal things to fight it - leveled out, throttled back. They didn't work. I thought the airplane was going to shake itself to pieces. All of a sudden the rudder froze, and the flutter stopped.*"

They were extremely lucky - a structural failure saved the day for a balance weight had broken loose and jammed the rudder.

Whatever it was that caused the Dash 80 to shake, rattle, and roll, it was not great enough to prevent Johnston from doing a seemingly impromptu barrel roll in front of 200,000 or more spectators. Then, for anyone who had missed it, he rolled Dash 80 again.

The legend that had grown up around the demonstrations have reached almost mythical proportions - over the years the story has been embellished with the telling until it became a part of aviation folklore.

It started from the second National Turbine-Powered Air Transportation meeting of the Institute of Aeronatical Sciences held in Seattle. Delegates gathered to hear a panel symposium on the first year of Dash 80 flying delivered by the team from Boeing who were directly involved. Boeing Chief engineer George C Martin presented the panel. Joseph 'Joe' Sutter, in charge of aerodynamics work on the prototype; Tex Johnston, Calvin E. Pfafman, assistant project engineer - systems, and Donald W Finlay, Boeing chief of preliminary design.

The reports covered the year's activities; by now Boeing was calling the 367-80 the '707' - note the inverted commas, meaning pseudo 707. They detailed how the testing programme had influenced production design, what uses had been made of test results and how the tests were contributing to the ongoing programmes in the growth of this family of aircraft.

The two phases of the test programme were outlined by Sutter. The first he called a check of basic design concepts and objectives of the aircraft, together with analysis to discover further needs. In Phase II, fixes were incorporated in the prototype and the aircraft reflown to check their validity. '*We have done a year's flying. In June of this year we have been*

Delegates to the National Turbine-Powered Air Transportation meeting of the Institute of Aeronatical Sciences watch a flyby of the Boeing 367-80, by now termed the '707'. Just visible under the tail is the dummy refuelling boom fitted for formation trials with a B-52. (Boeing via Peter M Bowers)

The Boeing 367-80 with a dummy refuelling boom in formation with a B-52. (Boeing via Peter M Bowers)

able to finalize the airplane's configuration; the airplane can be pinned down so production can go ahead and meet delivery schedules.'

Sutter showed a chart detailing test areas which, as he pointed out, covered checks from ground handling through a complete high speed programme.

Pfafman provided insights into systems and structural dynamics. He told of problems encountered and corrections made. He brought out several specific items in which complete information could be obtained only through prototype testing. Flight test results on the lateral control system was one instance cited. The system consisted of four ailerons and eight spoilers. The ailerons were interconnected by a cable system and were tab powered. The spoilers, connected in pairs, were hydraulically powered and, at the outset, were actuated by one control valve in each wing.

Among items which Pfafman said could not be evaluated without flight testing were control loads, spoiler synchronisation, control sensitivity and the up-float loads of ailerons and of spoilers.

As a result of flight test, it was possible to lower lateral control centering force since satisfactory centering of the ailerons was obtained in flight even though centreing was not positive on the ground.

The simplified single-valve control for the spoilers in each wing was found to be erratic in ground check, due to differences in line length and system friction. Individual control valves for each pair of spoilers were installed to solve the problem.

In lateral control sensitivity, he went on, the characteristics without dive brakes were good, but with the dive brakes partially up it was necessary to add a mechanical linkage to reduce the sensitivity.

Up-float loads on the ailerons were found to have been predicted accurately, requiring only adjustments

with the tab. Spoiler up-float loads proved to be less than had been determined in wind-tunnel tests, greatly simplifying the design.

Tex Johnston spoke of '707' flight characteristics and safety aspects. '*We have had considerable experience with swept-wing aircraft, the B-47 and the B-52, and have had no adverse problems from the handling characteristic standpoint. This airplane is as good in all respects, and better in some.*'

It seems that Johnston was particularly pleased with the lateral control system which gave excellent handling characteristics in low speed or cross wind operations. The plane's high speed capability, new to commercial transport aircraft, called for the lateral control spoiler configuration in conjunction with ailerons. Used as drag devices on approach, he said, they permittted practically any angle of approach desired.

Johnston characterised takeoff, climb-out and cruise conditions as entirely normal save that the pilot's duties were considerably reduced by the engine, and thus resultant flightdeck, simplicity.

Rudder, aileron and elevator controls on the '707' were manual and, in Johnston's terminology, '*...very light. In either low or high-speed range it is possible to actuate full control with one hand and without experiencing muscular exertion.*'

In high speed tests Johnston said a Mach number and airspeed placard had been placed on the aircraft when he felt it had exceeded the maximum flight speed it might ever approach in use. This was where neither stability nor buffeting problems had intruded. Trim changes necessary in all high-speed aircraft at high Mach numbers he described as easy to make on the '707.'

'*At these* (high) *speeds the airplane can be flown hands-off. The airplane is solid. We have no flutter problems and no stability problems.'*

He went on to describe letdown characteristics at high speed with lateral control spoilers used as dive brakes as very good. *'With this configuration, we can make descents at as much as 12 to 13,000 feet per minute from altitude to the deck.'*

Donald W Finlay, who supervised the structure of the '707' from its inception and now headed the preliminary design section at Boeing, presented some aspects of future planning to conclude the panel presentation.

'We believed that there was a place in the world for a whole family of airplanes of this type. The '707' family concept showed a wide range of weight from a basic commercial model to the heaviest military transport and tanker ultimately desirable from the fundamental design. A growth parallel to such weight spread, had been achieved with the B-47.'

The prototype was built lighter than the ultimate objectives, but heavy enough to reveal in tests all about large, high-speed jet aircraft not available from contemporary data or through model work.

'We recognized the physical problems of changing the strength, changing space for cargo and fuel as the airplane grew. We had to plan ahead, with a tooling philosophy.'

A number of other papers were presented to the conference. A year earlier at the first one, Boeing's

'707' had just made its initial flight; now the facts of 200 hours airborne were available.

To the initiate, there was a sound backgrounding all sessions of the turbine meeting. This roar of jet engines was brought into the open in an address by Vice Admiral Charles E. Rosendahl, Ret., executive director of the National Air Transport Coordinating Committee. He challenged industry and airlines with the statement that the noise problem in connection with jet aircraft could not be ignored. *'You cannot persuade people that the industry which has produced so many miracles cannot control sound.'*

Anticipated economics of the projected Douglas DC-8 jet transport were presented by Ivar L. Shogran, chief project engineer of the series. Of particular interest to delegates was the statement that the jet airplane's economy in comparison to the current DC-7 was expected to be better down to ranges as low as 500 miles.

Raymond D Kelly, United Air Lines' superintendent of technical development, reported on the ground handling of jet transports which he called 'a new machine tool for the airlines.' Cutting of ground time he listed as a major factor in the economics of jet transports. *'...Each wasted minute of ground time deprives a jet of almost nine flight miles.'*

It was during this conference that Tex Johnson

The famous - or should that be infamous? - barrel roll of the Dash 80 over Lake Washington.(via Peter M Bowers)

heard rumours: '*I'd heard that Douglas was telling people our prototype was an unstable airplane, and I believe that when you fly for a company, you sell the product by demonstrating what it can do.*'

On 7 August 1955 conference attendees moved to the shores of Lake Washington for the Gold Cup hydroplane races. The American Power Boat Association Challenge Cup, known to all as the Gold Cup, is to power boat racing what the Super Bowl is to football, what the Kentucky Derby is to horse racing, what the World Series is to baseball, and what the Indianapolis 500 is to automobile racing, and is the ultimate prize that every competitor strives to win at least once, and the race was watched by tens of thousands around a three mile course. William Allen asked Tex Johnson to fly the Dash 80 over the course as a kind of demonstration.

Johnston, wearing a flight suit and his trademark cowboy boots, was in the pilot's seat. Alongside him, in the co-pilot's seat, was Jim Gannett. A Boeing engineer, along for the ride, was in the cabin with a camera.

Co-pilot Gannett had an inkling of what was coming several hours earlier, when Johnston flew the aircraft through a couple of rolls during a test flight. Allen, however, had no idea. When he looked up and saw his company's biggest investment on its back, he looked like a clinical example of apoplexy, according to people seated near him. After rolling the aircraft for the first time as he passed over the race course, Johnston made a wide turn and then returned - repeating the roll.

The crowds below oohed and aahed. They had just witnessed aviation history. Carl Cleveland, then head of Boeing public relations, says that at the time

of the manoeuvre, he was on a yacht in Lake Washington with assorted bigwigs in the airline industry, including Bill Allen: '*After the first barrel roll, Bill Allen turned to me and said, 'I don't think we should have anything in the papers about that.' But I said, `All those people just saw it. I don't know how we can stop it.*'

It was rumoured that Boeing surpressed the story, but Cleveland always claimed that the reporters covering the race simply forgot to mention it '*...for some damned reason.*' He thought that members of the press - mostly sports writers - were more interested in the outcome of the race than in what was happening overhead.

Everyone loved the stunt, but William Allen, Boeing's President, never got over it. He fired Johnston at least a thousand times before they met the next morning and cooler heads prevailed. Nonetheless, the infamous manoeuvre was a forbidden subject in Allen's presence for many years. At his retirement dinner in 1980, he was given a huge photograph taken from one of Dash 80's windows while the Dash 80 was upside down. He left it behind.

The stunt may have impressed airline executives, but it didn't cure the problems in Dash 80's tail fin. Boeing eventually discovered that changing the fin's internal balance weights, increasing its size, and adding an electronic yaw damper and a hydraulically boosted rudder control ended the problems with flutter, yaw, and Dutch roll.

It has often been said that since Tex Johnston did this with the Dash-80, no one since had deliberately rolled a jet airliner. It is possible however, that the loss of a Lufthansa Boeing 720 - D-ABOP - on 15 July 1964 during a training flight was another such

Piling on the flight time! As the Dash 80 entered its third one hundred hours of flying, on one week it was flown flown by pilots of four American and one foreign airlines. Here is Captain 'Gus' Sommermeyer of United Airlines in the captain's seat with Tex Johnson alongside. Given the positioning of Tex's 'bone dome', this must have been taken pre-flight! Pilots from American, KLM, Northwest, Pan Am and United took turns at the controls. (Boeing via Peter M Bowers)

occasion, but this time with tragic results. It seems that the pilot-in-command was 'proving it could be done' to his companions on board; he sucessfully accomplished one roll, but on the second attempt the aircraft lost control when inverted, broke up and crashed near Nuremberg, killing the three on board.

Initial Airline discussions

Having successfully attracted orders for the C/KC-135A variant from USAF, Boeing moved their attention to winning orders from the airlines for the 707. The Dash-80, however, suffered the same fate as the Model 247 - the cabin was not large enough. Boeing then tried to save money by going on a charm offensive to the airlines, trying to justify the use of the same 144 inch width fuselage (and therefore making use of the same fuselage tooling) as the KC-135 which they thought was sufficient for four First Class, five Standard Class or six Tourist Class seating but the airlines demanded even more room and eventually the fuselage width was increased by another four inches over the KC-135 and the length was extended by a further ten feet.

A series of protracted discussions with the airlines began, and Pan American in particular, due to their transatlantic services, to try and convince them of their need for jet aircraft. Since the existing piston engined aircraft were capable of flying New York to London direct, Pan American and the other major airlines were unwilling to accept less range in the next generation of airliners and the 707,

as originally proposed, was marginal in this respect. Boeing were reluctant to modify the design, while Douglas, who had a much better relationship with the airlines, had recognised the importance of the 707 on air travel and announced the launch of their DC-8 competitor on 7 June 1955. The original DC-8 was also marginal on range but was still a paper exercise, so Douglas offered modifications to produce a heavier, longer range variant to meet the airline's requirements powered by Pratt and Whitney JT4As.

As a result, Juan Trippe and Pan American decided on the Douglas DC-8 and ordered twenty-five for transatlantic services but, because the 707 had an unassailable lead in terms of time, they also ordered twenty 707s to protect their commercial interests and to act as insurance across the Atlantic until the DC-8s were available.

These historic orders were announced on 13 October 1955. Pan Am intended to use the new type on tran-Atlantic and trans-Pacific services from December 1958, the last of the 20 being in service by November 1959.

Both Boeing and Pan Am's Sales and Public Relations people made much of the reduction in flight times. *'Transoceanic non-stop flights will be made in about half the present scheduled time. Jet*

Above: Walt W Braznell, Director of Flying Operations, American Airlines in the right hand seat of the Dash 80.

Left: C R Smith, President of American Airlines (left) and William Allen of Boeing sign the contract for Boeing 707s to be delivered in 1959. (both Boeing via Peter M Bowers)

flight will carry the passenger above the weather. The Boeing 707 Jet Stratoliner will provide soothing, vibration-free travel to the far reaches of the earth.'

Juan Trippe went on record as saying: '*The planes will provide a new high standard in speed and in passenger comfort in Pan American's pattern of non-stop over-ocean service.*

'*The vibration and noise caused by propellers will be eliminated. In fact, there is complete absence of all vibration and the sound of the jet turbine engines is audible only to passengers in the very after part of the cabin.'*

Pan American later disposed of the DC-8s and continued to operate 707s right up to the introduction of 747s and beyond; they ordered their last ones in late 1967 and withdrew them in early 1981, a full 22 years of service by the type.

Boeing reacted to the disappointment of being second-best in the eyes of Pan American by announcing new variants of the 707 - the original version ordered by Pan American was powered by the JT3C engine of 12,500lbs thrust, and they now announced that this was to be known as the 707-120 and there would be JT4A powered 707-220 and 707-320 variants.

The 707-120 was offered with two fuselage lengths, the standard and a special short version while the 707-220 was offered with the JT4A turbofans of 15,800lbs thrust, again in both fuselage lengths and the 707-320 was the long range version, it had a lengthened fuselage, greater wing span, more fuel capacity but the same engines as the -220.

When Rolls-Royce Conway 508 engines were specified in place of the JT4A, the 707-320 became the 707-420. this proliferation of models meant that the break-even point for the 707 was pushed a long way back. As a result of these improved versions, Pan American decided in December 1955 to amend its order from twenty 707-120s to six 707-120s and fourteen 707-320s.

Following Pan American's decision to take air travel into the jet age, other airlines were faced with the decision of following suit and remaining competitive or falling behind the pace makers and as a result sales teams from Boeing and Douglas were busy with potential customers.

Boeing received their next orders, however, not from another transatlantic carrier, but from a domestic trunk airline, namely American Airlines, who ordered thirty 707-120s on 9 November 1955. The last five of this order were subsequently cancelled when 720s were ordered in their place.

The early JT-3C engines were incredibly noisy, so various styles of noise-reducing nozzles were experimented with. A least ten different styles were flight-tested after more than two hundred paper designs were studied. This one, in front of test pilot Jim Gannet and flight test engineer Bruce Mengel was not accepted. (DGR Photo Library)

Walt W Braznell, Director of Flying Operations, took part in some of the demonstration flying aboard the Dash 80 on 15 September 1955, as was reported in *Flight Deck*, American Airlines publication for pilots and flight engineers: '*I had been asked to take a look at the Boeing 707 cockpit as part of an evaluation team looking over new airplanes. En-route to Seattle I was informed there might be a ride in the 707 in store for us. I visualized the usual bucket seat, windowless flight associated with prototype demonstrations, with the added attraction of a glimpse of the instrument panel over someone's shoulder - if you were lucky.*

In Seattle I read in the paper that Boeing was demonstrating the 707 and some of the airline people would be permitted to occupy the right-hand pilot's seat.

Tex Johnston welcomed our group aboard the 707. I noticed immediately the right cockpit seat was filled - with Tex Johnston. Motioning to the left seat, Tex asked of Dan Beard and myself, who wanted the first go at it.

The thought immediately occurred to me that

In a Manhatten NY warehouse Boeing and the Teague organisation built a mock-up of the Boeing 707 airliner. Walter Dorwin Teague Associates was one of the USA's leading industrial design companies and, under the direction of Frank J Del Giudice, came up with the design and layout of not only the mock-up but also equipment for the interiors of the actual aircraft. They also produced a brochure for perusal by potential airline buyers.

Come aboard THE **707**

☞ '...Four lavatories are available in the 707, styled to duplicate the effect of a small power-room in a private home'

✐ '...Five abreast seating provides seat-widths equalling those of conventional four-abreast airliners. Versatility permits change to either four or six-abreast configuration while retaining comfort.'

☞ '...Cantilevered seats permit unobscructed legroom, armrests fold up. Opaque window shades provide restful darkness. Smoke-tinted shade cuts glare, permits view'.

☞ '...Dual galleys permit greatest flexibility in food service. As many as 180 meals can be served.'

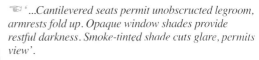

☞ '...Galleys on the 707 are equipped to serve the most tempting of cuisine, in the best tradition of every airline'

A stream of airline executives and such luminaries as Charles Linbergh - at the time an advisor to TWA - were led through the interior mock-up. Boeing added some Hollywood style effects, such as recordings of engine noise and cabin announcements in order to give the impression of jet flight.

☞ '...While a lounge is available fore or aft, it may be removed and replaced with additional seating.'

☞ '...The possibilities for color and decor is evident in one version of the 707 club-like lounge.'

(a) Johnston considered Dan and me finished jet pilots or (b) he knew his craft was so easy to handle that even a couple of desk pilots could not get into trouble with it. The answer of course was that Johnston knew Dan had little experience on jets, I had none at all, and both of us were desk pilots.

I bowed to age and Dan took over first. For the next hour-and-a-half we really had fun. For myself the flight was easily the most exhilarating of my flying career, and I'll include my solo ride in this statement.

To me, a most remarkable part of the experience was that I felt so at ease in a completely strange airplane. The operational simplicity was obvious and invited quick confidence.

While weather threatened to close the field (which had neither GCA nor ILS) and thus held our flight to low altitudes, 2000 and 3000 feet, Tex had no reluctance to demonstrate engine and engines out (on the same side) performance. As a matter of fact, we did slow flight and stall nibbles with gear

and flaps down while 2000 feet above terrain. My impression from these maneuvers was that the airplane has the greatest forgiveness factor of any I have ever flown.

I had heard stories about the complexities of air starts. Had gathered such was like betting on the Irish Sweepstakes. Tex demonstrated the simplicity of air starts by flicking a switch and

Above: Braniff officials aboard the Dash 80: J H Alexander, R V Carleton and Robert E 'Bob' Sawyer. In the right hand seat is Dix Loesch of Boeing. (Braniff)

Below: Three SABENA vice presidents fly aboard the Dash 80. From left to right: M C Stainler, Anselme Vernieuw and Fecicen Pirson. (SABENA Belgian World Airlines)

From the lack of view out of the windows, it is thought that both these were posed pictures taken on the ground.

Above: Henri J Lisieur and Max Hymans of Air France appear delighted with their trip aboard the Dash 80. (Air France)

Left: The ice machine flown on the Dash 80 to test the effects of ice formation on the engine pylons.

Below: the fifth engine fitted to the Dash 80 for 727 design trials so as to test the effects of an aft mounted engine.

placing the throttle in the Idle-Start position. The simplicity of this operation is a good example of many such comparisons of the jet operation versus present-day airplane operation. Tex had us chuckling like a bunch of kids watching a magician pulling rabbits out of a hat.

The acceleration and deceleration capabilities of the 707 were of course very impressive, but even though expecting great things in the way of a quiet, vibrationless cockpit, I wasn't ready for what I found. You must experience it to believe it. The only thing disturbing the churchlike quiet of the front end was the 'clacking' of the fuel totalizer, a sound problem that must be brought to the attention of the instrument manufacturer.

Braniff followed on 1 December 1955 with an order for five 707-220s for use on its hot and high South American routes, then Continental announced an order for four 707-120s on 12 December 1955.

Overseas orders came in from Air France who wanted ten Intercontinental 707s, with options on more; SABENA Belgian World Airlines announced its order for three - later increased to four Intercontinental 707s - on the same day; 28 December 1955.

On the down side, the expected United sales were lost to Douglas, they ordered thirty DC-8-21s on 25 October 1955 and were followed by National and Eastern. Both United and Eastern later ordered 720s however, and all three subsequently operated large 727 fleets.

By the end of 1959, a hundred 707s had rolled off the production line at Renton, and the first of several hundred KC-135s had been delivered to the USAF's Strategic Air Command. The Dash

80's career as a prototype and dealer demo was finished, but Boeing was not yet ready to put it out to pasture. Although it was very different to any of the 707s - or KC-135s for that matter - and was by no means a jet airliner, it was to become involved in a great number of test programmes to improve the safety, efficiency and comfort of commercial aircraft.

Most of these trials began after the 707s started to roll off the Seattle production line and included noise reduction, cabin interior linings, Boundary Layer Control and slotted flap studies.

A number of design studies involved major changes in the Dash 80's appearance. By all accounts it seems that for a period in 1959 it was fitted with a large nose radome for the Bendix AN/AMQ-15 weather reconnaissance radar that was later used on WC-135Bs. The Dash 80 was also fitted with addtional equipment to collect high altitude data and to monitor drop and rocket sonde weather probes.

In the early 1960s, Dash 80 was used to test a

By the time this picture was taken in 1959, the Dash 80 had grown all sorts of lumps and bumps, and a new nose. There are different engines and pylons on the inboard positions, and the airframe carries a few roughly patched up marks. (DGR Picture Library)

modification that would later show up in the 727, with a fifth engine fitted at the rear of the fuselage to validate this location for the 727's engines.

These tests led in turn to a long stint with NASA and Boeing testing wings that could generate enough lift for the aircraft to remain airborne at extremely low speeds. Dash 80 had averaged 612 mph during a transcontinental speed record flight in 1957. Now it was creeping around Seattle skies at 80 mph and landing at 92 mph. Dismayed commuter airline pilots had to S-turn their Douglas DC-3s on final approach to Boeing Field to avoid overrunning what appeared to be a 707. To preserve control at such ridiculously low speeds, the Dash 80 sprouted a profusion of leading and trailing-edge devices on its wings.

Gannett continued to fly Dash 80 throughout the low-speed tests, but Johnston and Loesch had moved on and were replaced by S. Lewis Wallick, and Thomas Edmonds. In test of leading-edge slats for the wing, engineers experimented with the curve of the slats by applying fibreglass to the devices and shaping them between flights. Leading-edge symmetry was critical—without it, the aircraft tended to roll uncontrollably in a stall. This imprecise shaping of the wing made for occasional imbalance and some very sporty flying. Edmonds recalls a day when one flight was enough: *'We stalled, rolled over to about 90 degrees to the horizon, did a split-S, and ended up headed in the opposite direction. We looked around, kind of startled, and decided there was no point in doing any more stalls that day.'*

The Dash 80 wore its high-lift wings to the end of its career, and Boeing and NASA engineers tested a series of design ideas that depended on solid control at slow speeds. The aging aircraft was landed on grass, dusty lake beds, soft earth, and even mud, using a landing gear system being considered for what would become Boeing's ultimately unsuccessful submission for what would eventually become the Air Force's enormous C-5A Galaxy transport. The landing gear spread the weight of the aircraft over twenty tyres instead of Dash 80's ten. The tyres' flotation allowed the aircraft to land on dust-covered mud only marginally more supportive than yogurt.

In 1965, with a long needle-like sensing unit, a comical face painted on its nose in honour of its 11th anniversary, and computer-mediated controls, it imitated the landing characteristics of a series of supersonic designs for NASA. A second set of controls enabled the copilot to take over and fly the airplane normally, a precaution that allowed the computer to crash without the Dash 80 following suit. The Dash 80 also tested scores of cockpit instruments and controls, some of which later showed up in the video display cockpits of the 757 and 767.

On 22 January 1970, after completing the last of a series of flights designed to test an automatic landing system for the space shuttle, Dash 80 went into retirement. Its logbook showed 1,691 flights over sixteen years for a total of 2,349 hours and 46 minutes, but it was not quite closed.

As a company-owned aircraft it played a vital part in the success of the Model 707 and related C/KC-135 families, but was also modified in an almost unbelievable number of ways to test features for later versions of its own family, and also structural, aerodynamic and power plant aspects of other Boeing aircraft. with the development of heavy military transports capable of operations from relatively small and unprepared airfields close to combat areas.

After 2,350 hours and 1,691 flights the aircraft

Blown flaps and high lift wings (above), and high-floatation landing gear that could not be retracted (left) were just some of the devices tested on the Dash 80.

Below: A needle nose sensing unit - with a comical face painted on it in honour of the 11th Anniversary of the Dash-80s first flight - was used to test computer-mediated controls for the landing characteristics for a number of supersonic designs.
(all DGR Picture Library)

was withdrawn from use in 1969 and placed in storage at Davis-Monthan Air Force Base near Tucson, Arizona. In 1972 there was a huge international aviation trade fair planned for Washington Dulles Airport under the title of Transpo '72. A star attraction was to be N70700 and so the Dash 80 was ferried back to Seattle, where Boeing employees refurbished the airframe, fitted a 707 nose and repainted it in the original house colours. On 26 May Boeing donated the 367-80 to the Smithsonian Air and Space Museum, which had designated it one of the twelve most significant aircraft of all time. At that time the National Air and Space Museum had not even opened its new building on the Mall in Washington and the Dulles exhibition centre and resoration facility was only a distant dream, so the Dash 80 returned to the Arizona desert.

For the next eighteen years the aircraft was stored at the 309th Aerospace Maintenance and Regeneration Group (AMARG). In 1988 it was noticed that the condition of the machine was starting to deteriorate, so arrangements was made with the Smithsonian for Boeing to conduct a full analysis of the aircraft's structural and operational condition. before being retrieved by Boeing. The arrangement was simple: the aircraft would return to Seattle and Boeing would act as its custodian until the museum could build an annex.

Early in April 1990, with Boeing project pilot Paul Bennett at the controls, it was flown from Arizona to Boise, Idaho, for refuelling, then from Boise to Moses Lake, Wash., to prepare for the

N70700 - the famous Boeing 367-80 - The Dash 80 On display at the Steven F. Udvar-Hazy Center, an annexe of the Smithsonian Institution's he National Air and Space Museum near Washington DC.

Right: the flight deck area can be seen through a bulkhead displaying part of the aircraft's history. This area is not usually open to members of the public.

brief flight home to Seattle on 19 May.

Over the next year or so Boeing used the Dah 80 in numerous public events and flew it a few times, including on 15 July 1991, to commemorate the 75th birthday of The Boeing Company.

In 1996 the Smithsonian finally found someone to support the annexe concept: Steven F Udvar-Hazy, the CEO of International Lease Finance Corporation and a good Boeing customer, but it was not until 2002 that plans were made to return the Dash 80 to the museum.

In the spring of 2003 a completely new restoration team was selected, the aircraft was taken out of storage in Plant 2 and the machine was prepared once again for flight.

This occurred on 2 August, and the next day it flew at Seafair over the same hydroplane course where Tex Johnston performed his barrel rolls 48 years earlier.

Three weeks later, on 24 August, the Dash 80 left Seattle for the last time. The flight plan included stopping for fuel, first in Rapid City, South Dakota followed by two days at Wright-Patterson Air Force Base in Dayton, Ohio. Sitting on the tarmac in Dayton next to the aircraft was a KC-135, the first derivative of the Dash 80.

The Dash 80's final flight was to Dulles International Airport near Washington, DC on 27 August 2003, where it was met by crowds of specators and media. The aircraft was then put on display in the Steven F Udvar-Hazy Center, an annex of the Smithsonian Institution's National Air and Space Museum, located adjacent to Dulles Airport in Chantilly, Virginia.

Chapter Five

'Passin Gas'... and so much more.
The 135 series.

Boeing may well have been busy both designing and building a jet tanker/transport as well as the next generation civil airliner in the shape of the Model 367-80 as a company funded prototype, but that was not the only machine which the United States Air Force was interested.

The USAF considered several other proposals including a tanker version of the Douglas DC-8 airliner, a proposed Douglas turboprop design, their own design as well as two from Boeing - one at a take-off weight of 261,00 pounds and one at 295,00 pounds. The turboprop option, although slow, was initially favourite but was later dropped.

At Strategic Air Command's Requirements Conference in November 1953, General Curtis LeMay called for two hundred jet tankers. The Air Force announced a design competition for a jet tanker

on 5 May 1954, inviting Boeing, Convair, Douglas, Fairchild, Lockheed, and Martin to participate. At that point Boeing's leaders could only forge ahead with the Dash-80, which had its first successful flight test on 15 July, and pray that it would win the competition.

From as early as 1949, the Lockheed Aircraft Corporation had been quietly working on their own jet airliner design, the Model L-193, named the Constellation II, with a swept wing and engines mounted at the tail. Lockheed proposed the same as Boeing - both an airliner and tanker version.

Lockheed sought input from Howard Hughes' Trans World Airlines for the airline's requirements and several sub-variants were developed. Technically, they were quite advanced. Notably, they featured unconventional engine installations such as a

The Dash 80 being formated on by a B-52 during a simulated tanking, watched by a T-33 chase aircraft.

staggered configuration with four turbojets mounted on the aft fuselage sides, with the inboard engines mounted aft of the outboard pair but fed by side-by-side intakes. Another configuration had either four or five turbojets mounted side by side beneath the fuselage. Others had a swept wing with the engines mounted at the tail similar to an Ilyushin Il-62 or Vickers VC-10. It was designed to be slightly smaller than the Boeing 707 and Douglas DC-8 of the time. Lockheed used features seen in its previous designs, including tip tanks similar to the Lockheed Constellation and a double-deck fuselage similar to the Lockheed Constitution. A modified L-193 - supposedly designated the CL-291 - was entered into the SAC tanker competition,

On the Dash 80's seventh flight in July 1954 it practised a mock refuelling sortie with a B-52 and on 3 August 1954, with the jet-tanker design competition still in progress, the Air Force decided to buy interim tankers. The Air Force Secretary, Harold E. Talbott, announced an order to buy twenty-nine tankers from Boeing. Less than two weeks later the Air Force said it would buy a further eighty-eight Boeing tankers. It looked as if Boeing was set to win the competition, but it didn't.

In February 1955 the Air Force announced that Lockheed had won the competition and at least one of its tankers would be funded for construction. In the very same announcement, however, Talbott said the Air Force would buy an additional 169 tankers from Boeing. By some accounts the aircraft was designated KCX-LO, - presumably standing for 'Tanker Cargo Experimental - Lockheed' and was re-designated the CL-391 to take into account a number of USAF changes. The same accounts suggest that first prototype would have been the XK-1.

By now Boeing was suggesting that the KC-135 could be delivered two years earlier than the Lockheed design, and was able to be put into squadron service four years earlier. So despite having won the aerial refueling competition and was apparently preferred by the USAF over the Boeing KC-135 Stratotanker orders, the Lockheed proposal was cancelled.

A few months later, in June, the *Chattanooga Times* uncovered that Talbott was using Air Force stationery to solicit business from contractors who sold to the Air Force for an engineering firm of which he owned fifty percent. After a swift Congressional investigation, Talbott resigned from his position as Secretary in August.

Right: Boeing employees installed insulation-soundproofing material in the interior of the first KC-135. (DGR Picture Library)

General Curtis Emerson LeMay, Head of Strategic Air Command, who did so much to promote the KC-135 and the B-52, one of the prototypes of which he is seen in here. Upon receiving his fourth star in 1951 at age 44, LeMay became the youngest four-star general in American history since Ulysses S. Grant. (USAF)

Possibly as a result of the Congressional Investigation, extreme political pressure was brought to bear to attempt to overturn the purchase of KC-135As and even cancel the programme. Protracted contract negotiations eventually led to the placing of orders for 810 aircraft but only 732 tankers were delivered - eighty-eight were built as variants after SAC realised its potential for other duties such as Airborne Command Posts and Reconnaissance platforms as well as a transport for MATS.

Some myths die hard, and it is important to dispel the suggestion that the KC-135A was somehow a military version of the Boeing 707 airliner. It was not. The KC-135A (or Boeing 717) preceded, and paved the way for, the commercial machine which became so successful with the world's civil carriers. Without doubt, both shared a common heritage in the vision

of Boeing's engineers and finance people, and both are progeny of the private Model 367-80 prototype.

The K-135A flew eighteen months before the first genuine 707, however, and differed from it in several important respects, having a more narrow fuselage and completely different cross-section. It was so different in fact that the two could not be produced on the same factory jigs.

Boeing eventually received USAF approval to use the KC-135 assembly process for the 707 models since USAF did not pay any development costs, and provided Boeing assured that the 707 would not cause problems with KC-135 production, and they would pay a 'royalty' per 707 airframe built with KC-135 tooling.

Publically, Boeing credited the major role in driving the speed of KC-135 production through on schedule to a planning committee. Meeting once a week, it grasped problems as they arose and set out to solve them.

For instance, when a report came that certain forgings were not going to be available on time, the committee acted. A committee member representing the materiel department contacted the sub-contractor making the rough forgings and persuaded him to go on a seven-day work week. Another member representing traffic arranged for high-speed shipments. A quality control member established priority for the receipt and inspection of the forgings on arrival. A member representing the Boeing machine

shop set up an accelerated schedule of machine work on the rough forgings. Result: the finished forgings were delivered to the assembly line on time.

A wide range of problems were brought to the committee as the KC-135 production picked up. Each item was tackled from the viewpoint that no delay in production would be tolerated. In consequence, the first production KC-135 was expected to roll out of the Renton factory door on schedule in the summer of 1956.

Clearly, however, other factors besides the planning committee's determination contributed to the KC-135 programme. Harvey Kent, factory manager of the transport division, went on record saying that the aircraft was engineered to the highest degree of good production practices he had ever seen. This, he claimed, not only made production easier, but held costs to a minimum, with consequent

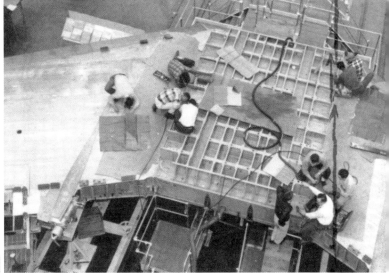

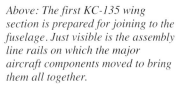

Above: The first KC-135 wing section is prepared for joining to the fuselage. Just visible is the assembly line rails on which the major aircraft components moved to bring them all together.

Left: The assembly line for the KC-135. It was extended in the winter of 1956.
(both DGR Picture Library)

The first KC-135, 55-3118 'City of Renton' nears completion at Renton, with the KC-97 production line behind. (USAF)

savings to be passed on to the Air Force.

Having a prototype machine built and flying was of great value to both KC-135 production and commercial airliner production. By late 1956, the Dash 80 had undergone extensive tests on the ground and more than 400 hours of flight test, so Kent estimated that the experience gained cut production time on the first KC-135 by at least 20 per cent.

The horseshoe-shaped KC-97 final assembly track was reduced to a single line with an assembly line for the KC-135 established alongside it. Aircraft on the two lines stood almost wing tip to wing tip, so the transfer of skilled employees from one operation to the other could be done with a minimum of expense and wasted motion. In the autumn of 1956, the last KC-97 was completed, the KC-135 final assembly line was lengthened into an S shape and production accelerated.

One of many effective steps taken to aid KC-135 production was the construction of a full-scale mockup of the tanker/transport. The mockup was constructed from engineering drawings which included design refinements made as a result of experience building and flying the Dash 80. The mockup proved the feasibility of all installations.

Even before any aircraft flew, Boeing began testing a static airframe at Seattle. To achieve this result a partial fuselage, complete with wing centre section and front and rear spar fittings, was subjected to various forces in a water tank and after a simulated 70,000 hours flying it was damaged to check for potential problems. It seems Boeing had learned their lesson from the De Havilland Comet tragedy.

This test airframe, built between the seventh and eighth aircraft, was not allocated a construction number by Boeing. There were some minor design changes as a result of the tests and these were incorporated in actual production aircraft while data from the trials and the later cyclic test airframe were used in the reskinning programme.

The static test 'airframe', part of 45 feet wide, 100 feet long and 24 feet high KC-135 aircraft was taken from Renton, Washington, to a 'torture chamber' at Boeing's Seattle Plant. (DGR Picture Library)

The first order of twenty-nine aircraft were built under the Boeing designation of Model 717-100A with constructors numbers 17234 to 17262 and USAF serials 55-3118 to 55-3146. Unsubstantiated rumours abound about the USAF ordering the KC-135 following a roll by the Dash 80 during a test flight - the feeling being that this demonstrated that the aircraft was capable of 'combat manoeuvres'; but that myth has never been proven!

Following the initial order Boeing had to modify the design concept to reflect the USAF requirements; these were increasing the length by eight feet three inches and making the fuselage twelve inches wider and two inches deeper, to 164 inches. The rear cargo door was deleted, leaving just the forward fuselage door which opened upwards and outwards and increasing the gross weight to 316,000 pounds, which was 68,000 pounds more than the first civilian 707s.

Thousands of Boeing employees observed the roll-out of the first KC-135 - a ceremony that was accompanied by a low-level flyover of the Dash 80 and a B-52 bomber. A predictable group of dignitaries was assembled for the occasion, including Boeing President William Allen, Air Force Lt-Gen Clarence S Irvine (deputy chief of staff for materiel), Renton's Mayor Joseph R Baxter, and Karen McGarrigle who had the distinction of being 'Miss Renton 1956'. Miss McGarrigle christened 55-3118 *City of Renton*,

although it was the mayor's wife who swung a bottle of Cedar River water against metal for the event, assisted by Renton factory manager Harvey Kent.

Engineering ground tests of engines and pre-flight work on *City of Renton* began during the week of 23 August 1956. Kent reported satisfactory progress with Boeing's 'shakedown', Air Force inspections and taxi runs, and indicated that the first eight production tankers would take off from Renton and land at Boeing Field in Seattle for delivery to the Air Force. The ninth airframe was to go to the nearby Moses Lake Flight Center for delivery.

Dix Loesch, now the project pilot on the KC-135 programme, told the gathered press that the first nine production tankers would undergo an estimated 1,380 hours of flight testing, with one airframe to be subjected to three months of sub-zero investigations in simulated Arctic conditions in the climatic hangar at Eglin AFB, Florida. Aircraft 1, 2, and 3 were scheduled for flight testing by the company at Boeing Field while Aircraft 5 through 9 were scheduled for the Air Force at Edwards AFB, California; Loring AFB, Maine (an operational SAC base); Eglin; and a special adverse-weather testing location at Ladd AFB, Alaska.

At the end of August 1956, Air Force Secretary Donald A Quarles announced that the production of Stratotankers would be speeded up, a previously-planned production rate of 20 per month to be realised 'substantially sooner'. General LeMay had told the Senate Armed Services Sub-committee of SAC's need for more jet tankers. '*We* [can] *increase our intercontinental strike capability considerably from our planned base structure and with the same*

Left: Mrs Joseph Baxter breaks a bottle of Cedar River water over the nose of City of Renton.The Cedar River provides drinking water for the greater Seattle area and drains into Puget Sound via Lake Washington and the Lake Washington Ship Canal.

Below: 55-3118, the first KC-135, is rolled out alongside the last KC-97, 53-3616, built. (USAF)

size bomber force if we [have] *more jet tankers than we are now programmed to have'*.

LeMay compared the KC-135A to the piston-engine KC-97: *'The slower conventional tanker, in order to make proper contact with its bomber, must depart several hours before the bomber. The bomber, forced to wait on the ground, is then exposed to enemy attack. The airplanes we are now refuelling are jet airplanes.*

'A jet tanker has the same general performance characteristics as the bomber, and therefore can accompany the bomber, eliminating the rendezvous problems. In addition, the performance of the jet tankers is such that the refuelling altitude is at a height above most of the weather ...and adds to range because the bomber does not have to descend to piston-engine altitudes to receive its load of fuel'.

Ten days ahead of the planned schedule, just before 1pm on 31 August 1956, *'City of Renton'* made a trial taxi-run at Renton and took position at the south end of the runway for its maiden flight. Aboard were Boeing's chief of flight test, Tex Johnston, and senior experimental test pilot Dix Loesch, the latter occupying the left-hand seat as pilot-in-command. Loesch took the KC-135A aloft and after one hour nineteen minutes landed at Boeing Field in Seattle. Also on board was Boeing President William Allen. He commented on the trouble-free flight: *'In the first place it was remarkable that the plane was in the air about a week and a half ahead of schedule and in the second place, it was my first time to fly a new-type airplane on its maiden flight'*.

From the outset of its rigorous flight test programme it was apparent that the KC-l35A had been designed to a standard of performance consistent with LeMay's high expectations. Powered by four Pratt & Whitney turbojets which were as advanced as anything in their day. It was a heavier and more solid aircraft than its 707 civilian contemporary and thus needed a runway as long as 13,700ft in tropical weather, a distance which would have been completely unacceptable for an airliner.

After three test flights and three hours thirty-eight minutes in the air, *City of Renton* was laid up at Boeing Field for installation of additional equipment and flight test instrumentation. By October 1956 the KC-135A was flying again, and made its first successful delivery of fuel in flight, to a B-52.

'The KC-135 has had fewer systems problems than any plane I know of', Loesch was quoted in one press statement.

Loesch could not have predicted how successful the KC-135A would be, but the flight test programme continued through the end of 1956 with so little

difficulty that all scheduling goals were exceeded. On 24 January 1957 *City of Renton* was officially delivered to the US Air Force, Maj Erich Schleier signing its acceptance.

In early 1957 *'City of Renton'* took part in Phase II flight testing which showed that it could off-load nearly 80% more fuel than the KC-97 at altitudes up to 35,000 feet - compared to the KC-97's ceiling of 18,000 feet. It was not all roses however, as the aircraft suffered from severe rudder flutter at high speed, it experienced 'Dutch Roll' - exactly the same as with the Dash 80 - especially during landing and refuelling, the boom required high stick forces and the aircraft suffered from 'unsafe' take-off control with an engine out. Boeing had intended to fit a yaw damper as part of the autopilot but its development was delayed 'so the Dutch Roll remained a problem even when the yaw damper was fitted as it was considered ineffective. *'City of Renton'* had J57-P-29A's of 10,500 pounds of dry thrust or 12,100 pounds with water injection while all subsequent aircraft had J57-P/F-43W's of 12,925 pounds thrust with water injection.

Take-off power was marginal when fully loaded and in an attempt to increase power a demineralised water injection system was installed to boost power by 2250 pounds of thrust per engine, but the original system was designed that one pump control system powered the left hand engines and one the right with catastrophic results when one side's system failed on take-off. It was later redesigned so that one provided power to the inner engines and one to the outer pair.

The engine-out performance on take-off and climb out remained critical and was only really cured with the KC-135E and KC-135R/T re-engining programmes. Later the -43W was replaced by the -59W which was identical except that the titanium parts were replaced by steel ones as a cost saving move (in 1950's costs the saving was in the order of $100,000 per engine even though there was a weight penalty of 400 pounds per engine). Incidentally, the letter P related to engine built by Pratt & Whitney and F meant it was assembled by Ford Aerospace, otherwise they were identical.

The rudder flutter problem which plagued both the Dash 80- and the KC-135 design was helped by adding extra layers of aluminium to the top of the fin and fitting dual rudder dampers while a hydraulically powered boom improved its operation but was not perfect. The fitting of a tall fin - increasing its height by forty inches - and powered rudder boost reduced the pilot's input during instances of engine-out and was introduced on the 583rd KC-135A produced (62-3532) and subsequently refitted to the remainder.

The second aircraft, 55-3119, was used for static air load survey tests while five others were involved in over 1000 hours of acceptance testing. 55-3121 was flown to Wright-Patterson AFB for adverse weather tests that would take it to Elgin's climatic hangar and then included Arctic icing trials and cold temperature soaks down to -65° Fahrenheit followed by high temperature trials in Arizona; 55-3122 in performance evaluation; 55-3124 in stability tests and 55-3125 and 55-3126 *City of Moses Lake* both took part in functional tests and 56-3591 was used by Boeing for refuelling compatibility testing.

Normal flight crew was four; pilot, co-pilot, navigator and boom-operator or 'boomer', while power was provided by four Pratt & Whitney J57-P/F-43WB non-afterburning turbojets of 11,200 pounds thrust dry and 12,925 pounds thrust wet with water injection. This meant that the aircraft was restricted to a minimum 13,000 foot long runway when fully loaded even when using water/methanol injection as take-off run was 9,250 feet at normal operating weight when at sea level and 59° Fahrenheit. Although the original USAF requirement

KC-135 55-3118 in flight with the Dash-80 and T-33 chase aircraft. (DGR Picture Library)

The classic water-methanol 'smokey-joe' take-off is demonstrated by this unidentified KC-135. The smoke stopped as soon as the water-meth was switched off. (USAF)

was a maximum take-off weight of 295,000 pounds, Boeing showed that the airframe was capable of operating at 325,000 pounds, but the engines had insufficient power for this weight. At hot or high elevation airfields the aircraft could not take off fully laden! The J-57 engines gave the KC-135A a top speed of about 600mph, a ceiling of 45,000ft and a range of 9,942 miles using all internal fuel. Mission range was 2900 nautical miles with a transfer of about 95,000 pounds of fuel. The use of water/methanol injection led to a characteristic black smoke trail on take-off but as soon as the injection was switched off the trail ceased, KC-135As carried a 700 gallon water tank for take-off, but supplies of sufficiently pure water was sometimes a problem, especially on overseas deployments.

Initially fuel was carried in six wing tanks as well as an integral centre wing tank and two fuselage tanks, one forward and one aft of the wing although later a rear upper deck tank was also fitted - the body tanks were beneath the main deck and comprised several cells in each. There were two refuelling pumps installed (one forward, one aft) and fuel could be moved from tank to tank in flight. The KC-135A could either use all the fuel itself or off-load it to a receiving aircraft (a minimum 300 US gallons is retained in each main wing tank) and the maximum fuel load is 30,000 US gallons - or 195,000 pounds - while comparative figures for the KC-135R are 31,725 US gallons. or 203,300 pounds.

There was a distinct difference in service-life ideals between the civil and military variants; the civil 707s were designed to be fail-safe while the KC-135, which would probably fly a lot less, was designed to a safe-life requirement including the use of different aluminium alloys in the fuselage and on the lower wing surfaces (7178 in the military version and 2024 in the 707). The original specification was for a life of only 10,000 hours which was reached by some of the aircraft in the early 1970s.

The use of the 7178 aluminium alloy led to fatigue problems caused by engine exhaust impinging on the rear fuselage,but this was cured by the fitting of twenty-five stiffeners around the fuselage between the rear of the

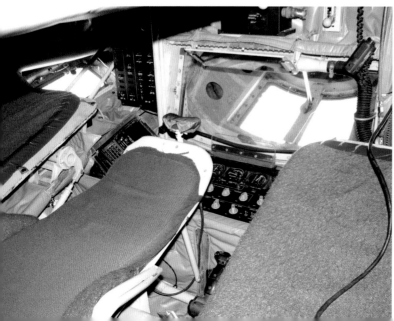

The boomer's position in the rear of a KC-135. The centre couch, complete with head/chin rest belonged to him, those either side was for either Instructors or observers. (USAF)

Above: The boomer's position from outside and below showing the three windows there and the aerodynamic visor raised. The rear fuselage also clearly shows the additional stiffeners fitted to the KC-135s to help prevent damage caused by engine exhaust efflux.

Below: the business end of the high speed refuelling boom, showing the probe in the retracted position. (both USAF)

135A was 31,200 US gallons, carried either in the wings or under the main cabin - all of which could be used by the tanker to extend its own range or transferred to receiver aircraft at a rate of up to 1,000 US gallons per minute. The fuel in the wing was usually for tanker use while the fuel intended for transfer was normally carried in the lower un-pressurised fuselage compartments.

The initial means of transfer was the Flying Boom nozzle but this was later changed to allow probe and drogue refuelling from the boom since the majority of US Navy and NATO air forces use this method'. Two types of Flying Boom could be fitted, one for use at all speeds and one that can only be used up to 330 knots. The boom is normally against the underside of the rear fuselage when not in use and operated in cone of movement; plus 12.5°, minus 50° vertically and 30° horizontally either side of the flight datum.

Operation of the boom is from a pod under the fuselage, where the boom operator lays on their stomach facing rearwards with the controls in front of them, also fitted are additional positions for use by instructors, students or observers. The boom contains a probe which extends to make contact with the receiver's refuelling receptacle, when contact is made fuel is transferred.

By June 1957, testing and deliveries of the KC-135A were proceeding so smoothly, with so little difficulty, that Boeing could only get their achievements into local newspapers by trotting out another beauty queen - Margery Barr, who held the title *Miss West Seattle* - and posing her with a 135. Like many stories in aviation, the KC-135A was now something of a non-story. The media only carried reports when an aircraft splattered against a mountainside or disintegrated above a crowded city, not when a flight development and production effort proceeded with minimal difficulty.

Even at the end of June when the first three KC-135As to reach SAC were delivered to the 93rd Air Refueling Squadron, part of the 93rd Bomb Wing at Castle AFB, California (the first of these being 55-3127), the event was newsworthy only because of the presence of Colonel Winston Close, the Wings deputy commander. Close, by all accounts, had scored a hat trick, picking up the first B-29 manufactured by Boeing in Wichita in 1943 and also the first B-52D!

A myriad of variants

When is a KC-135 not a KC-135? With well over sixty variants of the basic aircraft a KC-135 may not be a tanker at all but may be, instead, a transport, a

wing fillet and the dorsal fin. Using data from the cyclic test airframe and in-service histories it became apparent that wing underskins were an area of concern so from 1975 onwards the entire tanker force was modified with new lower wing skins to increase the expected life to approximately 30,000 hours.

Absolute maximum fuel capacity of the KC-

The refuelling boom was far more than just a tube within a tube, as this picture of six booms undergoing deep maintenance shows. The boom adjacent to the one being worked on shows some of the mechanism involved in controlling it via the flying 'vanes'. (USAF)

command post or a reconnaissance aircraft. One of the KC-135's many roles is the test function. Others carry out full-time or part-time duties which may or may not require the aircraft to be modified.

It may seem obvious, but the first thing is to look at the designation. KC aircraft are usually tankers, but not always. C aircraft - for cargo - are always transports, not just usually, but some of the time VC aircraft are transports, too, used to carry dignitaries. EC aircraft have an electronic role of some sort and are usually flying command posts. RC aircraft have the reconnaissance role.

Every machine in the KC-135 Stratotanker series has such a prefix, but machines derived from the Boeing 707 airliner have wholly different designations. The US Air Force's system for designating its aircraft dates to 1924 and is straightforward enough but is far from perfect, so there are inconsistencies.

Fuselage differences: A narrower double-lobe fuselage 128 feet 10 inches long with very few windows identifies one of the many machines in the KC-135 series. A fuselage with larger width, full double-lobe cross-section, windows (sometimes) and greater length identifies a military derivative of the Boeing 707 airliner.

Other external features peculiar to the KC-135 series and not found on derivatives of the Boeing 707

airliner include the plain pylon struts which support the engines (the 707 having some or all struts terminating in a ram air inlet for cabin, air-cycle conditioning) and, of course, the boom operator's position and high-speed refuelling boom pivoted under the rear fuselage.

Powerplant differences: All KC-135A tankers and some other members of the family were originally powered by the annular-intake Pratt & Whitney J57 (civil designation JT3C) two-spool, axial-flow turbojet engine with water injection which produced about 13,000 pounds thrust at 8,200 rpm and was notorious for smoky take-offs. Thrust reversers were not fitted. This engine weighed 3,870 pounds and had a diameter of 38.90 inches. It was the same powerplant employed by the B-52 Stratofortress.

All C-135B variants, all Boeing 707 derivatives (except the E-6A and Saudi KE-3A) and many rebuilds of the KC-135 series were powered by the Pratt & Whitney TF33 (civil designation JT3D) turbo-fan engine which produced about 18,000 pounds thrust at 8,700rpm and was developed from the J57 through removal of the first three compressor stages and replacement by two fan stages, the result being a nacelle which was longer and more perfectly cylindrical in appearance. Thrust reversers were employed. This engine weighed from 4,130 pounds to 4.570 pounds with a diameter of 53 inches.

Newer KC-135R and French C-135FR aircraft employed the F108 - as called in US military use, and known in civil use as CFM56-2B-1 and manufactured by CFM International, a consortium of General Electric and France's Sociefe Nationale d'Etude et de Construction de Moteurs d'Aviation (SNECMA). Saudi KE-3As and the E-6A had the almost identical CFM56-2A-2. This engine weighed 4,612 pounds and is 95.7 inches in length. A subsonic turbofan in the 20,000 pounds thrust class, it was shorter and, more importantly 'fatter' than other powerplants. It is not an exaggeration to say that this engine on the KC-135R gives the illusion of almost dragging the ground, the simple result of its girth.

Vertical fin differences: Early KC-135A tankers were delivered with a manually-operated rudder. These so-called 'short-finned' aircraft had a height of thirty-eight feet five inches and were identifiable by the fin cap being mounted directly above the rudder. They were retrofitted, and later production KC-135s were delivered with a powered rudder. This produced a forty inch fin extension and was identified by a fin extension above the rudder with the fin cap installed on top, the height of the aircraft being increased to forty-one feet eight inches.

Firstly, let us look at the new-build aircraft, as supplied from the original Boeing C/KC-135 production line. This comprised of 732 KC-135As, 4 RC-135A, 10 RC-135Bs, 15 C-135As, 10 C-135Bs and 12 C-135Fs.

KC-135A

The first order of 29 aircraft were built under the Boeing designation Model 717-100A with constructors numbers 17234 to 17262 and USAF serials 55-3118 to 55-3146. The order was placed by the USAF on 5 October 1954.

The first three aircraft were delivered to 93rd ARS at Castle AFB, CA on 30 April 1957 and they began KC-135A operations in June 1957. Eventually deliveries of the KC-135As peaked at 15 aircraft a month and all 732 were completed by 12 January 1965, when 64-14840 was delivered to 380th ARS.

C-135A

Both Boeing and Douglas proposed swing-tail cargo aircraft to USAF in the late 1950s to update their strategic airlift capability. This resulted in forty-five Boeing C-135A aircraft ordered without the refuelling system as cargo or troop transports with the Model number 717-157 following President Kennedy's decision to create a quick-

The classic Strategic Air Command photograph - a B-52 tanking with a KC-135A.

Boeing C-135A-BN Stratolifter 60-0376 of MATS landing at Prestwick in 1961. The aircraft has dayglo red areas by the cockpit and at the base of the vertical fin.

response capability. The C-135A was not as advanced as the proposed designs and was basically a KC-135A minus the refuelling boom, a strengthened floor and fuel dumping facilities - not a specific transport aircraft although they were seen as an interim aircraft before the C-141 Starlifter was delivered. Seating capacity was increased to 126 troops up to a possible maximum of 160, and additional 'passenger' facilities were installed, such as toilets and increased soundproofing.

C-135s had a cargo handling system built in but this reduced the capacity of the cargo compartment and was seldom used. The requirement for a fork lift truck with ten foot reach also caused some loading problems. The last thirty were completed as Model 717-158/C-135Bs. Following delivery of the Starlifters the C-135s were relegated to other missions such as command support, airborne command posts and test beds.

RC-135A

Nine RC-135As were originally ordered in 1962 to replace a fleet of RB-50 Superfortresses although this was later reduced to four due to cost overruns. These aircraft were built as Boeing Model number 739-700 for reconnaissance duties but were the last of the variants of C/KC-135s delivered to the USAF in the mid 60s, although they were not declared fully operational until about 1971. They were built with the J57-P turbojets of the KC-135As but carried cameras just aft of the nose undercarriage bay in place of the forward fuselage fuel tank while the refuelling system was omitted with a fuel dump tube replacing it. They were used for photographic and surveying work and their cameras could distinguish ten foot objects from a height of 40,000 feet. In 1972 they were relegated to support aircraft status then, in the late 70s, they were converted to tankers as KC-135D. Mission crew was nominally ten but not all crew members flew all missions.

63-8061 was one of four RC-135As and was used by the 1370th Photo Mapping Wing. Note the camera bay under the lower front fuselage. (author's collection)

Boeing C-135B-BN Stratolifter 62-4137 of MATS gets airborne from Prestwick, Scotland in 1963.

C-135B

The original order for C-135As was for forty-five aircraft but only the first fifteen were completed as such, the remaining thirty being built as C-135Bs. The power units were Pratt & Whitney TF33-P-5 turbofans (the military designation of the JT3Ds of 16,050 pounds thrust used to power civilian 707s) and this extra thrust required modifications to the horizontal and vertical tail surfaces resulting in the new Boeing Model number 717-158.

Like the C-135A they retained the boom operators pod but the refuelling probe was deleted. Maximum load was 89,000 pounds or 126 combat troops or 44 litters and 54 seats in med-evac role but they were used mainly as transports until superseded by the Lockheed C-141 Starlifter. Some were used as transports for middle ranking staff, others were converted to weather reconnaissance aircraft as WC-135Bs. On 20-21 February 1963 a C-135B flew from Clark AFB in the Philippines to McGuire AFB, a distance of 9,868 miles to set a new world record for transport aircraft. The last C-135Bs were converted to RC-135Ws in the mid 1990s, Most of the C-135Bs were modified to reconnaissance variants or other designations but three were lost while still operating as C-135Bs, one during the Cuban missile crisis while supplying the Guantanamo Naval Base in Cuba.

KC-135B

These were fitted with the flying boom installation but were also provided with air refuelling receptacles so their normal eight and a half hours endurance could be extended by in-flight refuelling. KC-135Bs were powered by the TF33-P turbofans (but without thrust reversers) as the C-135B and were used as Airborne Command Posts. The cargo deck was divided into office, communications and living compartments; the plan being that at any one time a command post aircraft would be airborne (with one on standby) with a staff officer - that is a general or above - capable of maintaining communications with the Armed Forces in case of war. This operation ceased in early 1990 following the ending of the Cold War and they now stand runway alert. Shortly after delivery the majority of the aircraft were re-designated EC-135C with SAC while the remaining three became EC-135J with National Command Authority.

61-2667 was originally built as a C-135B Stratolifter, but was converted to WC-135B standard in 1965.
(author's collection)

63-8054 was built as a KC-135B and was later converted to an EC-135C (author's collection)

RC-135B

Similar to the RC-135As but fitted with TF33-P turbofans without thrust reversers, these were electronic intelligence (ELINT) aircraft and were the first variant specifically built for use as a reconnaissance platform. They were the final aircraft produced from the original C/KC-135A family with the last deliveries made in 1965 and were delivered direct to Glenn L Martin Co for storage prior to conversion to RC-135Cs.

C-135F

The French Air Force (Armee de l'Air) ordered twelve tankers in 1962 to refuel their Mirage IVA strategic nuclear bombers and they were delivered in 1964. They were originally ordered with turbofan engines but the French accepted J57 engines because of costs. They do not have the 'K' tanker prefix as they were planned to be used ln the dual tanker/transport role, but are permanently fitted with the probe and drogue adapter since the French employed this refuelling system. They were test flown using USAF serials and reserialled with the last five of the USAF serial in French

service. They were powered by J57-P turbojets, eleven being converted to C-135FR and operated by ERV.93.

Modifications

The basic design of the C/KC-135 was soon seen as being highly suitable for a number of specialised missions that spawned a proliferation of designations which emanated from the changes of role from one use to another, or in some cases also switches between services.

The following listing is an alphabetical order by prefix letter.

C-135A 'Falsies'

Three KC-135As were built to partial C-135A standard prior to delivery of the proper aircraft; these were 60-0356, 60-0357 and 60-0362 and were referred to as C-135A 'Falsies' due to the refuelling system. The C-135As were built with the boom operators pod in place but no refuelling probe while the three converted tankers could be reconverted to tankers if required. They were converted into KC-135A-II 'Office Boy' by Ling Temco Vought (LTV)

12739 of the French Armee de l'Air coded 'CK' formerly 61-2739 of the USAF. (author's collection)

Scenes from inside an EC-135 in the role of Airborne Command Post

. Top left, the Intel Team, top: the Data Operator. Above and left: the Battle Staff.

Below: the lumps, bumps and aerials are clearly visible on this 'Looking Glass' aircraft flying 'on station'

(all 2AACS/USAF)

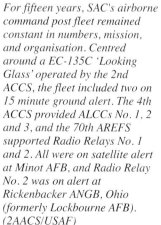

For fifteen years, SAC's airborne command post fleet remained constant in numbers, mission, and organisation. Centred around a EC-135C 'Looking Glass' operated by the 2nd ACCS, the fleet included two on 15 minute ground alert. The 4th ACCS provided ALCCs No. 1, 2 and 3, and the 70th AREFS supported Radio Relays No. 1 and 2. All were on satellite alert at Minot AFB, and Radio Relay No. 2 was on alert at Rickenbacker ANGB, Ohio (formerly Lockbourne AFB). (2AACS/USAF)

NKC-135A of the US Navy's Fleet Electronic Warfare Systems Group (US Navy)

from September 1961-April 1963 and re-designated as RC-135Ds by January 1965.

EC-135A

These aircraft were fourteen KC-135As converted with additional avionics to act as radio relay link aircraft in support of the SAC Post-Attack Command Control System, an airborne command and communication system with the capability to take over from destroyed ground installations following a nuclear attack. The first machine, 62-3579, was delivered to Andrews AFB on 2 September 1964 followed by two more in November and the other eleven were redesignated on 1 January 1965. The air refuelling system was retained but the aircraft could also be refuelled to enable an extended flight envelope of up to seventy-two hours duration.

They were powered by the J57-P turbojets but received extra antenna. All were either reconverted to tankers, withdrawn from use or modified to EC-135Ps. The five FY58 aircraft were transferred to USCINCPAC as 'Blue Eagle' airborne command posts in 1965 while the remainder operated as 'Looking Glass' machines, so called as they mirrored SAC's underground command post. Those converted were known as (RT) aircraft.

GKC-135A

The 82nd TW at Sheppard AFB, TX used one retired tanker for training on the heavy airframes in the USAF's inventory. The aircraft was handed over in October 1992 and received the above designation.

GNC-135A

This ex-test aircraft was withdrawn in June 1976 and transferred to Chanute AFB, IL as an instructional airframe, and broken up in October 1991 with the aft fuselage moving to Wright-Patterson AFB, OH.

GNKC-135A

55-3124 was a retired tanker, previously used as a test airframe. Located at Sheppard AFB, TX it was used as a ground instructional airframe by the 82nd TW.

JNKC-135A

Sixteen early KC-135As were dedicated to full-time testing roles and were given the J-prefix to show their status as test aircraft. Those converted to NKC-135A status were intended to be long term test airframes and not be converted back to tanker configuration.

NC-135A

60-0377 started out as a standard C-135A Stratofreighter. It was converted to the NC-135A configuration when it was adapted to be the B-2 avionics testbed, on which the radar and navigation systems were tested and validated with over 300 sorties, before the B-2 took to the air. (In some sources, it's referred to as an NC-135A and a C-135E,

At some stage in its life 717-148 60-0377 was used as an avionics test aircraft for the B-2 'Spirit' stealth bomber. (author's collection)

USAF NKC-135 'Big Crow' with oversized nose at a forward deployed operating base.
(TSgt Robert J Horstman USAF)

but there's no indication that these are correct). After the B-2 program came to an end, the aircraft was retired and put into storage at Edwards AFB.

KC-135A Relay

During the conflict in South East Asia the USAF converted two KC-135A to communications relay role to provide airborne communications capability for tactical aircraft conducting combat operations where they operated as 'Combat Lightning' aircraft. They acted as communications relay between the EC-121T airborne warning and control aircraft and the ground processing station for operational combat missions as well as MEDEVAC and rescue ops, and could also pass information between ground units. Modifications included numerous small antennae on both the upper and lower fuselage and they carried an AN/ARC-89 communications relay set internally. Following conversion by LTV Electrosystems the first two, (61-0271, 61-0280), arrived in Japan in September 1966 and operations began in October. They were later supplemented by two EC-135Ls until five more converted KC-135As were delivered. While the primary role was radio relay they could also act as tankers in an emergency. Following withdrawal from SE Asia in 1973, two were converted back to tankers while the others lost some of the radio relay equipment and were also used as

tankers but retained their antennae as well as provision for relay gear. At least two other KC-135As were converted to Relay role in the late 1970s.

NKC-135A

Three C-135As were converted to NC-135A for the Atomic Energy Commission, they were developed under the 'Rivet Digger' programme to monitor Nuclear Test Ban Treaty violations. Following conversion by General Dynamics, one was assigned to each of the AEC labs and were used to monitor atomic fireballs, optical and spectral data collection and radiation analysis. They were later reassigned to Air Force Systems Command.

These were modifications to the original tanker aircraft that would prove uneconomical to reconvert to that purpose. Different aircraft were converted for different purposes, some by alternative services such as the US Navy. They were used in a wide range of trials ranging from weightlessness training for astronauts, through ECM and related fields, ALL, airframe icing trials, communications research, advanced air refuelling techniques to some reconnaissance system testing including some highly classified programmes. All were later assigned to Air Force Systems Command except the USN examples.

Some of the many programmes undertaken by the NKC-135A fleet include High Energy Laser and

Airborne Laser Lab (55-3123); winglet testing (55-3129); celestial navigation testing (55-3134); 'Big Crow' ICBM vulnerability programme (55-3132); and ALOTS (Airborne Lightweight Optical Tracking System) testing. The pod was mounted on the a C-135 cargo door and could be fitted to the aircraft when needed. 55-3123, the aircraft in the USAF Museum, was used as the original Airborne Laser Lab and is credited with shooting down five Sidewinder air-to-air missiles and a target drone! 55-3129 was employed by NASA to test Whitcomb winglets to determine fuel cost savings but the programme was not proceeded with while others have been used for various ECM equipment testing. In the case of 55-3135, converted to TF33-PW-102 (JT-3D) turbofan engines and used for refuelling tests with new aircraft while the 'Big Crow' aircraft (55-3132) was also re-engined in January 1991 having been fitted with IFR in 1986. 55-3134 and 56-3596 were transferred to the US Navy for the Fleet Electronic Warfare Support Group (FEWSG) which was later named Fleet Tactical Readiness Group (FTRG) in September 1994 then Fleet Information Warfare Center (FIWC) in October 1995. They were allocated US Navy serials 553134 and 563596 respectively and used for ECCM (Electronic Counter-Counter Measure) training and testing and resulted in the service's later order for E-6A aircraft. One of the FTRG aircraft, due a major service, was flown to Davis-Monthan AFB in mid-1995 following a period of storage at Greenville, TX and was followed by the other eight months later.

EC-135B

Two aircraft from the original C-135B T/RIA (Telementry/Range Instrumentation Aircraft)

conversions were themselves converted in 1979/80 to EC-135B ARIA configuration following the installation of PMEE (Prime Mission Electronic Equipment) from two EC-135N ARIA's (60-0372, 62-41333), when they were demodified for other uses. Subsequently the PMEE was installed in C-18A's 81-0891/6 respectively when they were converted to EC-18B ARIAs. The EC-135B retained the TF33-P-5 engines of 18,000 pounds thrust.

The two EC-18B Advanced Range Instrumentation Aircraft were retired 24 August 2001. Both EC-18Bs assigned to Edwards AFB were transferred to the Air Force's Joint STARS programme by September 2001. The costs associated with maintaining the aircraft and its capability became a major factor in ending the ARIA programme.

The 452nd Flight Test Squadron at Edwards Air Force Base operated a variety of unique, highly modified C-135 and C-18 aircraft to plan and execute DoD, NASA, and operational flight test programmes. Missions supported include worldwide telemetry gathering, international treaty verification, spacecraft launches, ballistic missile defence, electronic combat and vulnerability analysis, aircraft icing tests, and aerial refueling certification.

The 452 FTS accomplished its primary mission using the Advanced Range Instrumentation Aircraft (ARIA) and the Cruise Missile Mission Control Aircraft (CMMCA). The ARIA, which originally stood for Apollo Range Instrumentation Aircraft, travelled the globe and served as airborne tracking and telemetry data-recording and relay stations. They flew over land where ground tracking stations are limited by geographical constraints and over broad ocean areas where tracking stations do not exist. The

The ARIA nose with its ten foot diameter cover off, revealing a seven foot diameter steerable radar dish. (USAF)

OC-135B from the 55th Wing, Offutt AFB, Nebraska, seen arriving for Royal International Air Tattoo 2000 held at RAF Cottesmore in the UK (author).

93

unit supported a variety of national and international customers, both military and commercial, including NASA and Department of Defense missions supporting unmanned space launches, cruise missile tests, Army, Navy and Air Force ballistic missile tests and space shuttle launches.

The Advanced Range Instrumentation Aircraft (ARIA - pronounced Ah-RYE-ah) were EC-135E and EC-18B aircraft used as flexible airborne telemetry data recording and relay stations. These aircraft were designed and developed to supplement land and marine telemetry stations in support of DOD and NASA space and missile programs. The ARIA have the capability to acquire, track, record, and retransmit telemetry signals, primarily in the S-band (2200-2400 MHz) frequency range. ARIA possesses a sagging and misshapen nose as its most distinguishing feature, earning it the nicknames 'Droop Snoot' and 'Snoopy Nose.' The bird's bulbous beak is actually a ten-foot radome housing a seven-foot steerable dish antenna.

OC-135B

Three WC-135Bs were converted by 4950th TW at Wright Patterson AFB, OH to OC-135B standard for operation under the 'Open Skies' treaty. Under this treaty the US was allocated up to 42 flights annually over former Eastern Bloc countries. They are fitted with various cameras (one panoramic, two oblique mounted framed cameras and one vertical mounted framed camera) and the first example was rolled out on 30 June 1993 and was delivered to 55thW on 19th November 93. They are powered by the TF33-PW-102 (JT-3D) engines removed from airliners, but one of the proposed airframes was placed in storage at Davis-Monthan AFB, AZ on 28 September 1993 and replaced by another. Since they are operated in civilian airspace they must comply with ICAO Stage 3 noise regulations and the USAF announced plans to hush-kit the aircraft with new QNC Stage 3 hush-kits, the first one flew with the hushkit in early 1996 although the requirements for the other two was later dropped. A programme to remove the flight engineer's station from the OC-135B's led to their redesignation as OC-135Ws. The aircraft had provision to carry up to thirty-eight crew, the first training flights took place over USA between 24-31August 1994 with a team of American and Ukrainian observers on board.

62-4125, one of five VC-135Bs. (USAF)

TC-135B

One WC-135B which had been utilised by several units as a flight deck crew trainer was converted to this designation and was known as the 'Silk Purse' trainer, and used to train OC-135B 'Open Skies' crews under the designation WC-135W following the removal of flight engineer's station.

VC-135B

Five aircraft from an original C-135B order were converted as VIP transports with special facilities justifying the V-prefix. They were originally used for high ranking staff but this perk was reduced during the Carter administration and the aircraft were downgraded to C-135B again.

C-135B (T/RIA)

Four aircraft from the C-135B production line were converted by Douglas at Tulsa, OK from 1967 with a ten foot 'platypus' nose extension to house a seven foot diameter radar dish for special electronic work; they also carried a theodolite pattern on the starboard fuselage side just behind the cockpit to aid in tracking. They were used as Apollo support aircraft designated T/RIA (Telemetry/Range Instrumented Aircraft) and although similar to the ARIAs did not carry the ALOTS pod. They retained the TF-33-P-5 turbofans and remained as C-135Bs until the remaining three aircraft were converted from 1980 onwards.

Ten C-135Bs were converted by Hayes International in 1965 to WC-135B for weather reconnaissance role for operation by the Air Weather Service. Used to provide low to medium altitude weather reconnaissance (and complemented by high altitude U-2s) they replaced WB-50s and were easily identified by the sampling points mounted on the over-wing escape hatches which were used to gather ambient air for subsequent analysis. They retained the fuel dump facility and had the ARR system installed. Two of the aircraft were converted to C-

135Cs for Military Airlift Command and one for Air Force Systems Command. One of the MAC aircraft was loaned to Tactical Air Command for use as an E-3A trainer at Tinker AFB, OK until replaced by two converted 707s operated by Boeing. Three more were converted to OC-135B, one to WC-135W and the remainder were stored.

61-2666 and -2672 provided atmospheric sampling missions around the world during April and May 1986 following the Chernobyl nuclear reactor accident in the Ukraine, then another was used in 1993 to collect data that confirmed the Peoples Republic of China had performed a nuclear test at Lop Nor on 5 October. They were also used during NASA Space Shuttle launches.

C-135C

Three aircraft - 61-2668, 61-2669 and 61-2671 - were demodified in 1974 from WC-135B back to a transport role. They retain the air-refuelling capability and were the only C-135 transports to have this facility. Also one of the C-135Bs was converted to C-135C status and operated as a VIP aircraft for Pacific Air Forces based at Hickman AFB. HI.

EC-135C

Seventeen KC-135Bs, either already delivered or on order, were redesignated EC-135C on 1 January 1965 and were equipped with communications gear to allow them to operate in the 'Looking Glass' Airborne Command Post role replacing KC-135As. They retained the TF33-P-9 turbofans and were fitted with the refuelling probe in the nose, interestingly they could also draw fuel through the flying boom by reverse action in an emergency. These aircraft carried a variety of antennae including a 'saddle' antenna, various blade and dipole antennas. HF probes and a VLF trailing wire antenna. They received several updates and were equipped with AFSATCOM UHF communications equipment. Three were converted

This KC-135D was previously an RC-135A before conversion (via Simon Peters)

An RC-135 Rivet Joint reconnaissance aircraft moves into position behind a KC-135T/R Stratotanker for an aerial refuelling over Southwest Asia 14 March 2006. (US Air Force photo by Master Sgt. Lance Cheung)

to EC-135J 'Night Watch' machines in the mid 1960's with a fourth conversion undertaken from May 1979-February 1980. Up to 1990, and the ending of the Cold War, one EC-135C was airborne at any one time flying eight hour missions - now they stand runway alert. Beside the Staff officer in charge as Airborne Emergency Actions Officer, there is his 10-man staff on board as well as the standard five-man flight crew. Four aircraft (62-3581, 62-3585, 63-8046 and 63-8054) were fitted with the MILSTAR system from 1990 onwards, but this was removed and used to upgrade E-6As to E-6B standard for the USN. Following the introduction of the E-6A into the ACP function, the EC-135Cs were retired to Davis-Monthan AFB, AZ by October 1998 when the E-6Bs become operational (the similar last remaining EC-135J was retired in October 1993). The type was officially retired in a ceremony at Offutt AFB, NE on 25 September 1998.

RC-135C

The ten RC-135Bs ordered by USAF were delivered direct to Glenn L Martin Co. at Baltimore, MD (later Martin-Marietta) and placed in long term storage pending the installation of reconnaissance equipment. The first one was delivered on 27 January 1967 and all ten were in service by the end of the year, allowing the RB-47Hs operated on SIGINT missions to be retired. The refuelling boom was replaced by the dump tube and the boom operator's position was turned into a camera bay occupied by a KA-59

camera. Modified and re-designated RC-135B aircraft were used for strategic reconnaissance duties, equipped with the AN/ASD-1 electronic intelligence (ELINT) system. This system was characterised by the large 'cheek' pods on the forward fuselage containing the Automated ELINT Emitter Locating System (AEELS – not Side Looking Airborne Radar – SLAR, as often quoted), as well as numerous other antennae and a camera position in the refuelling pod area of the aft fuselage. The aircraft was crewed by two pilots, two navigators, numerous intelligence gathering specialists, inflight maintenance technicians and airborne linguists. When the RC-135C was fully deployed, SAC was able to retire its fleet of RB-47H Stratojets from active reconnaissance duties. All ten continue in active service as either RC-135V Rivet Joint or RC-135U Combat Sent platforms.

KC-135D

The RC-135As delivered to Military Airlift Command were turned over to SAC in 1972, initially as command support aircraft but were quickly converted into KC-135D tankers, they were given a unique designation because they were originally built with a flight engineer on the flight deck. They have since been updated with the retrofit of TF33-PW-102 turbofans without further change of designation. They underwent a cockpit update to bring them in line with the KC-135Es also operated by the unit, they were due to be re-engined with CFM.56-2As and then operated under the KC-135R MDS.

RC-135D

Three KC-135As were redesignated on 1 January 1965 as RC-135Ds 'Office Boy' for use in 'Rivet Brass' SIGINT operations - later used on 'Burning Candy' missions. The refuelling boom was replaced by the fuel dump tube and air-refuelling equipment installed; they also had SLAR antenna fitted in a cylinder shaped fairing below and slightly forward of the wing on both sides of the fuselage and an elongated Hognose radome as well as fence aerials above the fuselage. They retained the J57-P turbojets so had restrictive range, the last 'Burning Candy' mission being flown 13 March 1975 when they were replaced by RC-135Ms and Vs. The RC-135Ds were declared surplus and were converted back to KC-135A tankers, later KC-135R and they retain the ability to air-refuelled. A fourth aircraft (59-1491, the 'Wanda Belle' airframe) was operated with the RC-135Ds but retained its RC-135S designation.

C-135E

Three C-135As were retrofitted with the TF33-PW-102 turbofans and redesignated EC-135Ns later C-135Es for use in combat support roles.

EC-135E

This designation refers to surviving C-135N conversions that were re-engined with TF33-PW-102 turbofans. They have been replaced in their original A/RIA role by ex-airline 707s converted to EC-18B standard and are now used as test aircraft with 412thTW. One was ALOTS capable while two supported cruise missile testing.

KC-135E

ANG and AFRes (later AFRC) units usually operated from noise sensitive civilian airports rather than remote military bases and the noise of a water injected fully laden KC-135A was louder than most fighters with afterburners on. Also, the safety implications in densely populated areas from an engine loss on take-off was enormous (and some, such as Salt Lake City, UT and Phoenix-Sky Harbor, AZ also suffered from altitude or high temperatures) so the USAF had to look at alternatives. With the demise of many airline 707s the United States Air Force took the opportunity to buy the surplus airframes and use the engines to re-engine the KC-135As with the civilian JT3D

A KC-135A is re-engined with JT3Ds from former civilian Boeing 707s at MASDC, Davis-Monthan Az, 1984. (USAF)

(designated TF33-PW-102). Over 150 aircraft were modified and the former KC-135A were re-designated the KC-135E.

In an attempt to improve the performance the first contract was signed with Boeing on 18 September 1981 with a scheduled delivery of the first aircraft on 30 January 1982. The first aircraft (59-1514. one that was air-refuellable) was delivered to Boeing on 30 September and after re-engining flew again on 10 January 1982 and was returned to USAF four days ahead of schedule on 26 January. The first 18 aircraft converted were all special purpose airframes (EC-135s, RC-135s plus some NKC-135s and C-135Ns). Donor 707s were flown to AMARC at Davis-Monthan AFB, AZ where they were stripped and the parts shipped to the BMAC conversion line at Wichita, KS. Changes were the JT-3D engines (redesignated the TF33-PW-102 by the USAF) including thrust reversers, removal of the water injection system, new brakes plus the horizontal stabiliser. In the cockpit there were new throttles and various instruments from the 707 - besides the new engines the provision of a yaw damper with the increased size of the new stabiliser finally eliminated the problem of 'Dutch Roll' on final approach.

Improvements included an increase in available take-off thrust from 13,750 to 18,000 Ib. per engine meaning a fully-laden KC-135E required 2000 feet less runway than a KC-135A to get airborne. The new engines also gave 12% better fuel consumption, 60% noise reduction, 90% reduction in pollution and an amazing estimated 400% increase in reliability.

The initial contract covered 128 airframes but was extended to 161 airframes and this option provided USAF with a cost effective and quick programme for upgrading the underpowered KC-135A airframe. Two KC-135Es (57-2589 and 59-1514) were operated by 55th Wing in addition to the ANG and AFRC aircraft. In 1996 the first KC-135E from 196thARS/CA ANG was delivered to Boeing-Wichita for conversion to KC-135R standard.

The -135E fleet was slowly modernised over a fifteen year period, largely as a result of funds added by Congress for the KC-135E to R engine conversion programme. The Air Force initially replaced the TF33 engines on 20 Guard and Reserve KC-135E aircraft with CFM-56 engines at a cost of about $436 million. These aircraft represent the last of the KC-135s for which re-engining funds were approved. The last four aircraft were completed in fiscal year 1998. By the completion of the programme, it had installed CFM-56 engines on 410 KC-135s. However, the

March 2004 Defense Science Board Task Force Report on Aerial Refueling Requirements found that ' *Usage, which induces material fatigue, is not the driving problem. Total flying hours are relatively low for the KC-135s: the current airframe average is about 17,000 hours. Fatigue life is estimated to be 36,000 hours for the E, 39,000 hours for the R. Cycles are commensurately low on average (3800 for the R and 4500 for the E). Thus, the airframes should be capable to the year 2040 based on current usage rates.*'

The KC-135 Assessment Report. published by the Air Force Fleet Viability Board. Wright-Patterson AFB in September 2005 estimated, with numerous caveats, that KC-135E aircraft upgraded to the 'R' configuration would remain viable until 2030.

The E-model economic service life was markedly different because of the difference in age and technology of some of its major components, most notably the engines. The basic airframe should, in theory, last as long as the R-model, but the age of the engines points to the likelihood that upkeep could become expensive in terms of parts and maintenance man-hours. The TF-33 (E-model) engines were previously used but refurbished to an expected 6,000 hour service life. The TF-33 began to need another major overhaul around the turn of the century. Additionally, since the TF-33 did not meet FAA Stage III noise requirements for the year 2000, more time and money would have be expended to ensure compliance.

There was also a major problem with the KC-135E engine struts obtained from retired 707 and 720 airframes. Because of their exposure to engine heat, severe heat-induced corrosion and fatigue have occurred. The Oklahoma City Air Logistics Center at Tinker Air Force Base depot developed an interim strut repair for about $100 thousand per strut, awaiting an Fiscal Year 06 program initiation of a fully reworked strut repair with a cost of about $1 million per strut.

The March 2004 Defense Science Board Task Force Report on Aerial Refueling Requirements found that 'The struts that attach the engine to the wings of the KC-135E models are a prime example of the problems of aging and environment. The struts are near the end of their service life due to exposure to high temperatures and corrosive environments and, assuming the KC-135Es are not retired, a major structural repair to the KC-135E struts is planned.'

On 16 September 2004 Gen. John W. Handy, commander of Air Mobility Command, directed twenty-nine KC-135Es with identified engine strut problems be removed from the flying schedule while

Air Force leaders evaluated a report from the Fleet Viability Board and recommendations of the Oklahoma City Air Logistics Center's KC-135 system program office.

NKC-135E

Two of the original test aircraft have been re-engined with ex 707 JT3D engines, the first being the fully instrumented tanker used in refuelling trials (55-3135) in March 1982 while the 'Big Crow' NKC-135A was retrofitted with TF33-PW-102 engines from October 1990 to January 1991 and then returned to the same test duties with 412thTW. It had been fitted with ARR in 1986 to extend the aircraft's range and mission capability which had been curtailed by the removal of most of the fuselage fuel tanks to allow ECM equipment installation.

RC-135E

Originally designated C-135B-II, project name Lisa Ann, the RC-135E Rivet Amber was a one-of-a-kind aircraft equipped with a large 7 MW Hughes Aircraft phased-array radar system. Originally delivered as a C-135B, 62-4137 operated from Shemya Air Force Station, Alaska from 1966 to 1969. Its operations were performed in concert with the RC-135S Rivet Ball aircraft. The radar system alone weighed over 35,000 pounds and cost over US$35 million in 1960 dollars, making Rivet Amber both the heaviest C-135 aircraft flying and the most expensive Air Force aircraft for its time. The radiation generated by the radar was sufficient to be a health hazard to the crew, and both ends of the radar compartment were shielded by thick lead bulkheads. This prevented the forward and aft crew areas from having direct contact after boarding the aircraft. The system could track an object the size of a soccer ball from a distance of 300 miles, and its mission was to monitor Soviet ballistic missile testing in the reentry phase. The power requirement for the phased array radar was enormous, necessitating an additional power supply. This took the form of a podded Lycoming T55-L5 turboshaft engine under the left inboard wing section, driving a 350kVA generator dedicated to powering mission equipment. On the opposite wing in the same location was a podded heat exchanger to permit cooling of the massive electronic components on board the aircraft. This configuration has led to the mistaken impression that the aircraft had six engines. On 5 June 1969, Rivet Amber was lost at sea on a ferry flight from Shemya to Eielson AFB for maintenance, and no trace of the aircraft or its crew was ever found.

EC-135G

Three KC-135As and one EC-135A were converted by TEMCO to EC-135Gs and although redesignated in 1965 they were not fully operational until 1967. They were modified to ALCC in 1968 and offered radio relay service between NCA (National Command Authority, a euphemism for the US President) and SAC's command structure. They retained the standard boom refuelling system and were also fitted with aerial refuelling receptacles. Following the ending of the Cold War in the early 90s they were retired in May 1992 and stored.

EC-135H

Commencing in late 1964 LTV converted four KC-135As tankers/ACP's to EC-135Hs incorporating the 'Silk Purse' ACP role, allowing the Douglas C-118s to be retired. A fifth aircraft (61-0274) was similarly modified in 1968 as at least one EC-135H was on aerial alert until December 1969 when they began full-time ground alert. They had a dorsal 'saddle' antenna on the fuselage spine and various blade

62-4137, 'Rivet Amber'. The aircraft was originally called Lisa Ann, after Lisa Ann O'Rear, daughter of Big Safari program director Mr. F E O'Rear prior to changes in 1967. The additional underwing pods used to create the extra power required for the radar array are visible in this picture. (USAF)

62-4137 was a model RC-135E and the only one of its kind. Rivet Amber and Rivet Ball operated together as a team from Shemya. The location of the phased radar array within the fuselage is clearly visible. (USAF)

antennae as well as trailing wire antenna while improvements were made to the radio and communications equipment. The interior was originally fitted out for sixteen battle staff personnel, thirteen command staff, two radio operators, two switchboard operators and one secure communications teletype operator, but later this was changed to nine CINCEUR personnel and four Supreme Allied Commander Europe battle staff. They retained the boom refuelling equipment and also have the aerial refuelling receptacle system and were re-engined in 1982 with TF33-PW-102 engines from retired airliners. They were operated by USAFE (USAF Europe) prior to deactivation in 1991.

GEC-135H
Two retired Electronic variants were handed over at Sheppard AFB, TX as ground instructional aircraft with the TTC, later 82nd TW.

EC-135J
Four KC-135Bs that were modified to EC-135Cs

were later converted to EC-135Js - the first one from 1965, two more were redesignated on 31 May 1967 and a final one was converted from May 1979 to January 1980 as Airborne National Command Posts for the National Command Authority and are fitted with a dorsal 'saddle' antenna. They were modified with fifteen operating stations and expansion of the EC-135Cs communications capability. The mission suites were removed and installed in E-4As and the aircraft were transferred to PACAF as 'Blue Eagle' EC-135P replacements in short term. Two were retired from service in March 1992 while one of the remaining pair crashed days before being placed in storage, the final one was retired in October 1993.

C-135K
In late 1996 one of the remaining EC-135Ks was redesignated as C-135K and is operated as a VIP aircraft for CINCPAC by 89thAW from Hickam AFB, HI.

59-1491 was a RC-135S and operated in concert with 62-4137, 'Rivet Amber'. On 13 January 1969 59-1491 was returning from a reconnaissance mission when it landed back at Shemya. The aircraft hydroplaned and slid off the ice covered runway, plunging into a 40 feet ravine and was written off. (USAF)

EC-135K

Originally two KC-135As were converted to EC-135K standard to provide communications links and accurate navigational data to TAC aircraft on long deployments, (with effect from 1 June 1992 the name of the operating command was changed to ACC). They were originally known as 'Head Dancer' for their role in fighter deployments to Europe and Asia. The boom refuelling was replaced by the fuel-dump pipe. Following the loss of one of the original aircraft, a third conversion (59-1518) was made - both the survivors were retrofitted with TF33-PW-102 turbofans. One of these aircraft was the first production aircraft which first flew on 31 August 1956 and was delivered on 24 January 1957, they were transferred to 89thAW in late 1995. The first production aircraft was finally retired in October 1996, over 40 years since its first flight.

EC-135L

Eight KC-135As were converted to EC-135L PACCS standard by Lockheed from 1965 to 1967 and replaced EB-47Ls as airborne radio relay radio and amplitude modulation dropout capability platforms. Their role was to provide secure radio links and had blade antennae above and below the fuselage for communications relay. They retained the boom refuelling equipment and also had airborne radio relay but were still powered by the original J57-P engines. Three were demodified to tanker status but two of these were redesignated EC-135L again on 6 January 1971 then back to KC-135A again on 14 September 1971! Normal crew was four on flight deck and three mission staff and two were involved during Operation 'Desert Storm'.

RC-135M

Six C-135Bs were converted by LTV Electrosystems to RC-135Ms from early 1966 and received the extended nose of the RC-135D to cover radar antenna as well as tear drop blisters on either side of the rear fuselage, they were used for 'Rivet Card/Rivet Quick' operations.

The RC-135M was an interim type with more limited ELINT capability than the RC-135C but with extensive additional COMINT capability. They were converted from Military Airlift Command C-135B transports, and operated by the 82nd Reconnaissance Squadron during the Vietnam War from Kadena AB, gathering signals intelligence over the Gulf of Tonkin and Laos with the programme name Combat Apple (originally Burning Candy) There were six RC-135M aircraft, 62-4131, 62-4132, 62-4134, 62-4135, 62-4138 and 62-4139, all of which were later modified by E-Systems in the early '80s and were redesignated RC-135W, still with TF33-P-5 engines. They continued in active service as RC-135W Rivet Joints by the early 1980s.

EC-135N

Converted by Douglas, the EC-135N had the 'platypus' nose extension as well as provision for the Northrop A-LOTS pod. This was carried by four and was suspended from the cargo door and contained both a telescope and cameras. The fist flight of the ARIA aircraft was on 19 September 1966 and their main tasks were vehicle tracking and two-way voice relay between astronauts and mission control in Houston, TX. They were originally employed during the Apollo lunar landing programme and all eight were involved in the Apollo 6 mission in 1986. Total

58-0022 was an EC-135P that formed part of Operation Blue Eagle that provided five EC-135J/P command post aircraft to the Commander in Chief, US Pacific Command (USCINCPAC), which were based at Hickam AFB, HI. (USAF)

USAF RC-135M 62-4138 seen from a KC-135 tanker. (USAF)

crew could be 23 including 18 or 19 mission staff. After the Apollo flights finished, four of the EC-135Ns were redesignated Advanced Range Instrumentation Aircraft (ARIA) still with J57-P engines, but they were later re-engined with TF33-PW-102s, converted to EC-135E, and assigned to special test programmes. The aircraft have been replaced in the tracking role by EC-18Bs.

EC-135P

Five KC-135As that were the original EC-135As were redesignated EC-135P 'Blue Eagle' Airborne Command Post status on 31 March 1967 with the reverse refuelling system as well as the ARR equipment for extending their endurance. These aircraft were originally used by Commander in Chief, Pacific Command but later transferred to Commander in Chief, Atlantic Command and retained the J57-P engines although two (55-8109, 55-8022) were retrofitted with the TF33-PW-102 turbofans. Two extra aircraft have also been converted to this designation (61-0274 in 1988 and 55-3129 to replace 58-007)

KC-135Q

Originally considered for refuelling the Lockheed A-12 high speed and high altitude reconnaissance aircraft with its PF-1 fuel, the KC-135Q was also modified to handle the JP-7 fuel of the SR-71 Blackbird which was the follow-on from the A-12. Fifty-six KC-135As were then modified to KC-135Qs to support the SR-71 in USAF service and were operated by two squadrons attached to 9th SRW based at Beale AFB, CA. Internally they had a modified fuel system to handle the JP-7 fuel while externally they had a single antenna for secure communication with the Blackbird prior to refuelling, which was conducted at the extremes of either aircraft's operating limits. They also have

the ability to handle the standard JP-4 fuel used by the remainder of the USAF fleet, just an air purge is required between the two. With the retirement of the SR-71 the remaining aircraft were used to refuel the F-117A fleet. From late 1993 the KC-135Qs were fitted with the F108-CF-100 (CFM.56-2A-2) engines and Aerial Refuelling Receptacles and redesignated as KC-135T. 58-0099 was the last aircraft to undergo conversion to KC-135T standard when it departed Fairchild AFB, WA on 29 September 1995 for Boeing at McConnell AFB, KS.

KC-135R

Three original reconnaissance KC-135As were redesignated KC-135R on 1 June 1967 and a fourth (58-0126) was converted in 1969; their primary role remained associated with nuclear testing by foreign nations under 'Burning Light' but they had a secondary SIGINT role and supported RC-135M operations in SE Asia. Each one appeared unique but they all had an antenna along the top of the fuselage and were the only reconnaissance variants to retain the refuelling boom. The elongated nose first appeared on the KC-135R, as did the rear fuselage tear drop fairing. 55-3121 was modified with an ELINT capsule that was reeled out from the aircraft in flight; it eventually received five rows of fence aerials on the upper fuselage. 55-3121 was used in the CIA's 'Briar Patch' and 'Iron Lung' programmes while two aircraft had camera bays installed in the fuselage cargo door. Two retained their refuelling booms.

C-135T

C-135R 55-3121 was modified in 1969 by Lockheed Air Services to the unique KC-135T configuration under the Cobra Jaw programme name. Externally distinguished by the 'hog nose' radome, the aircraft also featured spinning 'fang' receiver antennas below the nose radome, a large blade antenna above the forward fuselage, a single 'towel bar' antenna on the spine, teardrop antennas forward of the horizontal stabilizers on each side, and the trapeze-like structure in place of the refueling boom. The aircraft briefly carried nose art consisting of the Ford Cobra Jet cartoon cobra. It was later modified into an RC-135T Rivet Dandy.

KC-135R

This is the definitive update programme for the KC-135A series. USAF evaluated various engines, including the TF33. JT-10D (which became the PW2037) and CFM.56 as well as possibly refitting retired 707-320 wings to the existing fuselage. The requirement was to be able to fly fully laden to a rendezvous point 2,000 nautical miles away, offload 91,000 pounds of fuel and then fly another 1,000 nautical miles before landing. Numerous proposals were put forward, with the five 'finalists' being:

KC-135P-7   This involved fitting TF33-P-7 engines that would increase thrust by 8,000 pounds per engine, increase the fuel load to 202,800 pounds and all-up weight to 315.400 pounds. This option would also have the 707 stabiliser fitted and strengthened undercarriage.

KC-135ME   A hybrid scheme involving the use of two engine types, the 'Mixed Engine' proposal involved the use of CFM.56 turbofans on the inboard pylons while retaining the J57 turbojets on the outer ones. Fuel capacity would remain the same as the KC-135-P-7 with a maximum all-up weight of 317,800 pounds and would again require

strengthened undercarriage and wider stabiliser.

KC-135H   This involved the KC-135-P-7 modifications with the addition of the 707-320 wing, leading to an all-up weight of 374,400 pounds.

KC-135X   The first of two proposals using four CFM.56s or JT.10Ds, the KC-135X also used the 707-320 wing and saw all up weight increase to 376,400 pounds. It also included the wider stabiliser and strengthened undercarriage.

KC-135Y   This also used the CFM.56 or JT.10Ds and the other changes from the KC-135X but with a new more efficient wing leading to an all-up weight of424,000 pounds.

As it happened USAF settled for a new engine (the CFM.56) but not the wing modification as the aircraft had already undergone modifications to their stabilisers. BMAC rolled out the first KC-135R on 22 June 1982 with a proposed service life through to 2050 and while original intentions were to re-engine 642 aircraft by 1993, budget restrictions kept the numbers down. The cost was $16.3m per aircraft but BMAC estimated fuel saving to be $1.1 bn over fifteen years. The increased power and more modern technology of the CFM.56 meant that the KC-135R was cleaner and quieter than its predecessors as well as more fuel efficient - in a typical flight profile of 2000 nautical miles to off-load point then 2000 nautical miles return the KC-135A could off load 40,000 pounds while the KC-135R could dispense 70,000 pounds - while at extreme distances from base it could off load more fuel than a KC-10A since it burned less fuel to reach the rendezvous point. Two Turbomach T-62T APUs were fitted as were strengthened undercarriage, yaw dampers, brakes and

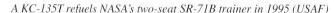

A KC-135T refuels NASA's two-seat SR-71B trainer in 1995 (USAF)

A KC-135R Stratotanker from the 434th Air Refueling Wing provides mid-air refuelling to a F-22 fighter aircraft. (USAF)

major instrumentation updates while a spine mounted refuelling probe allowed the KC-135R to be refuelled itself by other boom equipped tankers. Maximum unrefuelled range was increased to 11,309 miles and maximum weight to 322.000 pounds - surprisingly only 6,500 pounds more than the standard KC-135A. Initial deliveries to 384th ARW were in July 1984. The USAF planned to re-engine all existing KC-135As to KC-135Rs and the original batch was for 397 aircraft to be so converted, but the US Senate dropped funding from the project in Fiscal 1994 Defense Budget - also the ending of the Cold War meant that the number of tankers placed in storage increased and the programme was completed. Boeing-Wichita had also conducted the same updates on the KC-135Q and was due to start a similar one on some of the RC-135 variants although some ANG and AFRes KC-135Es began conversion at the beginning of 1996. Plans to introduce wing tip drogue re-fuelling system were initially dropped due to lack of funding but the aircraft were being fitted with the pallet/roller system to enable the aircraft to operate in the cargo role due to a fleet shortage caused by the late introduction into service of the C-17 Globemaster III and also the possible reduction in the C-17's inventory.

The Multi-Point Refueling System Program was an effort to enhance the efficiency and flexibility of the Air Force's air refuelling fleet, 45 KC-135R Stratotanker aircraft were outfitted to accept wing-tip, hose-and-drogue and air refuelling pods for refueling NATO and US Navy aircraft. US Navy and many NATO aircraft cannot be refuelled using the boom and receptacle refueling method of Air Force aircraft, and instead use a probe-and-drogue system where probes on the receiver aircraft make contact with a hose that is reeled out behind a tanker aircraft. KC-135s have been capable of refueling probe-and-drogue aircraft for years, by fitting a hose-and-drogue attachment to a tanker's refuelling boom. However, when tankers are flying with this configuration they are incapable of refuelling boom-and-receptacle aircraft. With the number of worldwide joint and combined military operations on the rise, the Department of Defense directed the Air Force to outfit part of its KC-135 fleet with the capability of refueling both probe-and-drogue and boom receptacle aircraft on the same mission. This also allows refuelling up to two probe-and-drogue aircraft at the same time.

The pods were very similar to the wing pods that were added to KC-10 Extenders. They contained a collapsible, funnel-shaped drogue on the end of a hose that can be reeled out to an awaiting aircraft with a refuelling probe. The hose was connected with a spring to provide constant tension, and the drogue was outfitted with small lights around it to aid night operations. Additional fuel controls, indicators, and circuit breakers had to be installed in the flight deck. Modifications to valves and a bladder cell in the fuselage were also necessary. Tubes, valves, and a vent system had to be modified in the wing fuel system to accommodate the new system. The wings were modified as well. They were strengthened to support new fuel tubes and wire bundles being installed on the aircraft for the installation of the pods, hardpoints, fittings, and pylons. Floodlights were added to engine pylons, wing pods, and boom area to assist in night refuelling. An aerial refuelling pod controller was added to the boom operator's station, so boom operators, in conjunction with the copilot, could monitor wing-pod refuelling.

Thirty-three pod sets were manufactured to outfit 45 KC-135R aircraft. The pods could be moved from one wing-pod-outfitted tanker to another, thereby remaining mission-ready, even when a particular aircraft was not. Managed by the KC-135 Development System Office at Aeronautical Systems Center, Wright-Patterson Air Force Base, Ohio, the programme completed the engineering, manufacturing and development portion of the programme in 1998 year and began follow-on operational test and evaluation early in 1999. The programme included an installation rate of about six aircraft per year, and initial operational capability in February 2000 with twelve aircraft. All forty-five aircraft were expected to be operational by September 2008. The forty-five modified Stratotankers were to be assigned to active units at McConnell and Grand Forks Air Force Bases; MacDill Air Force Base, Fla.; Fairchild Air Force Base, Wash.; guard and reserve bases at March Air Reserve Base, Calif.; and overseas at Kadena Air Base, Japan, and Royal Air Force Mildenhall, in the United Kingdom.

The C-135Rs were also subject of the Pacer CRAG (Compass Radar and Global Positioning System) Program which was designed to extend the functional life to 2040, the airframe's projected decommissioning date. The Pacer CRAG avionics upgrade to the KC-135 fleet was a commercial off-the-shelf modification program that would eliminate the need for a navigator on most missions. Pacer CRAG upgrades allowed the aircraft to be flown by a pilot, co-pilot and boom operator. The new design could also quickly be reconfigured for a navigator if the mission required it.

The existing cockpit consisted of electro-mechanical equipment of 1950s technology with individual control panels and instrumentation distributed throughout. Failure rates were high and repair capability had been restricted significantly as technology has changed. Not only were repairs to the KC-135's existing avionics suite costly for the Air Force, but they also meant more down-time for the tanker while repairs were made.

The project provided for a major overhaul of the KC-135 cockpit to improve the reliability and maintainability of the aircraft's systems. In addition, the programme met the congressionally mandated requirement to install the global positioning system in all Defense Department aircraft by the turn of the century.

Other modifications included state-of-the-art colour weather radar, improved compass and radar systems and an on-board global positioning system. An additional safety measure, the traffic collision avoidance system or TCAS, was also installed which

Doing the elephant walk! Twelve KC-135Rs line up on the taxiway, just before takeoff, at the Kadena Air Base in Japan (USAF)

1

2

3

4

5

KC-135R 57-1439 walkround McDill AFB, 2 March 2017

(all pictures Dennis Cole)

1. The crew access door, along with the access ladder.

2. The view up the access ladder into the area immediately aft of the flightdeck.

3. USAF tankers now have reasonably low-visibility markings applied. The cargo door is open, with a pick-up truck mounted airstair in position.

4. Nose gear details. Many airframes bear 'scars' in the shape of patches as testiment of nearly 60 years of use.

5. Wing mounted lights.

6. 1439 6 AMW 927 ARW denotes the aircraft's tail number - 57-1439 - 6th Air Mobility Wing, 927th Air Refuelling Wing.

6

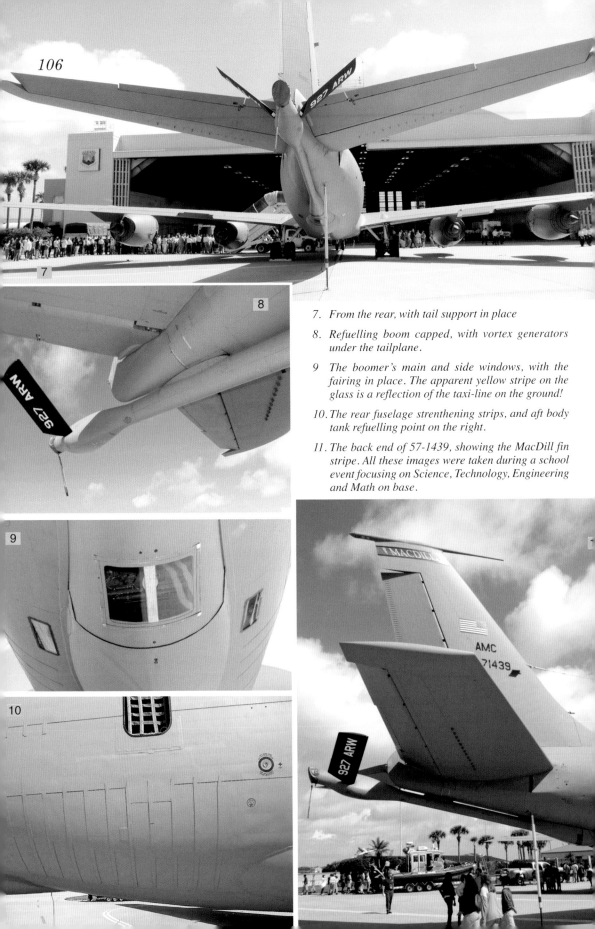

7. From the rear, with tail support in place

8. Refuelling boom capped, with vortex generators under the tailplane.

9 The boomer's main and side windows, with the fairing in place. The apparent yellow stripe on the glass is a reflection of the taxi-line on the ground!

10. The rear fuselage strenthening strips, and aft body tank refuelling point on the right.

11. The back end of 57-1439, showing the MacDill fin stripe. All these images were taken during a school event focusing on Science, Technology, Engineering and Math on base.

12. The 'front office' the flight deck of KC-135R 57-1439, showing the semi-glass cockpit, with CRT screens for the main flight displays. Later, KC-135R Block 45 Upgrade aircraft have been fitted with fully digital displays.

13. The main landing gear, showing the intricate array of elements that go into the doors.

14. From the somewhat gloomy rear fuselage, looking forward, showing the myriad of pipes and trunking in the roof.

15. Entry to 'the hole', otherwise known as the boomer's position. There are two hatches, either side of the rack of oxygen bottles.

16, 17, 18, 19 Four views taken down in the boomer's position, with the aerodynamic visor - the zinc-chromate yellow item - in the lowered psition. The panels and gauges show their age and amount of use.

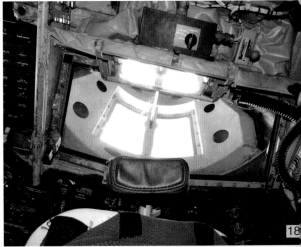

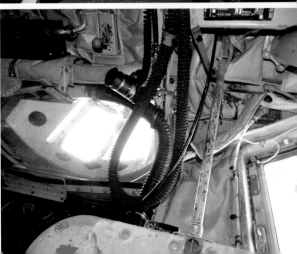

20. *The area immediately aft of the flight deck, with the cargo door in the raised position.*

21. *KC-135s were designed with three roles in mind: tankers, cargo and people carriers. The main cabin floor is fitted with a pallet roller system, and each side of the fuselage has seats for the carriage of troops. The main fuel tanks for the tanking role are underfloor in the aircraft's belly.*

helps with formation flying. The Pacer CRAG digital system includeD a more accurate and reliable altimeter, compass, airspeed indicator, and other navigational equipment, replacing the KC-135's outdated inertial navigation and doppler navigation systems.

One of the biggest benefits was that the system allowed pilots to view several functions through multifunction glass displays. As a result, pilots could concentrate on one area to view certain functions rather than looking at a number of instruments to get the same information. Using the improved radar, pilots could detect cloud formations, wind shear and other weather hazards. With GPS, pilots could identify their position anywhere in the world within a few metres.

AMC developed an integrated programme to enhance KC-135 cockpit avionics and reduce or eliminate the navigator requirement in KC-135s. The initial programme was to replace Compass, Radar and install GPS systems. Operational testing led to the addition of Traffic Advisory and Collision Avoidance System (TCAS). TCAS was an off-the-shelf fix to problems with formation station-keeping. The cost increased from $426.3M to $686.5M due to the TCAS requirement. Other recent additions to the Pacer CRAG program include Standby Air Data Indicator (ADI) and an Advanced Central Air Data Computer (CADC) for Reduced Vertical Separation Minimums (RVSM) certification an Enhanced Ground Proximity Warning System (E-GPWS), and a Reduced Vertical Separation Minima (RVSM) Compliant Air Data Computer. These systems will serve as the foundation for future Global Air Traffic Management (GATM).

Growth in air traffic volume spurred on initiatives to manage increasingly congested airspace and improve safety. Global Air Traffic Management (GATM) technology was needed to comply with proposed changes; aircraft without GATM equipment would be prevented from using heavily traveled air corridors. Exclusion of US strategic mobility aircraft from the world's busiest air routes would increase fuel costs and travel time while decreasing allowable cabin loads and delaying force deployments. GATM elements included data links replacing voice communication, integrated global positioning and flight management systems, and automatic aircraft position reporting instead of radar monitoring.

As an added safety measure for formation flying, TCAS gave pilots the ability to see other aircraft and provided advance warning of possible mid-air collisions. GPS receivers provided aircrews with near-pinpoint navigational accuracy. These new systems are primarily controlled through flight-management computers that automate many aircrew functions and reduce the overall workload.

The programme was structured in two segments, Block 10 and Block 20. Both blocks underwent stringent testing to assess the new systems' operational effectiveness and suitability. Production kits began delivery by the contractor in mid-1997, with installations immediately following at the Oklahoma City Air Logistics Center.

Block 10 replaced the APN-59 radar with a Collins commercial colour weather radar on 128 Air National Guard aircraft. These aircraft eventually transitioned to the Block 20 upgrade.

Block 20 was a fleet-wide modification. It includes the same Collins radar, new aircraft heading references, and installation of GPS equipment. The N-1 and J-4 compass systems were replaced by a GPS inertial navigation system and the existing Carousel IV-E inertial navigation system. Two flight-management, system-control display units also provided access to the fuel-savings advisory system.

A data-transfer and storage system allowed crews to access 50 flight plans with up to 200 waypoints each. Information was viewed on the same multifunctional displays used in Block 10, but in Block 20 the displays replace the horizontal situational indicators and attitude directional indicators at the pilots' stations. Information projected on the displays was selectable by each operator and included radar and route-of-flight mapping, and orbit patterns for air refuelling. All aircraft had wiring to the navigator station for placement of these same units, should the mission dictate. A new glare shield houses the radar and multifunctional display control panels. Some of the old round-dial instruments and warning lights were removed and their data viewed on the new displays. The upgrades provide a cleaner layout to the entire instrument panel.

Some KC-135Rs were fitted with Reduced Vertical Separation Minimum (RVSM) equipment, known as the Pacer CRAG Block 25 configuration. In an effort to deal with the tremendous growth of air traffic, International Civil Aviation Organization member nations have agreed to comply with RVSM as one of many planned air traffic management changes. RVSM reduces the vertical separation between aircraft from 2,000 to 1,000 feet at altitudes between 33,000 and 37,000 feet. The RVSM kit consists of Group B components and Group A hardware including wiring harnesses, pitot static tubing and metal fabricated parts. Due to receptacle type variations, modifications required to the GFP RVSM kits will vary from aircraft to aircraft. With the high utilisation of these aircraft, minimum aircraft down time and flexible scheduling of modification dates were necessary to meet a critical operational requirement.

In order to maintain the KC-135 fleet, in 1999 Air Mobility Command developed a new 'block 30' programme to perform additional modifications to the fleet at the same time as Pacer CRAG modifications. Some additional modifications under the block 30 programme included enhanced ground proximity warning system, which uses aircraft position and a digital terrain database to provide look-ahead awareness to the aircrew. The Reduced Vertical Separation Minima, equipped the fleet to operate in reduced vertical separation airspace. This included an additional digital air data computer, new digital altimeters and digital airspeed indicators. The navigation and safety modification installed a flight

The earlier NKC-135A AIT 55-3128 with spray rig extended and right, a close up of the spray 'head'. Its use gave rise to a crazy decades-long conspiracy theory that 'the establishment were using aircraft to spray chemicals into the atmosphere to alter the weather or reduce the population known as 'chem-trails'. (USAF)

data recorder, cockpit voice recorder and emergency locator transmitter. This initiative brought a large package of modifications together, essentially into a single modification, termed the block 30 airplane. This programme had the effect of reducing the amount of time that each aircraft is unavailable to the KC-135 fleet.

KC-135R AIT

The Airborne Icing Tanker (AIT) is a modified KC-135R Statotanker aircraft, that simulates rain and ice, allowing the military to determine their effects on aircraft. Such an aircraft allows testing to occur at Edwards Air Force Base rather than having to deploy other locations throughout the world.

The Air Forces only AIT was modified by BAS Systems in Mojave, CA, after receiving modifications to its navigation system that will bring it in line with operational KC-135 aircraft.

The $12 million AIT programme, which began in February 1999, reinstituted an environmental test capability to simulate airborne rain and ice conditions under controlled conditions.

The AIT conducted testing on a number of DOD aircraft, as well as Federal Aviation Administration certification testing on commercial aircraft.

It was a multi-service project, Edwards AFB having lead responsibilities for the project, the Army providing system and user requirements and the Navy heading up a team to design and build the spray array system. The Air Force was responsible for the instrumentation, water, boom and bleed air systems, as well as integration of all the components onto the airframe. The 412th Logistics Group instrumentation division designed the on-aircraft system and installed it on the aircraft.

C-135FR

In a programme approved in January 1980 and starting in 1984, the eleven remaining C-135Fs delivered to France were converted with the CFM International CFM.56-2A-2 to make them identical (engine and systems wise) to the KC-135Rs used by the USAF, the first delivery being in August 1985. Problems with corrosion and possible cracks in the undercarriage resulted in three USAF KC-135Rs being loaned to the Armee de l'Air while repairs were conducted. They were delivered on 19 December 1992 with a projected stay of eighteen months and were noted at Birmingham, AL in June 1994 awaiting attention but two returned on extended loan and were

A stunning picture of a re-engined 'Combat Sent' aircraft (USAF)

replaced by purchased aircraft, this time stored KC-135As being converted to KC-135R standard. After repairs one of the C-135FRs, (12736/93-CH), was returned to Boeing in May 1993 and fitted with wing mounted hose and drogue pods as well as retaining the flying boom installation, thus enabling three aircraft to be refuelled simultaneously. First flight was in October 1993 and the remaining ten aircraft were converted by Air France.

RC-135S
The RC-135Ss were converted from NKC-135A or C-135B for Telemetry Intelligence (TELINT) to gather information on Soviet missile tests and to confirm compliance with the SALT treaty. From 1958 this mission was flown by EB-47E(TT) aircraft but these lacked optical collection capability so NKC-135A 59-1491 was allocated to the 'Nancy Rae' programme in 1962 to assist in the development of this option. It was redesignated RC-135S on 1 March 1963 when transferred to SAC. The first one was later renamed 'Wanda Belle' but was lost in 1969 (it retained the J57-P engines while other RC-135S were converted C-135Bs with TF33-P-5 turbofans). The configuration varied between the aircraft and also at different stages of their operational life. Consistent was the elongated nose and IFR but there were varying numbers of antennae on the forward fuselage and the addition of round circular windows with sliding covers. Initially used for 'Rivet Ball/Cobra Ball' operations, they later had cameras fitted and then flew 'Burning Star' missions - during

the mid-1970s they had the starboard wing painted black (including insides of the nacelles) for anti-glare projects. They were on standby at Shemya AFB, AK until 31 March 1975, when they began world-wide deployments with a typical crew of four on the flight deck and twelve mission specialists. Plans were proposed to re-engine with the F108-CF-100 but this was later dropped due to Congressional Budget Restrictions. In 1995 the decision was taken to convert the stored RC-135X 'Cobra Eye' aircraft into a RC-135S by Raytheon E-Systems. On 1 June 1998 the USAF announced that all RC-135 variants would be re-engined with the F108 engines between August 1998 and 2002.

TC-135S
Following the loss of the RC-135T, an EC-135B was converted by E-Systems from early 1985 to serve as a training aircraft for the RC-135S crews since the aerodynamic effects differ from the standard aircraft. It did not carry the sophisticated electronic equipment of the RC-135Ss, was powered by TF33-P-5 engines, and had IFR systems but no boom. On 1 June 1998 USAF announced that all RC-135 variants would be re-engined with the F108 engines between August 1998 and 2002.

KC-135T
Following retirement of the SR-71 Blackbird the remaining KC-135Qs, which were used to refuel these high flying reconnaissance aircraft with their special JP-7 fuel, were adapted by the fitting of F108-

Two Cobra Ball aircraft on the flightline at Offutt Air Force Base, Nebraska in 2001.(SRA Jeremy Smith, USAF)

Right: the interior of the main cabin of a Cobra aircraft. (USAF)

CF-100 (CFM.56) engines and ARR to KC-135T standard for use as general tankers (they can also handle the standard JP-4 fuel). All surviving KC-135Qs were converted by the end of 1995, the last aircraft, 58-0099 entering the process at the end of September 1995.

RC-135T

One of the first KC-135Rs (and later RC-135Rs) was redesignated in May 1971 and operated as 'Rivet Dandy' mission aircraft with flight crew of four and mission crew of eleven. It was de-modified to a trainer in July 1973 and the PMEE transferred to 58-0126. It retained the hognose and wingtip static boom while the IFR was inactivated. It was retrofitted with TF33-PW-102 turbofans in 1982 then used as a training aircraft for RC-135 pilots and navigators. It was due to be replaced in mid 1985 by a newly converted TC-135S and move to 55thSRW as a trainer but was lost before the transfer.

RC-135U

Three RC-135Cs were converted by General Dynamics to RC-135Us starting July 1970 and the only original external difference was the addition of

a extended tailcone and a fairing on the fin above the rudder. Later modifications included the fitting of a chin radome, a large SLAR fairing on each side of the fuselage just behind the cockpit and 'Rabbit Ears' antenna arrays above. Aircraft flew 'Combat Sent/Combat Pink' missions during the latter stages of the Vietnam conflict.

RC-135V

Commencing in 1972 E-Systems converted one RC-135B and seven RC-135Cs to RC-135Vs to provide

I cannot let this chapter on the KC-135 pass by without mentioning an alleged 'incident' at the 1987 Finningly Battle of Britain Airshow. At the time it was the fashion for units or groups to 'zap' - that is to apply a sticker - to each other's aircraft. One 'group' although not official, was a squad of girls called 'Pilot's Pals' organised by former RAF member Joseph Merchant, who owned and ran a publishing organisation of the same name that produced specialist calenders. Joe's girls - who were all into serious fun, chaos and mayhem - were special guests at the show. With their black flying suits and white boots and belts drew a lot of media attention.

Legend has it that Joe was determined that his organisation was going to make its mark with the biggest, boldest zap ever - and it would be applied to the biggest aircraft at the airshow.

One of the participants on static display was KC-135E 63604 of the Kansas Air National Guard. There were rumours that certain display routine patterns chalked on the display briefing boards bore a strange resemblance to the erect male organ, but that was vigorously disputed by a certain YUGO Cars-sponsored wing-walker, claiming that a Boeing Strearman could not fly that pattern! On the Saturday evening after the first day of the show there was a barbeque on base, hosted by the Dominie Squadron. The girls and Joe were the centre of attention amongst the air and ground crew alike.

As dawn broke on the Sunday morning there was much attention around the tail of the KC-135 - which now bore a three foot diameter 'zap' of the puppy in a bone-dome that was the logo of Pilots Pals. Word has it that the Station Commander 'was not amused' having such a thing done to an aircraft guesting on his airfield, and so the zap was quickly removed, and just as quickly vanished, allegedly to surface again in a crew room in the USA. Joe and the girls of course, denied all knowledge of it - and no pictures seem to have been taken of the event - or if they were, they have been kept quiet!

COMINT and ELINT. Both the large SLAR fairings referred to above in the RC-135Us and the elongated nose of other reconnaissance variants were fitted and there were also other blade antennae under the fuselage. The RC-135Vs could also be used as an Airborne Command Post and as combat support aircraft on missions like policing the no-fly zone in Iraq or patrolling over Bosnia. One RC-135U (63-9792) was converted to RC-135V status by E-Systems in 1976/77. Power was from TF33-P-9 engines but budget approval was granted to re-engine with F108-CF-100s although nothing was finalised and Boeing, in association with Rolls-Royce/Allison Engines put forward an unsolicited proposal to re-engine the whole RC-135 fleet (as well as AWACS and J-STAR aircraft) with engines leased from the suppliers to save the USAF money over their planned service life. On 1 June 1998 USAF announced that all RC-135 variants would be re-engined with the F108 engines between August 1998 and 2002.

OC-135W

Following the removal of the flight engineer's station from the three OC-135B 'Open Skies' aircraft they were redesignated OC-135W.

Opposite page: an unusual vertically down view of a Türk Hava Kuvvetleri (the aerial warfare service branch of the Turkish Armed Forces) KC-135R in formation with the Turkish Stars aerobatic display team, flying Northrop NF-5s. The THK operate seven KC-135Rs that received the Pacer CRAG upgrade. The aircraft were operated by the 101st Squadron, stationed at Incirlik Air Base. (Türk Hava Kuvvetleri)

RC-135W

The six RC-135Ms were converted by E-Systems and redesignated as RC-135W standard following rebuild in the 1980s and were equipped to a similar standard to the RC-135Vs but with additional antennae. Currently powered by TF33-P-5 engines they were due to be re-engined with F108-CF-100s but this option was ater cancelled. Three C-135Bs were modified by Raytheon E-Systems from 1996/97 to RC-135W status to join the hard pressed 'Rivet Joint' fleet. On 1 June 1998 USAF announced that all RC-135 variants would be re-engined with the F108 engines between August 1998 and 2002.

TC-135W

One C-135B was converted to the TC-135W, a similar aerodynamic platform to the RC-135W, but without the delicate avionics, to serve as a training aircraft, it was also powered by TF33-P-5 engines but reengining was planned but not completed initially although USAF gave approval on 1 June 1998 for reengining of all RC-135 variants with F108s.

WC-135W

In 1995, to consolidate disparate airframes, all former WC-135Bs not otherwise converted and redesignated were given the WC-135W MDS even though each undertook different missions! 61-2665 was used as a trial aircraft for the OC-135 fleet and was fitted with Stage 3 hush-kits before being retired to AMARC, 61-2666 was leased to (Raytheon) E-Systems from May 1995 as a trials aircraft and a trainer while the third aircraft, 61-2667, was used as a flight deck trainer operated by 55th Wing for EC/RC-135 crews and was known as the Silk Purse trainer.

RC-135X

The sole RC-135X Cobra Eye, 62-4128, was converted to RC-135X for use in the SDI 'Star Wars'

project to gather information on Soviet missile tests. This was done during the mid-to-late-1980s making use of a C-135B Telemetry/Range Instrumented Aircraft. When the funding for its project, titled 'Optical Aircraft Measurement Program', finished the aircraft withdrawn from use. In 1993, it was converted into an additional RC-135S Cobra Ball. In late 1995 it began conversion to RC-135S configuration by Raytheon E-Systems and was re-engined with F108 engines.

EC-135Y

Two EC-135Ns were converted to EC-135Ys with additional equipment for use by CINCENTCOM. They are powered by TF33-PW-102s from retired airliners and were both active during Operation 'Desert Storm', both as support for General Norman Schwarzkopf and, occasionally, as a tanker as they retain the boom.

RC-135W Rivet Joint (Project Airseeker)

The United Kingdom bought three KC-135R aircraft for conversion to RC-135W Rivet Joint standard under the Airseeker project. Acquisition of the three aircraft was budgeted at £634m, with entry into service in October 2014. The aircraft formed part of 51 Squadron RAF, based at RAF Waddington along with the RAF's other ISTAR assets. They are expected to remain in British service until 2045.

The RAF had gathered signals intelligence with three Nimrod R1s, converted in the 1970s from the Nimrod MR1 maritime patrol aircraft. When the time came to upgrade the maritime Nimrods to MRA4 standard, Project Helix was launched in August 2003 to study options for extending the life of the R1 to 2025. The option of switching to Rivet Joint was added to Helix in 2008, and the retirement of the R1 became inevitable when the MRA4 was cancelled under the UK's 2010 budget cuts. The R1's

A Royal Air Force Rivet Joint aircraft arries at Mildenhall before taking up duties from RAF Waddington. The aircraft carries the 51 Squadron 'droopy goose' emblem on the fin. (USAF)

ZZ664 with the 100th Anniversary markings of 51 Squadron on its fin. This version of the 'droopy goose' appears to be not quite so droopy! Although the aircraft retains the boomer's position, it does not carry the full refuelling boom. (USAF)

involvement over Libya in Operation Ellamy delayed its retirement until June 2011.

Helix became Project Airseeker, under which three KC-135R airframes were converted to RC-135W standard by L-3 Communications, who provide ongoing maintenance and upgrades under a long-term agreement. The three airframes are former United States Air Force KC-135Rs, all of which first flew in 1964 but were modified to the latest RC-135W standard before delivery. The three airframes are the youngest KC-135s in the USAF fleet.

51 Sqn personnel began training at Offutt in January 2011 for conversion to the RC-135. The first RC-135W (ZZ664) was delivered ahead of schedule to the RAF on 12 November 2013, for final approval and testing by the Defence Support and Equipment team prior to its release to service from the UK MAA. The second one was once again delivered ahead of schedule on 4 September 2015 at RAF Mildenhall in Suffolk. The third is scheduled to be delivered and fully operational by December 2017.

Extending the life - KC-135R Block 45.

It was through the activities of AMARC that the 418th Flight Test Squadron at Edwards, along with a multitude of testers, the KC-135 Block 45 test team were able to complete a series of tests to help extend the aircraft's service life for decades.

"There are currently around 400 KC-135s that enhance the Air Force's capability to accomplish its primary mission of Global Reach while providing aerial refueling support to Air Force, Navy, Marine Corps and allied nation aircraft. These aircraft also provide mission support including cargo, aeromedical evacuation, personnel transport, and a variety of other specialized missions," said Major John Mikal, 418th FLTS KC-135 Block 45 lead project test pilot.

'Increasing the life expectancy of the current Air Force tanker fleet is critical. Ongoing upgrade programs help to ensure there is no gap in these mission capabilities, while the new KC-46 program starts replacing the aging KC-135 fleet."

The Block 45 modification was needed to extend the KC-135 aircraft as a viable weapon system through fiscal year 2040. The Block 45 systems mitigate capability gaps and improve overall KC-135 shortcomings in reliability, maintainability and supportability.

At the initial start of the KC-135 Block 45 program, it was originally estimated that testing would end in March 2011, but the technical challenge of integrating the new digital systems proved to be very challenging, according to the test team.

'It took an amazing amount of ingenuity and hard work by the collective KC-135 Block 45 upgrade team, due to the program experiencing a two-month stop in test in early 2012 to determine the cause of a structural coupling event which occurred during flight test. While clearing the aerial refueling envelope, the performance of the new autopilot altitude hold was so good, re-adjustment was required to improve stability during aerial refueling coupled flight.'

Along with the 418th, the massive, multi-year task required support from more than ninety members to overcome technical hurdles and prevent the very real threat of program cancellation. Of those included, individuals were acquired from the 412th Test Wing, 412th Operations Group, 412th Test and Engineering Group, 773rd Test Squadron, 775th Test Squadron, 370th Flight Test Squadron, 445th Flight Test Squadron, the KC-135 Special Programs Office, Rockwell Collins, Air Mobility Command Test and Evaluation Squadron Detachment 3, AMC Air, Space and Information Operations (A3), and McConnell Air Force Base, Kan.

'There were only two KC-135 aircrew in the

The old, and the new!

The KC-135R Block 45 Upgrade required a massive update to the flight deck, moving from analogue instrumentation in the pilot's centre console above, to a fully digital verson, as seen on the right. (USAF)

A flight test crew from Edwards AFB evaluate the glass cockpit of a Block 45 KC-135R. (USAF)

418th FLTS when the program started. Eventually, the 418th FLTS KC-135 aircrew numbered four; even so, Test Operations was largely instrumental in supporting the program with their KC-135 aircrew,' said Major John Mikal.

Most notably though was the Edwards team, which was able to complete the final testing $200,000 below cost and three weeks ahead of new schedule through extremely efficient testing and test execution flexibility despite regular scope changes, priority changes, funding rebaseline, weather cancellations, maintenance issues, resource rescheduling/constraints, and the ultimate challenge of addressing the AR oscillation issue with no additional schedule or funding impacts.

Maj John Mikal: *'In the end, the Global Reach Combined Test Force test team proved to be a pivotal contributor, bringing this challenged program to a successful completion. Successful completion of this program has secured the opportunity to field Block 45 to the KC-135 fleet, while preventing the otherwise inevitable reduction in overall mission effectiveness due to avionics obsolescence and CNS/ATM airspace access issues. Without the KC-135 Block 45, 88-percent of the USAF tanker assets would eventually be unable to complete their mission.*

The Block 45 modification was needed to extend the KC-135 aircraft as a viable weapon system through fiscal year 2040. The Block 45 systems mitigate capability gaps and improve overall KC-135 shortcomings in reliability, maintainability and supportability.'

Tanking with the 100 ARW

In 1976, due to budget reductions, Strategic Air Command consolidated its Strategic Reconnaissance assets. The 99th Strategic Reconnaissance Squadron and its U-2s were returned from U-Tapao in Thailand and assigned to the 9th Strategic Reconnaissance Wing (9 SRW) on 1 July 1976. This brought all the Strategic Reconnaissance assets of SAC under one wing at Beale AFB, California. The 9th SRW already controlled the 1st Strategic Reconnaissance Squadron, which operated the SR-71 Blackbird.

The U-2Rs of the 349th SRS and the AQM-34 Firebee/DC-130 Hercules drone operations of the 350th SRS were discontinued, the squadrons becoming KC-135 tanker squadrons of the 100th Air Refuelling Wing in support of the 9th SRS SR-71 Blackbird. The U-2Rs in South Korea became the 9th Strategic Reconnaissance Wing Detachment 2. The AQM-34s, associated DC-130

Hercules launch aircraft and CH-3 Jolly Green Giant recovery helicopters were reassigned to the Tactical Air Command 22nd Tactical Drone Squadron and remained at Davis-Monthan AFB.

With the redesignation, the 100th and its 349th and 350th Air Refueling Squadrons were moved administratively to Beale, taking over the assets of the 17th Bombardment Wing, which was inactivated. The 349th and 350th assumed the KC-135s of the 903d and 922d Air Refueling Squadrons. With the re-designation, the 100th ARW assumed responsibility for providing worldwide air refuelling support for the 9th SRW's SR-71s and U-2s on 30 September 1976.

The 100th ARW was inactivated on 15 March 1983 when its two KC-135 squadrons were reassigned to the host 9th Strategic Reconnaissance Wing at Beale, which became a composite wing under the one-base, one-wing concept.

After an inactive status for over seven years, SAC again reactivated the 100th, but this time as the 100th Air Division at Whiteman AFB, Missouri, on 1 July 1990, an intermediate command echelon of Strategic Air Command. It assumed host unit responsibilities at Whiteman. In addition, the division controlled the 509th Bombardment Wing, which was not operational while waiting for production B-2 Spirit stealth bombers to arrive and appropriate facilities for the B-2s to be constructed. It also controlled the 351st Missile Wing, an LGM-30F Minuteman II ICBM wing at Whiteman.

Air Force reorganization put the 351st MW under the reactivated Twentieth Air Force on 29 March 1991, and the 509th Bomb Wing took over host duties at Whiteman. As a result, SAC inactivated the 100th AD again on 1 August 1991.

Six months after its inactivation as an Air Division, and over 46 years after leaving England at the end of World War Two, the Air Force activated the 100 ARW, stationed at RAF Mildenhall, United Kingdom, on 1 February 1992. It was assigned to Strategic Air Command, Fifteenth Air Force, 14th Air Division. It was then reassigned to Third Air Force on 1 February 1992. From the time of its reactivation, the 100 ARW has served as the United States Air Forces Europe's lone air refuelling wing. It also serves as the host unit at RAF Mildenhall, where it deployed aircraft and managed the European Tanker Task Force. One of the Wing's honours is that it is the only modern USAF operational Wing allowed to display on its assigned aircraft the tail code

'Square D' 61-0267 of the 100 ARW at RAF Mildenhall. (USAF)

(Square-D) of its World War Two predecessor.

At the 100 ARW operations centre, the pre-mission briefing reviewed once again all the pertinent features of the day's task and rounded off the planning sessions which had been held earlier in the week. The briefing got underway with a roll call to act as a final check to confirm call signs, the aircraft to be manned and their locations on the airfield.

'Capt Smith?'

'All present'.

'Astra Eight One, 0267, Hardstand 28'.

'Capt Jones?'

'Present'.

'Astra Eight Two, 01 17 Q model, Hardstand 16'.

The customary time check followed: *'In 40 seconds, Gentlemen, it will be zero six zero two Local; 15… 10… 5, 4, 3, 2, 1- Hack! 0602 − is anyone for 03 ?'*

The resume of the day's mission, was straightforward. The Mildenhall Tanker Task Force was to provide air refuelling support for the redeployment of twenty-four F-16 Fighting Falcons from Spangdahlem AB, Germany to Shaw AFB, SC. A total of twenty aircraft would covering air refuelling sectors 1-5 and there would be twenty-four tankers from Pease AFB, NH covering ARS 6-10. The crews were referred to their

mission document packages containing all the relevant paperwork on timings, fuel offloads, communications frequencies, abort bases, etc. The information covered all four five-tanker cells so that any crew would be able to fly in any one of the twenty mission slots should last-minute changes necessitate a switch of tankers between formations or within cell sequences.

Next, the all-important weather forecast: in general, the outlook was favourable. Europe was covered by an area of high pressure which offered the prospect of another fine day, but there was some uncertainty about the time at which the mission could get under way as fog was covering all the bases in Germany. Spangdahlem was reporting three-tenths of a mile visibility with 200 feet obscured and not expecting it to lift before 08.00-09.00hrs, so there could be a delay in the fighters departure. Some mist and fog patches at Mildenhall were expected to disperse after sunrise, giving four miles visibility in haze for the early tanker take- offs. At the abort bases in the UK, everything was good, similarly at Lajes in the Azores, but Keflavik in Iceland was reporting strong winds gusting to 40 knots or more, with rain showers.

The briefing then turned to the airfield status and pre-departure procedures. The active runway was 29, all the navigation aids were operable and there were no restrictions. In assessing take-off performance, the crews were reminded that there was a downhill slope on runway 29, and if the action should switch to runway 11, a corresponding slight uphill grade in that direction. All taxi and take-off clearances were to be called by the cell leaders with the rest of the cell acknowledging the leader's radio calls. The Supervisor of Flying's last chance checks would be conducted on the hold line to one side of the threshold and, once cleared, the aircraft could proceed on to the runway.

Exploiting all the available surface, take-offs at Mildenhall were to be initiated from the end of the over-run beyond the threshold, so that tankers had to taxi to the extremity of the runway, pick-up the 180° guided turn-round line and line-up for departure.

Back in the days before the KC-135 were re-engined with the CFM-56s, it would have been at this point that crews using water injection for assisted take-offs would be reminded to get water on all engines before brake release rather than attempting to bring up the water on the roll.

'The old water technique', substantially increased the take-off power available from the KC-135's four J57 engines. At maximum dry power, these were rated at some 15,500 pounds thrust each, but with water injection the thrust rating is increased by about 4,000 pounds per engine, a useful gain for high weight take-offs. The various methods for coping with water supply problems were outlined, including throttle adjustments and application of power and water to two engines at a time.

Although the take-offs were scheduled at two minute intervals, it would take some time to get the five-aircraft formations together; the flight plan called initially for a fifty mile sector to the north and back to Mildenhall during which the cells were to form-up using differential airspeeds and, if necessary, some cut-offs on the turns.

After take-off from runway 29 the aircraft were to turn right to intercept the 335° radial from Mildenhall, proceeding out on this course to the fifty mile mark near Coningsby, then arcing eastwards over the Wash to maintain this distance from base until crossing the 010° radial from Mildenhall, at which point a right turn would be made on to the reciprocal heading of 190° to bring the cells southwards and back to a position overhead Mildenhall.

The basis of the air refuelling plan was that the third, fourth and fifth tankers in each cell would be solely responsible for the first three hook-ups, AR 1-3, each KC-135 taking two of the F-16s in the six aircraft receiver formations. At the conclusion of AR3, the three tankers which had worked AR 1-3 would break away from the cell, leaving the lead and number two tankers to take three F-16s each through AR4 and 5 to the mid-Atlantic rendezvous with the Pease TTF. This pattern of operation ensures that there are tankers with the receivers the whole way across the Atlantic, with a definite hand- off to the US-based KC-l35s taking place at mid-ocean, while the early break-away of part of the European TTF eases the traffic control situation during the tanker handover.

Accompanying the mission would be an EC-135, call sign Chine 99, tasked as Tactical Deployment Control Aircraft (TDCA) with an airborne movement control team aboard. The TDCA would join the stream at Land's End and

position five nautical miles behind the fifth tanker in the second KC-135 cell.

Interspersed through the briefing were re-caps on the altitude reservations - or 'ALTRV' as they are known in the trade - for each phase of the mission, the communications frequencies to be used and the procedures for ensuring correct fuel offloads and transmission of the latter information to the Wing's staff personnel flying in each cell who would, in turn, report the numbers to TDCA.

Before the gathering dispersed to individual tanker cell briefings, the floor was given over to the TTF Commander: *'It's been a long briefing and an early morning, and we've all got to go to work - so I'll keep this quick. Five-ship - its been a long time maybe since some of you have flown Five-ship cells; may I remind ya'll of the benefits of a good tight formation, especially if the weather gets tricky en-route.'*

We joined the crew of 'Astra Seven Three', the third tanker in the second cell, to sit in on the 'Astra Seven One Flight' briefing. There was a final check through the group's start-up, taxi, take-off, radio, en-route and tanking procedures, the objective being to ensure that the formation functioned as a cohesive unit and that airborne communications were kept to the minimum necessary. The cell leader was succinct: *'...as long as you're on your timings and have no problems, don't give me any calls at all. Try and hold the chatter down to an absolute minimum'.* Then it was out to the crew buses for the ride to the flightlines on the other side of the airfield.

Travelling round the perimeter road in the pale light of the sunrise, it became evident that Mildenhall was unusually well occupied that morning with about twenty-five tankers distributed on parking spots either side of the taxiway. As the bus passed along the flight lines, the distinctive Boeing 707-like shapes of the Stratotankers loomed out of the mist.

While the other members of the crew, co-pilot, navigator and boom operator continued with the preliminary check lists, the aircraft Commander left the aircraft to run a pre-flight eye over the Stratotanker's exterior in company with the crew chief. Starting up front with the nosewheel tyres, lights, doors and actuating panel, they proceeded

A Polish air force F-16 pilot receives fuel from a US Air Force KC-135 from the 100th Air Refueling Wing during a NATO exercise on 7 April 2009. The KC-135 Stratotanker is capable of delivering fuel to more than 20 F-16 aircraft in a single mission. (USAF photo by Staff Sgt Jerry Fleshman)

A KC-135 from the 100th Air Refueling Wing, RAF Mildenhall, England, refuels a pair of F-16 Fighting Falcons from Spangdahlem Air Base, Germany, during a multinational exercise on 7 April 2009. (USAF photo by Staff Sgt Jerry Fleshman)

via the nose-mounted pitot tubes and angle of attack indicator probe to the main gear bay. The right main gear was examined for any sign of hydraulic leaks, tyre wear, strut damage, and the engines for any post maintenance debris in the inlets or for loose cowling panels. The wing flying surfaces were scrutinised for any untoward signs and likewise the rear fuselage and tail; and then the reverse sequence followed on the left side of the aircraft. All was in order and was signed off accordingly.

Back in the cockpit, the pilots made contact with the ground crew below to check the responses of the moving surfaces against the stick and rudder pedal movements. A running commentary came up through the ground intercom as the cockpit controls and trim devices were positioned and re-positioned:

'*Stabiliser leading edge moving up... inboard tabs following*'.

'*Stabiliser leading edge moving down... inboard. tabs follow*'.

'*Rudder left... tab right*'.

'*Rudder right... tab left*'.

'*Rudder left... tab left*'.

'*Rudder right... tab right*'.

The most noticeable feature of the cockpit layout was the absence of a flight engineer's station, the right-hand seat immediately aft of the co-pilot being occupied by the navigator. So the fuel management task among other extras is also a front seat responsibility, and as the Aircraft Commander explained, it's really the co-pilot who is the flight engineer and who develops the knack of being able to look in several directions at once! The space between the central instrument panel and the throttle quadrant was occupied by a fuel panel. Criss-crossed by solid and broken lines, representing fuel lines controlled by boost pumps and gravity feed respectively, and with a myriad of valve controls and switches, the panel contained ten gauges - one for each tank, plus a total aircraft fuel gauge. That morning the Stratotanker was loaded with 145,000 pounds of fuel, considerably more than the aircraft's own weight of 108,000lb. Also included in the fuel panel instrumentation was a totaliser showing the cumulative fuel quantity offloaded and an indicator which marks the flow rate to the receiver. The offload flow rates vary a good deal between different types of receivers - with a B-52 on the boom the delivery is normally 6,500lb/min but it's about half that for an F-16.

The fuel valves enable the pilot or co-pilot to select the fuel routings between the tanks and the engines, or to the refuelling aircraft. Fuel can be taken out of any of the wing or fuselage tanks to supply the boom, but it is most frequently given to the receiver from the aft body tank as this simplifies the internal fuel movement needed to maintain the KC-l35's centre of gravity.

After the completion of the various pre- start check lists there was time for the crew to relax - or so we thought. The mission timings had been put back by an hour as the fog at Spangdahlem was holding up the F-16 departures and, in addition, Astra 73 and the rest of the second cell would have to wait a further thirty minutes while Astra 81-85 got away. As the first cell started up and made ready to taxi, the temporary lull in '1475' was interrupted by the news that Astra 83 was unable to go with the first cell and Astra 73 would have to take its slot. Suddenly it was all activity again, and we recalled the briefing remarks about any crew being able to refer to the mission document packages and fly in any one of the twenty tanker positions.

Now the new Astra 83 sortie was off and running; air was ducted from the ground power unit to No 4 engine, its RPM rose to 15%, the throttle was advanced, ignition, and the power was brought up to flight idle. All four engines were started in a prompt sequence and the ground crew were working fast to clear the aircraft.

Ground Crew: *'Ground calling'*.

Astra 83 Aircraft Commander: *'Go ahead'*.

Ground Crew: *'Roger sir; external power and air removed; chocks removed; all panels and hatches and secondary structures secure'*.

Astra 83 Aircraft Commander: *'And Ground, are we in a taxi configuration now?'*

Ground Crew: *'Roger sir'*.

Astra 83 Aircraft Commander: *'OK, you're cleared off. Thank you very much !'*

Ground Crew: *'Roger sir'*.

A quick check round the crew to make sure that all was ready for the move out, and then the aircraft started to taxi. Once established on the taxiway, there was a steady flow of pre-departure information. First was Astra 81, the lead tanker in the cell.

Astra 81: *'Astra Eight One Flight? ...are you ready to copy numbers?'*

Astra 82: *'Two'*... Astra 83: *'Three'* Astra 84: *'Four'*. Astra 85: *'Five'*.

Mildenhall Tower: *'Astra Eight One Flight, Roger. Temperature four two degrees; dewpoint three niner; pressure altitude minus two four two; altimeter three zero two one; wind calm, unstick wind calm. Visibility is three miles in fog; ceiling two zero thousand feet; and the visibility to the east through the south is two miles'*.

Then a call from the Mildenhall Consolidated Command Post (callsign 'Banner' to the Mildenhall Supervisor of Flying (callsign 'Foxtrot') enquiring as to the status of the American-based KC-135s:

Mildenhall Consolidated Command Post: *'Roger sir, be advised Pease Tanker Task Force take-off times are 24,25, 26 and 27'*.

It was then just past 09.30hrs Local at Mildenhall so the first cell of tankers had got airborne from the USA as scheduled, some twenty-five minutes before the initial European TTF take-offs. At the head of the queue on the taxiway, Astra 81 was being cleared out of the last chance check to be followed by Astra 82.

Mildenhall Supervisor of Flying: *'Eight One? Fox. Cleared the aircraft in take-off configuration, your APU doors are closed. Have a good flight! Break! Break! Astra Eight Two? Foxtrot. Turn in'*.

Astra 82: *'Eight Two, cleared in*.

Moments later, the Command Post was advising the departure of the first cell of six F-16 Fighting Falcons from Spangdahlem at 09.40hrs Local. Astra 83 was given a final look-over from the ground and the crew proceeded through the pre take-off checks while waiting for the preceding tankers to start the take-off stream at 09.50hrs Local. On the button, Astra 81 taxied out of the hold area, turned right down the over-run, made a U-turn at the far end and lined-up for departure. As the aircraft passed the threshold on its take-off roll, Astra 82 moved forward to repeat the procedure and then the Tower cleared us to the runway.

Mildenhall Tower: *'Astra Eight Three? When airborne, change departure control frequency. Wind calm, clear for take-off'*.

Established at the end of the over-run, the throttles were advanced, and the engine instrument needles spun round the gauges as Astra 83 wound up to take-off power. And then we were rolling, past Astra 84 on the hold area, over the threshold, accelerating down the runway centre line as '1475' picked up speed and the thousand foot markers were passed at progressively shorter intervals. A slight back pressure on the control column as we passed 160 knots and the aircraft rotated to lift-off after a 7,000 foot-plus run. The gear came up as we crossed the runway 11 threshold, and the 20° take-off flap setting was cancelled at 1,000 feet and 186 knots. Time to confirm our departure:

Astra 83: *'Honington Radar? Astra Eight Three is airborne Victor Mike'*.

Honington Control Zone: *'Astra Eight Three? Honington. Loud and clear and identified. Advise*

A Mildenhall 100 ARW KC-135 refuels an F-15C Eagle over Iceland during a training mission on 9 November 2013 (USAF Photo by Airman 1st Class Dana J Butler)

any change in flight conditions, climb Flight Level two four zero, report passing four thousand feet'.

Astra 83: *'Roger sir, cleared initial two four zero, report passing four'.*

Settled on the 335° course from Mildenhall, the navigator had the lead tanker, Astra 81, on the radar 20 miles ahead and Astra 82 was reporting in trail six miles behind Lead. Between the scattered cloud tops, the black smudges in the distance were resolving into KC-l35s as we closed on the first two tankers of the cell. As we skirted the Wash at 15,000 feet, Astra 81 turned right on to the fifty mile arc, followed by the rest of the Flight. On the inbound leg to Mildenhall the cell closed up with two to three mile separations between the first four tankers and with Astra 85, under Eastern Radar's guidance, cutting the corners at the rear to catch up the trail. The 'in the green' boom calls had been made to Astra 82 for relay to Mildenhall where, shortly afterwards, the formation turned right heading for Brize Norton and levelling the climb at 27,000 feet. Ground control switched from Eastern Radar to London Military and then at two-mile separations, the tankers were cleared under their own navigation from Brize Norton to Yeovilton.

Astra 81: *'Astra Eight One Flight, let's go left - Heading 230°.'*

Astra 82: *'Two'.* Astra 83: *'Three'.* Astra 84: *'Four'.* Astra 85: *'Five'.*

London Military Control: *'Astra Eight One? London Military'.*

Astra 81: *'Roger Mil, Astra Eight One. We're at Flight Level two seven zero at this time'.*

London Military Control: *'Roger Eight One, you're identified, radar control Flight Level two seven zero. Confirm all tankers Flight Level two seven zero. And you read me loud and clear?'*

Astra 81: *'That's affirmative sir. Read you loud and clear. We've got five KC-135s, all level two seven zero'.*

On a converging course for a rendezvous with the tankers near Yeovilton, and then just past the southern fringes of London heading westwards at 26,000 feet, were six F-16 Fighting Falcons. Behind them, again at thirty minute separations, three more six-aircraft formations.

Nearly 250 aircrew in some seventy aircraft were about to make a reality of several hundred hours of flight planning in the US, Germany and the UK; they would demonstrate once more the vital but routine, nature of the aerial tanker lifeline which accomplishes the rapid and direct transfer of tactical fighter aircraft between the US and

A KC-135 from the 100th Air Refueling Wing supporting Saudi Arabian-led coalition forces during operations against extremist groups like al-Qaida in Yemen since February 2016. (USAF photo)

Europe.

As the tankers swung round to the south-west, contact with the lead F-16 formation, using the call signs Epson 11-16, was imminent.

London Military Control: *'Astra Eight One? London Military. The fighters are at fife fife miles range, just about to come on this frequency'.*

Astra 81: *'Astra Eight One copies'.*

Epson 11: *'Epson One One, check'.*

Epson 12: *'Two'* . Epson 13: *'Three'* . Epson 14: *'Four'* . Epson 15: *'Five'* . Epson 16: *'Six'*.

Epson 11: *'London Mil? Epson One One, Flight Level two six zero, looking for Astra Eight One'.*

London Military Control: *'Epson One One, Roger. You're identified, radar control Flight Level two six zero. Maintain two six zero. The tankers are right, in your one o'clock, range of fife zero miles at the moment. They are all at two seven zero - keep me advised'.*

Epson 11: *'Roger. We're maintaining a heading of two seven fife degrees at this time, and say the tankers heading please'.*

London Military Control: *The tankers are heading southwest for Yeovilton at the moment. I'll put them in an orbit overhead Yeovilton... just maintain your present heading'.*

Epson 11: *'Epson One One. Roger. Thank you sir'.*

Approaching Yeovilton and the join-up with the fighters, Astra 81 Flight secured clearance for

altitude separation in the trail, and the formation went to 500ft intervals in the 26,000-28,000 foot band. At the same time, Epson 11 Flight was instructed to drop a thousand feet to Flight Level 250.

Obliquely crossing the course of the F-16s, from right to left and 35 miles ahead, the KC-135s turned left from their 230° heading on to an easterly course of 090°. This change of direction set up the reciprocal leg of a racetrack pattern, and it took the tankers towards the oncoming fighters which were still maintaining their 280° westerly track. As the range decreased, Epson 11 called a radar contact *'on the nose at 12 o'clock'*. The tankers were requested to begin a gradual U-turn at 25 miles which would roll them out on a 255° heading, a few miles ahead of the fighters and on a near parallel course.

Epson 11: *'Astra Eight One? Epson One One. How do you read?'*

Astra 81: *'Roger, sir. I've got you Five by how many?'*

Epson 11: *'Roger, Five by Five. Say your distance off to Yeovilton'.*

Astra 81: *'Roger, we're in a left turn, currently crossing zero fife zero degrees on our heading. We are looking for three four zero and are continuing it all the way around, and we are fifteen miles west of Yeovilton at the present time'.*

Epson 11: *'Okay, I think I have a tally on all*

five of you'.

London Military Control: *'Epson One One? They're now left at eleven o'clock, range eleven miles, crossing left to right* .

Epson 11: *'Roger, One One has got a contact at my left, eleven o'clock, slightly high. Rest of Flight call contact.'*

Epson 11: *'Astra Eight One? Epson One One'.*

Astra 81: *'Roger Epson One One, this is Astra Eight One'.*

'Epson 11: *Roger we have contact with all the tankers; we'll be going to our appropriate tankers'.* Astra 81: *'Roger, sir'.*

The rendezvous of the first cell of tankers and their receivers was completed, and the combined formation proceeded west-southwest towards the first air refuelling sector. It had been an impressively smooth join-up reflecting the thoroughness of the mission briefings.

After the two cells were established on the same track, which would take them across Devon and Cornwall and out over the coast near Land's End, the tankers moved out from trail to a 20° right echelon formation with one mile lateral separations and maintaining the 500ft vertical

intervals in the Flight Level 260-280 'ALTRV'. As the AR1 sector approached, Astra 83's Boom Operator reported the fighters in sight, got the boom cleared down and switched to the 'Comm 1' channel to make contact with the F-16s.

Astra 83 Boom Operator: *'Epson One One, One Two? This is Eight Three Boom, how copy?'*

Epson 11: *'One One's loud and clear'* .

Epson 12: *Two's loud and clear'.*

Astra 83 Boom Operator: *'And I read you loud and clear, One One, One Two'.*

Epson 11: *'And One One cleared in?'*

Astra 83 Boom Operator: *'One One, you're cleared in pre-contact'.*

Both halves of the air refuelling equation made a close in visual check on each other, while Capt Wartburg notified the F-16s that he was increasing the airspeed slightly to restore the correct distance from Astra 82, which had pushed out to two miles ahead of us. Then Epson One One was cleared in to the boom.

Astra 83 Boom Operator: *'Eight Three, Contact!'*

Epson 11: *'Yes, One One's contact'.*

Astra 83 Boom Operator: *'Taking gas now'.*

Looking like a bandit! The lean mean look of some KC-135s has been enhanced over the years by extending the matt black paint of the anti-glare nose up and around the flight deck windows to give the machine the 'look' of wearing a bandit's mask. (Simon Peters Collection)

'*And One One you're taking gas*'.

Epson 11: '*Roger*'.

After about three minutes the boom operator advised an unscheduled disconnect light, though Epson 11 was reporting his fuel gauges were reading almost full. A reconnection was quickly effected for a top-up until:

Epson 11: '*And One One 's now showing full all the way across. How are you reading Eight Three ?*'

Astra 83 Co-pilot: '*Boom? . . . no flow 11.5*'.

Astra 83 Boom Operator: '*And One One, we've got no flow at 11.5*'.

Epson 11: '*All right to disconnect?*'

Astra 83 Boom Operator: '*Eight Three, disconnect*'.

Epson 11: '*One One, disconnect*'.

Astra 83 Boom Operator: '*And One One, you're clear dry*'.

The procedure was repeated with Epson 12, and the replenished F-16s took up a close escort formation on both sides of Astra 83. Towards the end of AR1, two of the fighters pulled ahead for a systems check hook-up on Astra 81 and Astra 82, to make sure all would be in order for AR4 and AR5, and then returned to the Astra 83-85 area of the formation. The AR1 leg was completed some fifty miles out from formation and was established along a 50° North latitude track, having turned due West some time earlier. After ARI the 'ALTRV' moved down 4,000 feet and the aircraft descended to FL210-230, with Astra 82 going into trail on Astra 81, and 83, 84 and 85 flying a 20° echelon off 82. The rear three tankers then conducted AR2 starting at 50°N10°W followed by the lengthier AR3 which took the mission out beyond 50°N20°W. At the conclusion of AR3, the KC-135s returned to trail formation prior to the division of the cell, which was to see Astra 81 and 82 taking the fighters out to mid-ocean while Astra 83-85 turned back for Mildenhall.

First, a check on the coordinates at the turn:

Astra 83 Navigator: '*Eight One? . .. Eight Three, say your present position*'.

Astra 81: '*Roger Eight Three, we're showing Fifty Zero Four North, Eighteen Twenty-One West*'.

Astra 83: '*Roger, thank you*'.

Astra 81: '*Have a good flight back!*'

Astra 83 Navigator: '*Zero eight one is the heading*'.

Astra 83 Pilot: '*Eight Four and Eight Five? Eight Three is turning right now to zero eight one*'.

As we flew back towards the Bristol Channel and the UK West Coast, the crew settled into some paperwork and Boom took orders for their own fuel supply in the form of lunch. Away to the right, the Astra 81 and Epson 21 Flights were on the westerly track and could be heard over one of the Comm channels.

A call to London Military control to confirm Astra 83 Flight's route via Brecon, Brize Norton and Daventry also brought confirmation that the Flight could move to the ten-mile separations, as per the flight plan, for individual recoveries back at Mildenhall. The separation was effected by speed variation with Astra 83 going to 330 knots, Astra 84 establishing at 310 knots and Astra 85 dropping back to 285 knots.

Before initiating the descent from our en-route height of 22,000 feet, the Aircraft Commander briefed the crew on the approach and landing procedures, and then called up the Mildenhall Command Post to advise of our estimated time of arrival and fuel remaining 'over the fence', and the maintenance write-ups which would need to be actioned after our return. Banner Control logged the details and provided the base weather and landing details.

'*Wind two four zero degrees at fife knots; six miles visibility; six-eighths Alpha Q at eight thousand; ceiling measured at temperature fife six degrees. QNH three zero decimal one seven; pressure altitude minus two zero fife; and the active runway two nine. Be advised, sir, the ILS is inoperative at this time. Your parking spot is fifteen*'.

Initially cleared down to eleven thousand feet by London Military, Astra 83's descent was authorised to five thousand feet after handover to Eastern Radar; past the former airfield at Alconbury, we turned further right to transit south of Mildenhall on the downwind leg, being given renewed clearance down to 2,200ft by Honington Zone. Another change of control brought instructions from Mildenhall Approach to turn left on to the base leg and finally we touched down almost imperceptibly, and rolled out along the centreline; it was 14.06hrs local, and the mission had lasted just over four hours. The working day, however, was already eight hours old and for the crew it would last a good while longer as they went through a mission debrief.

Replacement - the KC-X saga.

Around the turn of the century moves were starting to be made in Washington DC and Washington State to find a replacement for the ageing design.

KC-X Tanker Options

Fuel the Fight. Anytime. Anywhere.

Northrop and EADS based their design for the KC-X on the A330, while Boeing baased theirs on their 767. After losing out on the contract, they then claimed if they knew the Air Force wanted a larger aircraft, they would have based their scheme on the 777.

The initial plan was for the USAF to lease Boeing KC-767 tankers on a sole-source basis; at that time Boeing was claimed to be the only American company with the requisite industrial capability to manufacture large-body aircraft. As such, the KC-767 was selected in 2002 and in 2003 was awarded a US$20 billion contract to lease KC-767 tankers to replace the KC-135.

Led by Senator John McCain, several US government leaders protested the lease contract as wasteful and problematic. In response to the protests, the Air Force struck a compromise in November 2003, whereby it would purchase 80 KC-767 aircraft and lease 20 more.

Yet in December 2003, the Pentagon announced the project was to be frozen while an investigation of allegations of corruption by one of its former procurement staffers, Darleen Druyun (who had moved to Boeing in January 2003) was begun. Druyun pleaded guilty of criminal wrongdoing and was sentenced to prison time for '...*negotiating a job with Boeing at the same time she was involved in contracts with the company*'. Druyun, would serve nine months at a minimum security prison and another seven months at a

halfway house or on home detention. She also was fined $5,000 and ordered to perform 150 hours of community service.

As part of the plea bargaining, Druyun admitted that she did '...*favor the Boeing Company in certain negotiations as the result of her employment negotiations and other favors provided by Boeing to the defendant.*'

Previously, Druyun had admitted to negotiating a post-government job with Boeing, but steadfastly maintained that she had never favoured them at the negotiating table.

Prosecutors said Druyun admitted to favouring the defence contractor after failing a lie detector test. She also confessed to altering a personal journal to make it appear that there were no conflicts with Boeing.

Her plea agreement outlined four specific contract negotiations where she favoured Boeing: Druyun agreed to a higher price than appropriate for a proposed deal to lease 100 tanker aircraft from Boeing, which she called 'a parting gift' to her future employer. She also shared a competitor's proprietary data with Boeing. In 2000, Druyun agreed to pay $412 million to Boeing as a settlement over a clause in a C-17 aircraft contract. She admitted to favouring the payment because her son-in-law was seeking a job with Boeing. In 2001, Druyun oversaw a $4 billion award to Boeing to modernise the avionics on C-130J aircraft. She admitted she favoured Boeing over four competitors because the company had given her son-in-law a job. In 2002, Druyun awarded $100 million to Boeing as part of a restructuring of the NATO Airborne Warning and Control System contract. She said the payment could have been lower, but she favoured Boeing because her daughter and son-in-law worked there and she was considering working there as well.

On 30 June the Department of Justice released the result of its own and other departments investigations.

'*Deputy Attorney General Paul J. McNulty announced today that the United States reached final agreement with The Boeing Company on a record $615 million settlement to resolve criminal and civil allegations that the company improperly used competitors' information to procure contracts for launch services worth billions of dollars from the Air Force and the National Aeronautics and Space Administration. Assistant Attorney General Peter D. Keisler, and the US Attorneys for the Central District of California and the Eastern District of Virginia, Debra Wong Yang and Chuck Rosenberg, joined Deputy Attorney General McNulty in the announcement.*

Boeing has agreed to pay a total of $615 million dollars to resolve the government's investigations and claims relating to the company's hiring of the former Principal Deputy Assistant Secretary of the Air Force for Acquisition and Management, Darleen A. Druyun, by its then Chief Financial Officer, Michael Sears, and its handling of competitors information in connection with the Evolved Expendable Launch Vehicle (EELV) Program and certain NASA launch services contracts.

"The American people rightly expect government officials and contractors to act with integrity," said Deputy Attorney General Paul J. McNulty. "The outcome of these investigations sends a clear message to those doing business with the government: harsh consequences await anyone whose conduct falls short of the highest legal and ethical standards."

The $615 million settlement includes a $565 million civil settlement and a $50 million monetary penalty according to a separate criminal agreement. The amount is a record for government

procurement fraud, for the Department of Defense (DOD), and for NASA.

Under the agreement with the US Attorneys' Offices, the United States agrees not to bring criminal charges related to the conduct that is the subject of the settlement agreement in part because the company is fully cooperating with the government's investigation. Boeing has agreed to accept responsibility for the conduct of its employees in these matters, continue its cooperation with federal investigators, pay a monetary penalty of $50 million, and maintain an effective ethics and compliance program, with particular attention to the hiring of former government officials and the handling of competitor information. The US Attorneys' Offices may seek to prosecute Boeing for charges relating to the Druyun conduct, or to assess a further penalty of up to $10 million, if during the two year term of the criminal agreement, an executive management employee of Boeing commits federal crimes as outlined in the agreement, and the company fails to report the misconduct to the Department of Justice.

The settlement with the Justice Department's Civil Division provides for Boeing to pay $565 million in exchange for a complete release from any civil liability arising from the Druyan matter as well as the Evolved Expendable Launch Vehicle Program (EELV) and certain NASA launch services contract.

The government's investigation focused on Boeing's relationship with the former Principal Deputy Assistant Secretary of the Air Force for Acquisition and Management, Darleen A. Druyun. Druyun was the Air Force's top career procurement officer before she retired from the Air Force in 2002. In that position, she wielded influence over billions of dollars in contract awards, modifications, and settlements. In 2000, Boeing, at Druyun's request, hired Druyun's daughter and future son-in-law. Then in 2002, Boeing's then Chief Financial Officer, Michael M. Sears, recruited Druyun for an executive position with Boeing following her retirement. During this period (2000 - 2002), Druyun was responsible for dozens of Boeing contracts, as well as for the controversial $23 billion procurement to lease a fleet of KC-767 aerial refueling tankers that has since been canceled.

Sears and Druyun both pleaded guilty to violations of the conflict of interest statutes. In documents filed with the criminal court, Druyun admitted that Boeing's favors in hiring her children and in offering her a position influenced her contracting decisions.

The government's investigation also focused on the EELV program, with which the Air Force sought to usher in a new generation of space launch vehicles to serve the government's critical satellite needs through 2020. Air Force strategy called for two sources to reduce the risk of failure and cost through competition. Those sources ended up being Boeing and Lockheed, with Boeing's low pricing leading the Air Force to favor Boeing in awarding it 19 of the original 28 launch services contracts awarded in October 1998. The United States alleged that, prior to this award, Boeing obtained more than 22,000 pages of documents from Lockheed Martin, certain of which contained confidential competition-sensitive or other proprietary information that related to Lockheed's EELV program and that some of this information was used to unfairly assist Boeing in the EELV competition. When this was subsequently discovered by the Air Force, it sought to 'right the wrong' by re-balancing the contracts, at great expense. Boeing's conduct resulted in a record 20-month suspension of three of its business units from government contracting.

NASA also had launch services contracts with Boeing and Lockheed that required the contractors to compete for missions. The United States alleged that Boeing's possession and use of Lockheed's proprietary information, including additional documents obtained through different channels than the EELV documents, plus the unfair advantage the company had gained in the EELV, enabled Boeing to persuade NASA to award 19 missions, known as the 19 Pack, on a sole source basis. The United States further alleged that the lack of competition plus Boeing's false claims for certain costs, resulted in Boeing charging NASA much more for the 19 Pack than NASA should have paid.

NASA Inspector General Robert W. Cobb expressed his appreciation for the 'superb efforts of the DOJ, DOD, and NASA team that brought about this historic settlement. In addition to fulfilling our statutory mandate to protect the public's and NASA's fiscal interests, this settlement also serves as a testament for holding accountable those who abuse the government's procurement system. Indeed, the settlement represents a significant accomplishment in our continuing fight against fraud, waste, and abuse.'

"Now, the Boeing settlement is behind us," said Dr. Ron Sega, Under Secretary of the Air Force. "It wasn't a proud time in their history and in some ways it wasn't a proud time in our history, but Boeing is a competent and capable contractor and we look forward to a positive working relationship."

"This settlement sends a clear message that integrity in DOD contracting is indispensable and that the American public deserves no less than honest government and aggressive vigilance over the expenditure of the nation's resources," said Acting Department of Defense Inspector General Thomas F. Gimble.

The Druyun investigation was conducted by the US Attorney's Office for the Eastern District of Virginia, the Mid-Atlantic Field Office of DCIS (DOD OIG) and the Air Force Office of Special Investigations. The EELV and 19 Pack investigations were conducted by the US Attorney's Office for the Central District of California, the Air Force's Space and Missile Systems Center at Los Angeles Air Force Base, the Western Field Office of the Defense Criminal Investigative Service (DCIS) within the Defense Department's Office of the Inspector General (OIG), the

Deputy Secretary of Defense William Lynn speaks about KC-X at a press conference at the Pentagon on 24 September 2009.

Air Force of Special Investigations, and the NASA Office of the Inspector General at the Kennedy Space Center. The civil investigation and negotiations were conducted by the Civil Division of the Department of Justice, with the assistance of the US Attorneys' Offices' civil attorneys and the investigative agencies.

The USAF then began the KC-X tanker replacement program. The DoD posted a request for proposal on 30 January 2007. The US Air Force's main requirements were 'fuel offload and range at least as great as the KC-135', airlift capability, ability to take on fuel in flight, and multi-point refuelling capability.

Two manufacturers expressed interest in producing this aircraft. The team of Northrop Grumman and European Aeronautic Defence and Space Company NV (EADS)/Airbus proposed a version of the Airbus A330 Multi Role Tanker Transport (MRTT), based on the Airbus A330-200. Boeing proposed a version of the KC-767, based on the Boeing 767.

Both competitors submitted their tanker proposals before the 12 April 2007 deadline. In September 2007, the USAF dismissed having a mixed fleet of new tankers from both Boeing and Northrop Grumman as being unfeasible because of increased costs from buying limited numbers of two types annually - after all, they were already operating a mixed fleet of Boeing KC-135s and McDonnell Douglas KC-10s. In December 2007, it was announced that the KC-X tanker would be designated KC-45A regardless of which design wins the competition. The DoD anticipated that the KC-45A would start to enter service in 2013.

On 3 January 2008, the competitors submitted final revisions of their proposals to the USAF. On 29 February 2008, the DoD announced the selection of the Northrop Grumman/EADS's KC-30.

A few days later, on 11 March 2008, Boeing filed a protest with the Government Accountability Office (GAO) of the award of the contract to the Northrop Grumman/EADS team. Boeing stated that there are certain aspects of the USAF evaluation process that had given it grounds to appeal.

The Air Force responded with a somewhat terse statement: '*Air Force officials received a copy of Boeing's formal protest March 11 on the KC-45A contract award, recently submitted to the Government Accountability Office.*

It is the company's right to formally submit a

protest. Air Force members will carefully evaluate the protest, defend their source selection decision and allow the GAO to make its final decision, officials said.

In order to protect the integrity of the procurement process, Air Force officials do not publicly comment on the merits or specifics on any issues under review.

Proposals from both offerers were evaluated thoroughly in accordance with the criteria set forth in the Request for Proposals. The proposal from the winning offerer is the one Air Force officials believe will provide the best value to the American taxpayer and to the warfighter.

Air Force members follow a carefully structured process, designed to provide transparency, maintain integrity and promote fair competition. Air Force members and the offerers had hundreds of formal exchanges regarding the proposals throughout the evaluation process.

Air Force officials provided all offerers with continuous feedback through discussions on the strengths and weaknesses of their proposals. Several independent reviews assessed the process as sound and thorough.

The protest was upheld by the GAO on 18 June 2008, which recommended that the Air Force rebid the contract.

'*The Boeing Company protested the award of a contract to Northrop Grumman Systems Corporation under solicitation No. FA8625-07-R-6470, issued by the Department of the Air Force, for KC-X aerial refueling tankers to begin replacing its aging tanker fleet.*

Boeing challenged the Air Force's technical and cost evaluations, conduct of discussions, and source selection decision.

Our Office sustained Boeing's protest on June 18, 2008. The 69-page decision was issued under a protective order, because the decision contains proprietary and source selection sensitive information. We have directed counsel for the parties to promptly identify information that cannot be publicly released so that we can expeditiously prepare and release, as soon as possible, a public version of the decision.

Although the Air Force intends to ultimately procure up to 179 KC-X aircraft, the solicitation provided for an initial contract for system development and demonstration of the KC-X aircraft and procurement of up to 80 aircraft. The solicitation provided that award of the contract would be on a "best value" basis, and stated a detailed evaluation scheme that identified technical and cost factors and their relative weights. With respect to the cost factor, the solicitation provided that the Air Force would calculate a 'most probable life cycle cost' estimate for each offerer, including military construction costs.

In addition, the solicitation provided a detailed system requirements document that identified minimum requirements (called key performance parameter thresholds) that offerers must satisfy to receive award. The solicitation also identified desired features and performance characteristics of the aircraft (which the solicitation identified as 'requirements,' or in certain cases, as objectives) that offerers were encouraged, but were not required, to provide.

The agency received proposals and conducted numerous rounds of negotiations with Boeing and Northrop Grumman. The Air Force selected Northrop Grumman's proposal for award on February 29, 2008, and Boeing filed its protest with our Office on March 11, supplementing it numerous times thereafter. In accordance with our Bid Protest Regulations, we obtained a report from the agency and comments on that report from Boeing and Northrop Grumman. The documentary record produced by the Air Force in this protest is voluminous and complex. Our Office also conducted a hearing, at which testimony was received from a number of Air Force witnesses to complete and explain the record. Following the hearing, we received further comments from the parties, addressing the hearing testimony as well as other aspects of the record. Our decision should not be read to reflect a view as to the merits of the firms' respective aircraft. Judgments about which offerer will most successfully meet governmental needs are largely reserved for the procuring agencies, subject only to such statutory and regulatory requirements as full and open competition and fairness to potential offerers. Our bid protest process examines whether procuring agencies have complied with those requirements.

Our review of the record led us to conclude that the Air Force had made a number of significant errors that could have affected the outcome of what was a close competition between Boeing and Northrop Grumman. We therefore sustained Boeing's protest. We also denied a number of Boeing's challenges to the award to Northrop Grumman, because we found that the record did not provide us with a basis to conclude that the agency had violated the legal requirements with respect to those challenges.

Specifically, we sustained the protest for the following reasons.

1. The Air Force, in making the award decision, did not assess the relative merits of the proposals in accordance with the evaluation criteria identified in the solicitation, which provided for a relative order of importance for the various technical requirements. The agency also did not take into account the fact that Boeing offered to satisfy more non-mandatory technical 'requirements' than Northrop Grumman, even though the solicitation expressly requested offerers to satisfy as many of these technical 'requirements' as possible.

2. The Air Force's use as a key discriminator that Northrop Grumman proposed to exceed a key performance parameter objective relating to aerial refueling to a greater degree than Boeing violated the solicitation's evaluation provision that "no consideration will be provided for exceeding [key performance parameter] objectives."

3. The protest record did not demonstrate the reasonableness of the Air Force's determination that Northrop Grumman's proposed aerial refueling tanker could refuel all current Air Force fixed-wing tanker-compatible receiver aircraft in accordance with current Air Force procedures, as required by the solicitation.

4. The Air Force conducted misleading and unequal discussions with Boeing, by informing Boeing that it had fully satisfied a key performance parameter objective relating to operational utility, but later determined that Boeing had only partially met this objective, without advising Boeing of this change in the agency's assessment and while continuing to conduct discussions with Northrop Grumman relating to its satisfaction of the same key performance parameter objective.

5. The Air Force unreasonably determined that Northrop Grumman's refusal to agree to a specific solicitation requirement that it plan and support the agency to achieve initial organic depot-level maintenance within two years after delivery of the first fill-rate production aircraft was an 'administrative oversight,' and improperly made award, despite this clear exception to a material solicitation requirement.

6. The Air Force's evaluation of military construction costs in calculating the offerers' most probable life cycle costs for their proposed aircraft was unreasonable, where the agency during the protest conceded that it made a number of errors in evaluation that, when corrected, result in

Boeing displacing Northrop Grumman as the offerer with the lowest most probable life cycle cost; where the evaluation did not account for the offerers' specific proposals; and where the calculation of military construction costs based on a notional (hypothetical) plan was not reasonably supported.

7. The Air Force improperly increased Boeing's estimated non-recurring engineering costs in calculating that firm's most probable life cycle costs to account for risk associated with Boeing's failure to satisfactorily explain the basis for how it priced this cost element, where the agency had not found that the proposed costs for that element were unrealistically low. In addition, the Air Force's use of a simulation model to determine Boeing's probable non-recurring engineering costs was unreasonable, because the Air Force used as data inputs in the model the percentage of cost growth associated with weapons systems at an overall program level and there was no indication that these inputs would be a reliable predictor of anticipated growth in Boeing's non-recurring engineering costs.

We recommended that the Air Force reopen discussions with the offerers, obtain revised proposals, re-evaluate the revised proposals, and make a new source selection decision, consistent with our decision. We further recommended that, if the Air Force believed that the solicitation, as reasonably interpreted, does not adequately state its needs, the agency should amend the solicitation prior to conducting further discussions with the offerers. We also recommended that if Boeing's proposal is ultimately selected for award, the Air Force should terminate the contract awarded to Northrop Grumman. We also recommended that the Air Force reimburse Boeing the costs of filing and pursuing the protest, including reasonable attorneys' fees. By statute, the Air Force is given 60 days to inform our Office of the Air Force's actions in response to our recommendations.

On 9 July 2008, Defense Secretary Robert Gates put the tanker contract in an 'expedited recompetition' with Defense Undersecretary John Young in charge of the selection process instead of the Air Force. A draft of the revised request for proposal (RFP) was provided to the contractors on 6 August 2008 for comments with the revised RFP to be finalized by mid-August. Proposals would be due in October 2008 and selection was to be done by the end of 2008. In mid-August, there was speculation that Boeing was considering a 'no bid'

position. On 21 August 2008 Boeing asked the DoD for an additional four months to submit a proposal centered on a larger aircraft, but they opposed further delay. Then on 10 September 2008, Defense Secretary Robert Gates decided that the new competition could not be fairly completed before the end of 2008. The DoD canceled the request for proposals and delayed the decision on when to issue another request until the new presidential administration was in office.

On 16 September 2009, Secretary Gates announced a renewed effort for the KC-X programme. The selection process was to be under the Air Force with a 'robust oversight role' by the Office of the Secretary of Defense (OSD) to prevent a repeated failure. On 25 September 2009 the USAF issued a draft request for proposals seeking comments for the official tanker replacement RFP. The RFP for a fixed-price contract specified 373 requirements for the new aircraft, and stated that the price of each tanker would be adjusted to reflect how much it would cost to operate over 40 years and how well it would meet various war-fighting needs. The initial contract would be for 179 aircraft for $35 billion.Northrop Grumman/EADS team claimed the requirement was advantaging Boeing and threatened to withdraw from the competition on 1 December 2009.

The fiscal 2011 Defense Department budget relegated $864 million in research and development money. A contract award was expected in summer 2010. On 24 February 2010, the US Air Force released the revised request for proposal for KC-X. The RFP called for the KC-X tanker to first fly in 2012 and aircraft deliveries to begin in 2013.

On 8 March 2010, Northrop Grumman followed through with their earlier threat and decided to not submit a bid for the KC-X tanker, stating that they believed the new evaluation methodology favoured Boeing's smaller tanker. EADS, however announced on 20 April 2010 that it was re-entering the competition on a stand-alone basis and intended to bid the KC-30 with final assembly to take place in Mobile, Alabama as planned under its prior teaming arrangement with Northrop Grumman. On 18 June 2010 the USAF announced that the decision would be delayed until November 2010.

On 1 July 2010, a surprise third bidder, consisting of the team of US Aerospace and the Ukrainian manufacturer Antonov announced its intention to bid in the competition. The two firms announced that they would be interested in supplying up to three types of aircraft to the United States Air Force. The types reportedly being offered were the four-engined An-124 and a twin-engined variant of the aircraft, the An-122. The third aircraft to be offered was known as the An-112, a version of the Antonov An-70, except with two jet engines. This tanker was proposed in the team's bid.

By 9 July 2010 bids from Boeing, EADS and US Aerospace/Antonov were submitted to the Air Force. However, the Air Force rejected the US Aerospace bid for allegedly arriving five minutes after the deadline, which US Aerospace disputed. US Aerospace filed separate protests with the US Government Accountability Office on 2 August and 1 September. The US Air Force proceeded with source selection while GAO investigated. The GAO dismissed US Aerospace's protest on 6 October.

In November 2010, the USAF mistakenly sent technical reviews of the other side's bids to each of the two remaining teams. At this time contract selection was postponed from late December 2010 until early 2011.

Boeing and EADS submitted their final bids on 10 February 2011. On 24 February 2011 Boeing's KC-767 proposal was selected as the winning offer. The tanker would be designated the KC-46A. EADS North America chairman Ralph Crosby declined to protest the award, saying that Boeing's bid was '...*very, very, very aggressive*' and carried a high risk of losing money for the company. Dr Loren B Thompson of the Lexington Institute agreed that Boeing's bid was very aggressive due to the Air Force's fixed-price contract strategy.

Further delays?
At the end of March 2017 the US Government Accountability Office (GAO) stated that the KC-135 replacement programme was at risk of further schedule delays.

In their latest report, it stated that the KC-46A manufacturer, Boeing, had struggled to meet key milestones throughout the duration of the programme and was at least one year behind by most measures. The company faced an uphill battle to keep the programme on time, even as it continued to meet cost and performance goals, the GAO said.

The most important deadline on the horizon is the October 2018 target date for 'required assets available,' which contractually binds Boeing to deliver the first 18 tankers and nine aerial refuelling

pods. The company has already slipped too far behind to meet its initial August 2017 benchmark.

Because of delays, Boeing will have to compress its original delivery timeline for those 18 aircraft from 14 months to 6 months.

'*This delivery period assumes Boeing will deliver three aircraft per month, a greater pace than planned during full rate production,*' the report stated. Twelve of those aircraft are already over seventy percent complete, GAO added, but the company was far from being in the clear.

Two major challenges stood in the way. First, Boeing may not be able to conduct an electromagnetic effects test scheduled for May 2017. The test, which is held at a specialized facility, will evaluate whether the KC-46 creates any electromagnetic interference. However, because the Federal Aviation Administration has yet to approve the aircraft's aerial refueling pod design, the Air Force will have to decide whether to test the aircraft and pods separately or risk pushing the test to a later date.

GAO also has questions about whether Boeing can finish developmental flight tests as quick as it plans, noting that the company '*...is projecting that it can complete test points … at a rate higher than it has been able to demonstrate consistently.*'

Boeing must finish an average 1,713 test points per month to enable the first aircraft deliveries in September 2017, but it has exceeded that number only once, when it completed 2,240 test points in October 2016, the report said. When looking at data from March 2016 to January 2017, the agency found Boeing's average completion rate was about 800 test points per month.

And so the story rumbles on.

Beyond Block 45 - Will the USAF be flying 100-year old tankers?
By March 2017 rumours started to appear that the US Air Force was strapped for cash to buy more than 179 of Boeing's KC-46 tanker to fully replace the legacy KC-135 fleet, and that the Air Force was looking instead to refit its sixty-year-old KC-135 Stratotanker with state-of-the-art survivability upgrades so it can fly for another forty years.

The Air Force was set to buy one hundred and seventy-nine next-generation KC-46s as the first step in an ambitious effort to recapitalize its tanker fleet. But even after Boeing's Pegasus is fully fielded in fiscal year 2028, the remaining three hundred KC-135s would be the backbone of the force until the future KC-Y or KC-Z comes online in the 2030-40 timeframe. In fact, the joint force will rely so heavily on the Stratotanker in the coming decades that the aircraft could be one hundred years old before it is sent to the boneyard, according to Gen. Carlton Everhart, chief of Air Mobility Command (AMC).

Questions were being asked as to why the Air Force studying how to make KC-135 survivable out to age 100. Analysts warned that the Air Force should not be too tied to old platforms, but why spend time and resources upgrading a 1950s-era weapon system instead of simply buying more fifth-generation KC-46s? It all comes down to budget limits, Everhart explained during a 2 March 2017 media roundtable at the Air Force Association's air warfare conference.

'It's all about the money, it's all about the resources, it's all about the continuing resolution (CR)' Everhart rold the media, referring to the stop-gap spending measure Congress used to fund the government through April pending agreement on a full appropriations bill. Operating under a CR for at least part of the fiscal year has become the new normal for the Pentagon, even though a CR limits funding levels for existing and new-start programmes and wreaks havoc on long-term budget plans.

'It's all about what can we afford to do in the timeframe we have.' Everhart said.

'Retiring KC-135s would not automatically mean more cash for KC-46s because the Defense Department could not easily transfer money between its operations and maintenance (O&M) and procurement accounts,' said Richard Aboulafia, an analyst with the Teal Group. *'The fundamental conundrum of Defense Department procurement is [that] procurement and O&M accounts don't talk to each other,'* He went on to explain that General Everhart was *'...just being realistic.'*

Modernising the KC-135 instead of buying more KC-46s would also allow the Air Force to add capacity in the near term, noted Todd Harrison of the Center for Strategic and International Studies. *'If the Air Force needs more tankers right now, adding KC-46s will not help because the additional aircraft will not be available until near*

the end of the current production schedule in the 2020s' he says.

In the meantime, the Air Force wanted to make sure the KC-135 workhorse could survive on a dynamic future battlefield. *'The service is currently remodeling the flight deck with new liquid-crystal displays, as well as a radar altimeter, autopilot, digital flight director and other computer module updates as part of a $910 million Block 45 upgrade program. But AMC is also beginning to look into what is needed for the next block upgrade'*, Everhart said.

Everhart wants to add Link 16 and beyond-line-of-sight communications so that KC-135s can exchange imagery and other data in near-real time with other aircraft in the fleet - a huge step up from current capabilities. He also wants to incorporate a layered defense approach, adding electronic countermeasures to protect against jamming, self-defense systems and maybe even signature management.

'We are going to be flying the KC-135 for quite a while, and it is going to have to participate in that networked, multi-domain command-and-control environment where the enemy is going to come after our tankers' said Brig Gen Jon Thomas, AMC director of strategic plans, requirements and programmes.

In addition, the Air Force is equipping the KC-135 with the FAA-mandated automatic dependent surveillance-broadcast (ADS-B), which uses GPS technology to determine an aircraft's location, airspeed and other data.

'KC-135 is a great platform, [but] it needs to be modernized...' said Everhart. *'...We will use that capable airplane to get us to bridge across [to a future KC-Z], along with the KC-46, and then as KC-46 brings on new electronics, brings on new things that it has, can that spin off and go back down to KC-135 to keep it just as viable"*

Harrison warned however that the Air Force should be careful not to box itself into a corner, because upgrading the KC-135 may ultimately come at the expense of long-term capability.

As he said; *'How much longer does the Air Force really want to be flying a 707 platform?'*

Chapter Six

'Big Ol' Jet Airliner'…

From the song *'Jet Airliner'* composed by Paul Pena in 1973 and popularized by the Steve Miller Band in 1977.

Having successfully attracted orders for the C/KC-135A variant from USAF, Boeing diverted their attention to winning orders from the airlines for the 707. The big 'problem' however was the size of the Dash-80's cabin which was just not large enough for the airlines. Boeing's charm offensive to convince them that the same 144 inch width fuselage as the KC-135 was more than sufficient for four, five or six across seating fell on deaf ears and Boeing eventually capitulated and increased it by four inches over the KC-135, at the same time extending the length by ten feet.

There then began a series of protracted discussions with the airlines and slowly the orders started to trickle in. Given the speed that the orders were coming in, the decision to secure military orders before seeking airline contracts seems to have been the correct one. Hopes to convert quickly the military selection of the Boeing tanker into orders from the leading airlines were frustrated by the caution which carriers showed toward jetliners following the tragic and untimely demise of the De Havilland Comet 1.

Less than six months after entering service with British Overseas Airways Corporation, the first Comet 1 had been damaged beyond economical repair in a take-off accident in Rome, Italy. Over the next seventeen months, five more Comet 1s were lost, the last two disintegrating in flight and prompting the grounding of the pioneering British jetliner.

Alarmed, airlines adopted a wait and see attitude pending results from a thorough accident investigation by the Royal Aircraft Establishment at Farnborough.

However, Boeing did appear to have an unbeatable lead, for by February 1955 it could boast Air Force contracts for no fewer than 286 KC-135As. The Douglas Aircraft Company meanwhile were unwilling to concede its 20-year lead as the world's foremost manufacturer of medium and long range airliners, and so decided to challenge Boeing. On 7 June 1955, before Boeing was able to secure a single order for its jetliner, Douglas confirmed that it would proceed with the development of a jet transport with performance surpassing that of the first Boeing 707 civil derivative of the 367-80 demonstrator.

The comparative fuselage widths of the Dash 80, KC-135/717 and the 707.

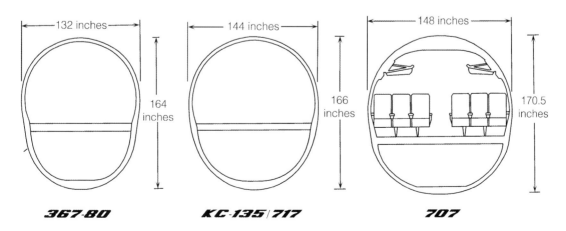

The Douglas DC-8 - this example being EC-ARB for the Spanish national airline Iberia. (author's collection)

The Douglas challenge was made even more dangerous for Boeing by the fact that the Southern California manufacturer had an intimate in-depth knowledge of what airlines needed as it had successfully developed its pre-war-designed, unpressurised DC-4 into the pressurised DC-6 and DC-7 series with ever-increasing speed, range, and payload that made them very commercially successful.

Douglas designed its DC-8 jet airliner to out-perform the initial 707 variant being marketed by Boeing. Douglas adopted a wider fuselage cross-section in order to increase seat width in first class and, more importantly, to offer better than spartan six-abreast seating in economy class versus the five abreast seating offered by Boeing. Douglas was quick to realise that airlines competing over the 'Blue Ribbon' North Atlantic route would want to offer nonstop jet service, as a multi-stop jet service would only be marginally faster than

nonstop piston- engine DC-7C service.

Convair, the dominant American manufacturer of short- to medium-range airliners, was also intent on challenging Boeing's lead by developing jetliners optimized for US domestic and shorter international routes. The company felt that a cruising speed higher than offered by either the 707 or DC-8 would be the key to success. Accordingly, in January 1956, the San Diego manufacturer announced the development of its Model 22 Skylark, a jet airliner slightly smaller but faster than the Boeing 707.

With the initial configurations of its 707 challenged at the lower end of the market by the smaller and faster Convair 880 and its turbofan—powered derivative, the Convair 990, and at the upper end of the market by the larger, heavier, and roomier Douglas DC-8 variants, Boeing was forced to depart from its original plans to offer the 707 only in long and short body versions powered by JT3C turbojets.

To meet the challenge from Douglas, Boeing was

The Convair 880 in the colours of Japan Air Lines. Initially the design was called the Skylark, but the name was later changed to the Golden Arrow, then Convair 600 and then finally the 880. (author's collection)

The fuselage of the 707/720 was made up of four sections. QEA502 was the nose section - from forward pressure bulkhead to aft of the passenger entrance door - for QANTAS Empire Airways (hence QEA) which became a -138, registered VH-EBB.
(DGR Picture Library)

forced to offer larger and heavier JT4A turbojet-powered, Rolls Royce Conway and JT3D turbofan-powered 707 models; at the same time, it addressed the Convair challenge with smaller and lighter 720 variants. In addition, in something of a series of unsuccessful attempts to regain the initiative, Boeing studied still larger and heavier variants, but none were built.

Production of the first 707s proceeded at Renton while Boeing was attempting to satisfy airline requests, but new orders were fairly slow coming in,

The first production 707, N708PA c/n 17586, was rolled out of the Renton plant on 28 October 1957 and took to the air for the first time on 20 December; the other aircraft used in the certification programme were N707PA and N709PA - all from the Pan American order. Performance guarantees as promised in contracts were met and the FAA issued

a provisional certificate on 15 August 1958 to allow crew training, route proving and familiarisation of airport personnel with the new generation of air transports. Pan Am then took delivery of N709PA, temporarily named 'Clipper America', and started crew training and route proving, the first visit to London being on 8 September 1958.

The route proving and crew training continued but BOAC, with the redesigned Comet 4, were not prepared to let Pan American start the jet age across the North Atlantic without a challenge and, in fact positioned a Comet 4 at New York's Idlewild Airport to start services as soon as New York Port Authority noise approval was granted.

The price on delivery of the first 707-100s was said to be about $6 million, although the declared value for insurance purposes of Pan Am's first aircraft was $4.5 million and BOAC's -436s cost about $5.1

PAA002 was the nose and forward fuselage barrel of the second 707 for Pan American Airways. As N707PA 'Clipper Maria' the machine was rolled out in February 1958 and delivered that December. Its first revenue services however were for National Airlines, who leased it for New York - Miami work early in 1959.
(DGR Picture Library)

The 707/720 line operated alongside the 717/135 production line for a number of years at Renton; final assembly of KC-135s can be seen top left. (DGR Picture Library)

million. The actual price paid depended on the number ordered, the amount of training and support purchased from Boeing and other factors.

The Approved Type Certificate (ATC) for the 707 was issued by the FAA on 18 September 1958 following noise measurements conducted at Le Bourget, Paris - the JT3C had multi-pipe nozzles to make the aircraft quieter but the engine noise problem was not resolved to an acceptable level until high by-pass engines were introduced. Boeing, in association with the engine manufacturers, spent a lot of resources on trying to cure - or at least improve the problem.

The first 707-121 to actually be supplied to Pan American was N710PA. It was delivered on on 29 September 1958 and was officially named '*Jet Clipper America*' on 16 October by the wife of the President, Mrs Mamie Eisenhower.

The historic *Clipper* names with Pan Am dated from the days of the Sikorsky flying boats of the 1930s. Most of the 707s reused historic *Clipper* (or *Jet Clipper*) names such as *Bald Eagle, Constitution* and *Friendship*. Special occasions were also marked:

At least one 707 was renamed for a new destination; *Clipper Beograd*, and for the Beatles' US tour in February 1964 one aircraft was temporarily redubbed *Clipper Beatles*.

Since the 707-121s were unable to fly the Atlantic non-stop, fuel stops were planned at Gander in Newfoundland or Shannon in Eire with proposed flight times of eight hours forty-five minutes westbound and six hours thirty five minutes eastbound - the speed increase was due to the prevailing jetstream.

The first 707 revenue earning service across the North Atlantic was made by N711PA operating as PA114 on 26 October 1958 between New York-Idlewild (now John F Kennedy Airport) and Paris-Le Bourget continuing to Rome; however BOAC had already started non-stop Comet services in both directions on 4 October 1958 between New York-Idlewild and London-Heathrow.

Despite the prestige of operating on the North Atlantic, Pan American leased time on some of its 707s to National Airlines for their Miami-New York services from 10 December 1958 to 15 May 1959 during the winter peak traffic on this route. In return Pan American leased Douglas DC-8 time from National in the summer of 1959 and this exchange of 707s was repeated from 1 November 1959 to 24 April 1960. An attempt to exchange stock as well as aircraft was not permitted by FAA.

A year after opening trans-Atlantic services, Pan Am inaugurated the first round-the-world jet service with its 707-321s, flown on 10 October by N717PA *Clipper Fleetwing*. The route started in San Franciso, heading to Manila via Hawaii, then Manila - Karachi - Rome - and then over the North Pole via Anchorage back to San Francisco. The flight took fifty five hours and sixteen stops over three days, but this was more of a publicity flight than a route- proving exercise.

Until the arrival of the 707, Douglas's DC-7C was the pride of the Pan Am fleet , but the jet soon showed its superiority in every respect. The 707 could fly nearly twice as fast with nearly twice the passenger load, and at a lower cost per seat-mile. Soon Pan Am was achieving 100 per cent load factors on the transatlantic routes and was paying off or amortising the cost of one 707 with the profits of each month's operations.

The 707-321 Intercontinental version, delivered from July 1959, extended Pan Am's non-stop destinations from New York as far as Frankfurt, Rome and Rio de Janeiro. By buying large numbers of -321C convertible cargo versions when they became available from 1963, Pan Am stole a march on its competitors with its 'cargo Clippers' and captured a large part of the civil long-haul freight market. During the Vietnam War, the airline received lucrative contracts to shift military equipment to the war zone as US involvement increased. This was something of a double-edged sword, for the military tasks impeded the growth of Pan Am's civil freight business until this was reorganised in 1966.

Introduction of the 707 led to problems at airports, not only due to a 50% increase in passengers carried over the DC-7Cs and Lockheed Constellations they replaced, but also because of their weight, runway length required and noise.

The early non-turbofan 707s required extra-long runways over the aircraft they replaced and many cities were reluctant to extend their municipal airport runways, causing delays in the introduction of new services. This runway length was not only for takeoff

The final assembly production line for the 707 at Renton. (author's collection)

Mamie Eisenhower christens Pan Am 707 N710PA 'Jet Clipper America' at Washinton's National Airport on 16 October 1958, watched by Juan Trippe. Four aircraft carried this name: N707PA (January to December 1958), N709PA (August-November 1958), N710PA (1958-1970) and N711PA (October- November 1958). It seems Boeing was uncertain over which aircraft would be ready on time for the naming ceremony and the transatlantic flight to follow directly afterwards, and so the manufacturer was hedging its bets. (Pan Am)

but also for landing; indeed at one stage deceleration parachutes as used by the military were considered but the introduction of the thrust-reverser overcame this problem.

Another problem was the weight of the aircraft, which were nearly twice as heavy as their predecessors so taxiways and parking areas also needed to be strengthened, while their increased length led to problems in parking at terminal gates. Up to this time aircraft usually parked side-on to the terminals but to fit the same number of jets in the equivalent space it became necessary to use nose-in parking, which was less convenient in terms of loading and unloading for only the forward doors could be used for passengers, slowing down the entire process. This soon became the recognised parking position - also needed then was a tug vehicle

Two views supposedly taken on the first Pan American service across the Atlantic to Paris on 26 October 1958.

Above Stewardess Hope Ryden offers a newspaper to a passenger. Left: A Pan American stewardess pours coffee for a passenger. The PAA logoed trolley and the artwork on the bulkhead somehow does not quite feel 'right'! There is some thought that these were shot in the Teague cabin mock-up in New York (both Pan Am)

Above: N712PA at Terminal 3 Idlewild - otherwise known as Pan American Worldport.

Below: a pair of Pan Am Stewardesses pose with a board promoting the new jet services. (both author's collection)

to push the aircraft back.

The success of the first generation jets and the introduction of tourist class led to more people flying which led to terminal saturation at many airports.

Aircraft noise also became an issue, the introduction of the early 707s and other first generation jet airliners matching an increase in complaints from the public living near airports. The silencing mechanism of the early JT3Cs and JT4As was rather crude, with a set of sound suppresser tubes mounted behind the main turbine assembly. When reverse thrust was selected clam doors closed and the exhaust gases were forced out forward through cascade vanes. When the later JT3D turbofans were introduced the noise was reduced on landing but the noise of approaching jets was also a problem. With flaps and undercarriage down and a nose high attitude, relatively high power settings were required, resulting in a high pitched whine. Eventually regulations were introduced by ICAO (International Civil Aviation Organisation) limiting the maximum permitted noise levels. Aircraft that failed to meet these limits from 1985 onwards were then banned from certain airports, but since then the regulations have been progressively tightened.

Boeing received few orders in 1958, but the USAF ordered three VC-137s, the military version of the 707-120s, for VIP use, South African Airlines ordered three 707-320s on 21 February 1958, Continental ordered one more 707-120 and American ordered twenty-five 720s, five of these being converted from the original 707-120 order.

Pan American was the first 707 customer, taking something of a gamble with the 707 - and the DC-8 for that matter - as much for Juan Trippe's desire not to be second in anything as for any other reason. One reason airlines were initially reluctant to embrace jets was their high purchase cost. In 1953 it was thought a four-engine jetliner might cost $4 million, compared to the $1.5 million price of a new DC-7. The final cost of a 707-100 was well over $5 million. (author's collection)

Getting orders from TWA

Ever since Boeing announced the development of the 367-80 various Boeing officials had tried to establish liaison with Howard Hughes and Trans World Airlines and periodically kept Ralph Damon, the President of TWA, and Robert W Rummel, who took the role of liason with Howard Hughes as majority stockholder, informed concerning Boeing's plans to offer and produce jets for the airlines.

Hughes, living up to his reputation of being incredibly secretive and of procastinating for as long as possible, refused to make a decision regarding purchasing 707s, so in October 1954 Ken Gordon of Boeing called Rummel, advising him that Boeing was having serious contractual discussions with Pan American and an unnamed airline. Gordon said Boeing expected to have contractual specifications completed by 15 November and to shortly work out option arrangements guaranteeing relative delivery positions between airlines.

Legend has it that Gordon told Rummel that Hughes had already contacted Wellwood Beall, Boeing's executive vice president, several weeks earlier, but since then Hughes had not returned Wellwood's calls. Gordon reiterated Boeing's desire to work with TWA and suggested early specification conferences. He invited TWA's senior management to visit Seattle and inspect the 367-80 prototype.

Rummel then discovered that Hughes had expressed interest to Wellwood Beall in procuring the first fifty Boeing jets, and Wellwood refused, explaining that such exclusivity was self defeating and contrary to Boeing policy because excluded airlines would likely turn to other manufacturers. This was a hard-learned lesson from the days of the Boeing 247!

Boeing's President Bill Allen wrote to Ralph Damon, advising that the 707 delivery schedule for any customer would be based on the order in which commitments were made and would take into account the quantity purchased by each. He also invited TWA to undertake specification and contract negotiations. Allen sent a copy to Hughes and identical letters to other major American airlines as well as some of the larger foreign airlines. Shortly thereafter, PAA, AAL, and UAL commenced negotiations in response to the invitation.

Rummel urged Hughes that exploratory negotiations be started with Boeing without delay, but Hughes appeared more interested in continuing talks with Convair for their Skylark design. Hughes is supposed to have told Rummel that the time 'wasn't right' to deal with Boeing, that he would 'handle that,' and that he would continue to work with Convair '...*to design the best damned airplane for TWA that can be designed.*'

Finally, in late December 1955 Hughes authorised negotiations to begin with Boeing for a 'stop-gap' fleet of eight 'domestic' 707s - the JT-3 powered versions. Hughes's belated authorisation triggered an intense negotiation in Seattle between Harry West and Robert Rummel for Hughes and Wellwood Beall and J B 'Bruce' Connelly, director of contract administration, cumulating in a letter agreement for the eight aircraft and executed on 6 January 1956.

These, and all subsequent 707s were actually ordered not by TWA, but by Toolco, the abbreviated, more familiar name for the Hughes Tool Company, which had been established in 1908.

It is worth considering a snapshot of Howard Hughes' myriad of companies and aeronautical activities. It had been established as the Sharp-Hughes Tool Company when Howard R Hughes Sr patented a drilling bit for oil rigs. He partnered with Walter Benona Sharp to manufacture and market the bit. Following her husband's death in 1912, Sharp's widow Estelle sold her 50% share in the company to Howard Hughes Sr in 1914. The company was

renamed Hughes Tool Company on 3 February 1915.

When Hughes Sr died in 1924, 75% of the company was left to Howard Hughes Jr, who at the time was a student at William Marsh Rice Institute . According to Howard Sr's will, his son was to initially receive a 25% share, his wife 50%, and the remaining 25% was to be divided between various family members. Since Howard Sr's wife had died some years earlier and the will had not been updated to reflect that, Howard Jr automatically inherited his mother's shares. Resentful of his relatives' attempts to run the business, Howard Hughes Jr had himself declared a legal adult, being the age of majority at the time, and bought out his relatives' minority share in the business.

Under Howard Jr's ownership, Hughes Tool ventured into the motion picture business via Hughes Productions during the 1920s, and into the airline business in 1939 with the acquisition of a controlling

The jet age arrived at San Francisco International Airport in March 1959 when TWA introduced Boeing 707-131 jetliners with nonstop service to New York Idlewild Airport (which was renamed JFK Airport in 1963). United then constructed a large facility at San Francisco for its new Douglas DC-8 jets, which were also flying nonstop service to New York. In July 1959 the first jetway bridge was installed at SFO, which was one of the first in the United States. (author's collection)

interest in Transcontinental and Western Air (later renamed Trans World Airlines).

In 1932, Hughes formed Hughes Aircraft Company as a division of the Hughes Tool Company. Hughes Aircraft thrived on wartime contracts during World War Two, and by the early 1950s was one of America's largest defence contractors and aerospace companies with revenues far outpacing the original oil tools business. In 1953, Hughes Aircraft became a separate company and was donated to the Howard Hughes Medical Institute as its endowment. Hughes Aircraft's helicopter manufacturing business was retained by Hughes Tool Co. as its Aircraft Division until 1972.

For a period of time in the 1940s to late-1950s, Hughes Tool owned the RKO companies, including RKO Pictures, RKO Studios, RKO Theatres, and the RKO Radio Network. For a brief period in the early-

1960s, Hughes Tool held a minority stake in Northeast Airlines. Hughes Tool's majority stake in TWA was sold off in 1966. Two years later, in 1968, Hughes Tool Company purchased the North Las Vegas Air Terminal.

In the late-1960s, Hughes Tool ventured into the hotel and casino business with the acquisition of the Sands, Castaways, Landmark, Frontier, Silver Slipper, and Desert Inn, all in Las Vegas. Hughes Tool also purchased KLAS-TV, Las Vegas' CBS affiliate. In the early 1970s, Hughes Tool ventured back into the airline industry with the takeover of the largest regional air carrier in the western United States: Air West, renamed Hughes Airwest following the purchase. Hughes Tool also briefly owned Los Angeles Airways, a small airline operating a commuter service with a fleet of helicopters.

But back to the 707 order. Hughes reconsidered

The flightline at Renton in March 1961. Visible are 707s for American, a 720 for Western, and aircraft for Braniff and Aer Lingus. The 'final assembly' of many 707s was carried outside at Renton, as the black and white picture shows - a number still need to have their vertical fins fitted. Flight testing could take three to ten hours of flying by Boeing, which was followed by an acceptance flight by the FAA and then it was handed over to the airline for its own acceptance tests. (both author's collection)

his stopgap position and during the first week of January agreed to negotiate for a sizable fleet of international 707s. Boeing tendered an offer to sell between twenty-two and thirty international 707s at a base price of $5,150,000 each, subject to cost escalation and adjustment for changes in the detailed specification.

By now the majority of Boeing's early production had been contractually committed to PAA and AAL, Braniff and Continental having agreed to later delivery positions. Boeing offered TWA some of the early delivery positions it had reserved to attract new customers. However, PAA and AAL had already obtained the earliest delivery positions, which, of course, was exactly what the Boeing delivery allocation system was designed to do: reward early customers with the best available positions while retaining some ability to attract additional business.

Immediately a series of arguments broke out. Hughes claimed preemptive understandings on delivery positions, which Boeing refused to acknowledge. Hughes also wanted the Boeing negotiations conducted in secret, and they were, at least in the beginning.

When the detail specification development period was reached, secrecy became impossible due to TWA technical experts, in concert with representatives from other airlines, participating in detail design standardisation activities. Due to Pan American and American Airlines specification negotiations having preceded TWAs, Boeing's standard specification was essentially what AAL had negotiated, revised slightly to take into account Pan American's unique requirements.

TWA also had unique requirements: flight deck

instrumentation and arrangements, air-conditioning system design and performance, the design of certain key aspects of the hydraulic and electrical systems, selection of accessories standard to TWA, autopilot selection, and others. Had Hughes been an earlier customer, Boeing could have complied with many more TWA requirements. The conferences were useful in many areas, and, while complete standardisation was not expected or achieved, they were helpful to all concerned because of the savings realised. As TWA was able to convince other airlines to adopt some of own its requirements, Boeing could comply with more of their specification objectives than had the conferences not been held.

The definitive contract for the eight Model 707-131 Boeings was executed on 2 March 1956, by Ayers for Toolco and Connelly for Boeing. This was not a sufficient number to preserve TWA's markets against the forthcoming onslaught by American and United. A contract for the purchase of eighteen international Model 707-331s was executed 19 March 1956, by C H Price for Toolco and Connelly for Boeing. Despite pressure from his own team of advisors and those from TWA management, Hughes took painfully long to increase his order in three stages, each involving extensive efforts to obtain earlier delivery positions.

Thus, on 10 January 1957, when the fifteenth domestic 707 was ordered, Toolco had on order a total of thrity-three Boeing jets. Then the bomb dropped: Howard Hughes sent out a short simple message to his staff to be passed on to TWAs top management: *'TWA has no rights whatsoever to the Toolco jets'*.

In air travel, they spell dependability with three letters

TWA. These letters do more than name an airline. They speak of a vast operation geared to a single effort: getting you there in comfort and on time. Of the StarStream* jet fleet, built to be best and maintained to stay that way. Of every convenience to speed your departure and return. And of people—20,000 TWA people here and abroad who know their work and do it proudly. Good reasons to look for the big red letters next time you fly. Nationwide . . . worldwide . . . depend on TWA.

*StarStream is a service mark owned exclusively by Trans World Airlines, Inc.

Life, wanted a long term financing plan for the jet order as it was becoming nervous about Hughes' borrowing to meet basic costs like payroll.

To ease the creditors, Hughes had Toolco accept the obligations for the jet order and in turn lease the aircraft to TWA. Aircraft orders were swapped with Pan American, something that pained Hughes to have to approach his rival Juan Trippe to help TWA out, and the Convair order was cut to twenty aircraft. Juan Trippe and Raymond Holliday, executive vice-president of Toolco, executed an agreement on 25 June 1959, assigning six of Toolco's eighteen international 707s to Pan American, subject to Boeing agreeing, which they quickly did. It still wasn't enough and some of Hughes' banks cut off his credit in March 1960. With the other creditors, a short term financing plan was arranged to allow TWA to keep operating provided Toolco assumed all financial liabilities for the airline as long as there was a change in management at TWA. To further put the brakes on Hughes, his shares in TWA were put into a voting trust which essentially shut out Hughes from the airline. While a financing plan agreeable to all the parties was eventually settled upon at the end of 1960, Hughes still found himself shut out of TWA

TWAs logo on the tails of their 707s became almost a symbol of the times...
...and also the inspiration of an icon of New York, the Finnish architect and industrial designer Eero Saarinen designed Trans World Airlines terminal.

Like everything concerning Howard Hughes, the whole saga was riddled with secrecy and mis-information. Accounts give various reasons why Hughes did what he did, but the overall concensus of opinion was that it was all to do with Hughes being cash-strapped.

Hughes pushed TWA's finances to the limit to get into jets and while the arrival of the Jet Age to TWA marked the beginning of its zenith, it also laid the groundwork for Howard Hughes' eventual exit from TWA despite the near-limitless capital that he could access from his own parent company, the Hughes Tool Company. In February 1956 he ordered the 707-120s, then followed in June 1956 with an order for thirty Convair 880s, and then more 707s in May 1957. The value of these three orders was $300 million. TWA raised additional funds with a one-to-one stock offering underwritten by Toolco that also gave Hughes 77% control of the airline. But the money raised from the stock offer wasn't enough and it seemed that TWA couldn't meet its payroll obligations for the first quarter of 1958. Hughes borrowed $12 million from the banks, but at this point, one of TWA's original 1945 backers, Equitable

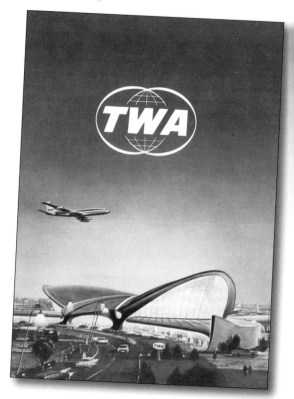

Above: Arrivals and departures board with information desk, TWA Flight Center, c. 1962.

Left" 'Miss Mary Tyler Moore, please pick up the white courtesy telephone'. Actress and dancer Mary Tyler Moore in the TWA Flight Center the same year. Note the TWA seating Chart behind her with details of Boeing Super Jet Flight 1. (both TWA)

and for six years lawsuit and countersuit after another were filed as he tried to regain control of TWA. He finally gave up in 1966 when in May of that year Toolco sold off its entire share of TWA stock and he was out of the airline business for a while.

Back in 1959, Hughes held tight reins on the delivery of the jets. It had been a regular practice to obtain authorisation from the TWA board for plant representatives to formally accept aircraft deliveries on completion of satisfactory acceptance flight tests and signal that final payments were ready for transfer. In this case, Howard telegraphically granted power of attorney to Edwin Zak, Maintenance Head for TWA's International Division, to accept one Boeing at a time, and then only when Hughes considered appropriate. He no doubt considered this degree of control necessary because of difficulty in mustering the necessary funds.

Shortly before the flight test phase, Hughes insisted that no one be allowed on the Toolco Boeings except the absolute minimum number of Boeing employees required to accomplish essential work and those known to be closely associated with Hughes.

It proved difficult for Boeing to make the first Toolco 707 ready for delivery. Repeated flight tests and some time-consuming modifications were required before proper system functioning was demonstrated. Everyone, including Hughes, was keen to see that the aircraft was delivered on time so that TWA jet services could be operated on the publicised date.

The start of service contingency time was all but used up by the time the airliner was ready. The aircraft had remained Toolco's, but last-minute arrangements were made to lease it to TWA on a day-to-day basis, arrangements that applied to all subsequent domestic and the first four international 707s.

After delivery, Robert Rummel flew in this first 707 with TWA Captain Gail Storck to San Francisco, where it was turned over to Flight Operations for

The TWA logo on the tail of their 707s beame used for everything from travel agents to clothing manufacturers. It was around this time that the 'If it's not Boeing tell them you're not going' started to appear. (author's collection)

FAA route proving flights. The inaugural flight occurred on schedule on 20 March 1959, with only minutes to spare.

Remarkably, that aircraft flew daily round trips between San Francisco and New York, and it performed flawlessly. It was operated an incredible twenty-one straight days without a single flight delay. And it operated with full passenger loads plus oversales passengers, who occupied the lounge seats. As Robert Rummel was to say afterwards: '*This incredible operating record is a tribute to effective jet planning and the fine TWA operations team that made it work.*'

A gradual expansion.
1959 saw 707 services start to spead around the world; American Airlines started New York-Los Angeles services on 25 January 1959, then gradually introduced 707s on all their long-haul routes while Trans World Airlines put their only 707-120 delivered on the New York-San Francisco route on 20 March 1959 followed by New York-Los Angeles in April after delivery of a second aircraft. QANTAS started jet services across the Pacific on 29 July 1959, then became the third operator of jets across the North

A line-up of 1956-ordered 707-131s for TWA are seen at Seattle in 1959. The aircraft in the foreground is fitted with noise reducing nozzles to cut down the sound generated by the JT-3C turbojets.

It consisted of two rings of eight exhaust pipes, and was first tested on the Dash-80 (right). (both John Stride Collection)

Atlantic on 5 September 1959.

Pan American put the 707-320 into service on 26 August 1959, initially from San Francisco to London, followed by the New York-London route on 10 October 1959, negating the need for refuelling. Braniff started its 'El Dorado' service from Dallas-Love Field to New York using 707-220s on 20 December 1959 with services to South America introduced on 1 April 1960.

Orders continued to be slow, Aer Lingus ordered a trio of 720s on 4 March 1959 initially to replace their L-1049Hs on the Dublin-Shannon-New York service with Boston added later although these were later superseded by 707s. The most significant order of the year, however, was from American in November for one 707-120 powered by Pratt & Whitney JT-3D turbofans of

17,000 pounds thrust.

On 10 October 1959 Pan American inaugurated the first all-jet around the world service when it started the San Francisco-Honolulu-Manila-Karachi-Rome-San Francisco service with 707-321 N719PA. TWA introduced 707-320s on the North Atlantic on 23 November with services between New York, London and Frankfurt, where their Lockheed Constellations had been uncompetitive alongside Pan American's 707s and BOAC's Comets.

Early problems.

Pan Am's great rival, American Airlines, was the first customer to put the 707 into scheduled domestic services. The first commercial coast-to-coast jet service was flown by N7502 *Flagship Oklahoma* from Los Angeles to Idlewild, New York, on 25 January 1959, returning the same day. The limited range of the 707-120 often led to weather diversions and occasionally to embarrassment. In October 1959 a New York to Los Angeles flight diverted to Phoenix due to bad weather at the destination and was impounded by local authorities, as Phoenix had no insurance cover for jets. It took five days to arrange the necessary documents so that the airliner could continue to Los Angeles.

After two months of having four of the new airliners in service, American discovered several indirect problems with the new jets. These included the difficulty of setting up a schedule based on predicted winds at the higher altitudes, which the airline's IBM punchcard computer was initially unable to deal with, and the US military occasionally blocked off 10,000 feet of airspace at a time when the jet routeings and altitudes available were already restricted. At that time there were only three transcontinental jet routes between New York and Los Angeles. Because of these and other factors, up to 66% of flights were late by ten minutes or more and a further ten per cent were early.

Air traffic control procedures also needed some adjustment for jet airliner operations. The regular reporting points were the same as for slower aircraft, so that the 707 crew could barely make one location report before passing the next checkpoint. American introduced a third pilot or second officer to handle navigation and communications duties. He would also take over the left or right seats or flight engineer's station if that pilot vacated it. This four-crew arrangement was also designed to ensure a constant visual scan in the increasingly crowded airways. American was the only US airline to adopt this crew arrangement and it was fairly short-lived.

Over in Europe there were similar problems. In Italy, the arrival of the 707s and DC-8s seemed to catch the authorities by surprise, even though they had experience of Comet operations in 1952-4. In 1958 the Italian Undersecretary for Civil Aviation refused to allow scheduled jet services as Rome's Ciampino Airport was overcrowded, the new Fiumicino Airport was not yet finished, and Milan's Malpensa Airport needed enlarging. Air traffic control was also considered inadequate and overall the 707 was thought to risk '...an undue strain on safety regulations'. The situation did not completely resolve itself until Fiumicino was opened in 1960.

British Certification problems.

Pilots had problems adapting to the slower increase in lift as power was applied during descents resulting in a number of abnormal situations. The popular press

A stunning picture of a 'bare metal' 707 with just 'BOEING 707 Intercontinental' on the fuseleage roof and tail - in fact it is N714PA prior to delivery to Pan American Airways (author's collection)

In March 1960, the Cunard Steamship Company bought a 60% shareholding in Harold Bamberg's British Eagle Airways for £30 million, resulting in a change of name to Cunard Eagle Airways. The support from this new shareholder enabled Cunard Eagle to become the first British independent airline to operate pure jet airliners, as a result of a £6 million order for two new Boeing 707-420 passenger aircraft. The order had been placed (including an option on a third aircraft) in expectation of being granted traffic rights for transatlantic scheduled services. Cunard's acquisition of a controlling stake in Eagle resulted in Bamberg's appointment as their new aviation director, hoping that his knowledge of the industry would help them to capture a significant share of the one million people that crossed the Atlantic by air in 1960. This was the first time more passengers chose to make their transatlantic crossing by air than sea.

In April 1960 the Government approved a range of new Colonial Coach fares for travel by British residents only on cabotage routes linking the UK with its remaining colonies. This was the right to transport goods or passengers between two places in the same country by a transport operator from another country. Despite opposition from IATA, British airlines - including British IATA members - were free to introduce them from 1 October 1960 as UK authorities controlled fares at both ends. Due to BOAC opposition, the aircraft were put on the Bermudan register to allow charters from London to Bermuda Via New York, but Cunard withdrew from partnership with Eagle Airlines in June 1962 and formed BOAC-Cunard instead. G-ARWD/VR-BBW served under the BOAC-Cunard, BOAC, BEA Airtours and British Airtours names until 1981. (DGR Photo Library)

were quick to provide coverage of these incidents, including the loss of control during simulated engine failure of both engines on one side of the aircraft causing the aircraft to dutch roll. This often resulted in incidents where engine pods were scraped along the runway on landing - something that could only happen with seven or eight degrees of roll! Rumour has it that many of BOAC's most distinguished old pilots - many who has served during the war - discovered that the lively, fast and lethal enthusiasm of the 707 for Dutch rolling made it only to easy to 'scrape a pod' and that after such an 'incident' they soon finished up in management!

Dutch roll was a problem inherent in swept-wing jets and was kept in check by the yaw damper function of the autopilot. The yaw damper could not be used at take-off or on the landing approach. Unlike piston transports, the 707 had to be 'flown' positively onto the runway rather than aimed at the threshold and 'floated' on. Pilots who tried to land the 707 like a piston risked undershooting the runway.

As a number of incidents and accidents during

crew training demonstrated. there were certain disconcerting characteristics. that neither Boeing nor the British Air Registration Board were happy about.

Pilots found the rudder system on the 707 somewhat different to what they had previously been used to. The original rudder system as fitted on the 707-120s had aerodynamic control only, but later variants have had power-boost assistance for bigger angles of rudder movement. For the first ten degrees deflection, the powered trim tab moved the rudder aerodynamically. Between ten and fifteen degrees the power booster began to take over and above fifteen degrees it was fully effective. However, this meant that there was no trim relief at higher angles and for structural safety reasons, the boost 'gave way' at air loads greater than 180 foot pounds of force. To use this effectively required training and practice as a heavy application of rudder gave a noticeable 'lag' as the booster became effective and then a rapid deflection to the booster's limit. The tendency was to add aileron and spoiler inputs, leading to an overcorrection and Dutch roll. A new booster that

Right: The ventral so-called 'ARB fin' on BOAC 707-436 G-APFB. When the marginal stability characteristics of the 707 in some modes was realised, Tex Johnston, backed up by the aerodynamicists, recommended a taller fin, a boosted rudder and the ventral fin seen here. Bill Allen and Boeing's board accepted his findings, as did the British Legend has it that when BOAC asked Johnston 'Who pays for it?' he replied with one word: 'Boeing'. This may have been an answer that reassured the customers and ensured the success of the 707, but it delayed profitability even further.

worked throughout the full range of deflection was designed to meet UK Airworthiness Registration Board (ARB) certification requirements and was later fitted to all 707s, but it was still not enough.

The situation was understood by pilots and proper corrective action was a matter of training and practice. But, apart altogether from any criticism of general handling, the characteristics of the system were such that, with the higher take-offpower available from the Conway and later J75 marks, the unmodified 707 could only be certificated to ARB standards by raising the minimum control speeds and thus unsatisfactorily restricting its take-off and landing performance.

There was a known requirement for increasing the keel area, indeed this was one demand from the British ARB; a modification that became known as the 'ARB fin' which not only increased stability but also acted as a tail bumper to prevent over-rotation on take-off. The ventral fins were of at least three different shapes, with straight or curved leading edges and different areas.

These changes also involved a rationalisation of the entire rudder-control system. The rudder was fully powered through its whole range of movement. The power supply and appropriate systems were duplicated for obvious safety reasons - and, more important, in order to provide maximum rudder deflection, without delay, in emergency conditions. Pressure was supplied at 3,000 pounds per square inch for low-speed flight and 1,000 pounds per square inch for high-speed flight, thus providing two different power 'ratios' with the changeover controlled by a Q-operated switch. The trimming system operated through the Q-pot mechanism, over the whole range of rudder movement.

'Q' feel is related to the aerodynamics and precise flight conditions that apply at the time of the control demand. As the aircraft speed increases so does the aerodynamic load in a mathematical relationship proportional to the air density and the square of velocity. The air density is relatively unimportant; the squared velocity term has a much greater effect, particularly at high speed. Therefore it is necessary to take account of this aerodynamic equation; that is the purpose of 'Q' feel. A 'Q' feel unit receives air data information from the aircraft pitot-static system. In fact the signal applied is the difference between pitot and static pressure, and this signal is used to modulate the control mechanism within the 'Q' feel unit and operate a hydraulic load jack which is connected into the flight control run.

In this way the pilot was given feel which was directly related to the aircraft speed and which greatly increased with increasing airspeed. It was usual to use 'Q' feel in the tailplane or rudder control runs; where this method of feel was used depended upon the aircraft aerodynamics and the desired handling or safety features. The disadvantage of 'Q' feel was that it was more complex and only became of real use at high speed.

There was no duplication in the yaw damper system, which remained inoperative during the take-off/climb and approach/landing stages of flight.

Most of BOACs -436s were delivered direct to London with empty cabins, but two were fitted with seats and galleys shipped out from the UK and picked up passengers from Montreal on the way.

Overall, problems with the aircraft itself included damage to skin, flaps and cargo doors by snow and slush thrown up by higher taxi speeds and trouble with the complex electrical wiring. The phenomenon of 'sonic fatigue' caused by engine noise created problems with certain areas of the airframe, in particular the tailcone. This was cured by replacing some magnesium components with aluminium ones and by lining the tailcone with fibreglass.

Spare parts availability was an early problem, made worse by minor changes on the Boeing line that came about as part of a pre-delivery design improvement programme which saw changes made between the specification given to the airlines and delivery itself, including everything from new doormats to leading-edge flaps. American found that if a part was to be changed on the production line, subcontractors would often stop making it immediately, leaving Seattle's stocks as the only source.

American Airlines Flight 514 was a training flight from Idlewild International Airport to Calverton Executive Airpark. On the afternoon of 15 August 1959, the Boeing 707 crashed near Calverton airport, killing all five crew members aboard. This was the first accident to involve a Boeing 707, which had only gone into service the previous year.

The aircraft, a 707-123 with registration N7514A, named '*Flagship Connecticut*' had accumulated 736 total flight hours. At that time The Calverton airfield was used frequently by American Airlines for training purposes for crew members on 707s, and was known then as the Grumman Aircraft Corp. field.

During the 1960s American Airlines advertised under the slogan 'Come Fly With Me' *that heavily featured their stewardesses dress in that 'swingin sixties' look. Their 707s were all named 'Astro-jets'.*

Below: American Airlines N7526A.
(both American Airlines)

The 707 departed Idlewild at 1:40pm local time, and accomplished high altitude air work after takeoff to permit sufficient fuel burnoff for airport transition training which was planned at Calverton, and arrived in the area around 3:11pm. Flight 514 accomplished several manoeuvres, including full-stop landings, crosswind landings and takeoffs, a high off-set approach, simulated engine out landings, and a no-flap aborted approach to landing. The aircraft did not retract its landing gear following the last aborted approach to landing on Runway 23, but continued in the traffic pattern at an estimated altitude between 1,000 and 1,100 feet. The crew reported on left base

American Airlines returned a number of their 'Astrojets' to Boeing for conversion to turbofan power, as the same time doing wing and tail modifications. The JT-3C was convertible to a JT-3D turbofan by adding a front fan and fourth stage turbine. This allowed the engine to handle two and a half times the air mass at takeoff, giving 50% more thrust, much better fuel consumption and reduced noise. (American Airlines)

leg for Runway 23, was given clearance to land, and was informed that the wind was from 230 degrees at 10 to 15 knots. As it approached the extended centreline of the runway, around 4:42pm, it made a left bank, steepening to approximately 45 degrees. The aircraft was then observed to recover immediately to level flight and to begin a bank to the right which became progressively steeper. The right bank continued until the aircraft was inverted, at which time the nose dropped and a yaw to the left was observed. The 707 then continued to roll to the right in a nose down configuration before the wings leveled. Investigation revealed the aircraft struck the ground in this attitude, in a nearly stalled condition, yawed to the left approximately twelve degrees, with considerable and nearly symmetrical power. The aircraft crashed in a potato field, a fire erupted on impact, and all five aboard were killed. The crash occurred only a few miles from the Brookhaven National Laboratories, a site of secret nuclear work.

The fire continued to burn for over an hour after the crash, hampering emergency crews in their efforts to remove the bodies of the crew. The Air Force sent several pieces of fire equipment to the scene. Eventually, a large crowd gathered at the crash site as word spread over radio and television newscasts, and people drove from resorts and towns in the area to see the wreckage.

The probable cause suggested was that '...*the crew failed to recognize and correct the development of excessive yaw which caused an unintentional rolling manoeuvre at an altitude too low to permit complete recovery.*' After the accident, the Federal Aviation Agency (FAA) discontinued the requirement that Boeing 707 aircraft make actual landings with simulated failure of 50 percent of the power units concentrated on one side of the aircraft during training flights, type ratings, and proficiency checks. These manoeuvres could now be simulated at an appropriate higher altitude. On 5 February 1960, Boeing issued a service bulletin for an improved rudder modification which added boost power to the wider ranges of directional movement, and gave increased control capability at low airspeeds and minimum gross weight. This modification also replaced the original rudder with an improved version.

Braniff Airways was to become famous for its more extreme fashion ideas worn by its stewardesses. Left is Emilio Pucci's Bubble Helmet designed supposedly in the days prior to the air-bridge to protect the coiffure from wind and rain on the walk from the terminal to the aircraft. A Braniff International stewardess models the plexiglass headgear at John F, Kennedy Airport, New York in 1965.

Braniff 720 N7077. (both author's collection)

Then Braniff International Airways lost its first Boeing 707-227 *El Dorado Super Jet* in a predelivery crash at Oso, some thirty miles north northeast of Everett, Washington, near Seattle. The aircraft came to rest on the banks of the Stillaguamish River.

Ship N7071 was the first of five Boeing 707's ordered by Braniff on 1 December 1955. Dubbed the El Dorado Super Jet, the big Boeing was the only one of its kind with the more powerful JT4A turbojet engines commonly found on the 707-320 series Intercontinental long range jet. The big Braniff engines did not require water injection on takeoff. The Series -227 featured the standard Boeing 707-120 fuselage which, combined with the powerful engines, created a long haul lower density airliner that was perfectly suited for the carriers US Mainland to South America routes.

This mix of power and lower capacity allowed Braniff to operate out of the higher elevation fields of South America where the jet was to be a planned mainstay. The smaller capacity also allowed for an increased profit spread, giving the fast 707 a

financial advantage over other jet aircraft. It was also the fastest 707, allowing it to be operated at top speeds of 636 miles per hour. Initial seating capacity was slated at 106 passengers but was increased to 112 seats with thirty-eight First Class and seventy-four Coach configuration.

N7071 was rolled out on 30 April 1959 and first flew on 11 June. Over the next four months numerous training and test flights were conducted in the Washington skies.

The flight proceeded as normal after departure from Renton. On board were eight persons including a FAA Inspector, a Boeing Flight Engineer, a Boeing Instructor Pilot, and another Boeing Pilot, and two additional Braniff personnel that included a Flight Engineer and Technical Training Instructor. There were two Braniff pilots up front including Captain M. Frank Staley and Captain John A. Berke as well as the Boeing Flight Instructor and Flight Engineer.

The Boeing Instructor executed a number of manoeuvres and then had the Braniff Captain demonstrate the same. The Boeing Instructor then began a series of Dutch Rolls and the Braniff Captain executed recoveries from each.

Boeing had instituted a maximum Dutch Roll bank angle of 25 degrees during any training manoeuvre on 707s. The Boeing instructor far exceeded this minimum with witnesses stating that the bank exceeded 45 degrees and upwards of 60 degrees. The Braniff pilot tried to recover out of a nose right angle and applied right aileron while the right wing was still moving in a downward motion and the aircraft immediately went into a 90 degree bank and yawed right at the same time.

The Boeing Instructor took control and immediately applied full left aileron and the aircraft began a violent roll to the left at which time the Number 1, 2, and 4 engines were ripped from their pylons. The Instructor began an emergency landing on the banks of the Stillaguamish River where N7071 ultimately crashed. Braniff Captain's Staley and Berke along with the Boeing Instructor and Boeing Flight Engineer were killed on impact. The other four personnel on board had shrewdly moved to the rear of the aircraft prior to impact and survived the accident. N7071 was a complete loss and the cost was absorbed by Boeing.

The Civil Aeronautics Board, who conducted airline accident investigations at that time, concluded that the aircraft engine pylons and nacelles had been overstressed and failed as a result of the improper inputs by the Braniff Captain trainee. The Boeing Instructor was faulted for exceeding the Boeing mandated 25 degree maximum bank angle during Dutch Roll training manoeuvres and it was pointed out that the Instructor had even been warned just prior to the accident by the Boeing Flight Engineer of the maximum bank angle during the training mission. The Boeing Instructor was also cited for allowing a pilot on his first training flight in the Boeing 707 to try to recover from such extreme gyrations.

Braniff would be allowed to use a Boeing 707-124 ordered by Continental Airlines for its training missions until Braniff's second -227 could be made ready for delivery. The Series -124 was not painted and was registered as N74612 and dubbed the *Silver Ghost* because of its lack of paint. The delivery of the *Silver Ghost* to Continental Airlines was delayed while Braniff was using the aircraft.

Three months after Pan American had started jet service, business was booming and the airline had already increased the accommodation in its 707-121s beyond the original 111 seat, two-class layout. However, the airline still faced problems as it had not yet resolved its dispute with members of the Air Line Pilots Association (ALPA). Thus, when on 3 February 1959, 707-121 N712PA (*Clipper Washington*) took off as Pan Am Flight 115, on the second leg of the daily Paris-London-New York flight, its two pilots were from management.

Captain W Waldo Lynch, who had logged 11,185 hours including 350 hours in 707s, was assistant vice president of communications for the airline. The copilot was Captain Samuel T Peters, then chief pilot of Pan Am's Pacific Division, who had logged 14,952 hours including 269 hours in 707s. These two veterans were assisted in the cockpit by John Laird, navigator, and George Sinski, flight engineer. In the two-class cabin two pursers and four stewardesses attended to the needs and comforts of 119 passengers, including the noted actor/dancer/choreographer Gene Kelly.

Bound for New York, with an intermediate fueling stop in Gander, flight PA 115 had taken off from London Heathrow at 18:45 GMT. Two hours later, the aircraft was cruising at 31,000 feet when Captain Lynch requested and obtained authorisation from Oceanic Control to climb to 35,000 feet before entering a frontal system with thunderstorms. As fate would have it, those additional 4,000 feet probably saved the lives of passengers and crew, changing the course of history for the 707 and Boeing.

After the aircraft reached flight level 35 while cruising at Mach 0.82, Captain Lynch left the cockpit to talk with Norman T. Blake, the Vice president of Pan Am's Atlantic Division, who was on board as a passenger/observer. Three hours and 20 minutes after takeoff, the aircraft was at 52.5 degrees N and 40.5 degrees W, some 500 miles east of Gander. Still in the cabin, Captain Lynch noticed a trim change, accompanied with buffeting, followed by a rapid build up of acceleration forces. In the cockpit, Captain Peters, who was checking notes on his clipboard after turning left 20 degrees to get on the new course requested by the navigator, also felt buffeting and positive acceleration forces building up rapidly. Buffeting increased, the lights on the copilot panel went out, and *Clipper Washington* went into a nose-down spiral to the right. PA 115 was in serious trouble.

While Captain Peters struggled to regain control by applying left aileron and rudder to stop the roll, Captain Lynch had a difficult time negotiating his way back to the cockpit due to the G forces. Once back in the cockpit, the first thing he did before even trying to get back into his seat was to pull all the

The Societé Anonyme Belge d'Exploitation de la Navigation Aérienne, better known internationally by the acronym Sabena or SABENA, was the national airline of Belgium from 1923 to 2001. Here is one of their 707-239s, OO-SJA.

Left: a period luggage label promoting 'Fly Boeing Jet Intercontinental' (author's collection)

stabiliser wheels to the 'up' position. First succeeding in getting the wings level, Lynch pulled back on the yoke as the aircraft passed through 8,000 feet, still going down. Finally, at 6,000 feet there were a few seconds of violent buffeting, but descent stopped and *Clipper Washington* pulled up into a fairly steep climb. At 9,000 feet the crew realised they had things back under control and the rate of climb was reduced. Flying the aircraft manually, Captain Lynch and his crew levelled out at 31,000 feet and cruised to Gander at Mach 0.79. The landing at Gander was uneventful.

Although knocked around, passengers and crew members suffered no serious injuries. The aircraft, however, had suffered what the Civil Aeronautics Board described as 'extensive structural damage.' The list of damage was impressive: wrinkles in the lower skin of both horizontal stabiliser with buckles in the centre section web and upper surface doubler; damage to both wing panels, including shear wrinkles in the rear spar webs; damage to outboard ailerons and their control rods; damage to the wing-to-fuselage fairings, with a three foot section of the right fairing having separated in flight; small amount of permanent set to both. wing panels; buckling to all four engine nacelle strut-to-wing fairings; and partial failure of the shear bolts in No. 2 and No. 3 nacelles and elongated fitting holes of all front spar-to-wing bushings.

The CAB concluded its investigation by

throttles back to idle. When Captain Lynch finally got into the left seat he saw the altimeter unwinding fast as the aircraft was passing through 17,000 feet after already losing 18,000 feet of altitude. He could not see the Mach meter, which was hidden by the control wheel. The artificial horizon was useless as it had toppled and the turn-and-bank indicator was full to the right with its ball left of centre. The horizontal stabilizer was in the full nosedown position and the electric trim button refused to work.

Taking over the control, Captain Lynch was assisted by the navigator, who kept calling the altitudes, and the flight engineer, who deactivated the stabiliser system and rolled up the two

ascertaining that probable causes were: '...*inattention of the copilot in the absence of the captain; the self-disengagement of the autopilot; autopilot disengagement light left i.n the 'dim' position and therefore not easily seen; and Mach trim switch not turned on'*.

Although not cited as a contributory factor, pilot fatigue most likely played a significant role. Management pilots had excessively long duty hours and insufficient rest time as Pan American struggled to maintain a full schedule while its ALPA pilots refused to fly 707s pending resolution of their pay dispute.

One cannot help but wonder what would have happened if Captain Lynch and his crew had not succeeded in regaining control. The loss of Clipper Washington in the Atlantic would likely have become an American counterpart to the Comet disaster off Elba in January 1954. At best, the 707 would have had to be withdrawn from use pending result of an accident investigation, a process that would have been made lengthy by the difficulty of recovering wreckage from mid-North Atlantic waters.

After the events of 3 February, *Clipper Washington* was ferried from Gander to Seattle for thorough inspection by Boeing; Once repairs had been made, the aircraft was returned to service.

Then, in Europe, Sabena Flight 548, operated by 707 OO-SJB, crashed en route from New York City to Brussels, Belgium, on 15 February 1961, killing seventy-three people, including the entire US figure skating team, which was on its way to the World Figure Skating Championships in Prague, Czechoslovakia.

The flight originated at Idlewild International Airport and crashed on approach to Brussels's Zaventem Airport. The Boeing had to abort its landing at Brussels because of an aircraft blocking one of the runways, and tried to climb and circle towards another one.

Under clear skies at about 10:00 a.m. Brussels time, the jet was on a long approach to runway 20 when, near the runway threshold and at a height of 900 feet, power was increased and the landing gear retracted. The airliner attempted to circle and land on another runway, but never made it back to the airport. The airliner made three 360 degrees turns to the left, during which the bank angle increased more and more until the aircraft had climbed to 1,500 feet and was in a near vertical bank. The 707 then levelled wings, abruptly pitched up, lost speed and started to spiral rapidly nose down towards the ground. It crashed and caught fire in a marshy area adjacent to a farm field near the village of Berg, less than two

miles from the airport, at 10:04 a.m. Brussels Time.

The wreckage burst into flames, though it is believed that all seventy-two on board were killed instantly. Theo de Laet, a farmer who was working in his fields, was killed by a piece of aluminum debris from the aircraft, and another farmer's leg was severed by flying debris.

The cause of the crash was never established, but is believed to have been a failure of the stabiliser-adjusting mechanism.

Further incidents and accidents

1962 and 1963 were not good years for Boeing, with several aircraft coming to grief. The first one was American Airlines 707-123B N7506A which crashed shortly after take-off from ldlewild, New York, killing all the occupants.

American Airlines Flight 1 was a domestic, scheduled passenger flight to Los Angeles International Airport. On 1 March 1962, the aircraft - having taken off two minutes earlier - rolled over and crashed into a swamp, killing all eighty-seven passengers and eight crew members aboard.

The flight crew consisted of Captain James Heist, First Officer Michael Barna, Jr, Second Officer Robert Pecor, and Flight Engineer Robert Cain. Also aboard were four stewardesses: Shirley Grabow, Lois Kelly, Betty Moore, and Rosalind Stewart.

The aircraft received instructions to taxi to Runway 31L at 9:54 AM EST, and clearance to proceed to Los Angeles non-stop under instrument flight rules (IFR) at 10:02 AM EST. Flight 1 became airborne at 10:07 AM EST. Following American Airlines procedures and Departure Control instructions, the aircraft initiated a left turn to a heading of 290. In the course of the turn, at 1,600 feet, the Boeing banked too far, flipped past 90 degrees, and began an upside-down, nose-first descent in a nearly vertical dive.

Flight 1 crashed into Pumpkin Patch Channel, Jamaica Bay, at 10:08:49, while angled at 78 degrees and on a magnetic heading of 300 degrees. Passengers aboard a Mohawk Airlines plane bound for Albany that took off immediately after Flight 1 watched the aircraft plunge into the bay. The airliner exploded upon impact, a geyser of brackish water and black smoke erupted from the site, and the scattered debris and fuel caught fire. Long Island residents described hearing explosions which shook the foundations of nearby houses, though no one on the ground is known to have witnessed the aircraft hitting the swamp. However, a few men at Naval Air Station New York / Floyd Bennett Field saw the massive geyser of water rising above the hangars, and one guard - at his post on a bridge that the aircraft flew over - saw it roll over.

A number of notable people were aboard Flight 1 when it went down in Jamaica Bay. They included: Admiral Richard Lansing Conolly, USN (retired),

In many respects Continental Airlines followed the theme of flying that was an adventure and a luxury.

Operating under the advertising slogan of 'The Proud Bird with the Golden Tail' their stewardesses followed the First Lady Jackie Kennedy chic.

Below: Continental Airlines 'Golden Jet' 707 N70773. (both author's collection)

president of Long Island University and Deputy Chief of Naval Operations; Johnny Dieckman, world champion fly-casting fisherman; George T. Felbeck, vice president of Union Carbide and operations manager of Oak Ridge, Tennessee. W. Alton Jones, multi-millionaire former president and chairman of Cities Service Company. Jones was found to be carrying $55,690 in cash, including a single $10,000 bill. Arnold Kirkeby, millionaire realtor and former head of the Kirkeby chain of luxury hotels; Louise Lindner Eastman, whose daughter Linda Eastman would later marry Beatle Paul McCartney; Irving Rubine, TV writer; Emelyn Whiton, 1952 Olympic sailing gold medalist and Peter F. Masse, president of C H Sprague & Son, an integrated coal company of New York and Boston. In addition, in the aircraft's hold were fifteen abstract paintings by the artist Arshile Gorky that were en route to Los Angeles for an exhibition - these were also destroyed.

The aircraft impacted into a remote area of marshland used as a wildlife sanctuary. Over three

hundred policemen and fire fighters, including 125 detectives attending a narcotics seminar at the Police Academy, as well as Coast Guard helicopters, were mobilized to the site within half an hour of the crash for rescue operations, only to find there were no survivors. The fire was under control by 10:50 AM EST, by which point only wreckage remained. Low tides aided search personnel in their attempts to recover bodies from the downed aircraft, but only a few bodies remained intact.

The Civil Aeronautics Board received notification of the accident at 10:10 AM EST and sent representatives to Jamaica Bay to start investigations. The flight recorder was found on 9 March and sent to Washington for analysis.

Investigators were unable to recover sufficient body tissue to determine whether the crew had been physically incapacitated at the time of the crash. Toxicology reports conclusively ruled out toxic gases, alcohol, and drugs as possible cause for the crash. Milton Helpern, the Chief Medical Examiner,

Above: 707 F-BHSB of Air France.

Left: Fifteen crew about to board an Air France Intercontinental 707 flight. The stewardesses uniforms were designed by Marc Bohan at Christian Dior for Air France in 1962, replacing a design by Georgette de Trezes. (both via Air France)

Above: Viação Aérea RIo-Grandense's (VARIG) 707 PP-VJA.

Right: like many airlines using the 707, VARIG pushed the glamour and 'executive exclusiveness of their jet service'. (author's collection)

decided that having relatives attempt visual identification of the crash victims was inhumane and ordered dental and fingerprint comparisons. In early July, the CAB announced their investigators believed that a cotter pin and a bolt missing from the rudder mechanism might have caused Flight 1's crash. Though considered to be a '...mechanic's oversight', the CAB nevertheless wired all 707 operators to inform them of the potential danger of the assembly.

In January 1963, the CAB released a Civil Aeronautics Board Aircraft Accident Report stating that the '...most likely abnormality' to have caused the crash was a short circuit caused by wires in the automatic piloting system which had been damaged in the manufacturing process.

CAB inspectors had inspected units at a Teterboro, New Jersey, Bendix Corporation plant and discovered workers using tweezers to bind up bundles of wires, thereby damaging them. The Bendix Corporation issued denials, stating that the units underwent sixty-one inspections during manufacturing, in addition to inspections during installation and maintenance work, and insisted that had the insulation on the wires been breached at some

point, it would have surely been detected and the unit replaced.

On 22 May 1962 Continental Airlines 707-124 N70775 operating their Flight 11 exploded in mid-air while cruising at 37,000 feet in the vicinity of Centerville, Iowa, while en route from O'Hare Airport, Chicago, Illinois, to Kansas City, Missouri. The aircraft crashed in a clover field near Unionville, in Putnam County, Missouri, killing all 45 crew and passengers on board. Remarkably, the airliner had been hijacked to Cuba the previous year as Flight 54. The investigation determined the cause of the crash was a suicide bombing committed as insurance fraud.

Passenger Thomas G. Doty arrived at the gate at Chicago O'Hare after the Continental airliner's doors had been closed. Although airline policy is that once the doors are closed they are not to be reopened, the

164

Above: N721US was a 720B of Northwest.

*Left: Advertising agencies were quick to latch on to both
the power of the jet and the mini-skirt in the 1960. It
became common practice to put a stewardess in the air
intake of a 707, as here with this Northwest girl.*
(both NWA)

Witnesses in and around both Cincinnati, Iowa
and Unionville reported hearing loud and unusual
noises at around 9:20 p.m., and some saw a big flash
or ball of fire in the sky. A B-47 Stratojet bomber
flying out of Forbes Air Force Base in Topeka,
Kansas, was flying at the altitude of 26,500 feet in
the vicinity of Kirksville, Missouri. The aircraft
commander saw a bright flash in the sky forward of
and above his aircraft's position. After referring to his
navigation logs he estimated the flash to have
occurred at 9:22 p.m. near the location where the last
radar target of Flight 11 had been seen. Most of the
fuselage was found near Unionville, but the engines
and parts of the tail section and left wing were found
up to six miles away from the main wreckage.

Of the forty-five on board, forty-four were dead
when rescuers reached the crash site. One passenger,
27-year-old Takehiko Nakano of Evanston, Illinois,
was alive when rescuers found him in the wreckage,
but he died of internal injuries at Saint Joseph Mercy
Hospital in Centerville, Iowa, an hour and a half after
being rescued.

FBI agents discovered that Doty, a married man
with a five-year-old daughter, had purchased a life
insurance policy from Mutual of Omaha for
$150,000, the maximum available; his death would
also bring in another $150,000 in additional insurance
(some purchased at the airport) and death benefits.
Doty had recently been arrested for armed robbery

doors were reopened and Doty was allowed to board.

Flight 11 departed at 8:35 p.m. The flight was
routine until just before the Mississippi River, when
it deviated from its filed flight plan to the north to
avoid a line of thunderstorms. In the vicinity of
Centerville, Iowa, the radar image of the aircraft
disappeared from the scope of the Waverly, Iowa,
Flight Following Service. At approximately 9:17 p.m.
an explosion occurred in the right rear lavatory,
resulting in separation of the tail section from the
fuselage. The flight crew initiated the required
emergency descent procedures and donned their
smoke masks due to the dense fog which formed in
the cabin immediately after the decompression. At
separation of the tail, the remaining aircraft structure
pitched nose down violently, causing the engines to
tear off, after which it fell in uncontrolled gyrations.
The fuselage of the Boeing 707, minus the aft 38 feet,
and with part of the left and most of the right wing
intact, struck the ground, headed westerly down a 10-
degree slope of an alfalfa field.

and was to soon face a preliminary hearing in the matter. Investigators determined that Doty had purchased six sticks of dynamite for 29 cents each, shortly before the crash, and were able to deduce that a bomb had been placed in the used towel bin of the right rear lavatory. Doty went into the lavatory with his briefcase and blew himself up, killing himself and everyone on board. His motive was so that his wife and daughter would be able to collect on the $300,000 of life insurance. His widow attempted to do so, but when Doty's death was ruled a suicide, the policy was voided and the widow was only able to get a three dollar refund.

This was followed Air France Flight 007, a charter flight operated by F-BHSM, carrying the elite of Atlanta, Georgia's arts community, crashed on 3 June 1962 while attempting to depart Paris's Orly Airport. The 707 carried 122 passengers and 10 crew and only two survived. The crash was at the time the worst single-aircraft disaster, the first single civilian jet airliner disaster with more than 100 deaths.

According to witnesses, during the takeoff roll on runway 8, the nose of Flight 007 lifted off the runway, but the main landing gear remained on the ground. Even though the aircraft had already exceeded the maximum speed at which the takeoff could be safely aborted within the remaining runway length, the flight crew had no other choice and attempted to abort the take off.

Stewardess recruitment, as advertised by Pan American.

N709PA in Boeing house colours before it was delivered to Pan American, only to crash on 8 December 1963 at Philadelpha, PA. (author's collection)

win your wings as a PAN AM® STEWARDESS

With less than 3,000 feet of runway remaining, the pilots used wheel brakes and reverse thrust to attempt to stop the 707. They braked so hard they destroyed the main landing gear tyres and wheels, but the aircraft ran off the end of the runway. The left undercarriage failed and a fire broke out. Three flight attendants initially survived the disaster. Two attendants seated in the back of the cabin survived, but the third died in the hospital.

Later investigation found that a motor driving the elevator trim had failed, leaving pilot Captain Roland Hoche and First Officer Jacques Pitoiset unable to complete rotation and liftoff.

The reasons for the charter flight was that the Atlanta Art Association had sponsored a month-long tour of the art treasures of Europe and 106 of the passengers were art patrons heading home to Atlanta. The tour group included many of Atlanta's cultural and civic leaders. Atlanta mayor Ivan Allen Jr. went to Orly to inspect the crash site where so many Atlantans perished.

During their visit to Paris, the Atlanta arts patrons had seen Whistler's Mother at the Louvre. In late 1962, the Louvre, as a gesture of good will to the

The frenetic glamour of the swinging sixties is probably best captured by The Beatles arrival in New York in 1964. Seen here with their manager Brian Epstein on the left are John Lennon, Paul McCartney, Ringo Starr and George Harrison in front of Pan Am's 707 N704PA.

The smell of the kerosene and the roar of the jets created a glamour and ambience that surrounded air travel - and nowhere was it more noticable than with the stews - and Pan American Airways certainly played that card to perfection! This is one of their 'graduation ceremonies'. (both author's collection)

BOMBAY · NEW YORK · 14ᵀᴴ MAY 1960

Mr. Peter F. Mehta,
Manager, USA & Canada,
Air-India International,
410 Park Avenue,
NEW YORK, 22, N. Y., U. S. A.

...AUGURAL FLIGHT · AIR-INDIA BOEING Ⓡ 707

Air India introduced the 707 on Bombay New York service on 14 May 1960, as shown here by VT-DJI. They marked the occasion with a First flight cover depicting the Maharaja of Air India giving a hookah to fellow Maharaja. The route and date of inaugural flight is printed in the top strip .
(via Air India)

people of Atlanta, sent Whistler's Mother to Atlanta to be exhibited at the Atlanta Art Association museum on Peachtree Street.

The crash occurred during the civil rights movement in the United States. Civil rights leader Martin Luther King, Jr. and entertainer and activist Harry Belafonte announced cancellation of a sit-in in downtown Atlanta - planned as a protest of the city's racial segregation - as a conciliatory gesture to the grieving city. However, Nation of Islam leader Malcolm X, speaking in Los Angeles, expressed joy over the deaths of the all-white group from Atlanta, saying '...*I would like to announce a very beautiful thing that has happened...I got a wire from God today...well, all right, somebody came and told me that he really had answered our prayers over in France. He dropped an airplane out of the sky with over 120 white people on it because the Muslims believe in an eye for an eye and a tooth for a tooth. But thanks to God, or Jehovah, or Allah, we will continue to pray, and we hope that every day another plane falls out of the sky.*'

These remarks led Los Angeles Mayor Sam Yorty to denounce him as a 'fiend' and Dr. King to voice disagreement with his statement. Malcolm X later remarked that '...*The Messenger should have done more.*' This incident was the first in which

Malcolm X gained widespread national attention. He later explained what he meant: '*When that plane crashed in France with a 130 white people on it and we learned that 120 of them were from the state of Georgia, the state where my own grandfather was a slave in, well to me it couldn't have been anything but an act of God, a blessing from God*'.

Nineteen days later Air France 707-328 F-BHST crashed into a mountain on descent into Guadeloupe killing 112. Operating as Air France Flight 117, this was a multi-leg international scheduled flight from Paris-Orly Airport via Lisbon, the Azores, Guadeloupe and Peru to Santiago, Chile on 22 June. The aircraft was just four months old.

The flight had been uneventful until approaching Pointe-à-Pitre. The airport is surrounded by mountains and required a steep descent. The weather was poor – violent thunderstorms and low cloud ceiling. The VOR navigational beacon was out of service. The crew reported themselves over the non-directional beacon (NDB) at 5,000 feet and turned east to begin the final approach. Due to incorrect automatic direction finder (ADF) readings caused by the thunderstorm, the aircraft strayed fifteen kilometres west from the procedural let-down track.

The plane crashed in a forest on a hill called Dos D'Ane (The Donkey's Back), at about 1,400 feet and exploded. There were no survivors. Among the dead was French Guianan politician and war hero Justin Catayée and poet and black-consciousness activist Paul Niger.

The investigation could not determine the exact reason for the accident, but suspected the insufficient meteorological information given to the crew, failure of the ground equipment, and the atmospheric effects on the ADF indicator. After the crash Air France pilots criticized under-developed airports with facilities that were ill-equipped to handle jet aircraft, such as Guadeloupe's airport.

Towards the end of 1962, VARIG lost 707-441 PP-VJB. Flight RG810 departed Rio de Janeiro-Galeão at 03:53 hours UTC on a scheduled flight to Los Angeles with en route stops at Lima, Peru , Bogotá, Colombia, Panama City, Panama and Mexico City, Mexico.

At 08:09 the flight reported to Air Traffic Control, Lima, at 36,000 feet, estimating Pisco at 08:13 and Lima-Callao Airport at 08:36 and requested permission to descend. Lima ATC advised of a DC-6, which had departed Lima at 07:35 and was also estimating Pisco at 08:13, when it would be cruising at 13,500 feet. After passing Pisco at 08:13, the crew started their descent. At 08:19 hours RG-810 reached 26,000 feet. Authorisation was granted to continue descending for a straight-in approach to runway 33. At 08:24 it reported to Approach Control ten minutes

from the station, at 15,000 feet, still in descent. By 08:30 hours it had reached 12,000 feet over Las Palmas. As it was too high for a straight-in approach to runway 33, Approach Control suggested that it make a 360-degree turn over Las Palmas and report again overhead Las Palmas. The aircraft continued descending. It turned slightly right of its 330 degree heading, passing east of Lima Airport, then made a left turn and passed over Lima-Callao Airport. It continued turning until it was headed south, passing west of Las Palmas in order to initiate the outbound procedure from the ILS back course, and then made a 180 degree turn to intercept the ILS back course of 327 degrees. However, it kept to the normal intercept course for almost three minutes before starting its turn to the north. Its heading was 333 degrees when it hit La Cruz Peak, about eight miles east of the approach track of the Morro Solar ILS back course.

The probable cause was recorded as: '...*A deviation, for reasons unknown, from the track prescribed for the instrument approach along the ILS back course of Lima-Callao Airport*'.

Not surprisingly, these accidents gave the insurance companies concern but the major airlines soon realised the premiums being requested were excessive for the risks involved and began to carry the hull risk themselves.

1962 may have been a bad year for accidents, but the jet passenger fatality per 100,000 miles and per 1,000,000 passenger miles continued to drop below the piston engined era - the increased

One airport that became synonimous with the 707 and Pan Am was Idlewild, also known at New York International. The terminal this Pan Am 707 is in front of was built in 1958 for the arrival of the jets. (DGR Photo Library)

D-ABOB, a 707-430 of the German airline Lufthansa.

Lufthansa operated a huge maintenance facility for both the 707 and 720. (both Lufthansa)

number of fatalities per incident tended to distort the figures. 1963 was marginally better for Boeing with only two losses, the first one involving Northwest 720-051B N724US, which crashed shortly after take-off from Miami.

Northwest Flight 705 was a scheduled passenger flight operated on 12 February 1963 which broke up in midair and crashed into the Everglades shortly after take-off from Miami International Airport in a severe thunderstorm. The aircraft was destined to Portland, Oregon, via Chicago, Spokane and Seattle.

Prior to leaving Miami, the flight crew questioned the ground controller at the airport about the departure routes being used, and he replied that most flights were departing *'...either through a southwest climb or a southeast climb and then back over the top of it.'*

After the jet lifted off from runway 27L, flown by Captain Roy Almquist, it made a left turn based on radar vectors from Miami Departure Control, to avoid areas of anticipated turbulence associated with thunderstorm activity. Another flight had followed the same guidance shortly before the jet took off.

While maintaining 5,000 feet and a heading of 300 degrees, Flight 705 contacted controllers and requested clearance to climb to a higher altitude. After a discussion between the flight and the radar departure controller about the storm activity, and while clearance to climb was being coordinated with

the Miami Air Route Traffic Control Center, the flight advised *'Ah-h we're in the clear now. We can see it out ahead ... looks pretty bad.'*

At 13:43, Flight 705 was cleared to climb to flight level 250. They responded, *'...OK ahhh, we'll make a left turn about thirty degrees here and climb...'* The controller asked if 270 degrees was their selected climbout heading, and they replied that this would take them *'... out in the open again...'* Controllers accordingly granted the jet clearance. Following some discussion about the severity of the turbulence, which was described as moderate to heavy, the flight advised, *'OK, you better run the rest of them off the other way then.'*

At 13:45, control of Flight 705 was transferred to Miami Air Route Traffic Control Center. There were communication difficulties, although after the jet was provided with a different frequency, the flight crew established contact with Miami ARTCC. Several minutes after contact, the airliner's altitude began increasing with a rate of climb gradually increasing to approximately 9,000 feet per minute. Following this rapid ascent the rate of climb decreased through zero when the altitude peaked momentarily at just above 19,000 feet. During this time the jet's airspeed decreased from 270 to 215 knots and as the peak altitude was approached, the vertical accelerations changed rapidly from +1G to about -2G.

In the next seven seconds, as the negative acceleration continued to increase at a slower rate, with several fluctuations, to a mean value of about -2.8G, the jet began diving towards the ground with increasing rapidity. As the descent continued with rapidly increasing airspeed, the acceleration trace went from the high negative peak to 1.5G, where it reversed again.

Below 10,000 feet the forward fuselage broke up due to the forces of the dive. The main failures in both wings and horizontal stabilizers were in a downward

BOAC produced a myriad of promotional material for the 707 for both public and travel industry alike.

G-APFE, which when operating as Speedbird 911 crashed onto the slopes of Mount Fuji in Japan on 5 March 1966. (author's collection)

On taking delivery of their first 707, BOAC made much of the event, sending out a lavish brochure to travel agents. 'Jet Powered by Rolls-Royce. The BOAC Rolls-Royce 707, biggest and fastest of the world's jetliners, is something special. It is powered by Rolls-Royce Conway jet engines. Four of these great by-pass turbo-jets drive the 707 through the sky. And what a performance they give! They sweep you along at ten miles a minute, anything from five to eight miles up and that's high above any tricks the Atlantic weather may play! At take-off, they develop a total thrust of 70,000 pounds. With these superb engines and a fuel capacity of over 19,000 Imperial gallons, BOAC's Rolls-Royce 707 has a range, with full payload, of more than 4,500 miles - over a thousand miles farther than London-New York! Thrust reversers, one installed in the tail pipe of each engine, provide something like 50 per cent thrust in the reverse direction - massive extra braking power from the Rolls-Royce engines when landing! Each engine also has a sound suppressor, so there's no jet roar to disturb you as you speed on your way. Flying in the Rolls-Royce 707 is supremely quiet and vibrationless!

Right: Handing over at Seattle. In front of the first BOAC 707 are, from left to right, Bill Carlyon and Tom Spalding (Boeing); Ivor Lusty (BOAC resident representative); Serge Gorney (Boeing); Charles Abell (BOAC chief engineer); J L Uncles (707 project engineer); Capt. H. J 'Dexter' Field (BOAC chief technical pilot); and Tom Gillan (BOAC inspector).
(all DGR Photo Library)

direction, and virtually symmetrical. The forward fuselage broke upward and the vertical stabilizer failed to the left. All four engines generally separated before the debris of the aircraft fell in unpopulated area of the Everglades National Park, thirty-seven miles west-southwest of Miami International Airport.

The report on the crash determined the cause was the unfavourable interaction of severe vertical air drafts and large longitudinal control displacements, resulting in a longitudinal upset from which a successful recovery was not made.

The second accident in 1963 occurred on 8 December when Pan American's 707-121B N709PA crashed on fire at Elkton, MD while awaiting permission to land at Philadelphia, PA. At 4:10 p.m. Eastern Standard Time (EST), the airliner, named *Clipper Tradewind,* serving the flight crashed while en route from Baltimore to Philadelphia, after being hit by lightning, killing all eighty-one on board.

The flight crew, Captain George F Knuth, aged 45, First Officer John R Dale, aged 48, Second Officer Paul L Orringer, aged 42 and Flight Engineer John R Kantlehner, operating as Pan Am Flight 214 had departed Isla Verde International Airport in San Juan, Puerto Rico, landed as scheduled at Baltimore's Friendship Airport. where sixty-nine passengers disembarked.

At 8:24 p.m., Flight 214 departed for Philadelphia with seventy-three passengers and eight crew members on board. Because of high winds in the area, the crew chose to wait in a holding pattern with five other airliners, rather than attempt to land in Philadelphia.

The flight reported over the New Castle Delaware VOR at 2042 and was instructed to hold at 5000 feet, west of the VOR. At 2058 a 'MayDay' transmission was heard from the flight. Shortly thereafter, the pilot of another aircraft radioed that 'Clipper 214 is going down in flames'.

Analysis of the debris showed evidence of a lightning strike to the left wing, specifically at the No. 1 reserve fuel tank, and evidence of a strike near connection points for the HF antenna. Samples of fuels were taken from San Juan, Puerto Rico, Idlewild, New York, and Baltimore, Maryland. The mixture of Types 'A' and 'B' fuels was studied, and not found to be a significant contributing factor. Testing of the aircraft's fuel tanks and supporting structures showed evidence of 'magnetic anomilies' which would be consistent with the lightning strike theory. Of the 140 ground witnesses interviewed, 99 reported sighting an aircraft or flaming object in the sky. Seventy-two said they saw lightning, and seven stated that they saw lightning strike the aircraft. Three other persons reported seeing a ball of fire appear at the fork-end of the lightning stroke.

Numbering system and more orders.
Since both of the offspring of the Dash 80 would be jet transports, the established Boeing model number system called for a number in the 700s to identify the two new aircraft. Boeing's marketing department decided that 'Model 700' did not have a good ring to it for the company's first commercial jet. So they decided to skip ahead to Model 707 because that reiteration seemed a bit catchier. Following that pattern, the other offspring of the Dash 80, the Air Force tanker, was given the model number 717 as

well as the Air Force designation of C/KC-135.

After 717 was assigned to the KC-135, the marketing department made the decision that all remaining model numbers that began and or ended in 7 would be reserved exclusively for commercial jets. Just to complicate things however, after the Boeing-McDonnell Douglas merger in the late 1990s, the model number 717 was reused to identify the MD-95 as part of the Boeing commercial jet family.

Other than the 717, the only other anomaly to the Boeing commercial jet numbering system was the Boeing model 720. The 720 was a short-range, high-performance version of the 707 and was first marketed to the airlines as the model 707-020. United Airlines was very interested in the 707-020 but had previously decided to go with Douglas and the DC-8. To help United avoid any negative public relations for going back to the 707, Boeing changed the name of the 707-020 to the 720.

This, however, was only the prefix part of the equation. Boeing introduced a further numbering system to enable any airline ordering original equipment to be identified by the sub-type designation. Since Pan American were the first customer for the 707-120 (as Boeing called the base model), their aircraft were designated 707-121 and subsequent orders for later versions were 707-321, -321B and - 321C (other Boeing types ordered by Pan American were 727-121, -221 and 747-121 etc. thus keeping the sub-type consistent).

The numbers between 21 and 99 were used first, including some allocated to airlines who did not order 707s, or some airlines who never ordered Boeing aircraft, then the numbers 01 to 19 were used followed by an alphanumeric system starting A0 to A9 then B0 to B9 etc. This has been followed by a numero-alpha system starting 1A to 9A then 1B to 9B etc.

Just to complicate things even further, Boeing may have considered the base model as the -120, -220 etc. but the FAA, who issued the initial type certificates, list the base models as -100, -200 etc!

On 23 January 1960 SABENA operated their first 707 service between Brussels and New York, followed a few days later by Air France who inaugurated 707 services on the North Atlantic on 2 February, followed by the central Atlantic routes on 20 June and those to South America on 16 August.

The German airline Lufthansa began 707-430 services between Hamburg, Frankfurt and New York on 17 March, so placing the first Rolls-Royce powered 707s in service, followed shortly by Air India, who started Bombay-London services on 19

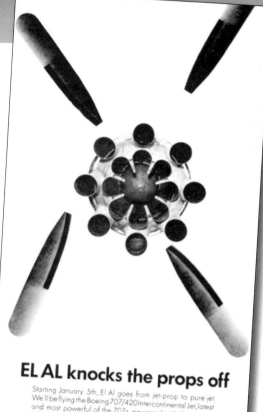

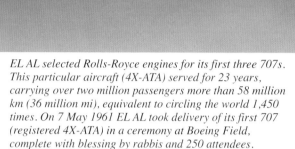

EL AL selected Rolls-Royce engines for its first three 707s. This particular aircraft (4X-ATA) served for 23 years, carrying over two million passengers more than 58 million km (36 million mi), equivalent to circling the world 1,450 times. On 7 May 1961 EL AL took delivery of its first 707 (registered 4X-ATA) in a ceremony at Boeing Field, complete with blessing by rabbis and 250 attendees. Captains Sam Feldman and Zvi Tohar commanded the delivery flight to Israel.

EL AL launched an extensive advertising campaign to promote its new pure-jet 707 service. This late 1960 image appeared in advertisements and also as a postcard issued by its New York office. (both EL AL)

EL AL knocks the props off

Starting January 5th, El Al goes from jet-prop to pure jet. We'll be flying the Boeing 707/420 Intercontinental Jet, latest and most powerful of the 707s, equipped with the superb Rolls Royce-Conway by-pass engines. We'll fly New York to Paris non-stop in 6 hours, 50 minutes, and one-stop to Tel Aviv in 11 hours, 50 minutes, without a change of planes. El Al jet flights to London begin in February, and Rome in March. See your travel agent or El Al Israel Airlines, 610 Fifth Ave., New York 20, N.Y., Plaza 1-7500

April with an extension to New York commencing on 14 May 1960.

No sooner had Pan American received its first 321B than it sparked the next development, which was the 707-320C when they announced an order for two aircraft in April 1962. The -320C was basically a -320B with a large forward cargo door, strengthened floor and undercarriage, while the payload was increased to 90,000 pounds - with passengers the payload of the -320B was space limited to about 50,000 pounds. This meant the -320C could carry a full payload coast to coast in the US or thirty-five tons across the Atlantic as the cargo could be loaded floor to ceiling and wall to wall (a cargo retaining barrier net, capable of withstanding 9G protected the cockpit). The original -320Cs were built as convertible aircraft, the length of time to convert from passenger to cargo depending on the airline and the amount of passenger equipment they left in the aircraft when in the cargo mode. Later, in October 1962, American ordered four non-convertible -320Cs with the windows blanked out. The -320C wing also had three (rather than two) leading edge flaps which made the ventral underfin optional - when these modifications were fitted to the -320Bs they were described as 'advanced' or -320BAs.

Since the increased capacity outstripped traffic growth, Boeing only received twenty-five orders in 1962, but one important order was placed by World Airways, who ordered two 707-320Cs, the first time a charter operator had ordered new jets. Previously, the charter operators were the customers when the trunk operators sold their front line equipment.

British Overseas Airway Corporation - BOAC - had expected to be the first airline to put the -420 into service but were delayed in introducing the type due to UK Airworthiness Registration Board modifications. They started London - New York services on 6 June 1960 when their 707-436s replaced Comet 4s, followed by services to Montreal and Toronto on 18 August 1960.

Such was the growing popularity of these early jetliners - and the growing success of the airlines publicity machines - it was not long before a new phenomenon started to appear; that of overbooking. In the days before highly technological computer reservations systems that are able to reserve seats months in advance with a very high degree of accuracy, and could also predict passenger and freight requirements to the same scale of accuracy and timescale, 'res systems' were either manual or card-index based. This could lead to accidental or deliberate over-booking to ensure full loads to take into account passenger no-shows.

One such event recorded by history relates to one Pan American 707 - it is also from the days that pre-date 'political correctness'.

Having originated in Buenos Aires and made several intermediate stops on its 'milk run' back to the United States, the aircraft arrived nearly full at Panama's Aeropuerto International de Tocumen. Most passengers were continuing on to Miami and New York, but a few deplaned, while many more expected. to board for the next legs to the States. Surprise, surprise, the flight was overbooked! The Pan Am staff at Tocumen were well used to this situation at their station, and so went through the usual routine of offering free booking, hotel accommodation, and meals to those passengers prepared to await later flights. There were no volunteers. It was time for the next step in the prescribed overbooking procedure: offering monetary compensation in addition to later booking, room, and board. There were still no takers. The Tocumen staff were at a loss when the Pan Am captain entered into the fray.

Unperturbed by the overbooking, he ordered boarding to commence while, with the help of his copilot and flight engineer, he went through the standard cockpit checklist. Midway through the boarding, the captain announced that there was a minor technical problem and that passengers were to return to the departure lounge while an engineering solution was devised. Of course, complimentary refreshments were made available to help passengers take the delay in their stride.

Having noticed that among the passengers there a group of young men on home leave after working in Veneezuelan oil fields, the captain surreptitiously passed on instructions to his senior stew. In the early years of jetliner operations the politically correct 'flight attendants' had yet to replace 'stews' when referring to stewardesses and stewards. The captain wanted the younger and more attractive stews were

to devote particular attention to the young oilmen and to make sure that these unsuspecting 'machos' would have unimpeded access to the free bar.

In the next hour, the 'technical problem' was fixed and boarding was resumed. This time the devious captain let his copilot and flight engineer handle the checklist procedure so that he could stand at the gate next to the boarding agents. When the unsuspecting young men, feeling good because alcohol made them believe that they had 'scored' with the attractive stewardesses, arrived at the gate, the captain was ready for them. Dutifully invoking the almighty FARs (Federal Aviation Regulations), he ordered the inebriated young men be denied boarding. Miraculously, there were now enough seats for all the other passengers and the flight departed without further delay. Archetypal the story may be, but problems were easier to solve in the days before political correctness was invented!

The 707 in popular culture

It is impossible to write about the Boeing 707 without touching on the glory and glamour of a time when, as one wag put it 'sex was safe and flying was dangerous'! Although there are many aspects of 707 coverage in the mainstream media - usually with this or that celebrity being photographed boarding, deplaning or sitting in a terminal somewhere about to board a 707, there are four aspects - one very real and tragic, two blockbuster best-sellers - one of which was made into a major feature film - and one current stage act that covers all aspects of social media that has allowed the airliner to enter popular culture.

The first was the very real and very tragic events of 22 November 1963 in Dallas, Texas. After landing at Love Field Dallas, President John F Kennedy and First Lady Jackie Kennedy stood in front of a shiny 707 for a series of live broadcasts that went nationwide of the Kennedys greeting well-wishers. The aircraft - full details of which is found elsewhere - was the first of two Boeing VC-137C aircraft specifically configured and maintained for use by the President of the United States. It was given the US Air Force serial number 62-6000. and given the unique call-sign 'SAM Two-Six-Thousand', 'SAM' standing for Special Air Mission'

The aircraft was built at Boeing's Renton plant at a cost of $8 million. Raymond Loewy, working with First Lady Jacqueline Kennedy, designed the blue and white colour scheme featuring the presidential seal that is still used today on Presidential aircraft.

Later that day in Dallas, after Kennedy's assassination made Vice President Lyndon Johnson the new president, images were flashed around the world of the VC-137C carrying the Johnsons, Jacqueline Kennedy, and John Kennedy's body back to Washington. To accommodate the casket, four seats and part of a bulkhead was removed from the passenger compartment; Johnson took the Oath of Office aboard SAM 26000 before takeoff.

Airport was a bestselling novel by Arthur Hailey about a large metropolitan airport and the personalities of the people who use, rely and suffer from its operation. It was adapted to make a major motion picture and inspired three sequel movies. It originated the 1970s disaster film genre.

The story takes place at Lincoln International, a

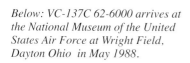

The most famous photo ever taken aboard a presidential aircraft was taken aboard VC-137C 62-6000. Hours after the assassination of John F. Kennedy on 22 November 1963, Lyndon Johnson, with Jackie Kennedy by his side, is sworn in just before take off for Washington.

Below: VC-137C 62-6000 arrives at the National Museum of the United States Air Force at Wright Field, Dayton Ohio in May 1988.

A photograph that is something of a puzzle - it was probably taken in a studio mockup of the cabin of the 707 used in the movie 'Airport'. It is suspected that some absent cast members were represented by 'cardboard cutouts' in those pre-Photoshop days! 1: Vern Demerest (Dean Martin) Captain, Trans Global Airlines. 2: Gwen Meighen (Jacqueline Bisset) Senior Flight Attendant and love interest of Captain Demerest 3: Tanya Livingston (Jean Seberg) Trans Global Airlines PRO and love interest of Mel Bakersfeld. 4: Mel Bakersfeld (Burt Lancaster) General Manager, Lincoln International Airport. 5: Harry Standish (Lloyd Nolan) Chief Customs Agent 6: Inez Guerrero (Maureen Stapleton) wife of bomber. 7: Ada Quonsett (Helen Hayes) stowaway passenger. 8: D O Guerrero (Van Heflin) suicide bomber. 9: Cindy Bakersfeld (Dana Wynter) wife of Airport Manager. 10: Anson Harris (Barry Nelson) Captain, Trans Global Airlines being checked by Capt Demerest. 11: Sarah Demerest (Barbara Hale) wife of Captain Demerest and sister of Mel Bakersfeld. 12: Joe Patroni (George Kennedy) trouble-shooter engineer on loan from TWA. 13: George Seaton, Director and Screenwriter. 14: Ross Hunter, Producer. (Photograph: unknown)

fictional Chicago airport based very loosely on O'Hare International Airport. Chicago is paralyzed by a snowstorm affecting Lincoln International Airport. A Trans Global Airlines (TGA) Boeing 707 flight crew misjudge their turn from Runway 29 onto the taxiway, becoming stuck in the snow and closing the runway. Airport manager Mel Bakersfeld is forced to work overtime, causing tension with his wife, Cindy. A divorce seems imminent as he nurtures a closer relationship with a co-worker, TGA customer relations agent Tanya Livingston.

Vernon Demarest is a TGA captain scheduled to be the checkride captain for TGA to evaluate Captain Anson Harris during TGA's Flight 2 to Rome. Flight 2, TGA's flagship service named *The Golden Argosy,*

is being operated by a Boeing 707. Although Demarest is married to Bakersfeld's sister, Sarah, he is secretly having an affair with Gwen Meighen, chief stewardess on the flight, who informs him before takeoff that she is pregnant with his child.

Bakersfeld borrows TWA mechanic Joe Patroni to assist with TGA's disabled plane. Meanwhile Bakersfeld and Livingston also deal with Mrs. Ada Quonsett, an elderly lady from San Diego who is a habitual stowaway.

Demolition expert D O Guerrero, down on his luck and with a history of mental illness, buys life insurance with the intent of committing suicide by blowing up *The Golden Argosy*. He plans to set off a bomb in an attaché case while over the Atlantic so that his wife, Inez, will collect the insurance money of $225,000. His erratic behavior at the airport, including using his last cash to buy the insurance policy and mistaking a Customs officer for an airline ramp agent, attracts airport officials' attention. Meanwhile Guerrero's wife finds a Special Delivery envelope from a travel agency and, realizing her husband might be doing something desperate, goes to the airport to try to dissuade him. She informs airport officials that he had been fired from a construction job for 'misplacing' explosives and that the family's financial situation was desperate.

Mrs. Quonsett manages to evade the TGA employee assigned the task of putting her on a flight back to San Diego, talks her way past the gate agent (passenger security screening did not yet exist), boards Flight 2, and happens to sit next to Guerrero. When the Golden Argosy crew is made aware of Guerrero's presence and possible intentions, they turn the plane back toward Chicago without informing the passengers. Once Quonsett is discovered, her help is enlisted by the crew to get to Guerrero's briefcase, but the ploy fails when a would-be helpful male passenger unwittingly returns the case to Guerrero.

Captain Demarest goes back into the passenger cabin and tries to persuade Guerrero not to trigger the bomb, informing him that his insurance policy will be useless. Guerrero briefly considers giving Demarest the bomb, but just then another passenger exits the lavatory at the rear of the aircraft, and the same would-be helpful passenger yells out that he should jump Guerrero, who has a bomb. Guerrero runs into the lavatory, locks it, and sets off the device. Guerrero dies instantly and is sucked out through the hole blown in the fuselage by the explosion. Gwen, just outside the door, is injured in the explosion and subsequent explosive decompression, but the pilots retain control of the aircraft.

With all airports east of Chicago unusable due to bad weather, they return to Lincoln International for an emergency landing. Due to the bomb damage, Captain Demarest demands the airport's longest runway, which is still closed due to the stuck airliner. Eventually Bakersfeld orders the aircraft to be pushed off the runway by snowplows, despite the costly damage they would do to it. Patroni, who is 'taxi-qualified' on 707s, has been trying to move the stuck aircraft in time for Demarest's damaged aircraft to land. By exceeding the 707's engine operating parameters, Patroni frees the stuck jet without damage, allowing the runway to be reopened just in time for the crippled *Golden Argosy* to land.

The movie used just one 707: a model 707-349, N324F, leased from Flying Tiger Line. It sported an El Al cheatline over its bare metal finish, with the fictional Trans Global Airlines (TGA) titles and tail.

Typical of Hollywood, there are some memorable quotes, two of which come from Joe Patroni and relate to the 707. On being informed by the junior engineer in the right hand seat that the manual said it was impossible for Patroni to have driven the 707 out of the snow Patroni replies *'That's one nice thing about the 707. It can do everything but read'*. And, tapping the belly of the safely landed 707 with the box of cigars he had won in a bet with Mel Bakersfeld *'Nice goin' sweetheart'*.

With the advent of 'the swingin sixties' there was something of a sea-change in how those working in the passenger cabin of the airliners were portrayed.

In 1930, the first stewardesses in America, or anywhere else, were hired by Boeing Air Transport, a forerunner of United Airlines. At that time, passengers had to worry not only about frequent crashes but also about sudden drops of altitude, which, in unpressurized aircraft, could rupture one's eardrums. That stewardesses were required to be registered nurses and were initially outfitted with white, hospital-style uniforms was intended to be comforting, to reassure nervous fliers that they would not spiral into a cornfield on the way to Grandma's or the anvil salesmen's convention; though it is quite possible to imagine the medical motif having the opposite effect.

In terms of her more concrete functions, an air hostess's duties in the early 30s might have included such pre-flight chores as loading baggage, dusting, making sure all the seats were screwed down tightly, and assisting to fuel the airliner. En route, she might have had to restrain passengers from throwing garbage and cigarette butts out of open windows.

By the 1950s, after the introduction of faster, safer, and pressurised aircraft, flying had evolved into a much less erratic proposition; passenger complaints now had more to do with lost luggage than with being killed. At some point during the decade, the number of air passengers in America first exceeded those who traveled by train; in 1957, a similar tipping point came for transatlantic crossings by air versus sea. In those days, commercial aviation was highly regulated. Among other things, the government dictated where and when the airlines could fly and how much they could charge; on transatlantic flights even the amount of legroom and the number and type of courses that could constitute a meal were prescribed by international agreement.

Not only did jets offer a faster, quieter, and smoother ride; *'You'll be able to stand a half-dollar on edge… You'll be able to hear the ticking of a* watch. *The flower you bought when you left will be fresh when you arrive,"* gushed a series of adverts for the 707, jets were sexy in the same early-60s way that the Kennedy administration and James Bond movies were, all kept aloft by an atmosphere of sleekness, power, and Cold War technology. For those who could afford it, jet travel made the world accessible in a way we now take for granted - and have maybe even begun to fear a bit - but was intoxicating at the time. This was when the jet set was born, when the fanciful premise of Frank Sinatra's 'Come Fly with Me' of casually floating down to Peru or sipping exotic booze in far Bombay on a whim, became a reality - at least for movie stars and international playboys of the jet set.

Coffee, Tea or Me? and its three sequels is a series of books that record the alleged memoirs of a pair of American stewardesses called Trudy Baker and Rachel Jones. The books depicts the anecdotal lives of two lusty young stewardesses, and was originally presented as factual.

The books were widely pontificated over by intellectuals and the media, trying to work out which airline they girls worked for: *'Written in the first person voice of Trudy Baker, the books describe a kind of glamorous lifestyle from the stewardess' point of view, working for two years for an unnamed American carrier out of a New York crewbase.*

They were written to emphasize the sexy parts of the job, although difficult experiences are also recounted, and reflects the shifts in society and culture then underway. It also contains content that could in later decades be deemed sexist, and dated descriptions of homosexuality'.

The books contain period references to television shows such as Batman and lists of celebrities the author's claim to have carried on their flights, as well as an incidental description of the airline introducing Boeing 727 into service. Other equipment mentioned includes the Boeing 707 and the smaller BAC 111. People's names are fictitious, excepting the famous, and there is no way to gauge the accuracy of any of the accounts.

The two most likely candidates for which airline the stewardesses supposedly worked for are American Airlines and Braniff International Airways, the only carriers who purchased BAC-111s to supplement fleets of Boeing 707s and 727s in the mid-1960s time frame of the novels.

The airlines themselves fed into the fantasy, These were the times when flight attendants were 'sexy stews, and when the 'sex sells seats' mantra drove some carriers to adorn 'trolley dollies' in hot pants and go-go boots.

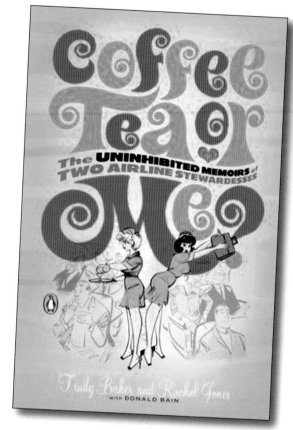

'We were envious of the Braniff uniforms', admitted one former Pan Am stewardess, who along with her sisters was still stuck in wool suits that looked like something Tippi Hedren might have worn or Jackie Kennedy. The owners of Braniff's rivals were certainly envious of its stock price, and soon every carrier's stewardesses had to have modish uniforms. Hems went up, colors got bolder, fabrics became more oil-based. United's new outfit was punctuated by a bright orange hat that looked like a cross between a jockey's cap and a mailbox. National promoted 'uniforms that purr', with hats and jackets made of simulated tiger fur - supposedly designed with the input of the stews themselves. The nadir, arguably, was the paper uniforms TWA introduced in 1968 to promote certain of its destinations. They came in four styles: a Roman toga, a faux-lamé miniskirt that was meant to represent Paris, 'penthouse pajamas' from Manhattan, and an English 'serving wench' outfit. The ads promised '...the end of routine travel with hostesses to match.' This proved to be remarkably true, since there was nothing routine about watching a stewardess whip out a roll of masking tape to repair her uniform, or, worse, catch on fire. (The uniforms' manufacturer had quickly run through its supply of nonflammable paper). The promotion lasted just seven or eight months.

Possibly this peaked in 1971 with the F. William Free advertising campaign for US carrier National Airlines. It was Free who came up with a

controversial 1971 advertising slogan '*I'm Cheryl –
Fly Me*', something which caused women's rights
groups to protest outside his office in New York City
carrying signs reading '*I'm Bill - Fire Me*'. The
campaign's notoriety paid off hansomely for
National, and they saw an increase in revenue per
passenger mile. The next year he created another ad,
'*I'm Eileen - Fly Me*', this time featuring an eight-
year-old girl who aspires to be a flight attendant. He
also reprised the original ad, saying: '*Millions of
people flew me last year*'.

In fact the four *Coffee, Tea or Me?* titles were
totally fictitious and were written by Donald Bain
while he worked as a New York City-based American
Airlines public relations person. The books became
spectacular best-sellers, created the template for the
image of the racy, jet-setting airline stewardess
aboard 707s as globe-trotting party girl in endless
pursuit of rich men and good times.

Then there is Pam Ann; and yes, you did read that
right! Pam Ann is the air hostess alter-ego of
Australian comedienne Caroline Reid. The name
Pam Ann being a play on words of that great 707
operator, Pan Am. In her shows - which are
absolutely brilliant, but decidedly 'adult' in content -
she refers to the so-called memories of the 'Golden
Age of Aviation', which for her, is the period between
the late 1950s and early 1970s when the 707 entered
widespread use, often contrasting it with mass air
travel of today, biting observations of the visual and
social changes like the lack of knives and glass on
the board.

Pam Ann is definitely from the days of the First
Class trolley-dollies and has a huge fan-base amongst
flight-crews with the slogan *No hablo clase
económia!* Her performances focus on the nuances
of air travel, identifying, parodying and satirising the
individual quirks of some of the world's biggest
international airlines and their media stereotypes. Her
style leans towards camp humour, in the vein of
Dame Edna Everage, Kathy Griffin and Chelsea
Handler.

Overall, she also plays with the stereotypical
views of airlines, like Virgin Airlines with model-
nymphomaniacs, Alitalia with '*...they think they are
all driving a Ferrari*'. Also generally she has at least
peeked inside into the current aviation industry, like
commenting accidents or airline retakes.

Around the world - from top to bottom!
In 1964 Captains Fred Lester Austin, Jr., and Harrison
Finch, two retired Trans World Airlines pilots,
attended one of several Explorer's Club meetings at
the invitation of John DuBois. The world famous
Explorers Club had been founded in New York City
in 1904 to promote the scientific exploration of land,
sea, air, and space. Noted explorer Lowell Thomas,
who was at that time the President of the Explorer's
Club, had voiced an opinion that all the memorable
flights in the lower atmosphere had been done.

Finch and Austin, however, noted that no one had
flown around the world over both Poles. The two
experienced pilots knew that prior to advancements
in aviation through the mid 1960s that an around the

Above: N332F Pole Cat , the first 'Combi' 707 of Flying Tiger Line.

Left: A newspaper cutting after the flight, showing Flight Commander Harrison Finch second from the left; Fred Austin, is second from the right, Lowell Thomas Jr is far right. In the centre of the picture is the main sponsor of the flight, Colonel Willard F Rockwell. (both Simon Peters' Collection)

world flight over the poles would have been impossible because aircraft did not have that kind of range or the navigational systems needed for such an unprecedented flight.

The pair began to investigate such a flight would entail. They were determined to be the first to accomplish it. According to Austin, they worked on the details of such a flight for about a year while in search of financing and attempting to secure a suitable machine.

Most of the airlines were very hesitant about leasing them an aircraft, but finally in early November the Flying Tiger line agreed to lease pilots Finch and Austin a 707. The introduction of jet transports revolutionised cargo operations, for no longer was it acceptable to process cargo by hand due to the speed between points, and new methods were introduced. Initially pre-loaded pallets were used but were superseded by containers designed to fit the internal fuselage contours.

The Flying Tiger Line, also known as Flying Tigers, was the first scheduled cargo airline in the United States and a major military charter operator during the Cold War era for both cargo and personnel.

Late in 1965 the US involvement in South Vietnam increased significantly, with the result that commercial airliners from Flying Tigers and other operators were chartered by Military Airlift Command (MAC) to supplement its C-135As and Bs until it received its C-141 Starlifters.

Harrison Finch knew John DuBois, a member of the Explorer's Club who had done aerial mapping of South America in the 1940. The two pilots came back to Finch's home town of DuBois, Pennsylvania to meet with DuBois to discuss the proposed flight and to invite him to join in for all the help he had given them.

DuBois suggested to Austin and Finch that they talk with Colonel Willard F. Rockwell, business magnate and the Chairman and founder of the Rockwell Manufacturing Company.

Within two days of securing an aircraft Colonel Rockwell agreed to provided $250,000 towards financing the historic flight that would be the first to circumnavigate the Earth over the two poles. With Rockwell as the principal sponsor, the flight was officially named 'The Rockwell Polar Flight.'

On 14 November 1965 the flight took off from Honolulu on a 26,230-mile, 57 hour, 27 minute flight around the world - from Pole to Pole. The pair leased a brand new Boeing 707-349C, registered N322F, from Flying Tiger Line. The airliner had only been delivered to them on 27 September 1965. Nick-named *Pole Cat* (some sources quote the name as

'*Polecat*'). It was crewed by five pilots, all rated captains. In addition to Austin and Finch, there were Captain Jack Martin, Chief Pilot of Flying Tigers Line, Captain Robert N Buck, TWA, and Boeing Senior Engineering Test Pilot James R Gannett. Three navigators and three flight engineers completed the flight crew. John Larsen, TWA's chief navigator, did most of the planning and the other two navigators and all three flight engineers were Flying Tiger Line employees.

The aircraft was fitted with a complex auxiliary fuel tank system that boosted its range to over 7,400 miles. Made from a rubber and nylon mix, each collapsible bladder carried 2,000 gallons of jet fuel with internal anti-surge mechanisms installed in the aircraft's main cabin aft of the flight deck and before the passenger compartment. In addition the aircraft carried over 5,000 pounds of scientific equipment for space, weather, navigational and radio research.

The airliner was equipped with an experimental Litton Systems Inertial Navigation System (INS) and the very latest Single Side Band (SSB) communications equipment from Collins Radio.

The flight departed Honolulu and flew to the North Pole where, at 31,000 feet over the Pole Finch and Austin were inducted into the Explorers Club. The 707 then headed south to London Heathrow, where they stopped for fuel. Unexpected runway restrictions limited the 707's takeoff weight, so they had to make an extra fuel stop at Lisbon, Portugal before flying to Buenos Aires, Argentina. After another fuel stop there, they continued south, circled the South Pole four times, then headed north to Christchurch, New Zealand. From there, they continued on to Honolulu where they arrived on 17 November.

Total elapsed time for the flight was 62 hours, 27 minutes, 35 seconds with just under five hours on the ground.

N322F was sold to Caledonian Airways in 1968 and registered G-AWTK. In 1970, Caledonian merged with British United and became British Caledonian. The aircraft was then registered G-BDCN, and named *County of Renfrew*.

1965 through 1967 were good years for Boeing with orders flowing in, although the airlines started to feel the pinch and had problems financing the massive sums of money involved in ordering new aircraft. So started the now common practice of aircraft leasing, in most cases, for ten years or so from a financing institution or some other tax advantage system.

High costs and service demand increased the utilisation of the 707, which led to some structural problems. The airframe was originally sold with a 30,000 hour fatigue life but some problems arose before this limit was reached. The first was in the tail assembly mounting when hairline cracks were detected in April 1966, which were cured by fitting a new mounting or reaming out the original bolts. Then in May it was found the 720s needed heavier wing skins on small sections due to taxiing loads. It became common practice for aircraft to have their operational life extended well beyond the 30,000 hour limit; a process that required major work including replacing fasteners and reskinning parts of the wings and fuselage. Some aircraft have exceeded 90,000 hours in service.

In one week in November 1966 Boeing took orders for fifty-one aircraft, including seventeen 707-320Cs for American as part of a thirty-eight aircraft order and ten 707-320Bs for QANTAS. 1967 looked to be a repeat of 1966 with the airlines prospering world-wide. The US and European charter airlines started making serious inroads across the Atlantic and the major routes looked ready for the Boeing 747.

Significantly, Pan Am started to suffer from reduced earnings and this was soon followed by other airlines - even so Pan Am ordered twenty-six 707s in 1967 as part of the total of seventy-five orders received that year. New services continued to be operated; Aerolineas Argentinas were able to start Buenos Aires - New York non-stop services on 2 February 1967 while Pan Am commenced New York - Moscow services on 15 July 1968, followed by a 15.5 hrs New York-Tokyo service on 1 September 1969. Continental started Los Angeles-Hawaii services in September 1969, followed by American on 1 August 1970, while Iran Air started 707 services early in 1970.

One thousand up!

In June 1967, Boeing delivered their 1000th civil jet when American accepted delivery of 707-123B N7584A, eight years and and nine months after delivery of the first 707-121 to Pan American. 1968 resulted in orders for thirty aircraft but traffic growth was much less than expected, it improved slightly in 1969 but not enough to give confidence to the industry. Orders for about twenty aircraft were received in 1969 followed by about ten in each of 1970 and 1971 which were two of the worst years in the industry's history up to that time and indeed in 1970 several airlines recorded lower traffic figures than in 1969.

The introduction of the 747 in January 1970 with Pan Am was basically the death knell of the commercially configured 707 although some airlines continued to place repeat orders or, in some cases, like CAAC, a new order for ten aircraft, but the production rate dropped to one aircraft a month in early 1971 and the writing was on the wall for the 707.

Boeing had been assigned to build the US SST competitor to the Anglo-French Concorde but this was cancelled in 1971 when US Congress withdrew its funding and the workforce in the Seattle area fell from a peak of 101,000 in January 1968 to 37,700 in late 1971; indeed in 1972 Boeing delivered a total of only ninety-seven jet airliners that included just four 707s, compared with a total of 376 just four years earlier when 111 707s alone were delivered.

Boeing offered the basic commercially configured 707-320B as the airframe for the Airborne Warning and Control System requirement drawn up by the USAF in 1963 to replace the EC-121s serving in the airborne early warning role and after evaluation were awarded the AWACS contract on 10 July 1970. This gave the production line a new lease of life with several military versions developed over

subsequent years (E-3A, E-6A etc.).

After the introduction of the 747 Boeing offered 'wide body' interiors to 707 operators, which included new seats, bigger and safer overhead lockers and other improvements, and some airlines took the opportunity to reduce the number of seats to give passengers more room, but they soon reverted to the higher density seating once traffic loads increased.

Boeing decided to look at re-engining the 707, either as new-build airframes or as retrofits, and built a prototype 707-720 powered by the General Electric/SNECMA CFM.56 turbofan of 20,000 pounds thrust - later increased to 23,000 pounds. This aircraft first flew on 27 November 1979 and was involved in a test and development programme, but the idea was abandoned since the availability of new (or retrofitted) 707s with the CFM.56 would seriously reduce the market for the new Boeing 757, the prototype of which was rolled out on 13 January 1982. The information gathered on the CFM.56/707 combination was not wasted since Saudi Arabia ordered this engine for its E-3A and KE-3A tankers followed by the RAF and French AF for their Sentry's and USN for their E-6A TACAMO aircraft and the re-engined KC-135R.

Eventually, on 1 September 1991, Boeing announced the closing of the 707 production line - at this time Japan were considering ordering E-3As but Boeing decided any future AWACS aircraft would be based on the Model 767. The last aircraft from the 707 line, a Sentry AEW.1 for the RAF, number 1012, was delivered to the UK on 21 August 1991, over thirty-three years after the first 707, while the last '707' delivery by Boeing was E-3C 73-1674 to USAF on 28 April 1994.

QANTAS were the first airline to dispose of 707s when, in 1967/1968, it sold its 707-120B short-body jets as they were replaced by new 707-320Bs. Eastern then traded its 720s into Boeing as part exchange for new 727s in 1969. As time went on this trade-in became quite common as the airlines found it difficult to sell whole fleets. In fact the 720, which got Boeing onto the short to medium haul routes were the first aircraft to be phased out -

Your first Boeing jet airliner flight

BOEING 707 and 720

VH-EBA, the first -138 model for QANTAS, on the ramp at Renton before delivery, in the company of unidentifiable TWA and American Airlines machines.

Initially the airline used the somewhat conservative 'classic' uniforms for their stewardesses, but as a new decade dawned, things progressed into the 'swingin sixties'. (author's collection/QANTAS)

replaced by the very successful 727 which overtook the 707 as the most popular jet aircraft and retained this position until superseded itself by the 737! Some of these 720s found their way into the European inclusive tour market, while Pan American were successful in selling most of their 707-320s to UK independent airlines and TWA sold their 707-120s to Israeli Aircraft Industries for overhaul, refurbishment and possible resale.

Many airlines, not being able to find a buyer for its aircraft, kept them in service until USAF announced in 1982 that it proposed to re-engine 128

KC-135As with JT3D engines removed from ex airliner 707s and both American and TWA disposed of entire fleets to Boeing Military Airplane Corp. for spares. Some of these were also converted to military use and parts were used in KC-135R updates, while some ex airline airframes were purchased by Omega Air/USAF as the basis of the E-8C J-Stars programme.

Some of the stored ex-civilian airframes were involved in tests to determine the survivability of aircraft after an on-board explosion in a programme of work run by the Federal Aviation Administration and Department of Defense. This programme of work commenced after the loss of 747-121 N739PA as Pan Am 103, when it crashed at Lockerbie, Scotland on 21 December 1988 killing all 258 on board as well as at least 11 on the ground following terrorist action. The work has also involved the

QANTAS was the only operator of the short-bodied 707. This aircraft is seen taking off with a spare engine slung in a pod on a pylon between the No.2 engine and the fuselage.

The QANTAS cabin staff uniform swung from the severe in the 1950s to the miniskirt in the 1960s. (both author's collection)

USAF and USN and four ex- USAF KC-135As were involved in further trials at Patuxent River NAS; new freight containers have been developed to reduce the risk of airframe loss based on an explosion similar to the one over Lockerbie. These new containers contain some of the blast and cause slight deformation of the aircraft skin, rather than skin rupture and consequent frame damage, and were available to airlines from late 1994. The new container is still within the ICAO weight limits although towards the upper end presenting a weight (as well as cost) penalty to airlines that used it.

Versions and variant in detail
707-120
Dated 16 November I951, layout drawings for the first design to bear a Model 707 designation show an aircraft with 35 degrees of wing sweep and four J57 engines in twin-podded nacelles, one under each wing. Intended to accommodate 72 first class passengers, this 707-1 had a fuselage width of only 122 inches, slightly less than featured by the most successful contemporary propliners. This shortcoming was corrected with the 707-2 layout which provided for a fuselage width of 132 inches. Although still less than the 139.3 inch maximum fuselage width of the Lockheed Constellation and Super Constellation propliner series, the 132 inch width was that of the upper deck of the Boeing 377 Stratocruiser, a propliner offering first class a four-abreast seating arrangement praised by passengers. Accordingly, this width was retained for the 367-80

and its intended 707-7 production jetliner version until the Air Force concluded that it would not provide clearance for efficient loading and carriage of standard military pallets on the upper deck.

In the meanwhile, mockups of airliner cabins had shown that a 144 inch fuselage width would not only provide for increased comfort in four-abreast first class seating but would also work for five-abreast tourist class and six-abreast economy class accommodations. Therefore, Boeing increased the width of its proposed Model 717 tanker and 707 jetliners to 144 inches before negotiations with airlines began in earnest. That width was found acceptable to the first commercial customer, since

Pan American was initially interested in the 707 only as a temporary aircraft that would enable it to match the anticipated introduction of transatlantic jet service by BOAC with De Havilland Comet 4s while waiting to build up its jetliner fleet with the larger, heavier, and more powerful Douglas DC-8.

Unfortunately for Boeing, because domestic trunk carriers did not face the competitive threat of Comet 4 operators, they did not plan on ordering two types of medium- to long range jetliners as Pan American had just done. Seeing merits in Douglas' arguments that the 147-inch fuselage width of its proposed DC-8 would provide for improved six abreast economy seating, United Airlines selected the Douglas jetliner over the 707 when in October 1955 it became the second carrier to order US jetliners.

In spite of the gamble it had taken with the private venture 367-80 jet transport demonstrator, Boeing was threatened with seeing its efforts frustrated by Douglas' superior understanding of airline requirements. The time had come for a painful reassessment by the management of the Seattle firm.

The perennial competition between American Airlines, United Airlines, and Trans World Airlines on US

Back in the day of the 707, South Africa was under the control of apartheid, as was the national carrier South African Airways. (both DGR Picture Library)

transcontinental routes provided Boeing with an opportunity of regaining the initiative. To be the first to offer jet service across the United States, American favored the 707 over the DC-8 but wanted jetliners offering the best possible seating in all classes of service. Putting pressure on Boeing, American Airlines got the Seattle manufacturer to increase the fuselage width of its 707 to 148 inches, 1 inch better than the DC-8 and 15 inches more than the Comet 4.

The wider fuselage was quickly adopted as the new Boeing standard, with specifications for the aircraft previously ordered by Pan American being changed accordingly.

The initial order for JT3C powered 707s was announced on 13 October 1955 when news of a twenty aircraft order placed by Pan American was released. This contract was for aircraft with 144 inch fuselage width but was later amended to cover

aircraft with 148 inch fuselage width. Moreover, Pan American subsequently elected in December 1955 to take only six aircraft as JT3C powered 707-121s while the balance of the original twenty aircraft order was switched to JT4A—powered 707-321s.

Proposals tailored to specific airline requirements were initially given sequential model numbers starting with 707-121, as first given to the JT3C-powered aircraft ordered by Pan American with 144 inch width fuselage but delivered with 148 inch width fuselage. The 707-122 designation at first identified the version proposed unsuccessfully to United Airlines with JT3C engines and 144 inch width fuselage. The 707-222 and 707-322 designations then briefly identified aircraft proposed to Scandinavian Airlines System respectively with JT3C and JT4A engines.

In addition to JT3C-powered aircraft with the standard 138 foot 10 inch long body, Boeing offered a short body version, with ten feet being removed aft of the wings to reduce fuselage length to 128 feet 10 inches. This machine was tailored for overwater service. Powered by four JT3C-6 engines and fitted with centre-section fuel tanks to increase fuel capacity from the basic 13,486 US gallons to 17,286 gallons., this 'short body' variant first appeared in a 120B layout drawing dated 7 September 1956.

The only airline to make use of the greater range of this version was QANTAS, as the Australian carrier had to contend with what then were unusually long overwater sectors, such the 2,080-nautical mile still-air distance San Francisco - Honolulu leg, the 2,269-nautical mile Honolulu - Pago Pago sector, and the 2,375-nautical mile Pago Pago - Sydney hop. Also, QANTAS had to navigate these sectors without

the luxury of any suitable diversionary jet airfields. The seven 707-138s built for the Australian carrier became the first 707s certificated to carry a spare engine in a pod mounted under the left wing inboard of the number 2 engine. Early production long-and short-body 707-120s were delivered with the so-called 'short' vertical-tail surfaces and manually operated rudder. However, as the result of modifications developed to obtain British certification of the 707-420 series, the fin was extended upward, the rudder was provided with hydraulic boost, and, in most instances, a ventral fin was added to improve handling in asymmetric engine conditions. These modifications were incorporated during production in late 1959, and most early production aircraft were retrofitted. The ventral fin, which was not always fitted or retrofitted, also helped to prevent the rear fuselage from hitting the runway during excessive rotation on take-off. Another modification had been retrofitted to the first 707-121s before they were delivered to Pan American and was incorporated early on during production. This was two segments of Kruger-type leading-edge flaps inboard of the number 1 and 4 engines, which delayed wing stall at slow speeds when deployed at the same time as the double-slotted trailing-edge flaps.

Structural differences between models were

In later years Braniff operated their four 707-220s in vivid colours of orange, yellow, blue and gold - below is N7099. Right: the interior of one of the Braniff 707s not long after delivery. (author's collection)

N-93134 was a 707-138B and was operated by the Boeing Company for a while as their Turbo-Fan demonstrator. It later went to QANTAS as VH-EBH 'City of Darwin'.

Left: 'Think of her as your mother' - contemporary American Airlines advertising.

version of their own product with wings of increased span and area.

To achieve the desired nonstop transatlantic capability without a payload penalty, not just between European capitals relatively close to the eastern shores of the Atlantic (such as London, Madrid, or Paris) and US or Canadian cities near the western shores (such as Boston, Montreal, or New York) but also from major metropolises further inland (such as Chicago, Frankfurt, Rome, and Zurich), required increases in fuel load and take-off weight. The distances between inland cities is substantially further than distances between coastal cities; for example, London - New York, uncorrected for winds, is only 3,005 nautical miles whereas Rome - Chicago is 4,176 nautical miles. Heavier take-off weights meant that to avoid downgrading airfield performance excessively, both power and wing area had to be increased while additional high-lift devices had to be provided.

The switch to Pratt & Whitney JT4A turbojets with dry takeoff thrust 17- to 35—percent greater than the wet thrust (i.e., using the cumbersome and noisy water injection system) of JT3C variants went a long way to keep take-off field length requirements within reason. Nevertheless, Boeing still needed to redesign the wings to increase area and provide space for additional fuel. This was accomplished by reducing trailing edge sweep between the wing fillet and the inboard engines

limited to the size and capacity of the centre fuel tank and to localised structural strengthening for models certificated for operations at higher weights. In addition, models differed in cockpit arrangements, avionics, and cabin layout and furnishing was specified by each customer. Thirty nine of these aircraft, including the three USAF VIP aircraft, were subsequently re-engined with turbofans as 707-120Bs.

707-320

Boeing still had to meet the challenge of the more powerful, heavier, and longer-ranged JT4A-powered version of the Douglas jetliner. Accordingly, keen on having Pan American move away from its initial preference for the Douglas jet transport, the Seattle manufacturer quickly proposed a JT4A-powered

and by extending the outboard panels to increase span from 130 feet 10 inches to 142 feet 5 inches and area from 2,433 to 2,892 square feet. The larger wings, however, retained the thirty-five degree of sweep at the quarter chord and two-spar structure of the original 367-80 wings. A collateral benefit from enlarging the wings was a reduction in cabin noise as the engines were moved further outboard, the centerline of the inboard JT4As of the -320 being 33 feet from the fuselage centreline, whereas that distance was only 27 feet 2 inches in the case of the inboard JT3C of the -120.

To increase lift, the larger wings were fitted with split fillet flaps on the trailing-edge between the fuselage and the inboard sections of double-slotted flaps and two additional sections of Kruger-type flaps on the leading-edge. This revised configuration enabled approach speed to be reduced from 145 knots for the 707-120 to 140 knots for the -320 in spite of the greater weight of the latter. Notwithstanding the use of more powerful engines and larger wings, however, the heavier 707-320 - with a maximum gross take-off weight between 18 and 28% greater than the 707-120 depending on configuration - still ended up having Federal Aviation Regulations runway length requirements some 12% greater than a fully loaded 707-120.

The 707-320 retained the newly adopted 148-inch fuselage diameter, but cabin length, from the cockpit door to the rear pressure bulkhead, was increased 6 feet 8 inches to 111 feet 6 inches. Standard seating was increased from 96 to 104 first-class passengers with 40-inch seat pitch and from 165 to 180 economy-class passengers with 34-inch seat pitch. With special seats and inflatable escape slides, the 707-320 was certificated to carry a maximum of 189 passengers in high-density configuration. Other structural changes included a strengthened undercarriage, stronger skin panels, and larger horizontal tail surfaces, with the span increased from 39 feet 8 inches to 45 feet inches.

Briefly marketed under the 'Intercontinental' name, the 707-320 was first ordered by Pan American on 24 December 1955 when the original 707 customer amended its

contract for twenty aircraft to cover six JT3C-powered 707-121s and 14 JT4A powered 707-321s.

The first of the larger and heavier models flew on 1 January 1959, and the 707-321 was placed in service by Pan American on 26 August 1959. Although rapidly supplanted by its turbofan-powered derivatives (the 707-420, 707-320B, and 707-320C), the JT4A-powered intercontinental version of the 707 sold better than the original JT3C-powered variant.

Initial deliveries were with short fin and manually operated rudder, but most -320 series aircraft were delivered with the larger surfaces and hydraulically boosted rudder. Aircraft delivered in the early configuration were retrofitted. According to their need, airlines specified different models of the JT4A turbojet with a takeoff thrust of 15,800 pounds for the JT4A-3 and -5, 16,800 pounds for the -9, and 17,500 pounds for the -11 and -12 models.

707-220

To match the capabilities of the JT4A-powered Douglas DC-8 Series 20 and to meet the

The quiet, spacious comfort and the incredibly smooth ride of the 707 will delight the whole family. You'll be secure in the knowledge that the 707 is made by Boeing, world's most experienced builder of multijet aircraft.

In the time it takes you to enjoy a leisurely meal aboard a Boeing jetliner, you'll span almost half a continent! Prompt service, too. For Boeing 707's are equipped with two efficient galleys, one forward, one aft.

A new kind of luxury awaits you. New spaciousness, new beauty everywhere, improved air and altitude conditioning. Comfortable seats. A cozy, relaxing lounge where you can enjoy congenial company and conversation.

Your first Boeing jet airliner flight

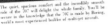

You'll be able to take your first flight in a Boeing 707 in just a few months, and it will be an exhilarating experience, even if you're a veteran airline traveler. Your first surprise will be the 707 cabin—more spacious, more luxurious than any you've seen before. From the moment of take-off you'll appreciate the truly

revolutionary advantages of jet 707 travel: a smoother, more solidly secure ride than you've ever believed possible. It's restful, serenely quiet. No vibration. Not even a sense of motion, yet you'll be cruising nearly 10 miles a minute! You'll arrive at your destination pleasantly refreshed, almost sorry the trip is over.

These airlines already have ordered Boeing jetliners:
AIR FRANCE • AIR-INDIA INTERNATIONAL • AMERICAN AIRLINES
BRANIFF INTERNATIONAL AIRWAYS • BRITISH OVERSEAS
AIRWAYS CORPORATION • CONTINENTAL AIR LINES
CUBANA DE AVIACION • LUFTHANSA GERMAN AIRLINES
PAN AMERICAN WORLD AIRWAYS • QANTAS EMPIRE AIRWAYS
SABENA BELGIAN WORLD AIRLINES
SOUTH AFRICAN AIRWAYS • TRANS WORLD AIRLINES
UNITED AIR LINES • VARIG AIRLINES OF BRAZIL

BOEING 707 and 720

707-420

The moment Boeing revealed the existance of plans to develop their airliner design all the major engine manufacturers contacted them, notably Rolls-Royce, who made it known that its Aero Engine Division had a novel 'bypass' turbojet, also known as a turbofan, under development. Fitted with a ducted fan ahead of its axial-flow compressor, the Conway turbofan was anticipated to have greater thrust and lower fuel consumption than the JT3C retained for the first 707s. Accordingly, as early as the autumn of 1954, Boeing studied variants of its projected 707-8, powered by Rolls-Royce Conway R.Co.5 bypass engines and with takeoff weight ranging between 205,000 and 235,000 pounds. The 707-420 intercontinental version, which began with a preliminary layout dated 30 December 1955 for a 296,000-pound airliner with R.Co.10s, evolved in parallel with the competing Conway-powered DC-8 Series 40.

Identical to the 707-320 in virtually all respects, but powered by Conway turbofans instead of JT4A turbojets, the 707-420 was expected to be particularly attractive to airlines in the British Commonwealth, as these carriers would not have to pay custom duties on British-manufactured engines.

The first contract for Conway-powered aircraft was not placed by a Commonwealth airline but by Lufthansa, which ordered an initial batch of four 707-430s in April 1956. Although the first Conway-powered had been ordered by the German carrier, the first to fly was one of the fifteen 707-436s ordered by British Overseas Airways Corporation in October 1956.

This flew on 20 May 1959 with a temporary US registration. Although the -420 was certificated in the United States on 12 February 1960 under an addendum to the ATC 4A26 for the -320, service entry was delayed until May 1960 by the need to redesign tail surfaces to meet British certification requirements. With the enlarged surfaces, the 707-420 was granted a British certificate by the Air Transport Licensing Board on 27 April 1960.

Even the re-designed tail did not prevent the loss of BOAC Flight 911 using 707 G-APFE operating

need of airlines operating from high elevation high-temperature airports, Boeing initially planned the 707-220 as a derivative of the JT3C-powered short-body version of the 707-120 with 144-inch fuselage width. It progressively evolved with an increase in fuselage width to 148 inches, lengthening of the fuselage to the standard 707-120 long body dimension, addition of 340 US gallon wing tip fuel tanks, installation of overwater equipment, and substitution of JT4A-3 engines for the initially intended JT3C-6s. This version was only ordered by Braniff Airways with JT4A-3s and standard long-body fuselage but without tip tanks or overwater equipment.

Only five 707-227s were built, the first flying on 11 May 1959, and certification was obtained six months later in spite of the crash of the first aircraft during an acceptance flight as we have seen earlier on 19 October 1959. The remaining four -227s were operated by Braniff on its Latin American network until the first quarter of 1971. After service with other operators, the last of the ex-Braniff aircraft was stored in December 1983 and broken up in May 1984.

under the callsign of Speedbird 911. This was a round-the-world flight that crashed as a result of an encounter with severe clear-air turbulence near Mount Fuji in Japan on 5 March 1966. The Boeing 707-436 on this flight was commanded by Captain Bernard Dobson, 45, from Dorset, an experienced 707 pilot who had been flying these aircraft since November 1960.

The aircraft disintegrated and crashed near Mount Fuji shortly after departure from Haneda Airport, at the start of the Tokyo-Hong Kong segment. All 113 passengers and 11 crew members were killed in the disaster, including a group of 75 Americans associated with Thermo King of Minneapolis, Minnesota, on a 14-day company sponsored tour of Japan and Southeast Asia.

The aircraft arrived in Haneda at 12:40 on the day of the accident from Fukuoka Airport where it had diverted the previous day due to conditions on the ground in Tokyo. The weather there had since improved behind a cold front with a steep pressure gradient bringing cool dry air from the Asian mainland on a strong west-northwest flow, with crystal clear sky conditions. During their time on the ground, the crew received a weather briefing from a company representative, and filed an instrument flight rules flight plan calling for a southbound departure from Haneda via the island of Izu Oshima, then on airway JG6 to Hong Kong at 31,000 feet.

At 13:42 the crew contacted air traffic control requesting permission to start engines, and amending their clearance request to a visual meteorological conditions climb westbound via the Fuji-Rebel-Kushimoto waypoints, which would take them nearer to Mount Fuji, possibly to give the passengers a better view of the landmark. The aircraft began taxiing at 13:50 and took off into the northwest wind at 13:58. After takeoff, the aircraft made a continuous climbing right turn over Tokyo Bay, and rolled out on a southwest heading, passing north of Odawara. It then turned right again toward the mountain, flying over Gotemba on a heading of approximately 298°, at an indicated airspeed of 320 to 370 knots, and an altitude of approximately 16,000 feet, well above the 12,388 foot mountain peak. The aircraft then encounted strong winds, causing it to break up in flight, and crash into a forest near the mountain.

The aircraft left a debris field ten miles long. Analysis of the location of wreckage allowed the accident investigators to determine that the vertical stabiliser attachment to the fuselage failed first. It left paint marks indicating that it broke off the port side horizontal stabiliser as it departed to the left and down. A short time later, the ventral fin and all four engine pylons failed due to a leftward over-stress, shortly followed by the remainder of the empennage. The aircraft then entered a flat spin, with the forward fuselage section and the outer starboard wing breaking off shortly before impact with the ground.

Several booked passengers had cancelled their tickets at the last moment to see a ninja demonstration. These passengers, Albert R 'Cubby' Broccoli, Harry Saltzman, Ken Adam, Lewis Gilbert, and Freddie Young, were in Japan scouting locations for the fifth James Bond film, *You Only Live Twice*.

Although some stress cracking was found in the vertical stabiliser bolt holes, it was determined by subsequent testing that it did not contribute to this accident. Still, it was potentially a significant safety-of-flight issue. Subsequent inspections on Boeing 707 and 720 aircraft as a result of this discovery did reveal this was a common problem, and corrective maintenance actions on the fleet eventually followed.

One day after the crash, speculation was that fierce winds above Mount Fuji were responsible. *The New York Times* reported: *"Despite these reports of a fire and explosion, aviation experts said that adverse wind conditions around the volcanic cone about 37 miles south of Tokyo may have caused the crash. The vicinity of the 12,388 foot peak is notorious for tricky air currents. Technicians in New York said that a condition could exist where turbulent air could have caused the aircraft to undergo a drastic manoeuvre that might lead to a crash. Such violent forces, they said, might have caused an engine to disintegrate, possibly setting fire to the wing or fuselage."*

The probable cause determination was: *"The aircraft suddenly encountered abnormally severe turbulence over Gotemba City which imposed a gust load considerably in excess of the design limit."*

With the Rolls-Royce bypass turbojet rapidly overtaken by the Pratt & Whitney JT3D turbofan, only thirty-seven Conway-powered aircraft were built.

720

Whereas the fuselage of the 707-120 had to be enlarged and the -220, -320, and -420 variants developed in response to Douglas' aggressive marketing moves, the Boeing 720 came about as a hastened response to Convair's January 1956 announcement of its Model 22 Skylark, later redesignated the Convair 880. Smaller than the JT3C powered 707-120 and Douglas DC-8 Series 10, the Convair airliner promised to be faster than its heavier competitors. While Douglas did not succeed with its proposed DC-9, at that time a smaller four-engined derivative of the DC-8, Boeing responded energetically to the challenge from Convair.

With United Airlines - a carrier which had just selected Series 10 and 20 DC-8s in preference to 707-120s but was known also to need smaller, shorter—ranged jetliners - as its initial target, Boeing started work in earnest on the 707-020 in February 1956. By the first week in March, the Seattle manufacturer had preliminary layouts for no fewer than twelve different configurations.

The baseline 707-020-1 retained the newly adopted 148 inch width fuselage and 130 foot 10-inch span wings of the 707-120 but had its fuselage shortened from 138 feet 10 inches to 115 feet 6 inches and was to be powered by four Rolls-Royce RA-29 Avon turbojets. The -2 had a one foot shorter fuselage and was designed around four Pratt & Whitney JT8A-1 turbojets. The -3, -4, and -9 retained the shorter -2 fuselage but were respectively matched to four Pratt & Whitney JT3C-6, General Electric CJJ80s, and Rolls-Royce RA-29 turbojets. The -11 and -12 were proposed Avon-powered developments with the -2 fuselage but a reduced gross weight and wings with different aspect and taper ratio.

Proposed with four JT3C-4 turbojets, the -10 had broader wings of reduced span - 120 feet - and area of 2,322 square feet. The more unusual variants, however, were the twin-engined 707-020-5, -6, and -7 with wings of even more reduced span and area - 101 feet 8 inches and 2,100 square feet. The designs were respectively proposed with two RA-29, JT3C-4, and JT4A-1 turbojets.

In spite of frantic design activities, it appeared for nearly twenty months that Boeing would be unsuccessful in its endeavor to block inroads by Convair into the jetliner market. Initial contracts for the Convair jetliner were announced in June 1956 with TWA, already a 707-120 and -320 customer, and Delta, a DC-8 customer, respectively ordering thirty and ten 880s. By October 1957, TWA had ordered

four additional 880s, while the Brazilian carrier REAL had become the first customer for a turbofan-powered derivative of the Convair jetliner (this model eventually was designated the 990). Boeing had yet to receive an order for its 707 derivative.

This short- to medium-range, reduced capacity derivative of the 707 was first called the Model 717, but that proved confusing since military C/KC-135 variants already used the 717 designation. Forty years later, that confusion was further compounded when, following the merger with McDonnell Douglas, the Model 717 designation was again used to identify the twinjet MD-95. Finally, to satisfy the launch customer's wish to have the new aircraft identified by a later numerical designation, it became the Model 720.

With inputs from the airlines, the 720 jelled progressively into a more direct derivative of the 707-120. As first sold to United Airlines in November 1957, when UAL ordered an initial batch of eleven aircraft, the JT3C-powered 720 had a standard 148-inch wide 707 fuselage with internal cabin length reduced to 96 feet, 6 inches from the 104-foot, 10-inch length of the -120 cabin. The shorter cabin of the 720 provided accommodation for 88 first-class passengers, a maximum of 141 economy-class passengers, or 115 passengers in a 30/70 mixed-class arrangement.

The basic wing layout of the 707-120 was retained but the wing leading-edge inboard of the inner engines was extended forward to form a 'glove,' thus increasing the wing chord and reducing the thickness/chord ratio for flights at higher speeds. The never-exceed Mach increased from 0.895 for the 707-120 to 0.906 for the 720-020, while fuel consumption was reduced.

Direct weight reductions resulting from the shorter fuselage and smaller number of seats, galleys, and lavatories also made possible the use of a lighter undercarriage and the deletion of one of the three

The first 720 - intended for use with United Airlines, hence the registration N7201U, in Boeing Company demonstrator colours. (DGR Picture Library)

turbocompressors for the cabin conditioning system. Thus, operating weight empty was reduced nearly eight percent from 118,000 pounds for the 707-120 to 110,800 pounds for the 720.

Power for the lighter Model 720 was provided by either four Pratt 8C Whitney JT3C-7s without water injection or four JT3C-12s with water injection, take-off thrust rating being 12,000 pounds for the former and 13,000 pounds for the latter. Airfield performance was improved due to the lower power and wing loadings but also by the addition of additional Kruger leading-edge flaps outboard of the engines.

Next to contract for 720s was American Airlines, with its order for twenty-five 720-023s later changed to include a mix of turbojet- and turbofan-powered aircraft, bringing the Boeing's order book to a total of 187 jetliners by the time Pan American started 707-121 operations in October 1958. That order book showed a 39% share of the four-engine jet airliner business. Four competitors, Douglas and Convair in the United States plus Vickers and De Havilland in the United Kingdom, respectively reported orders for 138 DC-8s in four variants, 87 Model 880s and 990s, 35 VC10s, and 33 Comet 4s. Although it led the pack, Boeing was nevertheless in a less than satisfactory position as the production break-even point for its early jetliners had been pushed further into the future by additional costs incurred in developing four additional models to fight off the competition.

The 720 prototype, intended for United Airlines, first flew from Renton on 23 November 1959. Being different from both the 707-100 and 707-300 already FAA-certificated, the 720 was covered by a new Approved Type Certificate, 4A28, issued on 30 June 1960. Boeing sold only sixty-four 720s.

The first 720 services were operated by United on 5 July 1960 between Los Angeles, Denver and Chicago while American introduced the type on 31 July between Cleveland, St Louis and Los Angeles. The first scheduled South African Airways 707-320 service was between Johannesburg and London on 2 October although the first, route-proving, flight was on 14 September .

In February 1961 Pan American, in one of their many repeat orders, ordered five 707-320Bs which were powered by JT3D-3 engines of 18,000 pounds thrust with an improved wing featuring full span leading edge flaps, improved trailing edge flaps and

redesigned wing tips which increased lift and reduced drag. These improvements increased the range of the -320B by about 15% over the earlier -320s.

Boeing were planning even more extensive development with the -520B offered to the airlines for 1963/1964 service introduction. This had increased power engines, a twelve foot fuselage stretch and modified wing, suggesting that it could

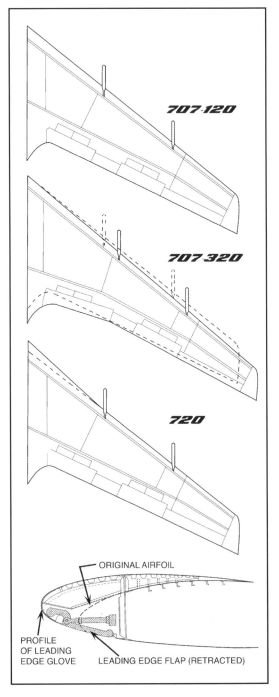

Evolution of a wing. The changes in the shape and size of the 707 wing from -120 model compared to the -320 series. The 720 wing was basically that of the -120, with a 'glove' fitted inboard of the engines to allow an increase in Mach number.

Olympic Airways operated a number of both 707s and 720s, SX-DBL, 'Evros River' was one of six 720s obtained from Northwest for their European services.

operate a round-the-world service with only two stops, but it never progressed past the design stage.

El Al started 707 services between Tel Aviv and New York on 5 January 1961, initially with a 707-441 leased from VARIG until its first two -458s were delivered in March and May 1961 respectively. American introduced the 720B and 707-120B into service simultaneously on 12 March 1961 and they started returning JT3C powered aircraft to Boeing immediately for conversion to JT3D power. In November 1961 one of Continental's 707-124s, N70773, clocked up 10,000 hours, the first 707 to achieve this milestone at an average utilisation of 10.8 hours per day - a usage rate that was much higher than piston engined aircraft due to the reduced maintenance requirements.

The first 707-320B flew on 1 February 1962 and was delivered to Pan American on 12 April with a provisional certificate, the full ATC being issued on 13 May. This was almost a year behind the corresponding Douglas model, the DC-8 Series 50, but the 707-320B soon entered service on long-haul routes like the 4,750 nautical mile London-Los Angeles service and the 4,600 nautical mile New York-Buenos Aires route. Indeed during tests one aircraft flew 5,080 nautical miles from Seattle to overhead New York and return to Seattle in 10 hours 15 minutes with almost 50,000 pounds of payload.

Things improved during 1963 for Boeing with about forty aircraft ordered, and the company were also busy building the initial 727s. The all-cargo 707-320C entered service on 17 June 1963 with Pan American and led to complaints from the all-cargo operators. The major US airlines were well up the list of purchasers with both Pan American and Trans World placing several orders as their excess capacity was taken up due to lower fares.

Air France replaced their earlier models with -328Bs on the longer non-stop services such as Madrid - Rio de Janeiro on 15 April 1963, while the CAB began to certificate the supplemental - or charter - airlines for Atlantic flights. 1964 again saw an improvement in orders with approximately seventy 707s or 720s ordered, again Pan American were in the lead with nineteen -320B and -320Cs.

QANTAS started non-stop trans-Pacific flights on 7 March 1965 following delivery of their first 707-320B while three weeks later a Pan American 707-320B en route from San Francisco to Honolulu suffered an explosion in the outer starboard engine shortly after take-off but landed safely.

The later built -320BAs were certified to higher gross weights and were fitted with the -320C undercarriages, these were known unofficially as -320BA-H.

1965 saw a huge milestone appear - the end of jet surcharges, designed to protect operators without jet aircraft. Although some piston-engined aircraft remained in service, the major routes like the North Atlantic were now all jet. Atlantic fares were coming down, due in part to the charter/supplemental airlines and simple competition and without doubt the fare paying passenger was the winner.

1965 saw an increase in orders with one hundred and twenty nine 707s and five 720s ordered including fifteen 707-321Bs and Cs for Pan American and a huge order of fifty-four aircraft for American. When finalised, American ordered twenty-seven -120Bs and five-320Cs as well as twenty-two 727-200s and the production rate was increased to ten per month. 1965 also saw the introduction of the JT3D-3B engine, which had modifications to the hot section eliminating the need for water injection. Trials were conducted with a 720B, later sold to Pakistan

NASA's N833NA made a number of remotely controlled approaches the final one being an overflight of the 'crash site' at Edwards before the deliberate crash landing.

On board the 720 were a number of adult and child crash test dummies. (both NASA)

International Airlines, into all weather landing systems. As a result, on 5 March 1965, the 707/720 series was certified for landings down to Category 2 limits (1200 foot horizontal and 100 foot vertical visual limits). Another huge area of debate was in-flight entertainment but this was eventually accepted by the airlines for long-haul flights and quickly became the norm.

One interesting 'loss' was deliberately crashed at Edwards Air Force Base, California, on 1 December 1984 while radio-controlled to a belly landing short of the runway and into obstacles.

The Controlled Impact Demonstration (CID, or colloquially, the Crash In the Desert) tests involved the efforts of NASA Ames Research Center, Langley Research Center, Dryden Flight Research Center, the FAA, and General Electric, and required more than four years of preliminary work. The aircraft was remotely controlled for the tests, and numerous test runs were undertaken prior to the actual impact.

The objectives of the CID programme were to demonstrate a reduction of post-crash fire through the use of antimisting fuel, acquire transport crash structural data, and to demonstrate the effectiveness of existing improved seat-restraint and cabin structural systems.

The Boeing 720 - tail number N833NA - was purchased new by the FAA in 1960 as a training aircraft. After more than 20,000 hours and 54,000 takeoff and landing cycles, it had come to the end of its useful life. The aircraft was turned over to NASA-Ames/Dryden Flight Research Center for the CID program in 1981.

The additive, ICI's FM-9, a high molecular-weight long chain polymer, when blended with Jet-A fuel, forms antimisting kerosene (AMK). AMK had demonstrated the capability to inhibit ignition and flame propagation of the released fuel in simulated impact tests. AMK cannot be introduced directly into a gas turbine engine due to several possible problems

Slapdown; Fitz Fulton found himself with an aircraft that was starting to dutch roll. Data acquisition systems had been activated, and the aircraft was committed to impact. The aircraft contacted the ground, left wing low, at full throttle, the aircraft nose pointing to the left of the center-line.

It had been planned that the aircraft would land wings-level, with the throttles set to idle, and exactly on the center-line during the CID, thus allowing the fuselage to remain intact as the wings were sliced open by eight posts cemented into the runway. This never happened.

The Boeing 720 landed askew. One of the Rhinos sliced through number 3 engine. The same Rhino then sliced through the fuselage, causing a cabin fire when burning fuel was able to enter the fuselage.

The cutting of number 3 engine and the full throttle situation was significant as this was outside the test envelope. Number 3 engine continued to operate, degrading the fuel and igniting it after impact, providing a significant heat source. The fire took over an hour to extinguish. The CID impact was spectacular with a large fireball created by number 3 engine on the right side, enveloping and burning the 720.

FAA investigators estimated that 23–25% of the aircraft's full complement of 113 people could have survived the crash. Investigators labeled their estimate of the ability to escape through dense smoke as 'highly speculative'. As a result of analysis of the crash, the FAA instituted new flammability standards for seat cushions which required the use of fire-blocking layers, resulting in seats which performed better than those in the test. (all NASA)

such as clogging of filters. It had to be restored to almost Jet-A before being introduced into the engine for burning. This restoration was called degradation and was accomplished on the 720 using a device called a degrader. Each of the four Pratt & Whitney JT3C-7 engines had a degrader built and installed by GE to break down and return the AMK to near Jet-A quality.

In addition to the AMK research, NASA Langley was involved in a structural load measurement experiment, which included using instrumented crash dummies in the seats of the passenger compartment. Before the final flight in 1984, more than four years of effort was expended in attempting to set up final impact conditions which would be considered to be survivable by the FAA.

Over a series of fourteen flights, General Electric installed and tested four degraders (one on each engine); the FAA refined AMK, blending, testing, and fueling a full size aircraft. During the flights the aircraft made approximately sixty nine approaches, to about 150 feet above the prepared crash site, under remote control. These flights were used to introduce AMK one step at a time into some of the fuel tanks and engines while monitoring the performance of the engines. During those same flights, NASA's Dryden Flight Research Center also developed the remote piloting techniques necessary for the Boeing 720 to fly as a drone aircraft. An initial attempt at the full-scale test was cancelled in late 1983 due to problems with the uplink connection to the 720; if the uplink failed the ground based pilot would no longer have control of the aircraft.

On the morning of the test, the aircraft took off from Edwards Air Force Base, California, made a left-hand departure and climbed to an altitude of 2,300 feet. The aircraft was remotely flown by NASA research pilot Fitzhugh 'Fitz' Fulton from the Dryden Remotely Controlled Vehicle Facility. All fuel tanks were filled with a total of 76,000 pounds of AMK and all engines ran from start-up to impact - a flight time was nine minutes - on the modified Jet-A. It then began a descent-to-landing along the roughly 3.8-degree glideslope to a specially prepared runway on the east side of Rogers Dry Lake, with the landing gear remaining retracted.

Passing the decision height of 150 feet above ground level, the aircraft turned slightly to the right of the desired path. The aircraft entered the well-known 707/720 situation; a Dutch Roll. Slightly above that decision point at which the pilot was to execute a go-around, there appeared to be enough altitude to manoeuvre back to the centre-line of the runway. The aircraft was below the glideslope and

below the desired airspeed. Data acquisition systems had been activated, and the aircraft was committed to impact.

The aircraft contacted the ground, left wing low, at full throttle, with the aircraft nose pointing to the left of the centre-line. It had been planned that the aircraft would land wings-level, with the throttles set to idle, and exactly on the centre-line during the CID, thus allowing the fuselage to remain intact as the wings were sliced open by eight posts called 'Rhinos' due to the shape of the horns welded onto the posts and cemented into the runway. However, the 720 landed askew, resulting in one of the Rhinos slicing through the number 3 engine, behind the burner can, leaving the engine on the wing pylon. The same rhino then sliced through the fuselage, causing a cabin fire when burning fuel was able to enter.

The cutting of the number 3 engine and the full throttle situation was significant as this was outside the test envelope. The engine continued to operate for approximately one third of a rotation, degrading the fuel and igniting it after impact, providing a significant heat source. The fire and smoke took over an hour to extinguish. The CID impact was spectacular with a large fireball created by the number 3 engine on the right side, enveloping and burning the 720. From the standpoint of AMK the test was a major set-back. For NASA Langley, the data collected on crash-worthiness was deemed successful and just as important.

The actual impact demonstrated that the anti-misting additive tested was not sufficient to prevent a post-crash fire in all circumstances, though the reduced intensity of the initial fire was attributed to the effect of AMK.

FAA investigators estimated that 23–25% of the aircraft's full complement of 113 people could have survived the crash. Time from slide-out to complete smoke obscuration for the forward cabin was five seconds; for the aft cabin, it was 20 seconds. Total time to evacuate was 15 and 33 seconds respectively, accounting for the time necessary to reach and open the doors and operate the slide. Investigators labelled their estimate of the ability to escape through dense smoke as being highly speculative.

As a result of analysis of the crash, the FAA instituted new flammability standards for seat cushions which required the use of fire-blocking layers, resulting in seats which performed better than those in the test. It also implemented a standard requiring floor proximity lighting to be mechanically fastened, due to the apparent detachment of two types of adhesive-fastened emergency lights during the impact. Federal aviation regulations for flight data

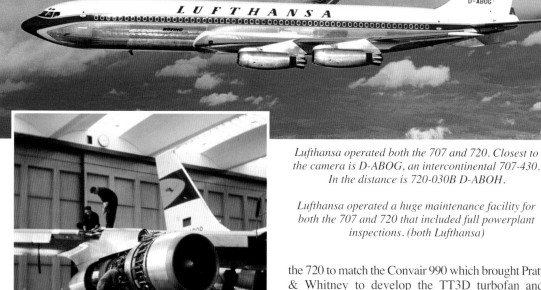

Lufthansa operated both the 707 and 720. Closest to the camera is D-ABOG, an intercontinental 707-430. In the distance is 720-030B D-ABOH.

Lufthansa operated a huge maintenance facility for both the 707 and 720 that included full powerplant inspections. (both Lufthansa)

recorder sampling rates for pitch, roll and acceleration were also found to be insufficient.

NASA concluded that the impact piloting task was of an unusually high workload, which might have been reduced through the use of a heads-up display, the automation of more tasks, and a higher-resolution monitor. It also recommended the use of a microwave landing system to improve tracking accuracy over the standard instrument landing system. In practice, the Global Positioning System-based Wide Area Augmentation System came to fulfil this role.

720B

Although preceded into the air and in service by the JT3D-powered 707-120B, the 720B is described first as it was the need for a turbofan-powered version of

the 720 to match the Convair 990 which brought Pratt & Whitney to develop the TT3D turbofan and Boeing to offer this turbofan not only for a 720 version but also for 707-120 and -320 derivatives.

Having ordered 707-123s in November 1955 when it became the second customer for Boeing jetliners, American Airlines amended its order in July 1958, canceling five JT3C- powered 707-123s but ordering twenty-five like-engined 720-023s.

Notwithstanding its 720 orders, American Airlines remained interested in the slightly smaller 990 which Convair was aggressively marketing with General Electric CJ-805-21 engines with a fan mounted behind the turbine. Fearing that American Airlines would reduce or cancel altogether its 720 order if Convair succeeded in promoting its 990 for luxury high-speed service to complement standard but slower 707-120 service, Boeing felt that it needed to have a turbofan-powered airliner. To achieve this goal, the Seattle manufacturer turned to Pratt & Whitney which, in mid-February 1958, had initiated the self-financed definition phase for a JT3D turbo-fan derivative of the JT3C turbojet with a two-stage fan and single-stage stator mounted ahead of the axial-flow compressor.

With its engineering staff reacting enthusiastically to the greater power, lower fuel consumption, and reduced noise promised by turbofan engines, American Airlines ordered twenty-five Convair 990s in October 1958. It also forcefully pushed Boeing into accelerating its development of turbofan-powered versions of its 707 and 720 and offering these derivatives at bargain basement prices. After haggling with Boeing for nearly a year, American finally renegotiated its contracts to have its 707-123s and 720-023s either re-engined with JT3Ds or delivered with these turbofans. Availability of JT3D-powered Boeing jetliners effectively ended Convair's hopes to remain an effective participant in the transport aircraft business.

Only thirty-seven Convair 990s were built while Boeing went on to build 644 JT3D-powered 707-120s, -320Bs, and -320Cs for airlines, to re-engine forty-nine 707-120s and 720s, and to deliver 126 JT3D-powered derivatives to government and military customers. For Boeing, the development of

the 720B to meet American Airlines' demands had proven an expensive undertaking, but it ended up firming up its position as the world's foremost jetliner manufacturer.

The first JT3D-powered 720-023B flew on 6 October 1960, three and a half months after the first JT3D-powered 707-123B. The Approved Type Certificate for the 720, ATC 4A28, was amended on March 3, 1961 to cover the 720B, and Boeing went on to build 89 JT3D-powered 720Bs for ten airlines. The 720B went into service on 12 March 1961, and the last 720B was delivered to Western on 20 September 1967.

In March and April 1962 EL AL accepted delivery of two Boeing 720Bs. This acquisition directly related to the Arab boycott. After the 1956 Sinai War, in order to reach Johannesburg, South Africa, without flying over or too close to Arab-controlled airspace, EL AL had to charter

EL AL launched an extensive advertising campaign to promote its new 707 service that later promoted its 720 flights. This late 1960 image appeared in advertisements and also as a postcard issued by its New York office. The airline also started to promote the country as a tourist destination to grab a share of the emerging affinity tour market.

Boeing 720 4X-ABB, was operating as EL AL Flight LY432 on 18 February 1969, a scheduled service from Amsterdam to Tel Aviv, with a stop at Zürich, Switzerland. The aircraft was taxiing for takeoff at Zürich when it was attacked by a squad of four armed Palestinian terrorists, members of the Lebanese-based Popular Front for the Liberation of Palestine. Several of the crew members were injured during the attack and the airliner was severely damaged. The co-pilot, Yoram Peres, died of his wounds a month later. An undercover Israeli skymarshal, Mordechai Rahamim, opened fire at the attackers, killing one. (both EL AL)

piston-engine aircraft from other airlines that took a circuitous route via North and Central Africa. The 720Bs had the necessary performance to allow EL AL to resume flying to South Africa with its own aircraft - via an exaggerated route stopping at Teheran, Iran - and they were chosen for that reason. With powerful Pratt & Whitney engines and an improved wing over that of the 707, the 720B could take off from 'hot and high' Teheran with sufficient fuel and payload for the desired flights.

As soon as possible, on 14 June, the 720Bs took over service from Tel Aviv east to Teheran, then flew southwest across the Persian Gulf to Central Africa, adding 2,400 miles to the trip to Johannesburg. A direct route south via the narrow Gulf of Eilat, over the Red Sea straits and then to South Africa was not feasible because of Egyptian hostility. This sixteen hour endurance test was one of the world's most circuitous air routes, with some twenty-five heading changes to prevent overflying hostile areas. Radio aids were sparse. High elevation and temperatures, plus a heavy fuel uplift, limited aircraft performance and thus the payload. Double crews had to staff the aircraft. To achieve the break-even point, the route had to show an 85% load factor.

Starting with the 1962 summer schedule, the 720B also replaced the Britannia on the Tel Aviv to Europe routes. This move secured a large slice of the international travel market, and the percentage of non-Jewish passengers edged closer to 40%. EL AL gained acceptance not just as an ethnic and immigrant carrier, but also as a successful and established international mover of passengers and cargo.

In 1965, to increase efficiency and performance of its 720Bs, EL AL replaced the original JT3D-1 turbofans with more powerful JT3D-3Bs. This also enabled standardisation with two Pratt & Whitney-powered 707-320B aircraft, ordered for delivery staring in late 1965.

During the early and mid-1960s EL AL developed the practice of maximizing the utilisation of each of its aircraft. In doing so, EL AL had to work with a very small fleet of only seven aircraft to service a far-ranging network from New York in the west to Teheran in the east, and south to Johannesburg; and it had to overcome limits on - and eventually the elimination of - passenger operations on the Jewish Sabbath and certain Jewish holidays.

EL AL achieved one of the highest aircraft utilization rates in the industry. To illustrate, on a typical schedule for a single 720B during summer 1964, the aircraft would operate between 07:00 on Monday and 16:30 Wednesday, Tel Aviv time, four roundtrips: to Zürich, Rome, Teheran and, via a European gateway, to New York. During this fiftey-seven and a half hour period the aircraft accumulated about forty hours flying time. It was then rolled into the hangar for an overnight maintenance check to be ready for an early flight the following morning.

Boeing 707s normally spent about thirty hours away from Tel Aviv on the New York run via Europe (except for the occasional nonstop flight). They typically would leave in the early morning and return the next day in the late afternoon for an overnight maintenance check before departing again on a similar schedule the following day.

EL AL's aircraft utilisation was such that it had a reserve aircraft factor of almost zero or, as one employee put it, '*one-half an airplane for three days a week, and none for the remaining four*'. During the Jewish Passover holiday in 1964, 707/720B utilization built up to an astonishing average of fifteen hours per day. Nevertheless, EL AL still managed to maintain an enviable on-time record and high safety standards.

707-120B

While the 720B was under development, the merits of incorporating the 'glove' wing leading-edge extension and turbofan engines into the larger 707–120B became increasingly obvious to Boeing and American Airlines. Other Boeing customers were not

CS-TBT of Transportes Aereos Portugueses - TAP - named 'Humberto Delgado' in the original livery. (author's collection)

CS-TBC of Air Portugal. (author's collection)

long to fully appreciate the potential offered by these upgrades, especially in terms of improved field performance and reduced fuel consumption. It was not surprising therefore that orders for the resulting 707-120B version quickly mounted.

The first of these aircraft, a 707-123B for American Airlines, flew on 22 June 1960, and ATC 4A21 was amended on 1 March 1961 to cover the 120B in its long body version required by most airlines. An additional amendment was approved on 24 July 1961 to cover the short body 707-138B version for QANTAS. Aircraft covered by these amendments included seventy-eight new-build aircraft (thirty-one -123Bs for American, forty-one -131Bs for TWA, and six -138Bs for QANTAS) as well as thirty-nine -120s modified and re-engined for Pan American (five -121s as -121Bs and one -139 as a -139B), American (twenty-three -123s as -123Bs), QANTAS (seven -138s as -138Bs), and the USAF (three -153/VC-137As as -153Bs/VC-137Bs).

707-320B

The grerater thrust and reduced fuel consumption of the JT3D were possibly of greater value to heavy, long-range airliners. However, having pioneered the use of JT3D with its 707-120B and 720B, Boeing was outpaced by Douglas when it came to using these turbofans to power long-range aircraft. Philipine Airlines became the first customer for JT3D—powered DC—8 Series 50 when it ordered two in May 1959. Douglas flew the first Series 50 on 20 December 1960 and obtained certification for this Series 30-derivative on1 May 1961. The first JT3D-powered Boeing 707-320Bs were ordered by Pan Am only in February 1961, and this variant first flew on 31 January 1962. The Approved Type Certificate 4A26 was amended by the FAA on 31 May 1962 to cover the Model 320B, and Pan Am started using it next day.

Apart from being powered by JT3Ds turbofans instead of JT4A turbojets, Model 320Bs differed from Model 320s in having wings of increased span and area as the result of the addition of extended outboard panels with curved wing tips, leading-edge extended forward between the fuselage and inboard engines, and revised trailing-edge flaps. Late production aircraft, referred to as Advanced 707-320Bs, added two segments of Kruger leading-edge flaps, further modifications to the trailing-edge flaps, and revised fan cowlings with larger blow-in doors to increase engine airflow on take-off. With all these modifications, maximum certificated gross take-off weight was increased to 335,000 pounds .

Four aircraft built for Northwest Orient Airlines with the 707-351B (SCD) model designation were the first 707s since the 367-80 to be fitted with side cargo doors (hence the SCD designation). Located forward of the wing on the port side of the fuselage for loading and unloading cargo on the main deck, the upward-hinging door measured 91x134 inches. Although the 707-351B (SCD)s were ordered as convertible aircraft and could carry freight, passengers, or mixed passenger/cargo loads, they lacked the reinforced flooring of the more fully modified 707-320Cs. The first 707-351B (SCD) flew on 15 May 1963, nearly three months after the first 707-351C for Pan American.

Including the four hybrid -351B (SCD)s for Northwest, Boeing built a total of 170 Model 320Bs for airlines customers with aircraft for late customers being identified by alpha-numeric designations after the manufacturer ran out of two-digit customer numbers. Aircraft built for airlines included three 707-312Bs for Malaysian Singapore, sixty -321Bs for Pan American, ten -323Bs for American, eight -328Bs for Air France, twelve -330Bs for Lufthansa, two -336Bs for BOAC, three -337Bs for Air India, two -344Bs for South African Airways, six -351Bs and four -351B (SCD)s for Northwest, three -358Bs for El Al, two -359Bs for Avianca, seven -382Bs for TAP, two -384Bs for Olympic, four -387Bs for Aerolineas Argentinas, and four -5J6Bs for CAAC.

In addition, Boeing built four aircraft for non- airline customers (two 707-353Bs as presidential VC-137Cs for the USAF, one -3F3B for the government of Argentina, and one -3L6B for the Malaysian government).

The last passenger-only 707 to be delivered to an airline was S/N 20457, a 707-336B which was handed over to BOAC on 17 April 1971. A number of passenger-configured 707-320Bs were later converted as freighters, while others were fitted with a new requirement; hushkits.

In the early seventies, the entry into service of wide bodied aircraft powered by substantially quieter high-bypass-ratio turbofans rendered operations by noisy first generation jetliners even more conspicuous. Accordingly, Boeing undertook to develop revised JT3D nacelles for its still-in-production 707. These nacelles were tested on a 707-331B (S/N 20059, N8730) leased back from TWA between January and July 1973. However, Boeing did not proceed with this scheme, as airlines showed little interest in noise reduction until the early eighties.

After production of civil 707s ended in 1978, the imposition of new noise emission rules by the FAA under FAR 36 Stage 2 and the International Civil Aviation Organization Annex 16 chapter 2 suddenly threatened restriction or grounding of ageing but still sprightly 707s, as well as other first-generation jetliners). To allow these aircraft to remain in operation with less wealthy airlines that could not afford new generation jetliners, several companies undertook to develop engine hushkits for JT3D powered 707s

Most successful of these hushkit conversions was that developed by Comtran International, Inc. in San Antonio, Texas. Using Rohr Industries' DynaRohr liners and featuring extended intake and fan exhaust ducts, Comtran Q-707 nacelles reduced the 100 EPNdB take-off footprint for a fully loaded 707 from 6.4 to 3.2 miles.

To reduce noise emission still further and bring 707s in compliance with Stage 3 noise requirements, Quiet Skies, Inc. and Burbank Aeronautical Corporation II were jointly marketing their Stage III hushkit in the late nineties. A 707-3J6B (S/N 20717, N717QS) fitted with these hushkit nacelles was demonstrated at the SBAC Air Show in Farnborough in September 1998.

707-320C

Combining the basic airframe and powerplant installation of the 707-320B, with all upgrades being similarly introduced during the course of production, with the main deck cargo door of the 707−351B (SCD) and a reinforced cargo floor with tie- downs, the 707-320C was built both as a convertible passenger/cargo aircraft and as a pure freighter. The first 707-321Cs were ordered by Pan American in April 1962, three months after rival DC-8-50CFs had been ordered by Air Canada.

The passenger/cargo convertible 707 first flew on 19 February 1963 and the 707-320C was certificated under an amendment to ATC 4A26 on 30 April. Following the launching of the wide-body 747, most airlines ordered convertible 707-320Cs in preference to all-passenger -320Bs. Production of the convertible aircraft thus greatly surpassed that of earlier passenger variants. In the end, Boeing built 305 Model 320Cs for commercial customers.

Another 707-320C and a -385C were initially retained by Boeing as development aircraft. In addition, Boeing built 29 Model 320Cs for government and military customers.

Most airlines ordered their -320Cs in convertible passenger/cargo configuration, but a number of customers ordered their aircraft in all-cargo configuration with all passenger amenities, such as galleys, lavatories, main cabin windows, and emergency oxygen equipment deleted. This enabled the operating weight empty of all-cargo configured aircraft to be 12,800 pounds, less than that of a

OD-AFX of Trans Mediterranean Airways - TMA. This 707-327C crashed at Beirut on 23 May 1979 during a training flight. (author's collection)

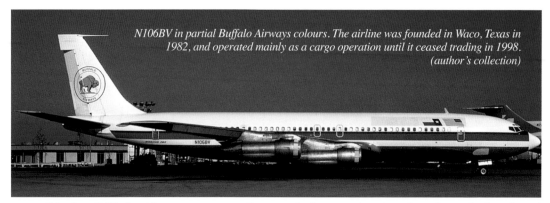

convertible aircraft fitted out for passenger operation and 19,600 pounds less than that of a convertible aircraft fitted out for cargo operation. Payload weight for all-cargo -320Cs was increased in the corresponding proportion.

Converted from the CFM56 test 707-700 aircraft, the last 707-320C was delivered to the Moroccan Government on 10 March 1982, 23 years and seven months after Pan American had taken delivery of the first 707-121.

Not counting the ex-airlines aircraft operated by the USAF and the USN with C-18 and 13-8 designations, Boeing included 196 passenger/ cargo convertible and all-freight -320Cs in its list of active aircraft as of 30 June 1998. Many of them were operated by air forces and government agencies.

707-700

Powered by four 20,000-pounds class CFM International CFM56 high-bypass-ratio turbofans, the 707-700 was an engine development aircraft using a 707-320C airframe. It first flew on November 27, 1979 and was then presented as the potential prototype for either re- engining existing 707—320B and -320C airframes or for a new production version. However, without a costly fuselage stretch, wing

redesign, and strengthened and lengthened undercarriage, the use of CFM56s proved unjustified for new production aircraft. Moreover, re-engining standard airframes was of little interest to major carriers, which by then were standardizing on later generation aircraft, and was too expensive for the smaller airlines building up their fleet with 707-320B/320Cs phased out by their wealthier competitors. Accordingly, plans to re- engine existing aircraft or to build new CFM56-engined 707s were dropped rapidly. Nevertheless, experience gained with the experimental CFM56-engined 707-700 proved valuable for Boeing as this high-bypass-ratio engine was adopted as the standard powerplant for the 737-300 and later variants of the Boeing twinjet and for re-engined KC-135s.

Proposed 707 Models

Then more familiar with the US military contractual practices, which often saw manufacturers' initiatives in proposing new models rewarded with 'cost-plus-fee' production contracts, Boeing also came up with a bewildering number of proposed 707 derivatives. As most of these proposals entailed major redesign, it was fortunate for the financial health of the company that none found customers as, having to be

9V-BBB of Singapore Airlines. (author's collection)

commercially priced as opposed to sold on 'cost-plus- fee' as were military derivatives, their success would have created a serious fiscal drain.

Often ignored by historians, some of these proposals provide interesting hindsight on the development of the first generation of jetliners and are thus worthy of being briefly described. They are listed in chronological order to show trends evolving between the mid-fifties and the early seventies.

Proposed shortly after the Conway-powered intercontinental 707-420 matured, the 707-520 designation first appeared in a preliminary layout dated 9 March 1956. It then called for a 707-120 development with 248,000-pounds gross weight and Rolls-Royce Conway R.Co.10 engines. This proposal died an early death as US carriers were not interested in a 'domestic' aircraft powered by British engines, while airlines in the Commonwealth found the Conway-powered 707-420 more attractive for intercontinental operations. Equally unsuccessful, a later 707-520B layout was prepared for a 707-320B derivative with a 12-foot longer fuselage and four 21,000 pounds Pratt & Whitney JT3D-5A turbofans.

In the spring of 1956, Boeing studied two configurations to be powered by four proposed Bristol 511 engines. Neither the 248,000-pound 707-620 based on the 707-120 with a ten-foot fuselage extension nor the 296,000-pound 707-720 derived from the 707-320 got the nod from airlines as the 511 remained a 'paper' engine.

Illustrated by a preliminary layout dated 8 April 1957, the 707-320-101 was a proposed 707-320 development with an enlarged lower lobe for additional passenger seating forward of the wing and cargo aft of the main gear well. Reflecting the elitist attitude still held by Boeing engineers that jet airliners would be used for premium service while 'steerage' passengers would be flown in obsolete propliners, this double-deck aircraft was laid-out to accommodate up to 199 first-class passengers, with 159 in the five-abreast upper deck and 40 in the four-abreast lower deck. An alternate cabin configuration provided for 200 coach-class passengers in six-abreast seating on the upper deck and 50 coach passengers in five-abreast seating on the lower deck. With all first-class accommodation in just-introduced, top-of-the-line Lockheed 1649A Starliners providing for only 62 seats in a four-abreast arrangement while all-economy Douglas DC-6Bs sat 102 passengers five abreast, airlines reacted negatively to the overly capacious double-deck Boeing jetliner proposal.

At the beginning of 1960, with the 707-120 and

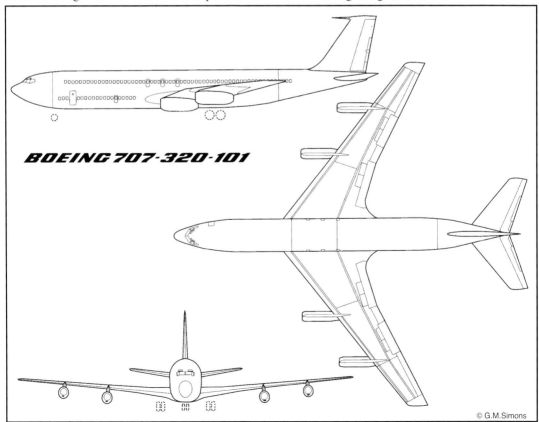

BOEING 707-320-101

© G.M.Simons

VT-DMN of Air India was a 707-437 named Kanxhwnjunga (K-2) after the world's second highest mountain. Sadly it crashed on Mont Blanc, Europe's highest peak, on 24 January 1966, sixteen years after the loss of another Air India aircraft - Lockheed Constellation VT-CQP crashed at almost exactly the same location. Also visible in the picture of a wet Renton ramp this day in March 1961 are 707s of Air France, Braniff, Western American Airlines and Aer Lingus. (John Stride Collection)

707-320 well established in revenue service and the Conway-powered 707-420 and lighter 720 about to enter service, Boeing set its sights on developing larger 707 derivatives so as to achieve lower seat-mile costs. Thus, the 707-520-X was to be a double deck aircraft with low-mounted wings and a fuselage length of 191 feet 7 inches, while the 707-520-2X was to be similarly configured but with a shorter fuselage. Proposed at the same time, the 707-520-X3 was to be a double deck aircraft with high-mounted wings spanning 142 feet 5 inches, the same as the 707-320 and -420, but with fuselage length of 144 feet 2 inches. In the real world, airlines judged these proposals to offer excessive capacity while the lack of suitable engines rendered further development of the 707 only of academic value.

In late 1964 Douglas announced plans to develop stretched versions of the DC-8 with all-economy seating for up to 259 passengers, and once again Boeing was caught wrong-footed.

Previously Boeing had derived much ill-placed pride from the fact that its 707 had a shorter and lighter landing gear than the rival DC-8 and that its first jet airliner had a convenient level fuselage attitude while on the ground whereas the DC-8 had an unsightly tail-high attitude. Later Boeing realised that Douglas, long a proponent of stretching basic designs to increase seating, had wisely chosen a

longer gear and tail-up attitude to endow its DC-8 with much growth potential. Unable to match the DC-8-61/63 capacity without an expensive redesign of the main landing gear and inner wing section of its 707, Boeing conceded this segment of the market to Douglas while concentrating its activities on developing the 2707, a supersonic transport aircraft - the aborted American SST - and the large capacity 747 (then primarily seen as a military freighter but also capable of being a 'Passenger Insurance' jet airliner in the event that the supersonic transport failed to materialise, which, of course, it did.

This is emblematic of the 'Boeing Knows Best' attitude demonstrated by many in the company, but hard financial success did come easily for the Seattle manufacturer. Often attributed to a supposed Boeing philosophy to offer many different variants of the basic design to meet different airline requirements, the profusion of 707 and 720 models was actually the result of competitive pressures. Without a doubt Boeing financial officers and its bankers would have preferred to see the company limit itself to offering models that retained the wings and fuselage cross-section of the Model 717/KC-135 but providing different seating capacities through changing fuselage lengths. This proved to be impossible when the original design itself was wrong and the airlines overwhelmingly favoured the wider fuselage cross-

Abel AG Airways was a short-lived Belgian carrier of the late 1970s, with 707-351C OO-ABA seen here. Part of the Abelag Aviation Group, the company operated flights to Mediterranean destinations. (author's collection)

section of the proposed DC-8. The resulting wider fuselage developed for the 707 was then retained as the company standard until the wide-body 747 was developed. For the 707/720 series, this constant section fuselage was offered in four lengths which became an inexpensive way to offer accommodation to meet customer requirements, ranging from 88 first-class passengers in the short fuselage 707-138 to 219 passengers in the 707-320C in a high-density configuration. Even the addition of a reinforced main deck flooring and a main deck cargo door to obtain the 707-320C was a relatively inexpensive exercise..

However, whereas changes in fuselage length, cabin configuration, and provision for carrying freight on the main deck all proved relatively easy and required limited additional investments, the engineering, manufacturing, and certification for wings of varying span, area, and plan proved expensive for Boeing. Its main competitor, Douglas, had planned its DC-8 with growth in mind and was thus able to keep to a minimum changes to the wings while its jetliner grew from the 265,000-pound Series 10 to the 355,000-pound Series 63AF. Conversely, not counting changes in high-lift devices, Boeing ended up having to offer five wing configurations for its first generation of jetliners which grew from the 190,000-pound 367-80 to the 334,000-pound 707-320C.

Bluntly put, Boeing had lacked a sufficient understanding of airline operations when it undertook to develop a jet airliner, so it was constantly forced to play catch-up with what was essentially an inferior design to moves by the more savvy Douglas and Convair, which were thoroughly familiar with the needs and preferences of the airlines.

To its credit, the Boeing management was willing to make up for errors resulting from this deficient understanding of the airline business. While this willingness drastically affected the financial bottom line for several years, it enabled Boeing to acquire the experience on which to build its future supremacy as a jetliner manufacturer. Significantly, Boeing did so by never repeating the costly errors of having to design too many different versions of its aircraft. Notably, 1,832 of its next jetliner, the 727 trijet, were built with only two different cabin lengths and common wings. The 367-80/ 707/ 720 lessons had been well learnt.

By the early seventies, just as the large-capacity 747 entered service and funding for the supersonic 2707-300 was terminated by Congress, US airlines experienced their worst downturn since the 1930s. As airlines sought to recover by providing more direct point-to-point services and increasing frequencies, Boeing again realised that an aircraft smaller than the 747 and more similarly sized to the

N7231T. On 8 February 1989, while operating as Independent Air Flight 1851, an American charter flight from Bergamo, Italy to Punta Cana, Dominican Republic, struck Pico Alto while on approach to Santa Maria Airport in the Azores for a scheduled stopover. The aircraft was destroyed, with the loss of all 144 on board. (author's collection)

UK 'Second Force' carrier British Caledonian operated a number of 707s, G-AWWD is seen here landing at London Stansted on 4 May 1973. (author)

stretched DC-8 might be needed. However, it was too late to develop such a derivative and no further 707 developments were undertaken.

Swing-Tail Proposals

A little known planned development of the freighter 707 derivatives were a pair of designs fitted with swing tails. In 1958, when the United States Air Force became painfully aware that its Military Air Transport Service (MATS) was without jet transports, Boeing actively promoted 707 derivatives suitable not only to military operations but also well tailored to commercial air freight operations.

The 367-80 had been designed with side cargo doors, but Boeing was initially unable to attract any USAF Military Air Transport Service (MATS) interest in a transport version of the KC-135. To spark Air Force interest in a KC-135/707 military transport derivative while offering to airlines a 707 version better suited to air cargo operations, Boeing studied a number of Model 707 and Model 717 derivatives fitted with the tail either swinging sideways or tilting upward to provide unfettered access to the main deck. In a memorandum dated 25 June 1958, Boeing

redesignated the 707 commercial cargo derivatives as Model 735s, while military cargo derivatives of either the Model 707 or Model 717 became Model 738s. Representative sideways-swinging tail and upward-tilting tail versions are illustrated.

Then, early in 1960, President Dwight D. Eisenhower approved a Pentagon decision to transfer a proportion of MATS traffic to the civil operators. The decision meant there would likely be a doubling-up of the military transport business that was currently being passed on to civil US carriers. The overall recommendation submitted by the Secretary of Defence was that MATS should withdraw from routine transport operations and a programme to this effect was to be completed by 1 May 1960.

Amongst the courses of action in the programme was one to the effect that suitable arrangements should be made for Government participation in the cost of developing long-range turbine-powered all-cargo aircraft. This meant that Douglas, Boeing and Convair were able to go ahead with the production of freight versions of their turbojet transports.

This in turn tied in with a programme proposed by Senator Almer Stillwell 'Mike' Monroney who

N29798 of InterAm. (author's collection)

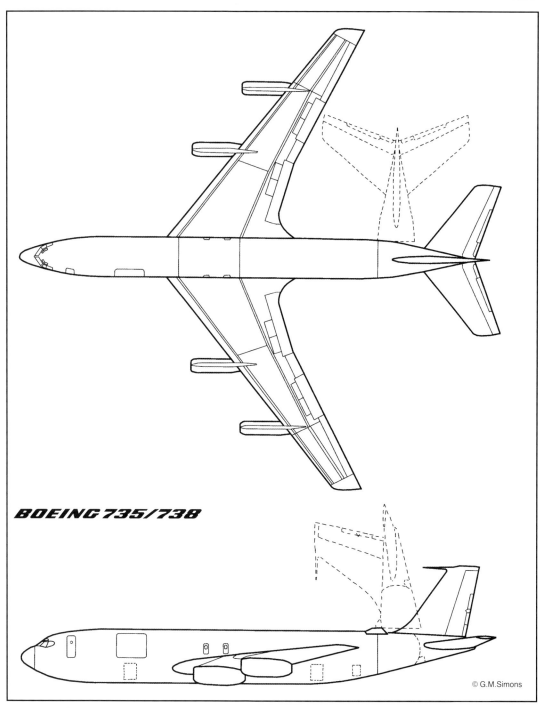

BOEING 735/738

© G.M.Simons

was suggesting that a series of ten-year loans to be guaranteed by the Civil Aeronautics Board for the purchase by operators of approved all-cargo aircraft following the transfer of much of MATS work to the civil carriers. The plans never really came to fruition from military or civil customers, and Models 735 and 738 remained stillborn.

For many less mainstream American carriers, such as Airlift International, Flying Tiger, Pacific Northern, Western and World Airways, the convertible 707-320C became available at the right time, as the US military involvement in Vietnam resulted in defence contracts to carry personnel and non-combat cargo between the United States and

MEA - Middle Eastern Airways - flew a number of 707s, with OD-AFL being shown. The aircraft was based at Paris-Orly following the Isreali occupation of the Lebanon in 1982, and was destroyed by shelling in Beirut on 21 August 1985. (author's collection)

bases in Southeast Asia. However, experience showed that when carrying cargo, 707-320Cs often 'cubed out' as average freight density was relatively low. It was not surprising therefore that a number of carriers followed the lead of Saturn Airways who, after obtaining three 707-379Cs, switched to stretched DC-8-61Fs which had a larger main deck.

'One careful owner...'

Established 707 and 720 customers began trading delivery positions fairly early in the game in order to build up their jet airliner fleet according to traffic demand. That process began when TWA, which had been frustrated by Howard Hughes during the initial buying phase, was forced to release six 707-331 delivery positions, and these aircraft were delivered new to Pan American in 1959-1960. TWA then had to make up for its inadequate fleet by leasing two Northwest Orient Airlines 720-051Bs in 1961-1962 before taking over two World Airways delivery positions for 707-373Cs in 1963.

The number of transactionsof this nature between established Boeing operators was, at first, relatively limited. However, when the larger, healthier carriers increased capacity by placing wide-bodied aircraft into service, 707s and 720s became available in fast-increasing numbers. At first, most were taken up by

established operators which used these pre-owned aircraft to build up their fleets at minimum costs. Later on, these first-generation machines were more and more frequently acquired by new entrants.

For the 720, the era of 'only one careful owner since new' got into stride in the early seventies with these JT3C-powered aircraft being rapidly disposed of by major carriers. The first airline to relinquish its entire fleet of early Boeing jetliners was Eastern, which traded its fifteen Model 720-025s back to Boeing between September 1969 and June 1970 to acquire more economical 727-225s. United and Braniff International were next, respectively storing or selling most of their twenty-nine Model 720-022s and five -027s in 1973. That same year, Western Airlines disposed of the two 720-625 and single 720-048 it had obtained in its merger with Pacific Northern Airlines. Abroad, the only original 720 customer, Aer Lingus, had been even quicker to dispose of its three 720-048s, selling one to Pacific Northern and one to British West Indian Airways in 1966, and one to Trans Polar in 1970. American Airlines, which had re-engined its 720-023s with JT3D turbofans, kept most of its 720-023Bs somewhat longer, disposing of the last in 1976.

Of the remaining fifteen JT3C-powered aircraft, three 707-124s were sold by Continental Airlines to

Tradewinds was a small UK cargo airline that used a number of 707-320Cs, with G-WIND seen here. (author's collection)

Boeing 720 N421MA in the colourful livery of Aerolineas de Guatemala Aviateca.
(author's collection)

TWA in December 1967. In turn, TWA disposed of these aircraft and of its last twelve -131s at the end of 1971. The more capable JT4A- and Conway-powered intercontinental models lasted longer with their original owners. British Airways progressively transferred most of its 707-436s to its charter organization, British Airtours, but retained ownership of four Conway-powered aircraft until 1981.

JT3D-powered 707-320Bs and -320Cs remained in production longer than all other 707 and 720 variants. 477 of these aircraft were delivered to airlines between April 1962 and January 1978, with peak deliveries occurring in 1968 when 118 were accepted by carriers. With so many being built for so long, and with their JT3D turbofans proving extremely reliable, it is not surprising that 707-320B/Cs remained in service with most major airlines until the early eighties. Many pre-owned JT3D-powered 707s then quickly found customers among smaller carriers, particularly for freight operations.

Early on, most 707s and 720s changing hands went to established Boeing operators, such as Pan American, which expanded its fleet with two ex-Western 707-1395, three ex-American 720-023Bs, and six ex-Lufthansa 720-030Bs. Later transactions, however, increasingly saw pre-owned aircraft being acquired by new jet operators.

Pre-owned 707s and 720s were acquired not just by scheduled carriers and charter airlines but also by a variety of other customers.

An Instant Airline...
Wet-leasing is a concept that is resorted to whenever an airline has a sudden but temporary need for extra capacity, for whatever reason. If a complete airliner, ready to go with full tanks and a crew on board, can be hired by the day, week or month, this makes more sense than buying an extra aircraft, training crews and

then, later, trying to find a buyer when the aircraft is no longer needed.

So it was in the early 1970s, when such aircraft as the 747, DC-10 and L-1011 were making an impact on the world scene, in almost every case by displacing 707s and DC-8s. Thus, plenty of the latter, which in the 1950s had thrust the world's airlines into the jet age, were coming on to the market, still with plenty of flight-time remaining on their airframes and at every depressed prices. This brought them within reach of carriers such as the UKs British Midland Airways (BMA), especially after the airline's capital had been increased to just over £5 million in September 1972.

Also, pilots and engineers qualified on the 707 were equally plentiful, and short-term contracts could be negotiated. BMA The era of the instant airline really began with the signing of a contract with Sudan Airways in November 1972. That airline's chairman, Mohammed Abdel Bagi, had been in Nigeria in during 1968-69 and saw how satisfied Nigeria Airways had been with BMA's wet-lease of a Vickers Viscount. His board agreed with the view that, in order to ease the transition from the Comet 4 to bigger and more competitive equipment, it made sense to hand the whole job to a reliable operator such as BMA. The initial contract covered full-time operation of both BMA's 707s until the end of 1973, together with all necessary management and training.

The two aircraft were to operate all the airline's 'Blue Nile' international services, until they could be handled entirely by the airline itself. In the event most of the Sudan staff were trained at Khartoum, but the flight crews and six of the stewardesses did come to East Midlands. The pilots all had British licences, and thus carried out much of their conversion flying on BMA services.

It speaks much for the company's political awareness and diplomacy that the first two 707s

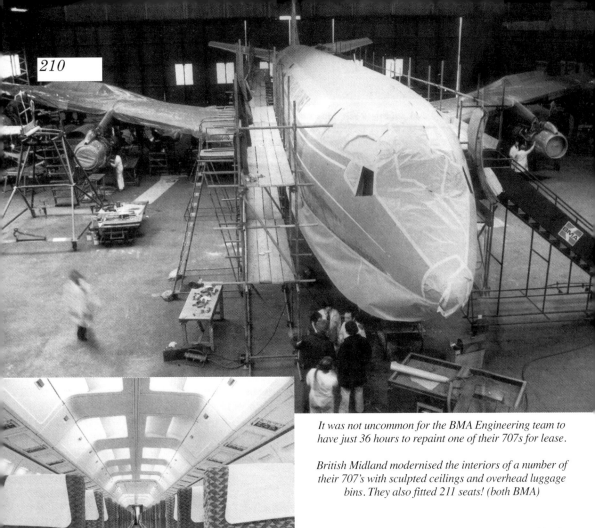

It was not uncommon for the BMA Engineering team to have just 36 hours to repaint one of their 707s for lease.

British Midland modernised the interiors of a number of their 707's with sculpted ceilings and overhead luggage bins. They also fitted 211 seats! (both BMA)

wove a path through what could have been a minefield during the 1970s without causing any conflict.

One diversion for BMA was the charter of a 707 on 4 April 1975 by the *Daily Mail* newspaper on behalf of Project Vietnam Orphans and The Ockenden Venture to rescue I50 orphan children from Saigon in the final collapse of South Vietnam. David English, the newspaper's editor, joined a group of doctors and nurses aboard G-AYVE. Everything went well until the arrival at Saigon; then officialdom reared its head to a point where the lives of many of the children were put at risk. Mr Hunt of the British

Embassy argued non-stop for six hours, while the children were packed in buses at temperatures well beyond 38°C. Even after the 707 had been loaded and started its engines, a fresh lot of officials arrived and reiterated that the children did not have permission to leave. After further long delays, and much signing of forms, takeoff clearance was granted - but Mr English was told that he had to stay in Saigon. Fortunately he was able to get back on board. Once airborne, with air conditioning working, the desperately exhausted and dehydrated children began to recover. According to Dr Grifiin, from Chislehurst, *'At least six of the children would have died in the next 60 hours if they had been left in Saigon... The cabin crew performed in a manner that can only be described as magnificent'* When the 707 landed at Heathrow the nursing teams and the four stewards had been working without a break for 29 hours. This was the only British aircraft to rescue Vietnam orphans, and the last aircraft of any nation to do so.

The airline learned fast, and decided to have its 707s upgraded in capability. The interiors were gutted, two extra emergency exits were inserted aft of the wing, with 'slimline' escape slides, and the

Another British charter service operator was British Midland Airways who had a fleet of 707s of assorted variants, but most were not flown by them, being leased out to other airlines around the world. Here though, in full BMA colours is -321C G-BMAZ. (author's collection)

whole interior trim was replaced, incluing the fitment of overhead 'bins'. New galleys were added, and finally 211 seats of new design, reputedly the largest number of seats ever certificated for the 707 were installed.

So success were BMA in building up its 'instant airline' reputation that in 1975 the number of 707s jumped from two to six, and by 1978 four more had been added, though the number in use at any one time seldom exceeded six. This was largely because of the effects of the 1973' fuel crisis. Suddenly the price of fuel sprang into the forefront of operating costs, and the early 707s powered by JT4A turbojets showed up very badly.

Though they might cost £5 million instead of £ I million, the later aircraft with JT3D turbofans were considerably more efficient, quite apart from having a better performance, and the last four comprised a 707-373C (leased from World Airways and retaining its US registration N370WA), two -338Cs from QANTAS and a -324C built for Continental but actually acquired from BCal. Between 1974 and 1982 the Boeings of BMA, with BMA crews, flew in the colours and on the services of such airlines as Air Algerie, Air Inter (France), Bangladesh Biman,

DETA (Mozambique), East African, Gulf Air, Iraqi, Kenya, Kuwait, Libyan Arab, Malaysian, Nigeria, Pakistan International, Sudan, Syrian Arab, Tunis Air and Zambia. The Maintenece Department of BMS often had just thrity-six hours in which to repaint the 707 in the complete livery of a new operator!

The ups and downs of the Various contracts resulted in equally dramatic changes in the number of aircraft employed. During one week the number of active 707s jumped from one to six. Often the airliners were inactive for weeks at a time, costing little but the parking fees racked up at East Midlands. Then, when a wet-lease came in it was controlled chaos while things were organised. The nucleus of company crews was augumented by short-term contract 707 pilots and flight engineers as required. Many were early retirees from British Airways, especially in 1976-79, while in 1978 six QANTAS first officers arrived on a similar release. All had the opportunity to broaden their experience in a way seldom possible on regular line flying with one operator.

For example, one route flown for DETA was Maputo (Mozambique) to Cuba, and others went to East Berlin and even to the central parts of the Soviet

British Midland's 707-320C G-BFLD. (author's collection)

Union. Three weeks were spent flying salmon from King Salmon Airport, Alaska, to Abbotsford, near Vancouver. Desert ibex were flown to Saudi Arabia - where they had been extinct - under a US- inspired project for reintroduction and conservation, while a Gulf Air cargo contract saw Rolls-Royce cars being airlifted to Britain for routine servicing!

Then a BMA Boeing was hijacked. In the small hours of 9 July 1977 G-AZWA, flying in Kuwait Airways colours, was hijacked by Palestinians while en route to Kuwait from Beirut. At Kuwait the passengers were exchanged for different hostages, and a relief crew was allowed on board. The hijackers demanded a flight to Aden, but Aden, Bahrein

and Doha all refused permission, and eventually a landing was made at Damascus. Fully fuelled, the 707 taxied out with orders to fly to Tripoli. The runway was blocked with trucks, but as Captain Ron Hardy was supposed to have said '...*with a gun at your head you simply obey*'. The terrorist on the flight deck spoke no English, but as Hardy began his takeoff he began screaming in Arabic and waving his automatic weapon. Hardy abandoned takeoff at 60 knots, and returned to the apron. The hijackers then fell out among themselves, and their leader, who appeared highly unstable, was disarmed. BMA management listened-in to the whole hijack on HF single-sideband radio at the operations room at East Midlands Airport.

BMA's instant-airline operations began to wound down from 1980, and to cease in 1982. From 1980 onwards the diminishing 707 fleet was employed mainly on conventional charters. It finally ceased operating in October 1984, most of that year having been spent on holiday travel to the Mediterranean resorts and transatlantic charters.

The bottom rung of the airline industry were the Air Travel clubs. They sprang up and blew away like dandelions. Probably the largest and most successful was the Denver, Colorado-based Denver Ports of Call operated flights for the Ports of Call Travel Club from 1967 to 1992. In its heyday, Ports of Call was the largest travel club in the United States, with at one time over 66,000 members.

The travel club had a private terminal separate from the main public terminal at Stapleton International, and operated their own domestic and international trips using specially outfitted private aircraft. They began by using large four-engined piston and turboprop aircraft, with pilots who were initially commercial airline employees who flew

UK charter operator Britannia Airways flew a number of 707s and 720s on inclusive tour and affinity charters during the 1970s. G-AYSI is seen here at the airlines Luton base. (Capt Mike Russell/Britannia Airways)

Denver Ports-of-Call flew worldwidw with their immaculate 707s.
Here N703PC is seen at London Stansted. (author)

Ports of Call aircraft in their off time, and later were full-time employees. The flight attendants stayed with each travel club group on a trip for up to a month as group tour guides.

As Ports of Call grew, more modern jet aircraft such as the Convair 990, Boeing 707 and Boeing 727 were acquired on the second hand market. By 1986, Ports of Call operated eleven Boeing 707-300 airliners, a B707-100, and a single B727-100. The club was widely visible from the Ports of Call Travel Club stickers displayed on many automobiles around Denver and throughout Colorado and the surrounding states. One trip in the mid eighties was 'Around the World' and circumnavigated the globe with multiple stops. Another of the more interesting trips flown by the club was the annual 'Mystery Trip', in which members signed up to be taken on a trip to an unknown destination. This annual event was so popular that the club would fill multiple B707s with nearly 800 people per trip.

Because of federally mandated aircraft noise restrictions, the company went public to raise funding to pay for the required hush kits on the aircraft. In an effort to increase aircraft use, the aircraft began operating as a separate charter company after being rebranded as Skyworld Airlines under FAR part 121, enabling them to operate non-travel club charter services as well. In the wake of public ownership, and after several leadership changes, the company essentially suffered a hostile take over. The new controlling interests liquidated the aircraft assets and shut down the airline portion, remaining open as a travel club without aircraft.

The travel club subsequently was forced to book member trips in blocks of seats on commercial airlines. Part of the mystique of the travel club genre of airlines was the enjoyment of special treatment. Instead of club members boarding private aircraft

The first Ambassadair 720, N8711E. The Ambassadair travel club was started by George Mickelsons after the shut down of Voyager 1000. Ambassadair operated until the launch of American Trans Air , which then took over Ambassadair Club flights. (author's collection)

Lloyd International was a UK-based charter operator. They acquired their first 707 in 1970, but ceased operations in 1972. Here their 707-324C G-AZJM is seen at London Stansted. (author)

from a terminal, groups were now shuttled over to Stapleton terminal to board whatever commercial flights were available to the trip destinations, although they were accompanied by a POC tour guide. With the loss of their own aircraft and the ability to fly directly to any desired destination, they were reduced to offering only the multiple connecting flights available commercially. As a direct result, club membership renewals quickly plummeted and the travel club eventually shut down completely in 1994.

Other 707s and 720s were operated in the USA by sports organisations such as the Los Angeles Dodgers major league baseball team, or worldwide by government and air forces and to corporations, either as staff transports or as testbeds for engines and aircraft systems.

One such test aircraft was 720-023B (construction number 18024) the 177th Model 707-type airplane made by Boeing. It was rolled out on 28 October 1960, registered as N7538A, flew on 14 January 1961 and was delivered to American Airlines on 3 February. This airline operated N7538A until August 1971, when it was

put in storage in Tulsa, Oklahoma.

Middle East Airlines (MEA), the largest airline in Lebanon, bought the airliner on 25 September 1971 and re-registered it as OD-AFQ. It was delivered to its new owner three days later. Like many, if not most MEA airplanes, OD-AFQ was forced to stay away from its main base in Beirut when Israel invaded Lebanon, in June 1982, and occupied a good part of the country until 1985. Based at Orly, Paris, the airplane occasionally flew passengers for Air France and Air Inter, another French airline.

Pratt & Whitney Canada (PWC) bought the Model 720B in December 1985 and re-registered it as C-FETB (FETB as in Flying Experimental Test Bed) on 10 January 1986. A series of modification were made after this date.

C-FETB did its flight acceptance flight on 9 October 1986, a PWC crew flew the airplane across the Atlantic on the 12th. Known internally as FTB1 (Flying test bed 1), C-FETB was thoroughly modified for its new role between October 1986 and January 1988. It was equipped to test a variety of engines, a large turbofan could take the place of the

G-APFG was a former BOAC and later BEA Airtours 707-436 On retirement it served as a trainer with Aviation Traders Engineering Limited at Stansted for many years before the fuselage was taken to Cardington near Bedford where it was used for water mist suppression tests to assist in developing a survivable cabin environment in the event of a fire.

The following engine types were tested on C-FETB: International Aero Engines (IAE) V2500 turbofan; PWC JT15D turbofan; PWC PW300 turbofan; PWC PW500 turbofan; PWC PW600 turbofan; PWC PT6 turboprop; PWC PW100 turboprop.

Eager to preserve this historically significant test bed, Pratt & Whitney Canada (PWC) and the Canada Aviation and Space Museum (CASM) came to an agreement that saw the 720 go on indefinite loan to the National Air Force Museum of Canada, in Trenton, Ontario.)

inside inner engine underneath the starboard wing. A small turbofan could be mounted on the starboard side of the forward fuselage. A turboprop could be mounted in the nose.

Terrorism and conflict.

Apart from aircraft lost through accidents, domestic and international terrorism for political ends saw the destruction of a number of 707s and 720s. On 13 September 1970, three airliners that had been hijacked by the Popular Front for the Liberation of Palestine - known as the PFLP - were blown up by terrorists in front of the the the world's media. The incident started some days earlier when four jet airliners bound for New York City and one for London were hijacked. Three aircraft were forced to land at Dawson's Field, a remote desert airstrip near Zarka, Jordan, formerly a British Royal Air Force base, that then become the PFLP's 'Revolutionary Airport'.

El Al Flight 219 was a 707, registered 4X-ATB that originated in Tel Aviv, Israel, and was en route to New York City. On board were 138 passengers and 10 crew members. The aircraft stopped in Amsterdam, Netherlands, and was hijacked shortly after it took off from there by Patrick Argüello, a Nicaraguan American, and Leila Khaled, a Palestinian.

Plans were to get four hijackers on board, but two were stopped from boarding in Amsterdam by Israeli security. These two conspirators, traveling under Senegalese passports with consecutive numbers, were prevented from flying on El Al on 6 September. They purchased first-class tickets on Pan Am Flight 93 and hijacked that flight instead.

Posing as a married couple, Argüello and Khaled boarded the plane using Honduran passports—having passed through a security check of their luggage—and were seated in the second row of tourist class. Once the plane was approaching the British coast, they drew their guns and grenades and approached the cockpit, demanding entrance.

After being informed by intercom that a hijacking was in progress, Captain Uri Bar Lev decided not to accede to their demands. Instead he put the aircraft into a steep nosedive which threw the two hijackers off-balance. Argüello reportedly threw his sole grenade down the airliner aisle, but it failed to

N1R 'Kay-O II' was a Boeing 720 used by the Los Angeles Dodgers baseball team. The jet was usually kept at Las Vegas' McCarran Airport. (author's collection)

explode, and he was hit over the head with a bottle of whiskey by a passenger after he drew his pistol. Argüello shot steward Shlomo Vider and according to the passengers and Israeli security personnel, was then shot by a sky marshal. His accomplice Khaled was subdued by security and passengers, while the aircraft made an emergency landing at London Heathrow Airport; she then claimed that Argüello was shot four times in the back after he and Khaled failed to hijack the airplane. Vider underwent emergency surgery and recovered from his wounds; Argüello died in the ambulance taking both him and Khaled to Hillingdon Hospital. Khaled was then arrested by British police.

TWA Flight 741, another Boeing 707, tail number N8715T was a round-the-world flight carrying 144 passengers and a crew of eleven. The flight on this day was flying from Tel Aviv, Israel to Athens, Frankfurt am Main and then to New York City, and was hijacked on the Frankfurt-New York leg.

It landed at Dawson's Field in Jordan at 6:45 p.m. local time. Hijackers gained control of the cockpit and a female stated, "This is your new captain speaking. This flight has been taken over by the Popular Front for the Liberation of Palestine. We will take you to a friendly country with friendly people."

Three other airliners were also hijackered. Swissair Flight 100, a Douglas DC-8-53, registered HB-IDD, and named *Nidwalden* was carrying 143 passengers and twelve crew from Zürich-Kloten Airport, Switzerland, to New York JFK. The plane was hijacked minutes after the TWA flight and diverted to Jordan. It also landed at Dawson's Field, increasing the hostage number to 306 hostages.

Pan American Flight 93, a Boeing 747, tail number N752PA named *Clipper Fortune* was carrying 136 passengers and seventeen crew. The

flight was from Brussels, Belgium, to New York, with a stop in Amsterdam. The two hijackers bumped from the El Al flight boarded and hijacked this flight as a target of opportunity.

The 747 first landed in Beirut, where it refueled and picked up several associates of the hijackers, along with enough explosives to destroy the entire aircraft. It then landed in Cairo after uncertainty whether the Dawson's Field airport could handle the size of the 747. Flight director John Ferruggio led the plane's evacuation, and is credited with saving the plane's passengers and crew. The airliner was blown up at Cairo seconds after it had been evacuated. The hijackers were arrested by Egyptian police.

Finally, on 9 September a fifth airliner, BOAC Flight 775 from Bombay to London via Bahrain and Beirut - operated by Vickers VC10 G-ASGN, was hijacked after departing Bahrain and forcibly landed at Dawson's Field. This was the work of a PFLP sympathizer who wanted to influence the British government to free Leila Khaled.

On 7 September the hijackers held a press conference for members of the media who had made their way to what was being called "Revolution Airport." About 125 hostages were transferred to Amman, while the American, Israeli, Swiss, and West German citizens were held on the planes.

As groups of the remaining passengers and crew were assembled on the sand in front of the media, members of the PFLP, among them Bassam Abu Sharif, made statements to the press. Sharif claimed that the goal of the hijackings was '*...to gain the release of all of our political prisoners jailed in Israel in exchange for the hostages.*'

In the United States, President Richard Nixon met with his advisers on 8 September and ordered United States Secretary of Defense Melvin Laird to bomb

Opposite page: A line up of German Cargo 707-320C-Hs at a very wet Frankfurt. Closest to the camera is D-ABUA with its cargo door open, with D-ABUO and D-ABUE behind. (Lufthansa GMbH)

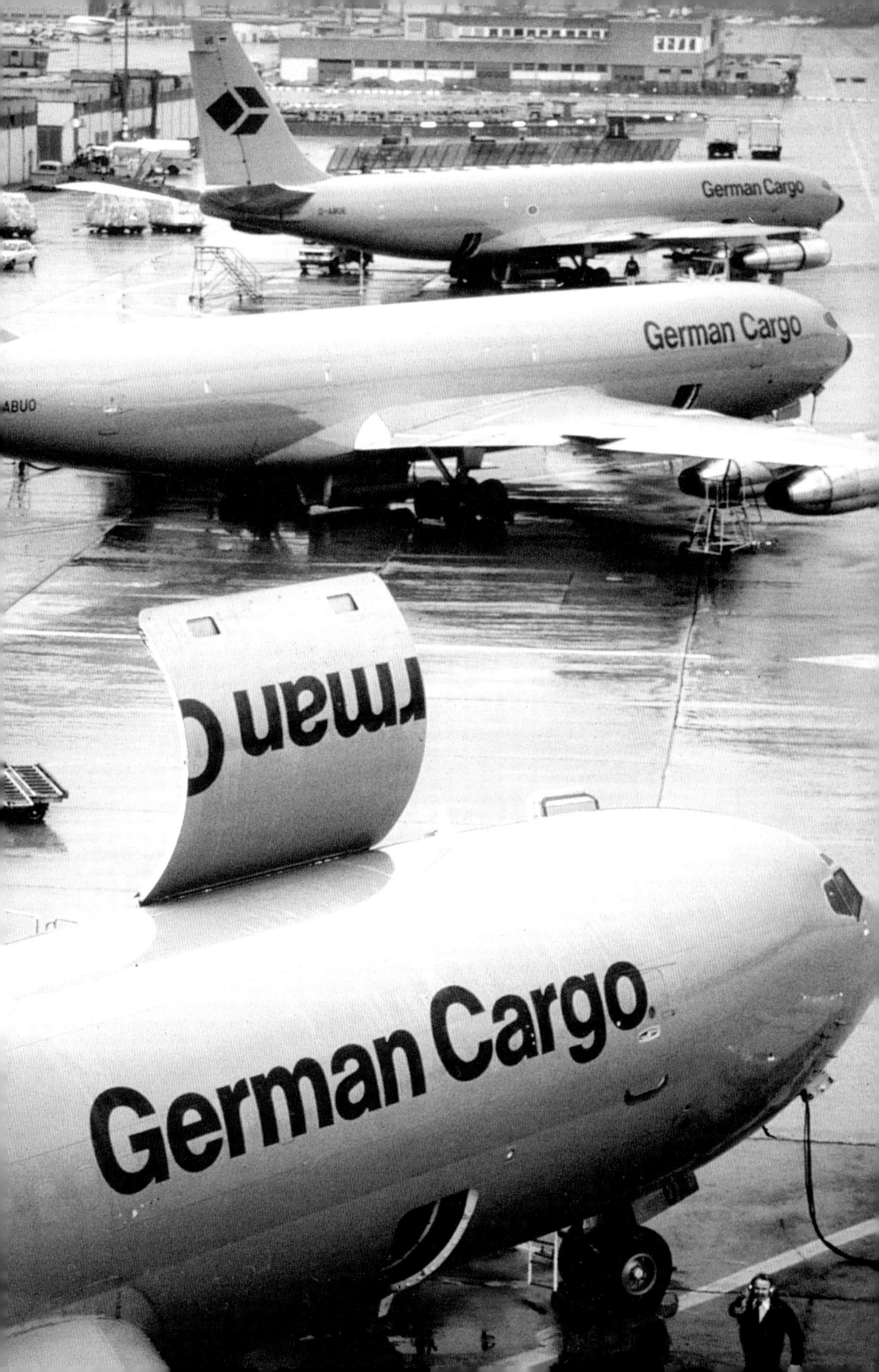
German Cargo
German Cargo
ABUO
German Cargo

BEA Airtours' G-APFD was originally delivered to BOAC in 1959 -it passed to Airtours in 1973. (author's collection)

the PFLP positions in Jordan. Laird refused on the pretext that the weather was unfavorable, and the idea was dropped. The 82nd Airborne Division was put on alert, the Sixth Fleet was put to sea, and military aircraft were sent to Turkey in preparation for a possible military strike.

In contrast, British Prime Minister Edward Heath decided to negotiate with the hijackers, ultimately agreeing to release Khaled and others in exchange for hostages. This was bitterly opposed by the USA.

On 9 September the United Nations Security Council demanded the release of the passengers, in Resolution 286. The following day, fighting between the PFLP and Jordanian forces erupted in Amman at the Intercontinental Hotel, where the 125 women and children were being kept by the PFLP, and the Kingdom appeared to be on the brink of full-scale civil war. The destruction of the aircraft on 12 September highlighted the impotence of the Jordanian government in Palestinian-controlled areas, and the Palestinians declared the city of Irbid to be 'liberated territory', in a direct challenge to Hussein's rule.

On 13 September the BBC World Service broadcast a government announcement in Arabic saying that the UK would release Khaled in exchange for the hostages.

Complicating the international crisis was the fact that Syria and Iraq, which had links with the USSR, had already threatened to intervene on behalf of Palestinian groups in any confrontation with the

Kingdom of Jordan. According to British documents declassified under the thirty year rule, an anxious King Hussein asked the United States and UK to pass a request to Israel to bomb Syrian troops if they entered Jordan in support of the Palestinians. When a Syrian tank crossed the border, Israeli aircraft overflew the area in warning.

King Hussein declared martial law on 16 September and initiated the military actions later known as the Black September conflict.

About two weeks after the start of the crisis, the remaining hostages were recovered from locations around Amman and exchanged for Leila Khaled and several other PFLP prisoners. The hostages were flown to Cyprus and then to Rome's Leonardo da Vinci Airport, where on 28 September they met President Nixon, who was conducting a State visit to Italy and the Vatican.

During the crisis, on 11 September President Nixon initiated a programme to address the problem of air piracy, including the immediate launch of a group of 100 federal agents to begin serving as armed sky marshals on US flights. Nixon's statement further indicated the US departments of Defense and Transportation would determine whether X-ray devices then available to the military could be moved into civilian service.

The PFLP officially disavowed the tactic of airline hijackings several years later, although several of its members and subgroups continued to hijack aircraft and commit other violent operations.

720 4X-BMA of MAOF, an Israeli charter airline formed in early 80's. MAOF used a pair of ex-Monarch Airline 720's around around Europe. (author's collection)

The passengers and crew were spared at Dawson's Field, which was not the case three years later at Rome's Leonardo da Vinci Airport.

On 17 December 1973, Pan Am Flight 110 was scheduled to fly from Leonardo da Vinci International Airport in Rome to Beirut International Airport in Lebanon and then on to Tehran, Iran. At the controls of the Boeing 707-321B, tail number N407PA, and named Clipper Celestial were Captain Andrew Erbeck,First Officer Robert Davison, and Flight engineer Kenneth Pfrang.

At approximately 13:10 local time, just as Flight 110 was preparing to taxi, a number of Palestinian people made their way through the terminal building, armed with automatic firearms and grenades. The terrorists removed submachine guns from hand luggage bags and began firing throughout the terminal, shattering windows and killing two. Crew on the flight deck of the aircraft were able to observe travelers and airport employees in the building running for cover. Captain Erbeck announced over the airliner's public address system that there was some commotion in the terminal and ordered all on board to get down on the floor.

Several of the gunmen ran across the tarmac toward the Pan American jet, throwing at least two phosphorus incendiary hand grenades through the open front and rear doors of the aircraft. The explosions knocked crew and passengers to the ground, and the cabin filled with thick, acrid smoke from the resulting fires. Flight attendants were able to open the emergency exit over the wing on one side of the aircraft; the other was obstructed by gunmen. The crew attempted to evacuate as many passengers as possible through the available exit, but twenty-nine passengers and Purser Diana Perez died on the aircraft, including all eleven passengers in the first class section. Four Moroccan officials heading to Iran for a visit, and Bonnie Erbeck, wife of the captain,

were among the dead. Captain Erbeck survived the attack. Also killed were fourteen Aramco employees and employee family members. The aircraft was destroyed.

Other gunmen later hijacked a Lufthansa 737and fled to Kuwait via Athens, Greece and Damascus in The Lebanon.

In many ways the Lebanon was pivotal to deliberate 707 and 720 destruction. Middle East Airlines (MEA) of Lebanon operated thirty- two 707 and 720 'Cedarjets' from 1968 and lost at least fourteen of them. Only one loss was an accident, the rest being the result of civil war and regional strife. The first was destroyed in 1968 within six weeks of delivery by Israeli commandos who landed by Super Frélon helicopter at Beirut Airport and blew it up in a retaliatory raid for a terrorist attack on Israeli passengers at Athens. During the Israeli invasion of 1982, Beirut Airport was shelled heavily, and no less than six 707s and 720s were lost on 22 June of that year alone. With a much-reduced fleet, no airport and not much of a country left, the battered but determined MEA continued in business by operating from France and by leasing many aircraft out.

Another incident happened on 20 April 1978, an involved a Korean Air Lines 707. The aircraft was HL-7429, a former Pan Am 707-321B, recently purchased from ATASCO and operating as KAL Flight 902 from Paris to Seoul via Anchorage with ninety-seven passengers and thirteen crew members. Soviet air defense fighters shot down KAL 902 near Murmansk in the Soviet Union, after the airliner violated Soviet airspace and failed to respond to Soviet ground control and interceptors.

KAL 902 had departed from Paris, France on a course to Seoul, South Korea. The aircraft's only scheduled stop was in Anchorage, Alaska, USA where it would refuel and proceed to Seoul, avoiding Soviet airspace. As the airliner passed over Alert, the

There seems to be few photographs of American Travel Air. Operating in 1983, this 720 was an ex Aer Lingus aircraft that flew for Ambassadair and American Trans Air prior to American Travel Air. In 1986 it was flying for Airfast. (author's collection)

Middle East Airlines (MEA) of Lebanon lost a number of 707s and 720s during that country's prolonged civil war. OD-AFP, closest to the camera was destroyed by Israeli shelling at Beirut, one of four MEA 720s lost that day. Sister airliner OD-AFE, the second in line in this picture was damaged that month but served with MEA until 1997. OD-AFQ later became an engine testbed with Pratt & Whitney of Canada. (author's collection)

northernmost permanently inhabited place in the world, 508 miles from the North Pole on Ellesmere Island - flight captain Kim Chang Kyu suddenly changed his course and headed southeast toward Murmansk.

The aircraft was not fitted with an inertial navigation system, and GPS navigation was not available at the time. Due to an error in calculating magnetic declination, the airliner flew in an enormous, right-turning arc. The location of the turn corresponded quite closely with the location of the North Magnetic Pole, which is likely to have contributed to, if not directly caused, the error.

It flew southeast over the Svalbard archipelago and the Barents Sea, past northern Scandinavia and into Soviet airspace.

Soviet air defence radar spotted the aircraft approximately 250 miles away from Soviet territorial waters. At first, the Soviets assumed it was a naval aircraft that was returning from a mission, and had forgotten to change its IFF transponder code. When the Korean aircraft passed over the Kola Peninsula at 21:19 (Moscow time), Soviet air defence dispatched Captain Alexander Bosov to intercept.

Bosov, who was flying a Sukhoi Su-15, incorrectly identified the airliner as a United States Air Force reconnaissance RC-135. When reporting back to Tsarkov, Bosov said he could see a maple leaf on the airliner's tail, implying that it belonged to NATO. After a few moments he corrected himself, stating that he could see Chinese characters and the maple leaf was actually a red stork with wings spread.

According to Kim's account of the attack, the interceptor approached his aircraft from the right side rather than the left as required by International Civil Aviation Organization regulations. Kim decreased his speed and turned on the navigation lights, indicating that he was ready to follow the Soviet fighter for landing.

Soviet reports, however, state that the intruder repeatedly ignored commands to follow the interceptor, and KAL 902 began drifting toward Finland. However, tapes released by Rovaniemi Area Control Centre show that Kim transmitted a call signal three times immediately prior to being shot down and attempted to communicate with the intercepting pilot.

Vladimir Tsarkov, commander of the 21st Soviet Air Defence Corps, ordered Bosov to take down the airliner, as it had failed to respond to repeated orders to land, and was approaching the Soviet border with Finland.

Bosov tried to convince his superiors that the airliner was not a military threat, but after receiving orders to shoot it down, he fired a pair of R-60 missiles. The first missile flew past the target. The second one hit the left wing, knocking off approximately four meters of its length. The missile also punctured the fuselage, causing rapid decompression and jamming one of the airliner's four engines.

After being hit, the airliner quickly descended from an altitude of 30,000 ft. It fell into a cloud, disappearing from Soviet air defence radars. Soviets mistook the part of the wing that had fallen off Flight 902 for a winged missile and dispatched another Su-15 interceptor to fire at it. Anatoly Kerefov, another Soviet pilot, replaced Bosov because his aircraft was running low on fuel.

For the next 40 minutes, Flight 902 flew across the whole Kola Peninsula at a low altitude, searching for a place to land. After several unsuccessful attempts at landing, Kim brought the airliner down on the ice of the frozen Korpiyarvi lake in Karelian ASSR, located approximately 87 miles from the Finnish border.

Finnish sources state that Soviet air defense did not have any information on the airliner's whereabouts after it disappeared from the radar. However, Tsarkov stated that Kerefov located Flight 902 and led it to the Afrikanda air base. Tsarkov went on to say that Kim fell behind and landed on the

Three views of 707 HL-7429 operating as Flight KAL 902 after it was downed by Soviet fighters on 20 April 1978, the airliner eventually making a forced landing onto the frozen lake at Korpiyarvi. The pilot managed to get it to stop just before it hit a stand of trees. Damage to the wing and fuselage is evident.
(all author's collection)

HL-7406 was built for Korean Airlines in 1971. In 1978 it returned the passengers from KAL902, brought down by Russian fighters near Murmansk, from Helsinki back to Seoul. On 29 November 1987 this 707 was brought down by a bomb left aboard by two North Korean agents and crashed off the Western coast of Burma, killing all 115 aboard. The agents, a 24-year-old woman and a 70-year-old man were arrested in Bahrain, but the man committed suicide soon afterwards. The woman was convicted but later pardoned by the South Korean government. (author's collection)

lake. Kerefov said he practically forced the aircraft to land on the ice of Korpiyarvi.

Soviet helicopters rescued the 107 survivors and transported them to the city of Kem in Karelia. The passengers were quartered in the garrison's Officers' Lodge. After two days at the Murmansk Airport, the passengers were released to the US Consulate in Leningrad. The crew was held for investigation and released after making a formal apology. The Korean pilots acknowledged that they deliberately failed to obey the commands of Soviet interceptors. They petitioned the Presidium of the Supreme Soviet of the USSR for pardon.

Eventually, the passengers were deported from the Soviet Union back to Seoul. The Soviet Union invoiced South Korea $US100,000 for caretaking expenses.

TASS, the official news agency of the Soviet Union, released a statement to the public on 30 April 1978. The Soviet Union refused to cooperate with international experts while they investigated the incident and did not provide any data mined from the aircraft's flight data recorder. The airliner was dismantled and all equipment transferred by helicopter onto a barge in Kandalaksha Gulf. The deputy chief commanding officer of Soviet air defense, Yevgeniy Savitsky, personally inspected the pilot's cockpit.

The incident was a major embarrassment to Soviet air defence because Flight 902 had already entered Soviet territory before it was intercepted. This led to a shift in command and contributed to the shooting down of another Korean Airlines flight, KAL 007, in 1983, which killed all aboard.

Drugs and arms - anything to anywhere.
The 'fall from grace' as it were in the twilight years of the 707/720 saw the type descend from the glory and glamour days of the high life with the jet-set in the late 1950s to to murky world of arms dealers and drug-cartels. A whole industry of less-than-legitimate customers thrived, with aircraft being repeatedly leased and sub-leased without the manufacturer having a say in such transactions. Some were shady drug-cartels, others arms dealers. Some operated 707 by 'front airlines' on behalf of organisations such as the Central Intelligence Agency.

Not surprisingly, some of these aircraft ended up being confiscated as the result of their use in drug-smuggling or illicit arms-smuggling activities. Others soldiered on, getting more and more decrepit.

As for the pilots operating these geriatric jets? They are anonymous, professional, highly paid and as mercenary as any of the combatants in the scores of wars from which they make their living. And when they fly their cargoes of weapons or troops into yet another bush conflict, their primary aim, after getting out alive, is to keep their actions secret.

In a rare breach of his profession's code of silence, one of the most experienced 'freelance cargo pilots' has spoken out about his career.

Brian 'Sport' Martin flew with the UK charter airline Dan-Air for a while. In 2000 he broke the code of silence to explain a little about his activities.

He describes how he has made his living flying armaments, including key components in nuclear weapons programmes, all over the world. Not only has he been able to work unhindered by Western governments, on several occasions - he claims -

British and American officials hired him for clandestine work. He talked about his work in the early nineteen eighties flying Chinese 'heavy water' - used in the construction of nuclear reactors and weapons - to India, Argentina and Libya.

I spoke with him at length at a Dan-Air reunion in 2000, and he was telling me about his recent times flying general supplies, and '...*whatever the military would turn up with*' to Ugandan-backed rebels in the east of Congo from Entebbe airport.

He said he had flown 707s registered in Swaziland for two Congolese carriers, Planet Air and New Goma Air, from Entebbe in Uganda, and Kigali in Rwanda.

'*We mostly carried brand new Kalashnikovs plus their ammunition. They were in quite beautiful condition. It was a standard operation for us. You don't really know there is a war on. You're not involved - you're just charter pilots.*' Many were recruited by companies based on England's south coast and in London. Others were hired by local agencies. One, Planetair, which employed Martin for the trips into Congo, had been mentioned in a report into the reasons for the ongoing wars in Africa published by the US State Department.

Sport also told me that he had flown samples of new Soviet weaponry, clandestinely obtained behind the Iron Curtain, to testing grounds on the east coast of America from East German airfields.

Although the pilots were unlikely to fall foul of British law, they were aware of the risks they were taking. Martin had been jailed in Venezuela and spent three days in a cell packed with violent and starved prisoners in Nigeria. He escaped only after paying a $10,000 bribe.

On other occasions he has narrowly avoided being shot down. While flying government soldiers into the Sudan, rebels attempted to down his 707 with Soviet-made surface-to-air missiles. By approaching airstrips at speed Martin had avoided being hit by anything other than heavy-machine gun fire.

Flying into the central African state of Burundi in the middle of a war also proved tricky. On his final approach into Bujumbura airport, Martin was unable to raise anybody in the control tower. When he finally did so he was told to abort the landing. While arguing with the controllers he heard a loud bang. The tower had been hit by a rocket and destroyed.

Further research into the activities of the arms smugglers - or drug dealers for that matter - is fraught with contradictions, difficulties and danger. Prior to my meeting with Sport Martin, I had met and talked with people like William 'Bill' Armstrong, founder of Autair International and the owner of, in his own words '...*more airlines than I care to remember*'. Bill knew and worked with such people as Texan Hank Warton and South African Jack Malloch. As I grew more and more 'trusted' by these people, plus getting to know some of the 'characters' that hung around the fringes of the embrionic aviation museum at Duxford in the early 1970s - and who still must remain nameless - I started to get an insight into the wheeling and dealings that went on between between contract pilots, multi-layered company ownership, fake aircraft registrations, government contracts, front companies and political machinations.

After talking with Sport Martin I did further research and uncovered a story that was typical - if there is such a thing - of these sorts of flying.

In August 1997 a newspaper report indicated that Occidental Airlines, a company based at Ostend Airport was under investigation by the public prosecutor of Bruges. Until 1998 Occidendal Aviation Services NV, as the company was officially registered at the Ostend Commercial Trade Register, had its own large warehouse next to the airport control tower. Apparently it was allegedly owned a former Belgian airline pilot, Ronald Rossignol, together with Brian Martin.

A search through assorted trade and telephone

EL-AKJ in full Occidental Cargo colours. (author's collection)

directories realed the following: *OCCIDENTAL AIRLINES, S.A.: P.O. Box 32, Ostend Airport, B-8400, Belgium; Phone 32 59 514340; Fax 32 59 510103; Code OCT; Year Founded 1995. Registered in Belgium and based in Nigeria, Occidental set up in 1995 to undertake international and regional all-cargo services. Flights commence with one each leased Boeing 707- 321C and B-707-328C. Flights continue in 1996-2000. during which years a B-707-347C is also acquired.*

Aircraft spotters are regarded by some in derogatory terms, but not me. They have an invaluable information network that can provide all sorts of details: *Occidental Airlines Fleet: 707-321C EL-AKJ c/n 19375; 707-3230 9G-ADS c/n 19587; 707-347C EL-AKU c/n 19964. The airline took delivery of a -320C in May 1995 to operate charters from Ghana to other points in Africa and to Europe. It is not confirmed whether the Liberian registered -347C is an addition or replacement from late 1995. Both were noted with no titles by late December 1995, the owned example being transferred to Analinda and operated for SABENA in early 1996. The -321C was leased from July 1996 to May 1998.*

Ronald Rossignol was the son of a senior political appointee in the office of P. Van den Boeynants, at the time when the latter was serving as Belgium's Minister of Defence. Ronald Rossignol had, prior to 1980, close connections with Brussels extreme right wing circles. Since 1980 it was alleged that he had been involved in business with the Congo's erstwhile President Mobutu. According to the Belgian newspaper *Le Soir,* his name appeared on Interpol lists and he was arrested in 1984 in France and accused of fraudulent bankruptcy, to the extent of some 800 million Belgian francs.

Despite the dubious past of Ronald Rossignol being placed once more under judicial scrutiny, a senior civil servant of the Flemish authorities, Paul Waterlot, responsible for Ostend Airport's promotion and information, defended Rossignol publicly in the press and reaffirmed in the name of the airport's management board, full confidence in the aims of, and the services provided by, Occidental Airlines.

The subject of the judicial investigation was a cargo of nearly forty tonnes of military equipment, to be sent to governmental or rebel forces in Angola. An Avistar Airlines Boeing 707 freighter, Cyprus-registered as 5B-DAZ, was chartered for the trip by Occidental Airlines. Pending a Belgian Customs investigation the consignment, consisting of Dutch Army surplus items, had been impounded in Occidental's warehouse for nine months. The cargo manifest showed an innocuous cargo of used clothing, vehicle parts and vehicles, but the cargo consisted of twenty tonnes of uniforms, an armoured car, multi-band radios and other equipment needed by a fighting force. After being impounded for nine months, the consignment was granted permission to be exported to England and was merely sent across the Channel by truck without arousing further interest.

On 12 May 1998 the Avistar aircraft took off from the civil airport side of RAF Manston in Kent, bound for Africa. The flight plan showed that the aircraft was bound for Kano in Nigeria to refuel and then to its reported final destination of Mmabatho in South Africa. After taking off from Kano, the aircraft temporarily disappeared. It never landed on Mmabatho's runway, actually too short for a fully-laden Boeing 707, but it was observed around 04.00 hours on 13 May on the ground at Cabinda, Angola and reappeared some hours later at Lomé in Togo, empty.

According to the UK newspaper *The Observer* of 14 March 1999, the same aircraft 5B-DAZ, which in 1997 made some twenty-eight flights from Ostend flew, in December 1998, a cargo of weapons and

Looking rather tatty, and completely unmarked apart from the registration 9G-ADS, this -323C of Occidental has all the passenger windows plugged up.
(author's collection)

Not terrorist related, but a dramatic image nevertheless: the aircraft is China Airlines 707-309C B-1826, which caught fire and burnt out after it undershot the runway at Manilla International Airport on 27 February 1980. Of the 135 occupanrts on board, only two passengers received fatal injuries. (author's collection)

ammunition from Hermes, the former Slovak state-owned arms' manufacturer in Bratislava, to the Sudan, in breach of an European Union embargo. The money paid by Hermes for the flight was split between the pilot, the crew and Ronald Rossignol, who acted as broker. While on its way for another delivery to the Sudan and again chartered by Rossignol, the aircraft left Bratislava on 7 February 1999, failed to achieve sufficient speed and ploughed into the mud at the end of the runway. Because of its long list of ongoing malfunctions, it was decided not to repair the aircraft.

Ronald Rossignol succeeded in his efforts to remain outside the grip of Belgian justice, which probably had insufficient legal grounds to take him into custody. The incapacity of local justice illustrates clearly the need for comprehensive international legislation and law enforcement, as well as underlining the ease with which arms' brokers are able to take advantage of gaps within and between national legal systems.

Into the twilight

Notwithstanding the availability of hushkits bringing JT3D-powered 7075 into compliance with Stage 2 and Stage 3 noise regulations, the number of civilian operators of early Boeing jetliners was fast dwindling.

Although by the turn of the millennium the 707 had all but completely left passenger service, numerous freight operators around the world continued to operate the type in ones and twos. Often subject to poorer operating and maintenance standards than they enjoyed in their heydays as part of a large passenger fleet, and periodically, the numbers of 707s in service was reduced by a mishap to one in some far-flung corner of the world. One such event which occurred without loss of life,

Two views of 707 ST-APY in Lake Victoria. (author's collection)

occurred near Mwanza, Tanzania, on 3 February 2000 and was not without its elements of comedy.

One-time Northwest Orient's N372US, 707-351C had served with BWIA and seven other lesser operators before joining Trans-Arabian Air Transport (TAAT) in 1985. Registered ST-APY in April, 1998, and long since converted to freight configuration, the airliner was en route on a night flight from Khartoum, Sudan to Mwanza on the Tanzanian shore of Lake Victoria to pick up a 38 tonne load of fish fillets from Vick Fish Processors for delivery in Europe.

When it went dark en route to Mwanza, the radio altimeter integral light was found to be unserviceable. The crew were not able to fix the problem and the continued using the FMS. The crew contacted Mwanza tower at 16:58 and were being advised that there was no power at the airport and that efforts were being made to use a standby generator. Further information passed on the crew reportedly included VOR, DME and NDB all unserviceable, weather: wind calm, 8 km visibility, temperature 25deg C and QNH 1015. The airport's elevation is listed as being 3763 feet /1147 metres. After holding for ten minutes, the airport generator came on and the runway lights went on.

The first officer, who was pilot flying, started a visual runway 12 approach. When well established on finals with full landing configuration, the captain told the first officer that he was too low, and a few seconds later he told the first officer he was too high. Both the captain and the flight engineer then told the first officer to go around. The first officer overshot and climbed to 5500 feet on the downwind leg. Turning on the left base the captain remarked that the turn was too tight: ".. *I will do a 360-degree turn to the right and position you finals*". The captain thus took over control and started a right turn at 4400 feet. Just before completing the turn, the first officer said: *"do not go down anymore, the altimeter is reading 4100 feet"*. Almost aligned with the runway, the first officer took over control again. At that same moment the aircraft bounced two or three times yawing to the left and came down to a halt in the middle of the lake, losing all four engines in the process, floating about 3 miles offshore. The external lights guided a fishing boat to the scene and the five crew were rescued uninjured. The next day the airliner was towed to the lakeshore, where it remained as a visual beacon for some years to come, and ironically, a home for relatives of the fish it arrived to pick up.

Chapter Seven

'Ladies and Gentlemen, from the Flight Deck...'

Of the many airlines using previously owned 707s, Dan-Air Services, part of the Davies & Newman Group is a good example, and Australian-born Operations Director Captain Arthur Larkman describes their introduction to service and use.

'It was Alan Snudden, the then Managing Director of Dan-Air, who started our entry in the long haul charter market using 707s carrying affinity groups. He had had many discussions with various people who had made the original proposal to engage in these charters. When Alan became convinced that this could be a sensible way for the Company to begin its expansion into the long haul market, he persuaded the Board to approve the plan.

When this decision was taken the first step was to set up a company entitled 'Dan-Air InterContinental' to deal with the commercial aspects of the operation. As the Government strictly limited the number of airlines who were permitted to operate scheduled flights on international routes, all other British carriers were limited to Charter flights. A method had already been devised which would enable the operation of consecutive flights. This was known as 'affinity group' charters and involved the targeting of groups of people who shared a common interest, most often members of clubs. These groups were offered a specially arranged flight to a trans-Atlantic destination at much reduced cost. When the number who wanted to travel was sufficient to fill the seats, the organisers would charter an aircraft. It was obvious that the real economies required a return load and a few people, like Ron

Bryant, saw the opportunity of putting together a sufficient number of these groups who could time their journeys so that an aircraft could carry a full load to a destination and return with another full load. When sufficient flights were programmed for this 'back to back' system, a much lower charter price could be offered and this attracted yet more groups. By diligent marketing it was expected that sufficient flights could be organised to support the operation of a long haul aircraft.

C.I.Smith, who had been appointed Projects Manager by Frank Horridge, was tasked with recommending suitable aircraft for our requirements. Pan-American were disposing of their Boeing 707-321s at a comparatively low cost at that time, and 'Charlie Item' proposed that the Company should buy them. The decision was made to purchase these aircraft, together with the full package of support including spares and training. Unfortunately the choice of aircraft was not a wise one as this series aircraft was an early type with high hours and, therefore, greater maintenance requirements. With its limited range when carrying a full load the type was not really a Trans-Atlantic aircraft. This decision was destined to present us with many problems on our future Trans-Atlantic operation.

Pan-American sent a technical lecturer to the UK to instruct the first course of pilots and flight engineers, which was conducted in the Training Centre which I had set up at Horsham. The subjects covered on the course were typical of those on all aircraft conversion courses and included the power plant and

A Travel Agent's display model announcing the new Dan-Air 707.

Right: at the office - Captain Arthur Larkman in the left hand seat of one of the Dan-Air 707s.

Below: the famous 707 vertical fin appeared on the Dan-Air Summer timetable for 1974.

DAN→AIR

TIMETABLE **SUMMER 1974**

Valid 1st April–26th October 1974

could be practiced. We were already equipped with projectors for transparencies, films etc. Examinations were held at regular intervals throughout the course and on its completion the CAA's exams were undertaken.

I joined the B-707 course at Horsham on the 11th. The crews on this course included Bob Atkins, John Cotter, George Sutton, Alan Farrar, Sam Bee, Bob Hope, Gordon Pumphrey, Ken Topliffe and Flight Engineers Bill Snow, Cliff Lewton, Ned Cleary, Alec Ewen and Tim Ware.

The Boeing ground course was completed on 29 January and the next day we flew to New York, where we were to be trained on the simulator at Pan-Am's Training Center at Kennedy Airport. We stayed at the Ramada Inn, which was sufficiently close to the airport boundary for us to be able to walk to and from the Training Center.

Pan-Am had arranged our accommodation very cleverly, for there was nothing to distract us from our studies. The facilities at the training centre were very good and the instruction was first class. The instructors were pilots who had been seconded from the line and were now occupied solely with training, although they were scheduled for occasional line flights to keep them current. One of my instructors was Bob Dooley, an ex-Airforce bomber pilot who before joining Pan-Am had been a Commander of Airforce One (the President's aircraft). One of Bob's recommended procedures for dealing with an emergency on the aircraft was to say-- 'Aw Sh-t', before dealing with the problem. This was wise advice, designed to avoid precipitate action before analysing the problem.

After returning to the UK I commenced the base training on the 707 which I had planned to take place

its accessories, the airframe, including the electrical, fuel, pneumatic, hydraulic, and electronic systems. Navigation Aids, emergency equipment and procedures, performance data, cruise control, flight planning and loading plus much more. To assist with the training we obtained system mock-ups, panel trainers and a Cockpit Procedure Trainer which was a flight deck mock up in which drills and procedures

at Newcastle as usual. The instructors were Bob Dooley and Al Bernstein, who worked us very hard but managed to make the experience very enjoyable. When this training was completed I returned to Gatwick to prepare the 707 line training programme. Pan-Am was sending to the UK the line training Captains who would fly with us on the line flights and complete our training. My priorities were to arrange their accommodation and to have their Licences endorsed by the CAA which would give them approval to fly in command of a British aircraft. I had already provided the CAA with all the details of the Pan-Am pilots, and the approvals were issued without any delay.

To save expense I housed them in one of the local guest houses and told them that this would be much more enjoyable than an impersonal hotel as they would be able to get to know more of English life in the countryside. My fingers were crossed as I

expected that they would demand accommodation in a hotel in a town. I had already visited several establishments in the area and selected those most likely to be acceptable. When the Captains arrived from New York it was a warm and sunny April day. I drove them to the first establishment on the list but there was no reply at the front door so we made our way to the garden at the rear. We were somewhat surprised to find the two youngish women who ran the guest house, with whom I had previously discussed the arrangements, were sitting in their swimming costumes alongside the small swimming pool. Introductions were made and while drinks were brought, one of the pilots spoke for the others when he said 'This will do just fine'. I left them there and never heard any complaint about accommodation!

The inaugural flight of our first 707, G-AYSL, on which my line training began, was to Niagara Falls. We set off with a full load of passengers and re-fuelled

The Captain's and First Officer's Control panels on Dan-Air's 707 G-AYSL.

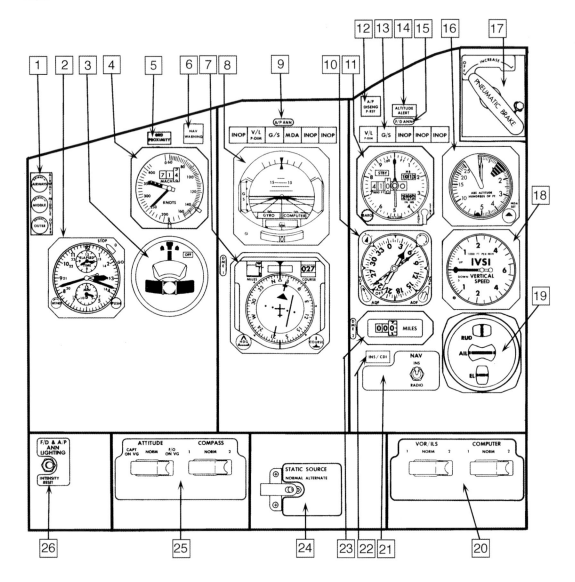

Captain's Panel

1 Marker Beacon System.
2 Clock.
3 Turn and Bank Indicator.
4 Machmeter.
5 Ground Proximity Warning Light.
6 Nav Warning Light.
7 Horizontal Situation Indicator
8 Attitude Director Indicator.
9 Approach Progress Display.
10 Radio Magnetic Indicator.

11 Servo-Pneumatic Altimeter.
12 Autopilot disengaged warning light.
13 Approach Progress Display.
14 Altitude Warning Light
15 Flight Director
16 Radio Altimeter
17 Pneumatic Brake Handle
18 Vertical Speed Indicator
19 Trim Indicator
20 Integrated Flight System Transfer Switches

21 Radio/Instrument Navigation System Selector.
22 Instrument Navigation System/CDI light.
23 Distance Measuring Equipment Indicator.
24 Pitot-Static Selector.
25 Integrated Flight System Transfer Switches
26 Flight Director & Autopilot Annunicator Lighting Intensity Reset Switch.

at Shannon as we were too heavy to carry the fuel required for a non-stop flight. We nightstopped at Niagara while another crew who had positioned there as passengers flew the aircraft back to Gatwick. From there another crew flew the aircraft to New York. The day after our arrival at Niagara we travelled by taxi to Buffalo where we took a scheduled flight to La Guardia. At La Guardia we again took taxis to John F Kennedy, New York's main international airport. We met our aircraft, Sierra Lima, there and flew it to Toronto, where another crew were waiting to take it to Gatwick. The aircraft was then flown to New York and was returning to Gatwick with a few empty seats which, to save airfares, we could use for our return to the UK From Toronto, therefore, we positioned on a scheduled flight to JFK, and then took taxis to the North Passenger Terminal where our aircraft was arriving. This complicated mixture of flights and travelling was the result of the many and varied destinations to which we operated and was to be the pattern of our existence for some years to come. After my return to the UK I attended three meetings in London with Air Spain in quick succession and two days later I flew IT charters on the 707 to Palma and to Prestwick, then from Luton to Munich, followed by a flight to Nairobi. After returning from Nairobi to Gatwick, a flight to New York followed--a busy April.

In June I flew several trips to Toronto from both Gatwick and Prestwick. At Toronto it was interesting to observe a variation on airport terminal arrangements that I had previously only seen in the

Above: Four of the Stewardesses who were to fly regularly on the 707. Left to Right: Miss Dilys Ruffle, Miss Riley Siponen, Miss C Brewen and Miss Jackie Gallagher, 707 Fleet Stewardess.

Below: 707 G-AYSL being loaded with passengers at London Gatwick prior to its first commercial service with the company on 8 April 1971. The flight, under the command of Captain Bob Atkins, Dan-Air's Chief Pilot, was to Niagara Falls, Canada.

third world. All arriving passengers exited Customs through a door which opened directly into the terminal landside area. Our 189 passengers had to force their way through at least as many welcoming relatives and friends crowding the doorway. It was completely chaotic and always took a long time for the hundreds of people and their baggage to become disentangled. A positive factor was the evident enthusiasm of the welcome, although if more than one aircraft had arrived, things tended to get out of hand. Among other flights I made that month were to Vancouver and to Seattle. One of the staff of Sea-Tac, our handling agents at Seattle, was Barbara Walder. Barbara later joined Dan-Air at Gatwick and was my Secretary for many years.

The 707 destinations were very varied and this made the operation much more interesting. For example one of the flights I made in October was from Toronto to Barbados. We were positioning empty to Gatwick from Barbados the next day and Bob Atkins and his crew who had slipped in Toronto from another flight, came as passengers with us to save airfares back to London. Everyone enjoyed the nightstop in Barbados and we all had an early morning swim on the day of departure to freshen up after our night out. On the long ocean crossing only the First Officer, the Flight Engineer and the 'galley hostess' were awake. At one stage in the flight the F/O went back to the cabin to chat to our passengers, and while there he asked the hostess on 'galley' duty to bring up two coffees for the F/E and myself. In the meantime the F/E had gone down into 'Lower 41', a

hold below the flight deck, to check some electrical equipment. When the hostess arrived with the two coffees I was alone, and she asked where the F/E was. Rather cruelly, I didn't tell her but asked her to look for him. In the meantime I told the F/E to remain in the hold. Several minutes later she re-appeared and in a very worried voice said she had looked everywhere and he wasn't on board. I called him on the intercom and said he could come up now and when he climbed up the ladder and opened the hatch in the flight deck floor she was greatly relieved.

One of a series we were operating was a weekly flight to Vancouver. The return flight to Gatwick was operated by a crew already at Vancouver, and the crew which had flown the aircraft in, remained in Vancouver for a week. The aircraft was fully occupied with flights to other destinations during this time before returning to Vancouver, when the slip crew in Vancouver would fly the aircraft back to the UK. The stopover in Vanvouver was always popular as it is a very attractive city with a great many amenities, and is surrounded by areas of interest such as Stanley Park, and skiing on Grouse Mountain which is in North Vancouver on the other side of the inlet. Because of my commitments I could not afford to stay away for so long, so I was able to fly on only one of these very popular trips. In September 1971 I operated a flight whose schedule differed from the usual flights. On this flight the crew had a four day slip in Vancouver and then we were rostered to travel to Seattle where we would meet the aircraft when it landed, and then fly it back to Gatwick.

The 707 was the largest company aircraft the Dan Air engineers at Lasham had to deal with up to this time. Nevertheless, the soon learned the ins and out of the big Boeing. (Dan Air Staff Aassociation)

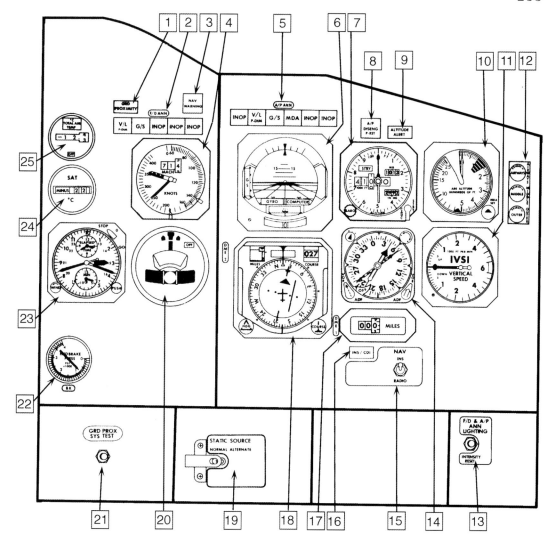

First Officer's Panel

1   Ground Proximity Warning Light.
2   Approach Progress Display. Clock.
3   Nav Warning Light.
4   Machmeter.
5   Flight Director
6   Attitude Director Indicator.
7   Servo-Pneumatic Altimeter.
8   Autopilot disengaged warning light.
9   Altitude Warning Light
10 Radio Altimeter
11 Vertical Speed Indicator

12 Marker Beacon System.
13 Flight Director & Autopilot Annunicator Lighting Intensity Reset Switch.
14 Radio Magnetic Indicator.
15 Radio/Instrument Navigation System Selector.
16 Instrument Navigation System/CDI light.
17 Distance Measuring Equipment Indicator.
18 Horizontal Situation Indicator

19 Pitot-Static Selector.
20 Turn and Bank Indicator. Integrated Flight System Transfer Switches
21 Ground Proximity test switch.
22 Hyraulic Brake Pressure Indicator.
23 Clock.
24 Static Air Temperature Indicator.
25   Total Air Temperature Indicator.

234

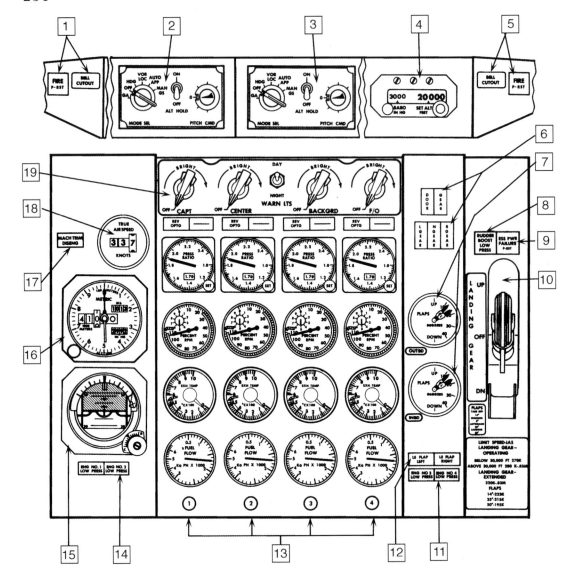

Pilot's Centre Panel and Light Shield.

1. Master Fire Warning Light and Bell Cutout Switch (Captain)
2. Flight Director (1)
3. Flight Director (2)
4. Altitude Selector/Control
5. Master Fire Warning Light and Bell Cutout Switch (First Officer)
6. Landing Gear Warning Lights and Gear Down Lights
7. Flap Position Indicators
8. Rudder Boost Low Pressure Warning Light
9. Essential Power Failure Light.
10. Landing Gear Lever
11. Engine No.3 & 4 Low Oil Pressure /Filter Bypass Warning Light.
12. Leading Edge Flaps Lights
13. Engine Indicators, Bottom to Top: Fluel Flow Ind; Exhaust Gas Temp (EGT); Tachometer; Engine Pressure Ratio (EPR) Ind; Thrust Reverser Operating Light.
14. Engine No.1 & 2 Low Oil Pressure/Filter Bypass Warning Light.
15. Standby Horizon Indicator.
16. Servo-Pneumatic Altimeter.
17. Mach Trim Disengaged Warning Light
18. True Airspeed Indicator.
19. Flight Deck Light Controls.

Al Bernstein, the Pan-Am training Captain, came to the UK in November in order to conduct the bi-annual Competency Checks on our crews and while he was here checked John Cotter and myself out as B-707 Base Training Instructors. This was carried out under the supervision of Captain Spence, a Civil Aviation Flying Unit examiner and Captain Harris, a Ministry Inspector. We were also cleared as Type Rating Examiners on the 707. Al gave me a hard time, covering every type of unusual situation that could arise when instructing a beginner on the type who could put the aircraft into a dangerous position. All types of emergency procedures were practiced, including failing two engines on the same side shortly after I had taken off. I completed the circuit and landed on two engines. The reason for this gruelling trial became clear when sometime later Al suggested I might like a job as a Training Captain with Pan-Am, an offer which I declined.

We purchased a second B-707 from Pan-Am. The Company was expanding rapidly and the administration was running hard to keep up, but the operations staff relished the challenge and the extra activity was absorbed with but little indigestion.

The number of crews on the 707 had to be increased with the addition of another aircraft, so in January '72 John Cotter and Bill Snow, and Tim Ware and I, went to New York to be checked out by the Pan-Am trainers while we gave the full course of conversion training to our crews on the simulator. They included Brian Martin and Brian Zeitlyn, Chuck Smith, Bill Grief and Pat Fry. I fitted in a full programme of training on both the B-707 aircraft and the simulator in New York.

TWA put their 707 simulator up for sale in October 1972 and, as it seemed likely that Dan-Air would expand this fleet. John Cotter and I took the opportunity, during a two day stopover in Toronto, to inspect the simulator which was housed in TWA's training centre in Kansas City. They accommodated us while we assessed its performance, as part of which we flew the same programme on it as we did

when air testing an aircraft for the renewal of its Certificate of Airworthiness. This is a very demanding test covering all aspects of the aircraft's capability including measurement of its performance with engine and systems failures. We found that it did not meet the requirements for CAA approval for mandatory 1179 Check items. This meant that we would have to continue bringing crews to New York to carry out the Mandatory Checks and training on the Pan-Am simulator which was approved.

In March of 1972 the Company organised a sales presentation tour in Western Canada. The Commercial and other Departmental Managers and our PR manager set off in the 707 which I flew to Prestwick where we picked up a reduced load of passengers bound for Calgary. As the aircraft was not full this allowed all our staff to travel together. Alan Snudden had asked my wife Joy to accompany us and assist the PR Manager in spreading the word. In Calgary a round of meetings with Tour Operators and Travel Agents followed, with cocktail parties held in the evenings. I didn't see much of Joy at these occasions as she was always surrounded with people. We then flew on to Edmonton where we repeated the process. The return flight was on March 16th, my birthday. We had passengers for Amsterdam and after unloading them there we positioned back empty to Gatwick. During this short flight the cabin staff asked me to come back and look at a problem in the cabin. Leaving the aircraft in the capable hands of Sam Bee I went back to find a birthday cake, covered in candles, awaiting me.

Air France found themselves short of aircraft in the early summer and contracted us to operate their scheduled services between Orly and Heathrow on our B-707. The flights went very well and the crews very much enjoyed the catering, which was uplifted in Paris. I was intrigued, when I flew the service, to find that the crew meals were accompanied by a carton of small bottles of wine, three red and three white, especially for the use of the flight deck crew. More crew training followed at Newcastle in July

707 G-AYSL awaits it's passengers at London Gatwick prior to its first commercial service with the company on 8 April 1971. (Dan Air Staff Association)

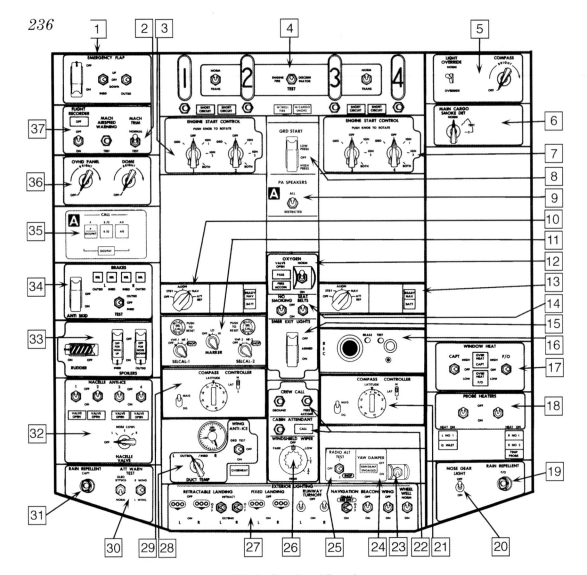

Pilot's Overhead Panel

1 Emergency Flap Switches
2 Mach Trim/Warning
3 Engine Start Controls
4 Fire Detection and Extinguishing Controls.
5 Lighting Controls
6 Hold Smoke Detection
7 Engine Start Controls
8 Ground Start Switch
9 PA Speakers
10 Internal Navigation System Mode Selector Switch.
11 SelCal Controls.
12 Oxygen Controls.
13 Internal Navigation System Mode Selector Switch

14 'No Smoking/Seat Belts' Switch.
15 Emergency Exits Lighting Switch.
16 Cockpit Voice Recorder
17 Window Heat Controls.
18 Probe Heater Controls
19 Rain Repellant Control; First Officer.
20 Nose Gear Light Switch
21 Gyro Compass Controls
22 Ground Crew/Cabin Crew Call Buttons
23 Yaw Damper Switch
24 Yaw Damper Light
25 Radio Altimeter Test Switch

26 Windshield Wiper Controls
27 Exterior Lighting Controls
28 Anti-Ice Controls
29 Gyro Compass Controls
30 Oleo Bypass Test Switch/Attitude Warning Selector and Test Switch.
31 Rain Repellant Control; Captain
32 Nacelle Anti-Ice Controls.
33 Rudder/Spoiler Control switches
34 Anti-Skid brake controls
35 Communications Call System
36 Main Cabin Lights
37 Flight Recorder ON/OFF

Not only did Dan-Air pilots have to learn about flying in to Hong Kong with the 707, but the Stewardesses had to learn about Far-Eastern cuisine! In the mortar-board and gown is Eva Lam, Manager of the Far East travel Centre's Chinese Department. The Dan-Air stewardesses are, from left to right:: Sue Evans, Lynne Boreham, Velma Sharma and Sue Hale. (Dan Air Staff Association)

where I flew with Ken Grover, Keith Moody, Tony Kirk and Stan Lee.

With the addition of a second B-707 the number of trans-Atlantic flights greatly increased. Toronto was now such a frequent destination that Jock Mills, with his wife, took up residence there as our Station Engineer. We had also based Alan Barker in Toronto as our Company representative. Alan had flown with us as a First Officer, but had recently lost his licence on medical grounds. The number of New York flights also increased. Charter aircraft were very often processed at the North Passenger Terminal (NPT), which was on the north side of JFK airport. The facilities were rather primitive although comparatively peaceful compared to the International Terminal in the central area.

One evening, when we had positioned from Toronto to JFK, we were parked at the NPT to embark the passengers waiting there for the flight to UK. The immigration official who met us on our arrival at the NPT told us that he could clear the passengers out of the country, but not the crew as they had not been cleared into the country. I suggested

that he should, therefore, clear us in to the country, but he replied that he was not empowered to deal with persons entering the country, even though we would be leaving the country as soon as our departure procedures were completed. He told us that only the Immigration Officer at the International Arrivals Terminal could clear us and we would have to enter the country there. He could not be persuaded of the illogicality of this so we had no choice but to comply. International Arrivals could only be reached by travelling through the local suburb of Jamaica as there was no connecting road within the airport boundary. We took taxis therefore, out of the Airport boundary, drove through the countryside, and then entered the Airport once again at the International Arrivals Terminal. When we entered the terminal we exited the country through Immigration Control, turned around and were cleared to enter again. The officials here saw nothing wrong with the process as the paperwork was now in order. We went back through the countryside to the NPT by taxi and were then allowed to leave the country.

A very stressful aspect of our turn-rounds at JFK

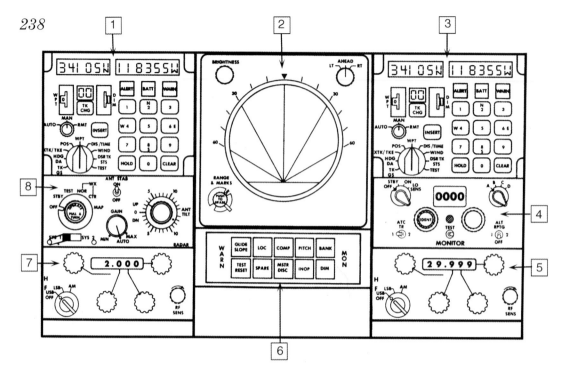

Forward Electronic Control Panel

1 Control Display Unit; Captain
2 Weather radar
3 Control Display Unit; First Officer.

4 ATC Transponder System
HF Radio Controls; First Officer
6 Instrument Comparator

Warning System
7 HF Radio Controls; Captain
8 Antenna Stabiliser Controls.

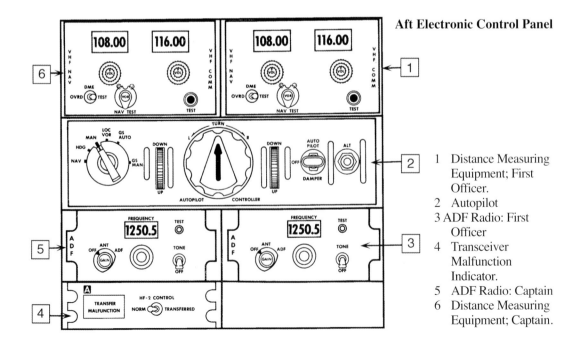

Aft Electronic Control Panel

1 Distance Measuring Equipment; First Officer.
2 Autopilot
3 ADF Radio: First Officer
4 Transceiver Malfunction Indicator.
5 ADF Radio: Captain
6 Distance Measuring Equipment; Captain.

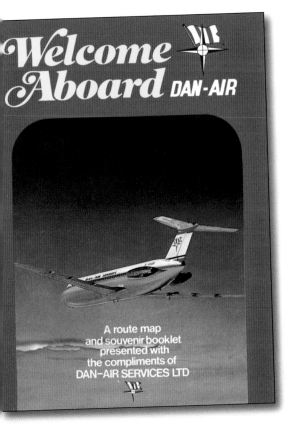

Two company in-flight magazines from the 707 period the upper one from 1973 when it was called a 'souvenir booklet' and below, No1 of the true Inflight Magazine, that used the flight-deck of a 707 as a backdrop. (Dan Air Staff Association)

was the handling process. Our contract with the handling agents required them to provide only steps if we were not on a finger, the ground power, and passenger handling. All other services were provided by a variety of individual suppliers. Preparing for departure was a test of how to bring order out of chaos. Because of the limitations on the amount of load our 321 series Boeings could carry, it was necessary to calculate exactly the maximum load we could uplift in the prevailing conditions. To do this the first information required was the breakdown of the load which had to be obtained from the agents, but was not usually provided until the last minute. From this I would calculate the total weight of the female passengers as well as that of the males, children and infants if any. The weight of the baggage and its distribution in the freight holds had to be calculated and all of this translated on to the load sheet to give the take-off weight and the balance of the aircraft. It was necessary to ensure that the final calculation was within the maximum limits dictated by the length of the runway in use, the wind speed and direction, and the temperature. This was done while sitting on the flight deck, as it was necessary to maintain radio contact with the handling agents and with the airport ground control. At the same time a queue of the suppliers would form at the flight deck door, all with their bills in hand for which they wanted payment in cash. I had to count out the dollars to the catering, cabin cleaning, toilet emptying, and water replenishment etc. suppliers, while attending to the many other pre-departure duties. It was not wise to fall out with any of these service suppliers, much as one was tempted to do at times, as practically every activity on the airport was controlled by the Mafia, and we all had heard tales of the troubles ensuing for unco-operative clients.

My duties with Dan-Air were as demanding as ever however, and I was also flying intensively. One of the flights in September was a very welcome change as it was chartered to carry a replacement ship's crew to a P&O cruise liner in Sydney, and to return the replaced crew to the UK.

In Singapore, on the return journey, I met up with John Cameron who in 1956 had persuaded me to join Dan-Air when he was Chief Pilot of the Company. After a disagreement with Laurie Moore he had resigned and joined Middle East Airlines. Subsequently he became Operations Manager of West African Airways but left them after he had refused to train some of their First Officers. West African had bought B-707s and they wanted all their indigenous pilots to be converted onto the aircraft, but John failed some of them as he considered them

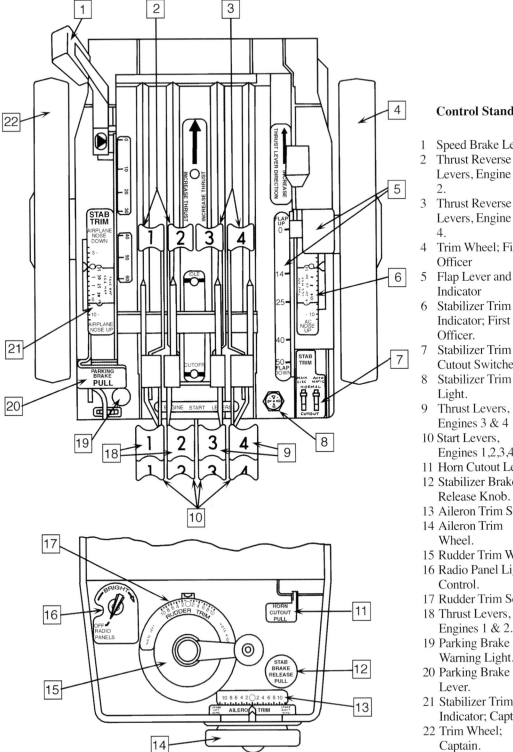

Control Stand

1. Speed Brake Lever
2. Thrust Reverse Levers, Engine 1 & 2.
3. Thrust Reverse Levers, Engine 3 & 4.
4. Trim Wheel; First Officer
5. Flap Lever and Indicator
6. Stabilizer Trim Indicator; First Officer.
7. Stabilizer Trim Cutout Switches.
8. Stabilizer Trim Light.
9. Thrust Levers, Engines 3 & 4.
10. Start Levers, Engines 1,2,3,4.
11. Horn Cutout Lever.
12. Stabilizer Brake Release Knob.
13. Aileron Trim Scale
14. Aileron Trim Wheel.
15. Rudder Trim Wheel
16. Radio Panel Light Control.
17. Rudder Trim Scale.
18. Thrust Levers, Engines 1 & 2.
19. Parking Brake Warning Light.
20. Parking Brake Lever.
21. Stabilizer Trim Indicator; Captain.
22. Trim Wheel; Captain.

to be below the required standard for that aircraft. He then rejoined Singapore Airlines and was now flying Boeing 747s.

Soon after returning to Gatwick from Sydney, I flew to Seattle and from there positioned to Los Angeles. The crew and I set off on a sightseeing tour but the famous sights are spread over such a wide area that we saw only a few of those that we had looked forward to.

In November I flew a party of golfers to West Palm Beach in Florida. The stopover was very pleasant but the return was a disaster. The so-called handling agents, who had been selected by London Office, were, in fact, a small flying club. They knew nothing about handling a large international flight with the result that the take-off was well delayed. When we were settled in the cruise, the pressurisation system began to fluctuate and Alec Ewen, the flight engineer, was unable to get it under control. I descended to a lower altitude but the problem continued with large surges in the pressure, so much so that the passenger oxygen masks were automatically released, although we were unaware of it until the hostess came to the flight deck.

The cabin was a ridiculous sight with the jungle of masks hanging from their tubes, and most of the passengers breathing from them, although the cabin pressure was sufficiently high to maintain the cabin altitude below 10,000 feet. We had no choice but to divert to Bangor, where the crew re-stowed the masks. There had been several reports in the Technical log of problems with the system but Lasham had not yet rectified it. Once again inadequate maintenance proved very costly to the airline. Our problems were not yet over as the weather at Gatwick, our destination, had deteriorated and by the time of our much delayed arrival, a howling gale was blowing across the runway. The wind speed was well above the aircraft's cross-wind limits, so we were forced to divert to Manchester. The passengers had to travel to London by coach, and I got the impression that they were none too pleased. When the aircraft returned it was taken out of service and the system was overhauled at last but, of course, the cost to Dan-Air Services of the incident was not shown on the Dan-Air Engineering balance sheet.

At the end of December 1972 The Company was contracted to position two 707s at Teheran to be exclusively employed in the carriage of Muslim pilgrims to Mecca during the period of the Hadj. Our crews stayed in the Teheran Sheraton which was more comfortable than we had anticipated. Both aircraft were engaged throughout the twenty-four hours in flying the pilgrims to Jeddah, the airport

Dan-Air put the 707 on just about every piece of literature it produced, including this Duty Free Tariff Card. (Dan Air Staff Association)

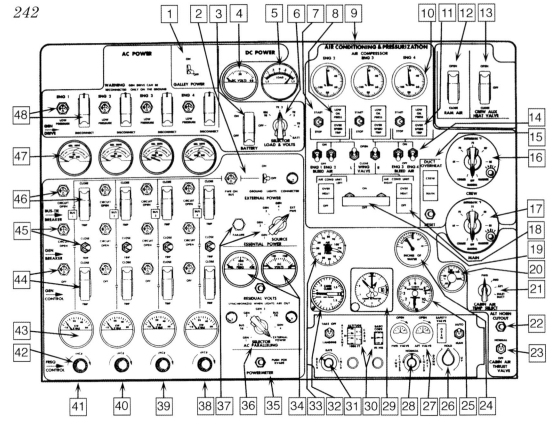

Flight Engineer's Upper Panel

1 Galley Power Switch
2 External Power Selector + lights.
3 Battery Switch.
4 DC Power Voltmeter
5 DC Power Loadmeter.
6 Selector, Load & Volts
7 Air Compressor Start/Stop Switch.
8 Air Compressor Low Oil Pressure Warning Light.
9 Air Conditionion & Pressurisation Panel (Engines 2 - 3 - 4)
10 Air Compressor Tachometer.
11 Air Compressor Overspeed Trip Light.
12 Ram Air Switch.
13 Crew Auxilliary Heat Valve Switch.
14 Engine Bleed Air and Wing Valve Switches.
15 Duct Overheat Warning Lights.
16 Cabin Temperature Selector: Crew Compartment.
17 Cabin Temperature Selector Main Cabin.
18 Air Conditioning Lights
19 Air Conditioning Unit Switches.
20 Cabin Air Temperature Indicator.
21 Cabin Air Temperature Source Selector.
22 Cabin Altitude Warning Horn Cutout Switch.
23 Cabin Air Thrust Valve Switch.
24 Conditioned Air Duct Pressure Indicator.
25 Cabin Diff. Pressure Indicator.
26 Pressurisation Manual Control Selector.
27 Outflow Valve Position Indicators.
28 Outflow Valve Balance Control.
29 Cabin Altimeter.
30 Altitude Selection Indicator & Barometric Correction Indicator.
31 Pressurisation Rate Selector.
32 Cabin Rate Of Climb Indicator.
33 Air Supply Duct Pressure Indicator.
34 Frequency Meter & AC Voltmeter.
35 KVARS Switch
36 AC Paralleling Selector
37 Essential Power Failure Warning Light & Selector
38 AC Power column Engine 4
39 AC Power column Engine 3
40 AC Power column Engine 2
41 AC Power column Engine 1
42 Frequency Control.
43 KW/KVAR Meter.
44 Generator Control Off Light & Switch.
45 Generator Breaker Circuit Open Light & Switch.
46 Bus Tie Breaker Light and Switch.
47 Generator Drive Oil Temperature Rise Indicator.
48 Generator Drive Low Pressure Light and Generator Drive Discconnect Switch.

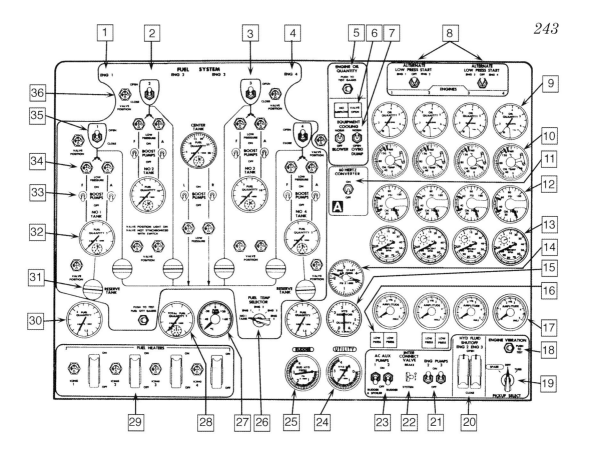

Flight Engineer's Lower Panel

1 Fuel System: Engine 1
2 Fuel System: Engine 2
3 Fuel System: Engine 3
4 Fuel System: Engine 4
5 Engine Oil Quantity Test Switch.
6 Equipment Cool Valves Warning Lights.
7 Equipment Cooling Switches.
8 Alternate Low Pressure Start Switch, Engines 1,2,3,4.
9 Oil Quantity Indicator, Engines 1,2,3,4.
10 Oil Temperature Indicator, Engines 1,2,3,4.
11 60Htz Converter Switch.
12 Oil Pressure Indicator, Engines 1,2,3,4.
13 N_2 Tachometer, Engines 1,2,3,4.

14 Start Air Pressure Indicator.
15 Hydraulic Reservoir Quantity Indicator Utility System
16 Utility and Auxiliary System Pump Low Pressure Lights.
17 Vibration Amplitude Indicator, Engines 1,2,3,4.
18 Vibration Monitor Test Switch.
19 Vibration Pickup Selector.
20 Hydraulic Pump Switches
21 Utility System Pump Switches.
22 Interconnect Valve Switch.
23 Auxiliary System Pump Switches
24 Utility System Pressure Indicator.
25 Rudder Hydraulic Pressure Indicator.
26 Fuel temperature Selector.
27 Fuel temperature Gauge

28 Total Fuel Quantity Gauge for usable fuel in all tanks.
29 Fuel Heater Switches & Fuel Icing Lights.
30 Fuel Quantity Gauge for each tank.
31 Fuel Crossfeed Selector, Engines 1,2,3,4.
32 Fuel Quantity Indicator, Engines 1,2,3,4.
33 Boost Pump Switches, Engines 1,2,3,4.
34 Low Pressure Lights, Engines 1,2,3,4.
35 Engine Fuel Shutoff Valve Switch, Engines 1,2,3,4.
36 Fuel Valve Position Light, Engines 1,2,3,4.

Dan-Air Engineering was part of the Davis and Newman Group of Companies and had a major facility at Lasham Airfield in Hampshire. Here one of the company 707 undergoes deep maintenance. (Dan Air Staff Association)

near Mecca. An impressive new terminal, the design of which was based on a very large tented encampment in the desert, handled an enormous flow of passengers pouring in from every Muslim country. The air traffic control system was not very advanced but the controllers achieved the remarkable feat of getting the aircraft, which were circling the airfield like a swarm of bees, safely onto the ground. Just as remarkably they succeeded in getting those on the ground into the air again and separated from the swarm of arrivals. It was an exciting experience, and I thought that maybe their faith in Allah had been justified throughout this period, as there were several near misses, but no accidents. The same process was repeated at the end of the Hadj when the hundreds of thousands had to be evacuated. The flights went smoothly and the passengers, many of whom had never flown before, behaved surprisingly well. We carried four of our own girls on each flight, from a team led by Val Barnett with the assistance of Susie Calderwood, and three Iranian hostesses as translators and cabin staff assistants.

I flew eight of these round trips in eight days, and then flew the aircraft back to Gatwick as there was a lull before the series of return flights began. The return to Gatwick was in order to operate a charter flight to Barbados, so there was no gap in the utilisation of the aircraft. Because we had full loads we had to refuel at Santa Maria in the Azores both ways. After a brief rest when I arrived back at Gatwick I flew the aircraft back to Teheran. During

the stay in Teheran I saw a lot of Joe Reaney, an old friend who had been a fellow pilot in Malayan Airways and was now flying with IranAir. He had flown the DC-7 with Dan-Air for a period but left when the Company had not provided War Risk insurance for the crew when he flew a charter to Biafra during the war being waged upon it by the Nigerian Government.

After I returned to the UK and waded through the backlog of office work, John Cotter and I flew a charter to Ankara and Karachi. After our return we both flew to New York in mid February 1973, where we commenced the conversion training for the additional crews joining the 707 fleet. While we were there we carried out all the Competency Checks and Instrument Rating Renewals for the current crews. During our stay in New York one of the Pan-Am instructors, who had flown with the US Navy, took us to dinner in the Mess at the Brooklyn Navy Yard.

Another concentrated period of 707 training took place in March 1973 when I went to Newcastle to base train two more crews including Pat Fry and Bill Grief. At that time all the emergency manoeuvres had to be practised in the aircraft in flight so that the time spent in the aircraft during Base Training was very extensive. With the advances in simulator technology which have been made since then, it is no longer necessary to do this and these manoeuvres are practised in the simulator. The high altitude procedures included stalling the aircraft in differing configurations of flap and Undercarriage positions and recovery from Dutch Rolls. This roll is an uncomfortable gyration of the aircraft during which the aircraft wings move up and down alternately while the whole aircraft slides from side to side at the same time as the nose swings back and forth and rises and dips. These effects result from the swept wing design which causes the centre of lift to move aft along each wing as it yaws into the airflow, then forward again along the retreating wing. The recovery is not difficult but the instructor had to keep his wits about him because the instinctive action of the trainee is to apply rudder to stop the nose swinging. The danger is that excessive use of the rudder makes the problem worse and can lead to a 'jet upset' – a problem which caused severe problems in the early days of B-707 operation when aircraft fell through thousands of feet. In some cases engines were shed from the wing as a result of these 'upsets'. It is essential for the trainer is to keep his feet firmly on the rudders so that they can't be moved by the trainee and to ensure that recovery is made by using the ailerons to damp down the rising wing. I mention this because Bill tried to apply violent rudder movement in the recovery and I had to use a good deal of strength to prevent any movement.

Another interesting exercise was the demonstration of 'Mach Tuck' which is the aircraft's progressive nose down attitude change as a result of increasing airspeed. The aircraft was set up in a .82 Mach cruise configuration (82% of the speed of sound), and the nose was then lowered 5 degrees. Initially, as the speed increases, the nose tends to rise but, because the increased speed moves the centre of lift further back down the swept wings, this has the effect of lifting the tail and pushing the nose down. The more the nose goes down the faster the airspeed increases and the more difficult it becomes to raise the nose. Reducing the power makes the problem worse as cutting the power on the under slung engines results in an increase in the nose down moment. Within 20 seconds, if uncorrected, the speed will increase beyond the maximum allowed, and if uncorrected could lead to a 'jet upset' which, on some occasions, resulted in the loss of the aircraft. To reduce height at the end of these exercises an Emergency Descent was made. Depending on the experience of the trainee these exercises could raise the adrenaline level of the Instructor quite considerably.

The Inclusive Tour (IT) activity was expanded and the number of B-707 flights was increased by the addition of series of flights from Manchester and Prestwick to North America.

In February John Cotter and I operated a flight to Bangor and Chicago where we nightstopped, while another crew picked up the aircraft. The hotel where we stayed in Chicago was one of the original hotels started by Conrad Hilton. It was famous then

Arthur Larkman,left, our B-707 on the tarmac at Teheran's airport along with Sam Bee and Ken Balsdon. (Athur Larkman)

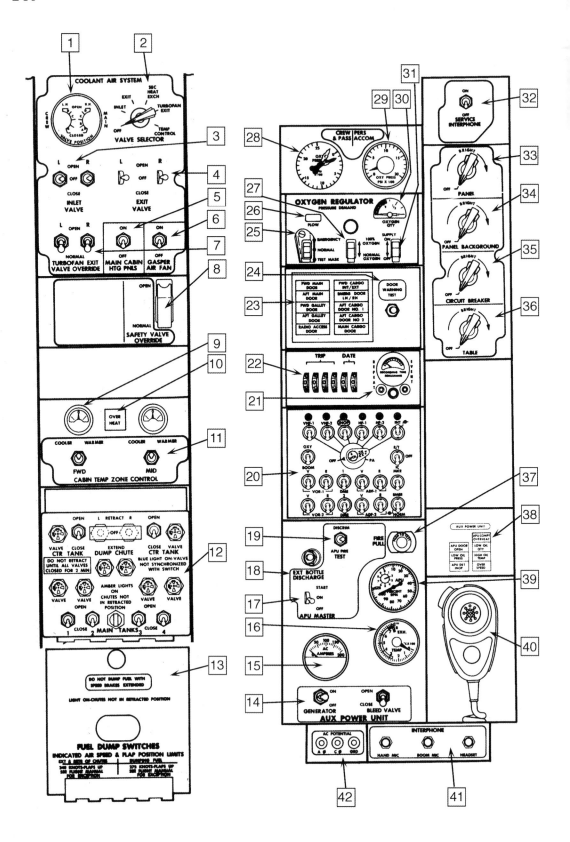

The long and short of it! A publicity photograph demonstrating that Dan-Air were able to offer aircraft for charter ranging from the 29-seat Nord 262 to the long-range 189-seat Boeing 707. (DASA)

for its new concepts in hotel accommodation and for its size. It set the pattern for the modern hotel chains with their standardised rooms and service. Fortunately the Chicago Hilton was one of a kind as it was reputed to have more rooms than any other hotel; it certainly was oversized. The rooms were comfortable and well appointed but the endless corridors were very off-putting, and one needed a route map to find the way around. One of the things which took me aback was the reaction at the check-in desk when I replied "cash" to their question of how I intended to pay the bill. Captains were supplied with Travellers Cheques to pay expenses because it had been decided not to issue them with credit cards. On extended flights the Captain carried many thousands of pounds in Travellers Cheques. Many hotels and

businesses either did not accept these cheques or applied a surcharge for cashing them, so I usually exchanged them for dollars at the airport. On this occasion I found that because of the enormous throughput of guests at the hotel they only accepted credit cards- money was not acceptable.

On another stopover in Chicago the Company had booked us into a hotel in suburban Albany. This was the area favoured by gangsters in pre-war days and the hotel manager was proud that many of the famous names of that time had stayed there. I could well believe it as several of the current occupants looked as if they were following in the tradition. We didn't stay there again. The booking of hotels for the crew was done by the operations staff at Gatwick and the choice of hotels was determined by the cheaper

Flight Engineer's Auxilliary Panels

1 Coolant Air System; Valve Position Indicator.
2 Coolant Air System; Valve Position Selector.
3 Coolant Air System; Inlet Valve Switches.
4 Coolant Air System; Exit Valve Switches.
5 Main Cabin Heating Panels Switch.
6 Gasper Air Fan Switch
7 Turbofan Exit Valve Override Switches.
8 Safety Valve Override Switch.
9 Zone Termperature Control Indicators.
10 Zone Temperature Control Overheat Light.
11 Zone Temerature Control Switches.
12 Fuel/Defuel/Dump Control System
13 Fuel/Defuel/Dump Control System Cover.

14 Auxilliary Power Unit Generator on/off Switch
15 Auxilliary Power Unit AC Output Gauge.
16 Auxilliary Power Unit Exhaust Temperature Gauge
17 Auxilliary Power Unit Master On/off switch
18 Auxilliary Power Unit Fire Bottle Discharge Button
19 Auxilliary Power Unit Fire test button
20 Interphone Selector Panel.
21 Flight Recorder Encoder: time remaining.
22 Flight Recorder Encoder: Digitizers
23 Door Warning Lights
24 Door Warning test button.
25 Emergency Oxygen Lever.
26 Oxygen Flow Indicator.
27 Oxygen Diluter Lever.
28 Crew and Passenger Oxygen Pressure Indicator.

29 Personnel Accomodations Oxygen Pressure Indicator.
30 Oxygen Quality Indicator.
31 Oxygen Supply Lever.
32 Service Interphone Switch
33 Panel Lighting Dimmer Control
34 Panel Background Lighting Dimmer Control
35 Circuit Breaker Lighting Dimmer Control.
36 Table Lighting Dimmer Control
37 Auxilliary Power Unit Pull to Test Switch
38 Auxilliary Power Unit Warning Lights.
39 Auxilliary Power Unit RPM Indicator.
40 Hand Microphone.
41 Interphone jack sockets.
42 AC Potential Lights.

quotes they received. This was a logical method if the hotel standard was satisfactory, as was generally the case. In earlier years some of the hotels arranged for us were disgusting, particularly in the UK where for several years after the war even the better hotels were very sub-standard. A wash basin in the room was considered a luxury. In fact they were very similar to hotels I encountered in Iron Curtain countries. Early in my time in the Company I discovered that if the room rate that the Company had contracted could be revealed, I could visit other hotels of a better standard and, obtain as good a rate and often better than that achieved by the Company, by meeting the Manager in a face to face negotiation. This was particularly true in North America where the business culture is open to making a deal on the spot. In Vancouver for example, I negotiated a price in the Bay Shore, the best hotel at that time, which was less than the inferior hotel which had been arranged for us.

From Chicago we flew another aircraft to New York where we slipped for three days, before flying yet another aircraft to Gatwick. During those days spent at Kennedy we had arranged to carry out a series of periodic checks on those crews who were due for them. With the only simulator approved for the conduct of these mandatory tests being the Pan-Am machine, John and I went to extraordinary lengths to arrange the programme in such a way as to get examiners and crews together in the most economical way. A large part of the potential cost was avoided because we had done a deal with Pan-Am for free travel for our crews on flights from London to and from the simulator. The cost of doing this was much less than doing the checks on the aircraft, even ignoring the increased cost of having the aircraft out of service.

The following month I flew to Ottawa and after a stopover there positioned with the crew to Halifax, Nova Scotia, by Air Canada. We were scheduled to nightstop there and take over an aircraft flying in from the UK the next day, which happened to be my birthday. We were to position the aircraft to Montréal, and from there to Gatwick with a fresh load of passengers. The next morning the weather was foul with low cloud and poor visibility in driving snow. We waited at the airport for news of the incoming aircraft and eventually heard that it was diverting to Moncton in New Brunswick. I hired three taxis to take us the 270 miles to Moncton. The journey was slow and depressing at first but eventually the weather began to improve and we stopped at a village for a quick snack. While I was sitting at the table Tony Kirk, who was acting as co-pilot, marched up to the table carrying a small sponge cake on which was a large lighted candle in the shape of a fir tree. The whole crew sang Happy Birthday while I blew out the candle. It brightened up the whole day for me.

Further flights to Canada and to Berlin for IT series followed as the summer season got into full swing. Further activity on the 707 was provided by another series for Air France operating their scheduled flights on the Paris/London route. In early April I operated a flight with mixed groups of passengers each heading for a different destination.

A classic scene at London Gatwick in the early 1970s; Dan-Air's 707 G-AZTG about to depart on another long-haul flight. In the background can be seen a trio of BEA Airtours Comets. (DASA)

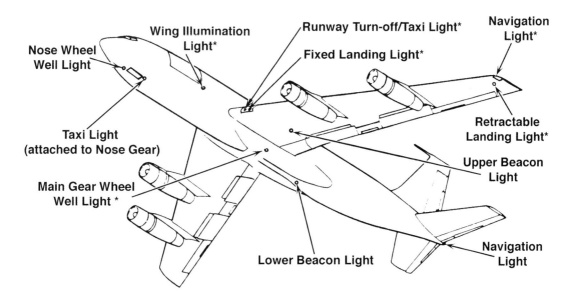

Exterior Lighting Positions and Controls on Overhead Panel on Flightdeck

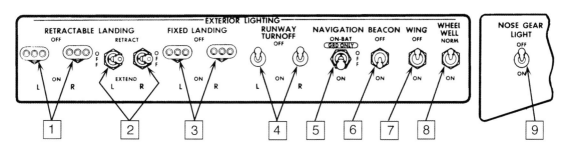

1 Left & Right Retractable Landing Light Switch: ON - Retractable landing Lights illuminate.

2 Left & Right Retract-Extend Switch. EXTEND - extends outboard landing lights. RETRACT - retracts outboard landing lights

3 Left & Right Fixed Landing Light Switch. ON - Fixed Landing Lights Illuminate.

4 Left & Right Runway Turnoff Light Switch. ON - Runway turnoff light illuminates.

5 Navigation Light Switch. ON BAT - Ground use only. Light supplied from 28V

DC Essential busses. ON - Power for light supplied by 28V AC bus.

6 Beacon Light Switch. ON - Beacon (anti-collision) lights illuminate and rotate.

7 Wing Light Switch. ON - Illuminates the tops and leading edges of the wings and engine nacell area.

8 Wheel Well Light Switch. NORMAL - Allows the individual lights to be controlled by switches near each unit. ON - Wheel Well Lights Illuminate.

9 Nose Gear Light Switch. ON - Nose Gear Taxi Light Illuminates.

We flew to Sondestrom in Greenland where we re-fuelled before flying on to Winnipeg. From there we flew to Toronto, then returned to Prestwick to off-load some passengers and from there we flew to Manchester where more dis-embarked and then carried on to Gatwick, all of which was accomplished

in three days. A relaxation in the requirements for single group affinity flights had made this possible and thus enabled us to operate more flights.

From mid October '75 to mid February 1976 I did not fly at all but at last managed to operate part of a Bangladeshi series. John Cotter and I positioned

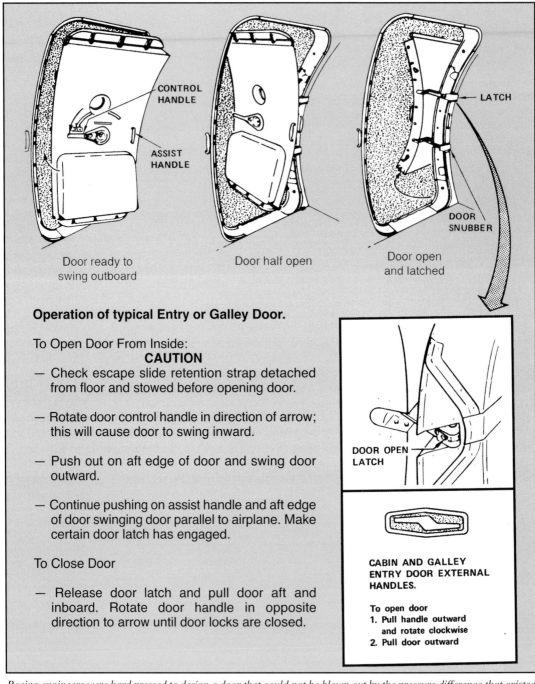

CONTROL HANDLE

ASSIST HANDLE

LATCH

DOOR SNUBBER

Door ready to swing outboard

Door half open

Door open and latched

Operation of typical Entry or Galley Door.

To Open Door From Inside:
CAUTION
— Check escape slide retention strap detached from floor and stowed before opening door.

— Rotate door control handle in direction of arrow; this will cause door to swing inward.

— Push out on aft edge of door and swing door outward.

— Continue pushing on assist handle and aft edge of door swinging door parallel to airplane. Make certain door latch has engaged.

To Close Door

— Release door latch and pull door aft and inboard. Rotate door handle in opposite direction to arrow until door locks are closed.

DOOR OPEN LATCH

CABIN AND GALLEY ENTRY DOOR EXTERNAL HANDLES.

To open door
1. **Pull handle outward and rotate clockwise**
2. **Pull door outward**

Boeing engineers were hard pressed to design a door that could not be blown out by the pressure difference that existed between the inside and the outside of the cabin. How could a door be opened outward and still fit as a plug inside the doorway? Four such doors are fitted on the Boeing jet liners, two passenger-entry doors on the left side and two galley-service doors on the right side.

When closed, the outward-opening, plug-type door seals the pressurised air in the cabin. It was opened by turning the handle which folds the door's upper and lower edges inward and rotates the door outward, edge first, through the doorway. In trials a door was tested under high pressures and in a cold chamber to make certain it could be opened even with a coat of ice covering it, and opened and closed more than 25,000 times in a life test.

the aircraft to Heathrow and as I hadn't flown for four months, he used this short hop to give me a three engined take-off and a three engined landing at Heathrow. A very busy 15 minute flight. This, plus the ensuing line check on the flight to Dubai satisfied the requirements for my authorisation to fly in command once again. Another crew took the aircraft on to Dhaka and back to Dubai where we waited to fly it back to London. We were dozing in the sun by the swimming pool the next morning when I heard the unmistakeable voice of Joan Buckett. She was an Australian girl who had been a hostess with us for some years and had left to take a cabin staff job with Gulf Air, based in Bahrain. She was with a group of five other girls, all Gulf Air hostesses, and four of them were also ex-Dan-Air. We had a very pleasant re-union until they departed on their flight that evening.

In March I managed to operate a flight to Pittsburgh, then nothing more until June when I flew another mixed group from Gatwick, Manchester, and Prestwick to Toronto, then returned via Boston and New York. In July I flew our newly acquired 707-321C freighter into Gatwick for the first time. It was fitted with very large doors and strengthened floor and with its sister aircraft subsequently flew many cargo flights. After all these years we were carrying freight again. A few days later I flew it to Venice on its first service with us.

While we awaited the decision on a suitable candidate for the operations management position, I agreed to fill the vacancy on a temporary basis. Frank Horridge finally came up with the solution to the problem and proposed that I become the Head of Operations. This was agreed, although I was far from enthusiastic about it and accepted on the understanding that I would serve only until a suitable person was found. Alan Snudden issued a memo in February, notifying the changes—

"As a result of the increasing flying programme and the need to integrate and improve the Company's Operations and Passenger Services function, it has been decided to appoint Captain Larkman, who has been actively engaged in re-organising our Operations Department, to the new post of Operations Services Director. He will be assisted by Mr J Stevens, the Operational Performance Manager. Captain Larkman will be responsible to Mr. F. Horridge, the Deputy Managing Director".

I invented my title of 'Operations Services Director' to avoid embarrassment to Bob Atkins, whose existing title was 'Operations Director, Flying', and the possible confusion of having two Operations Directors. John Stevens served with us for a period during which the Operations Control staff continued to develop the strategies of circumventing Air Traffic delays. This was a skill in which Dan-Air outshone all our competitors, much to their chagrin. Roy McDougall, the Operations Director of Britannia Airways, was particularly interested in Air Traffic Control (ATC) matters and had met John at various ATC conferences. In 1978 Roy persuaded him to join Britannia's Operations Department but, unfortunately for Roy, John had not yet mastered the arcane skills that Roy had hoped he would bring with him, and they were no farther forward. Other Managers in Operations were Eric Bristow, the Ops. Administration Manager, Thornton Simmons, who was Liaison Officer for the IAS freight contract on which our two 707-321C's were employed, and Dermot Mulvagh, the Passenger Services Manager.

Another responsibility which I assumed was to represent the Company on the National Aviation Security Commission (NASC). This Committee met regularly at the Department of Trade in London, where the policy for all aspects of Aviation Security including the procedures used by the airlines, the airports, the Police Services etc. were discussed and decided upon. We were regularly briefed by the Intelligence Services on their continuous assessment of all current and future threats, and planned the counter measures required to combat them. The number of aircraft hi-jacks taking place world wide

707 G-AYSL taxies in at Gatwick after another flight to the USA.

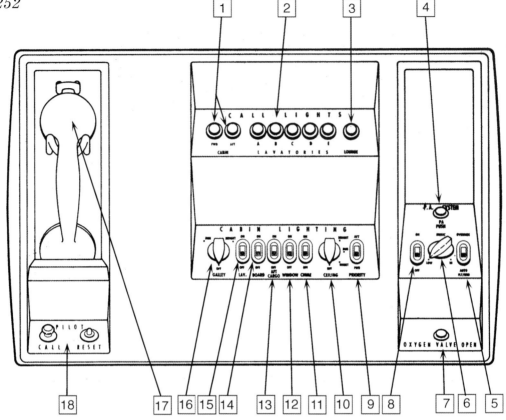

Cabin Attendant's Panel

1 Forward and Aft Toilet Call Lights (Press to Reset)
2 Passenger Call Lights. (Press to Reset)
3 Lounge Call Lights. (Press to Reset)
4 Public Address System Operate Button (Push to use)
5 Public Address System Override Switch
6 Music High/Low Selector
7 Oxygen Valve.
8 Tape Preproducer Unit Switch
9 Lighting Priority Selector
10 Ceiling Light Switch
11 Chime Switch
12 Window Light Switch
13 Aft Cargo Light Switch
14 Board Light Switch
15 Lavatory Light Switch
16 Galley Light Control
17 Handset.
18 Attendant to Pilot call Switch/Call Light and Pilot to Attendant Reset Switch.

remained high throughout this period and there was much terrorist activity.

The first two weeks of November were taken up with the training of crews converting onto the 707, who included Malcolm Grant and Pete Jamieson. After they completed their simulator training we set off from Gatwick to carry out the base training. I put Pete in the left hand Captain's seat so that he could fly the positioning leg up to Newcastle. This was his first experience of handling the aircraft after completing the simulator training. We took off and had just commenced the initial climb out of Gatwick when there was a fire warning on one of the engines. Pete calmly ordered the shut down and fire drill and landed the aircraft back at Gatwick. When we were

on the ground at Gatwick he told me that I had made him practice so many fire drills during the simulator training that he remained calm and carried out the procedures as a matter of routine. He said that he suspected that I was simulating the fault on the aircraft but, in fact, this time it was the real thing.

At the end of November I flew G-BEBP, our second 707-321C, out to Hong Kong and, fortunately, Joy was able to come with me. The aircraft had been chartered by Cathay Pacific to carry out freight services for them as they were short of an aircraft. I was very pleased to meet once again two Cathay staff who had been among Dan-Air's best traffic officers; Derek Smith, who had been our Traffic Superintendent at Gatwick, and was now

Cathay's Manager at Kai Tak, and Gerry Penwarden, who was now Cathay's Manager for the whole of South East Asia. They looked after us extremely well and made our stay very enjoyable. Joy accompanied me on a flight I operated from Hong Kong to Singapore, where we slipped for two nights. The morning after our arrival we were collected by Phil Caroline, who offered to take us on a tour of the city. Phil was a Singapore Airlines Boeing 747 Captain who had been my Best Man when Joy and I were married in Singapore Cathedral in 1953. I had visited Singapore many times over the years and was fairly familiar with the many changes which had been made to the city and, indeed, to the very shape of the island by land reclamation. Joy, however, had not been back since we left for the UK in 1956. We had lived in Singapore for several years so she was really looking forward to seeing it again.

We returned from Hong Kong in December with a load for Maastricht before finally landing at Gatwick in time for Christmas. This aircraft crashed just over five months later because of a design fault in its construction.

The report into the crash of G-BEBP made grim reading. We were flying on behalf of International Aviation Services Limited, who themselves were trading as IAS Cargo Airlines, who had been sub-contracted by Zambia Airways to operate a weekly scheduled all-cargo service between London Heathrow and the Zambian capital, Lusaka, via Athens and Nairobi. The aircraft - a 707-321C - had first entered service with Pan American World Airways in 1963. This aircraft was also the first convertible 707 built. We acquired it in 1976.

The flight originated from London Heathrow Airport to Athens Hellinikon Airport, which was uneventful; from Athens the crew flew to Nairobi . Departure from Nairobi for Lusaka on the final leg occurred as planned at 07:17, 14 May 1977.

The 707 cruised at flight level 310 for about two hours, after which it was cleared for descent to flight level 110. Flight level 110 was reached at approximately 09:23, and clearance was granted to begin descent towards a target of flight level 70. Just before 09:30, clearance to descend to 6,000 feet was granted, and moments later the plane was cleared to make a visual approach to runway 10. A few minutes later, eyewitnesses saw the entire right horizontal stabiliser and elevator detach from the aircraft. The aircraft lost pitch control and entered a nose-dive from about 800 feet to ground level, destroying the aircraft on impact. All six on board were killed.

A full investigation was launched by the Zambian authorities and then delegated to the UK Air Accidents Investigation Branch. The conclusions made are as follows: It was determined that the structure of the right horizontal stabiliser failed due to metal fatigue in the rear spar structure, and due to

Most of Dan-Air aircraft had nicknames, usually generated from their registrations. 707 G-AYSL was always known by the crews as old 'Spread Legs'. (Dan-Air Staff Association)

A company 707 rests between flights at Hong Kong's old Kai Tak airport. (Dan-Air Staff Association)

the lack of an adequate fail-safe structure or device should such an event occur. The investigation also identified deficiencies in the assessment of aircraft designs and their certification and in the way aircraft were inspected.

The crack found in the failed stabiliser after the accident was thought by investigators unlikely to have been detectable using normal testing means, such as fluorescent dye. It was also thought that the crack had been present for at least 6,000 flight hours before the accident, and before we had acquired Echo Papa from Pan Am.

Inspections of the Boeing 707-300 fleet, made as a result of the crash, found another thirty-eight aircraft with similar cracks.

1976 had been a mixed year for the Company but overall was quite successful. Profit before taxation was almost £2,000,000, an improvement of £500,000 over 1975's figure, even though the de-valuation of the pound had increased many costs, particularly that of fuel. The contracts for fuel supplies are always in US dollars, so this had made a very large impact on us. The number of passengers carried also increased to more than 2.8 million. The number of aircraft operated now totalled 55, with four 707s, six 727s,

six 1-11 500s, six 1-11 200/400s, sixteen Comets and sixteen 748s.

Possibly the last word on the Dan-Air 707 operation should go to Captain Keith Moody, who later became Fleet Manager on our 727 fleet.

'The 707 may have ruled the air - but it did not like short runways. The 707 may have been King of the skies, but it had a problem. It's performance was relatively sedate - fine if you had plenty of space and long, long runways. That was caused by the wing sweepback, which were great for high-speed flight, but they did not produce much lift at low speeds, meaning that it was imperative to bring the aircraft in fast, and that meant eating up massive amounts of runway before you could bring it to a stop.

It was a real man's aeroplane. When Boeing built it they decided that all of the pilots who were going to come on to it had previously flown piston engined aircraft, and were used to high forces needed to operate the flying surfaces. The 707 needed nearly 10,000 feet to get airborne or to stop safely.

There was no way we could use it on any of our mediterranean charters other than into places like Athens or Rome - we left those services to our Comets or 72s!

G-BEBP seen at Gatwick in a partial Dan-Air colour scheme with joint Dan-Air/IAS titling. (Dan-Air Staff Association)

Chapter Eight

Military 707s

The EC-137D; E-3 Sentry.
In 1963 the USAF asked for proposals for an Airborne Warning and Control System (AWACS) to replace its Lockheed EC-121 Warning Stars, which had served in the airborne early warning role for over a decade. The new aircraft design would be able to take advantage of improvements in radar technology, computer aided radar data analysis and data reduction. This would allow airborne radars to 'look down' to detect the movement of low-flying aircraft and discriminate - even over land at a range of 200 miles - a target

aircraft's movements, which up until then was impossible, due to the inability to discriminate an aircraft's track from ground clutter.

AWACS would be able to carry out the NORAD support role and also operate as a tactical command post for the direction of air and ground forces in specific battle situations.

Contracts were issued to Boeing, Douglas, and Lockheed, the latter being eliminated in July 1966. In 1967, a parallel programme was put into place to develop the radar, with Westinghouse Electric and Hughes Aircraft being asked to compete in

An unidentifiable USAF E-3 in flight. Apart from the huge rotodome, there are assorted 'lumps and bumps' along the aircraft spine. Particularly noticabler are the refuelling recepticle and markings. (USAF)

producing the radar system. In 1968, it was referred to as Overland Radar Technology (ORT) during development tests on the modified EC-121Q. The Westinghouse radar antenna was going to be used by whichever company won the radar competition, since Westinghouse had pioneered in the design of high-power RF phase-shifters.

Boeing were appointed in July 1970 as prime contractor for the system, which was to be based on the airframe of the Boeing 707-320B transport.

The first EC-137 made its maiden flight on 9 February 1972, with the fly-off between the two radars taking place during March–July that year. Favourable test results led to the selection of Westinghouse's radar for the production aircraft. Hughes's radar was initially thought to be a certain winner, simply because much of its design was also going into the new F-15 Eagle's radar programme. The Westinghouse radar used a pipelined fast fourier transform (FFT) to digitally resolve 128 Doppler frequencies, while Hughes's radars used analogue filters based on the design for the F-15 fighter. An FFT is an algorithm that computes the discrete Fourier transform (DFT) of a sequence, or its inverse. Fourier analysis converts a signal from its original domain (often time or space) to a representation in the frequency domain and vice versa.

Westinghouse's engineering team won this competition by using a programmable 18-bit computer whose software could be modified before each mission. This computer was the AN/AYK-8 design from the B-57G program, and designated AYK-8-EP1 for its much expanded memory. This radar also multiplexed a beyond-the-horizon (BTH) pulse mode that could complement the pulse-Doppler radar mode. This proved to be beneficial especially when the BTH mode was used to detect ships at sea when the radar beam was directed below the horizon.

Boeing built two prototypes of the EC-137D (later to be called the E-3A), the first of which (71-1407) first flew on 9 February 1972. To save costs, the endurance requirements were relaxed, allowing the new aircraft to retain the four JT3D (US Military designation TF33) turbofans. In basic E-3A configuration the heart of the aircraft was the AN/APY-1 surveillance radar, housed within a large 'rotodome' radar dish mounted on twin pylons above the rear fuselage and designed to turn at a rate of six cycles per minute. Data from the system were processed by an IBM CC-1 computer which provided information to the mission crew at up to nineteen situation display units (SDUs), while some thirteen different channels were provided for air-to-ground communications.

Two of the crew stations aboard a USAF Sentry. (USAF)

Approval was given on 26 January 1973 for full-scale development of the AWACS system. To allow further development of the aircraft's systems, orders were placed for three preproduction aircraft, the first of which performed its maiden flight in February 1975. IBM and Hazeltine were selected to develop the mission computer and display system. The IBM computer received the designation 4PI, and the software was written in JOVIAL. A Semi-Automatic Ground Environment (SAGE) or back-up interceptor control (BUIC) operator would immediately be at home with the track displays and tabular displays, but differences in symbology would create compatibility problems in tactical ground radar systems in Iceland, Europe, and Korea over Link-11 (TADIL-A).

JOVIAL was a high-level computer programming language, but specialised for the development of embedded systems; that is, specialised computer systems designed to perform one or a few dedicated functions, usually embedded as part of a complete device including mechanical parts.

JOVIAL was developed as a new 'high-order' programming language, beginning in 1959 by a team at System Development Corporation (SDC) headed by Jules Schwartz to compose software for the electronics of military aircraft. The name JOVIAL is an acronym for '**J**ules **O**wn **V**ersion of the **I**nternational **A**lgebraic **L**anguage.'

During the 1960s JOVIAL was a part of the US Military L-project series, in particular 465L (the SACCS project), due to a lack of real-time processing languages available. Some 95% of the SACCS project, managed by ITT with software primarily written by SDC, was written in JOVIAL. The software project took two years and no fewer than 1400 programmer years.

During the late 1970s and early 1980s, the US Air Force adopted a standardised CPU, the MIL-STD-1750A, and subsequent JOVIAL programmes were built for that processor. Several commercial vendors provided compilers and related tools to build JOVIAL for processors such as the MIL-STD-1750A, including Advanced Computer Techniques (ACT), TLD Systems, Proprietary Software Systems (PSS), and others.

JOVIAL was standardised during 1973 with MIL-STD-1589 and was revised during 1984 with MIL-STD-1589C. It is still much used to update and maintain software on older military vehicles and aircraft.

Modifications to the Boeing 707 for the E-3 Sentry included a rotating radar dome, single-point ground refuelling, air refuelling, and a bail-out tunnel or chute. The original design had two (one forward, and one aft), but the aft bail-out chute was deleted to cut mounting costs. Engineering, test and evaluation began on the first E-3 Sentry in October 1975.

The first of the planned thirty-four production aircraft - now named 'Sentry' - was delivered to Tactical Air Command's 552nd Airborne Warning and Control Wing (now the 552nd Air Control Wing) at Tinker AFB, Oklahoma received the first E-3 aircraft, commanded by Major James R Sterk, on 24 March 1977. Further development was already under way, however, and the 25th and subsequent aircraft were delivered with the much higher capacity IBM CC-2 computer, additional UHF radios, maritime surveillance capability and anti-jamming voice communications. These aircraft were later further upgraded to E-3C standard with five additional SDls and other alterations. The original batch of 'core' E-3As became E-3Bs following an upgrade to similar standard.

The 34th and last USAF Sentry was delivered in June 1984. In March 1996, the USAF activated the 513th Air Control Group (513th ACG), an ACC-gained Air Force Reserve Command (AFRC) AWACS unit under the Reserve Associate Program. Co-located with the 552nd ACW at Tinker AFB, the 513rd ACG performs similar duties on active duty E-3 aircraft shared with the 552nd ACW.

The E-3 Sentry's airframe is a modified Boeing 707-320B Advanced model. USAF and NATO E-3s have an unrefuelled range of some 4,000 miles or eight hours of flying. The newer E-3 versions bought by France, Saudi Arabia, and the United Kingdom are equipped with newer CFM56-2 turbofan engines, and these can fly for about 11 hours or about 5,000 miles. The Sentry's range and on-station time can be increased through air-to-air refuelling and the crews can work in shifts by the use of an on-board crew rest and meals area.

When deployed, the E-3 monitors an assigned area of the battlefield and provides information for commanders of air operations to gain and maintain control of the battle; while as an air defence asset, E-3s can detect, identify, and track airborne enemy forces far from the boundaries of the US or NATO countries and can direct fighter-interceptor aircraft to these targets. In support of air-to-ground operations, the E-3 can provide direct information needed for interdiction, reconnaissance, airlift, and close-air support for friendly ground forces.

On 18 November 2015, an E-3G was deployed to the Middle East to begin flying combat missions in support of Operation Inherent Resolve against ISIL, marking the first combat deployment of the upgraded AWAC Block 40/45. The $2.7 billion development effort started in 2003, with the first five aircraft achieving initial operational capability (IOC) in July 2015. The Block 40/45 Mission Computer and Display upgrade replaced current 1970 vintage mission computing and displays with a true open system and commercial off-the-shelf hardware and software, giving AWACS crews the modern computing tools needed to perform, and vastly improve mission capability. Estimated fleet upgrades are due for completion in 2020. The Air Force plans to convert twenty-four AWACS to E-3G standard, while retiring seven from the fleet to avoid upgrade costs and harvest out-of-production components.

NATO AWACS

The need for a European AWACS system came about after the Warsaw pact countries first acquired the capability of using their attack aircraft at very low altitudes so defeating friendly radar by operating 'out of sight' behind topographical features. It was obvious that a method had to be devised to counter the threat as the warning time of the enemy raider's approach had been reduced to less than two minutes. The answer was the E-3A Sentry.

Between 1968 and 1974 the NATO powers set up a high-ranking study group that recommended the American equipment. However, the initial proposals were too expensive for NATO Council members and cuts to numbers and ob-board equipment had to be made to keep the project within budget.

An organisation was set up in Brussels which was tasked with preparing the complete proposals for member countries approval including the number and configuration of aircraft and how these could readily fit into existing NATO ground-based air defence systems. Finally the overall cost had to be confirmed and a method devised so that this could be split fairly amongst the individual nations who had set the project up. On 7 December 1978 an inter-governmental agreement was reached and signed by NATO Defence Ministers thus giving the signal for the realisation of one of the most ambitious international defence schemes yet devised.

Headed by a German Major General, an organisation was set up to carry out this complex programme, given the title of NAPMO (NAEW Programme Management Organisation) on which all twelve NATO countries taking part were represented. They had three main tasks to accomplish. Firstly the actual procurement of the agreed eighteen aircraft modified to NATO requirements plus all the associated ground equipment and flight and mission simulators. Secondly the NATO Air Defence Ground Environment (NADGE) radar stations in Europe stretching from northern Norway to Turkey had to

LX-N 2000, one of the three 707-307Cs used by NATO as support trainers for their fleet of E-3As (NATO)

Sixteen E-3A aircraft are assigned to the NATO E-3A Component. Normally, only a certain number of the E-3As are at NATO Air Base Geilenkirchen at any given time. The remainder are deployed to the Component's Forward Operating Bases in Aktion, (Preveza) Greece; Trapani, Italy; and Konya, Turkey; and to the Forward Operating Location at Oerland, Norway; or to other allied airfields. Above: LX-N90454 comes in to land at Aktion National Airport in Greece. The bulges under the aircraft's chin house a suite of electronic warfare support measures.(Author)

Right: The flightdeck crew of NATO E-3s consist of Pilot, First Officer, Navigator and Flight Engineer. (NATO)

be converted to accept information provided by the E-3A's data link system. Finally an airfield base had to be found that would be suitable for the general headquarters but with four other forward operating bases established from which the aircraft could increase their range and ability to stay on station longer.

As from 1980 the NATO Early Warning Force Command was set up as a NATO agency under SACEUR in Belgium and co-located with SHAPE. It is commanded by a Major-General and the post is held alternately by the USAF and the German Air Force.

Out of the twelve nations taking part, one, Luxembourg, has not got an air force of its own and therefore the aircraft themselves were placed on the civil aircraft register of that country in a true spirit of compromise and in order to overcome the legal requirements of aircraft ownership.

The gigantic task of setting up what in effect was a new air force with all the necessary command structure, rules and regulations, its own police force and a complete training and spares organisation was not easy. Basically the NATO 'air force' is structured after the German Geschwader principle and has three component squadrons. Training and supply areas were based on American

systems which had already been established by the USAF although NATO's aircraft were differently configured and had a slightly modified task to their American counterparts. The common language was English and each nation contributed air crew members in numbers according to their financial contribution to the whole project.

Even though aircrew members with previous experience of AWACS operations such as the USAF personnel seconded to NATO's air arm, had to go through the training system again at Geilenkirchen before being declared operational.

In all thirty multi-national crews from eleven countries including the USA, Canada, Belgium, Denmark, Germany, Greece, Italy, Turkey, The Netherlands, Portugal and Greece make up the Component's Operational Wing with ten crews assigned to each of the three squadrons.

The E-3A Component was NATO's first operational flying unit with multinational manning. The Component commander's position is of Brigadier General rank and is held alternately by Germany and the USA. The Component's organizational structure comprises a Headquarters staff and five major functional elements (Operations Wing, Logistics Wing, Base Support Wing, Training Wing and Information Technology

The specially painted anniversary AWACS was first presented in 2007 as part of the celebration of the NATO E-3A Component's 25th anniversary. (NATO)

Wing). Each Wing is commanded by a Colonel, each from a different NATO member nation.

The Component's multinational, fully integrated workforce consists of more than 3,000 military and civilian personnel from 16 NATO member nations. This figure includes personnel assigned to support functions, such as the engineering support teams of the Bundeswehr Service Centre, National Support Unit personnel, and morale and welfare activities staff.

The Component operates sixteen (out of an original order for eighteen) Boeing E-3A AWACS aircraft and also operated three Boeing 707 Trainer Cargo Aircraft, but these were retired in 2011.

In terms of hardware, the flightdeck of a NATO E-3A is just like any Boeing 707 but with the addition of the navigator's equipment on the port side making it a little more cramped than its equivalent in an airliner.

With the first NATO E-3A being delivered green from Boeing's Seattle plant in February 1982, the internal equipment was fitted by Dornier-Werke at Oberpfaffenhofen. The last of the eighteen aircraft was delivered in mid-1985.

Each is fitted with high performance Pratt and Whitney TF-33-100A engines giving more power than the civil Boeing 707 equivalent and the internal structure is strengthened to allow for the weight of equipment carried, especially the rotodome. Internally the operational equipment is

sub-divided into four compartments excluding the flight deck. From front to rear these consist of the communications consoles including radio voice systems and the data transmission link. It is operated by two technicians who are responsible for maintaining the equipment whilst in flight and providing any of the many services that can keep the E-3A in touch with other agencies or aircraft. This is followed by the data processing system with a powerful computer which was somewhat old technology but at the same time thoroughly reliable and well-proven.

In the centre fuselage there are nine tactical workstations with multi-purpose consoles having a centrally mounted VDU display on which at a selection of various distance and scale modes all aircraft can be displayed or shipping search conducted. Each target is labelled and non-essential information taken off the screen at will.

At any one time the aircraft can watch over 312,000 square kilometres of the earth's surface and three NATO AWACS aircraft flying overlapping orbits can provide ground agencies with a complete radar picture of the whole of central Europe extending into the Warsaw Pact countries. The E-3A can detect low flying aircraft or missiles at a range of up to 400 kms and medium altitude targets up to 520 kms.

A popular myth from the early days of the

NATO AWACS was that they could detect an armoured column on the move - this was certainly not the case; or at least, not without one of the AFVs having a radar responder or an identifying signal that could also be picked up by the enemy. The AWACS task was with low flying aircraft and not the land battles as such.

However, there was one very useful secondary role that the E-3 could perform. If an aircraft within range declared any form of emergency, this signal could be accurately tracked until it landed safely.

One machine - LX-N90457 - was lost following multiple bird strikes on take off from Préveza-Aktion Airport, Greece on 14 July 1996.

The planned take - off time was 1815 hours local. The normal crew of seventeen had been reduced to fourteen for the mission due to an expected low level of air activity.

The take-off brief called for a rolling right seat take-off. At approximately 120 knots a flock of birds was seen rising towards the left side of the aircraft and sounds of impact along the left side of the fuselage were heard. The Aircraft Commander contemplated aborting the take - off at that moment, but elected to continue. The aircraft continued to accelerate with all engine indications normal. As the aircraft nose started to rise the crew saw a large black bird moving from left to right in close proximity to the aircraft. A noise, interpreted as the bird impact, was then heard on the right-hand side of the aircraft. The Aircraft Commander then elected to abort the take-off and initiated the procedure. The remainder of the flight deck crew responded accordingly. However, as the abort procedure was carried out, it became rapidly apparent that the aircraft would not be stopped on the remaining runway. The aircraft departed the

runway at approximately 60 knots down a sandy incline onto the landing lights support pier and into the Ionian sea. The main landing gear separated from the aircraft after contacting the rocks, while the aircraft continued forward, eventually coming to rest some five hundred feet from the end of runway 25R, rotated about sixty degrees to the right, with the aft section on the runway lighting support pier and the partly separated nose section resting in the sea.

On 23 June 2015, the first of the original eighteen NATO E-3A AWACS aircraft to retire, arrived at Davis-Monthan AFB near Tucson, AZ. The aircraft, LX-N90449, was placed in parts reclamation storage where critical items were removed by NATO technicians to support their remaining fleet of E-3A aircraft. It had accumulated 22,206 flight hours between 19 August 1983 and 13 May 2015 and operated out of twenty-one different countries in support of NATO operational activities. The aircraft was due in mid-July 2015 for a six-year cycle Depot Level Maintenance (DLM) inspection which would have been very costly. Without the inspection, the aircraft would no longer be allowed to fly. The so-called '449 Retirement Project' resulted in reclamation of critical parts with a value of upwards of $40,000,000. Some of the parts to be removed were no longer on the market or had become very expensive. The surviving sixteen aircraft of the NATO E-3A Component are all registered in Luxembourg as part of that country's contribution to the NATO AWACS programme.

Since coming into service in the early 1980s, the aircraft, their onboard systems and associated ground-based equipment have undergone regular upgrading. Three major programmes have been accomplished since the early 1990s. The Mid-

The demise of LX-N90457. The Sentry failed to stop on the runway and ended up in the water - not surprising considering the 9419 foot runway has its ends in either the Amvrakikoa Kolpos (Ambracian Gulf, also known as the Gulf of Arta or the Gulf of Actium) and the other in the Ionian Sea. (Σπύρος Σπυρίδων)

Term Modernization Programme, was completed in December 2008. It included the retrofitting of seventeen E-3As with improved navigation systems, digital communication systems and five additional workstations, as well as the enhancement of two Mission Simulators. As a result of this project the NATO AWACS will be able to continue to fulfill its intended role as an important NATO asset for maintaining peace and security.

The Component's two operational E-3A squadrons and its former TCA squadron have a total of thirty multinational aircrews from fourteen of NATO's twenty-eight nations: Belgium, Denmark, Germany, Greece, Hungary, Italy, the Netherlands, Norway, Poland, Portugal, Spain, Turkey, Romania and the United States. Canada withdrew its participation from the AWACS program in 2014. In addition, the Aircrew Training Squadron operates on an equally multinational basis under the direction of Training Wing.

The Component has approximately thirty military and civilian assigned personnel at each site; these are NATO personnel, but all are from the respective host nation.

The fleet of E-3s has remained in operation since the Cold War and has adapted its mission to emerging security threats, primarily in European airspace. Despite stringent self-imposed flight restrictions, including conducting a significant portion of training flights at different airfields throughout Europe and North America, E-3A operations in Geilenkirchen caused noise pollution, according to a recent study by the Netherlands National Institute for Public Health and the Environment, affecting over 40,000 citizens of Parkstad Limburg across the nearby German-Dutch border, who have formed an NGO aiming to stop AWACS flights. The Dutch government has asked for a mid-life upgrade of the AWACS fleet to include upgrading the engines to make the fleet meet the maximum noise levels allowed for civilian air traffic.

The unpressurised rotodome is thirty feet in diameter, six feet thick at the centre, and is held eleven feet above the fuselage by two struts. It is tilted down at the front to reduce its aerodynamic drag, which lessens its detrimental effect on take-offs and endurance (which is corrected electronically by both the radar and secondary surveillance radar antenna phase shifters). The dome uses both bleed air and cooling doors to remove the heat generated by electronic and mechanical equipment. The hydraulically rotated antenna system permits the Westinghouse Corporation's AN/APY-1 and AN/APY-2 passive electronically scanned array radar system to provide surveillance from the Earth's surface up into the stratosphere, over land or water.

Other major sub-systems in the E-3 Sentry are navigation, communications, and computers. Consoles display computer-processed data in graphic and tabular format on video screens. Console operators perform surveillance, identification, weapons control, battle management and communications functions. The radar and computer sub-systems on the E-3 can gather and present broad and detailed battlefield information. This includes position and tracking information on enemy aircraft and ships, and location and status of friendly aircraft and naval vessels. The information can be sent to major command and control centers in rear areas or aboard ships. In times of crisis, data can be forwarded to the National Command Authority in the US via RC-135 or naval aircraft carrier task forces.

Electrical generators mounted on each of the E-3's four engines provide the one megawatt of electrical power that is required by the E-3's radars and other electronics. Its pulse-Doppler radar (PD) has a range of more than 250 miles for low-flying targets at its operating altitude, and the pulse (BTH) radar has a range of approximately 400 miles for aircraft flying at medium to high altitudes.

Starting in 1987, USAF E-3s were upgraded under the 'Block 30/35 Modification Program' to enhance the E-3s capabilities. On 30 October 2001, the final airframe to be upgraded under this program was rolled out. Several major enhancements were made, firstly the installation of electronic support measures (ESM) and an electronic surveillance capability, for both active and passive means of detection. Also, Joint Tactical Information Distribution System (JTIDS) was installed, which provides rapid and secure communication for transmitting information, including target positions and identification data, to other friendly platforms. Global Positioning System (GPS) capability was also added. Onboard computers were also overhauled to accommodate JTIDS, Link-16, the new ESM systems and to provide for future enhancements.

All transmissions from a radar set are unique to that type of radar, and can be identified by anyone with a suitable radar frequency receiver and a decent database of radar parameters. 8

A dramatic head-on shot showing the huge rotodome on top of RAF E-3D Sentry XH103 'Happy' at RAF Waddington in early 1996. (author)

Squadron's E-3D Sentries are fitted with the Loral 1017 'Yellowgate' ESM system, unique to the E-3D within the AEW world, located in the aircraft's distinctive wing pods. This system gives automatic identification of radar transmissions together with a bearing of that radar's source. This allows the ESM operator some degree of identification of radar contacts in a tactical situation.

The E-3D can pass information by a variety of data links, and radios. Voice communication is achieved via satellite communications, UHF, VHF and HF voice radios. Data can be passed by data link. The main links include:

Joint Tactical Information Distribution System (JTIDS), which uses both Interim JTIDS Message Standard (IJMS) and Link 16 message standards. Link 16 is used to pass tactical information between the E-3D and the Tornado F3s and Typhoons. IJMS is the main NATO air-picture data link.

Link 11 is used to pass data to Naval Forces, UK air-defence sites and to some air platforms such as maritime patrol and Elint aircraft.

Seven different internal communication nets allow the crew to co-ordinate internally, either discretely or crew-wide. Three of these nets are capable of carrying classified information without risk of interception.

Sensor data is processed by the on-board computer, known as the 'mission computer' and presented to the E-3D mission crew via ten 'Situation Display Consoles.' The operators track these contacts – information such as position, heading, speed, height and identification is also stored in the computer. This track information can be passed to other computer systems, either on the ground or in ships and other aircraft, via data links.

The Radar System Improvement Program (RSIP) was a joint US/NATO development program. RSIP enhances the operational capability of the E-3 radars' electronic countermeasures, and dramatically improve the system's reliability, maintainability, and availability. Essentially, this programme replaced the older transistor-transistor logic and emitter-coupled logic electronic components, long-since out of production, with off-the-shelf digital computers that utilised a High-level programming language instead of assembly language. These hardware and software modifications improved the E-3 radars' performance, providing enhanced detection with an emphasis towards low radar cross-section (RCS) targets.

The RAF had also joined the USAF in adding RSIP to upgrade the E-3's radars. The retrofitting of the E-3 squadrons was completed in December 2000. Along with the RSIP upgrade was installation of the Global Positioning System/Inertial Navigation Systems which dramatically improve positioning accuracy. In 2002, Boeing was awarded a contract to add RSIP to the small French AWACS squadron. Installation was completed in 2006.

The USAF has a total of thirty-one E-3s in active service. Twenty-seven are stationed at Tinker AFB and belong to the Air Combat Command (ACC). Four are assigned to the Pacific Air Forces (PACAF) and stationed at Kadena AB, Okinawa and Elmendorf AFB, Alaska. One aircraft (TS-3) was assigned to Boeing for testing and development (retired/scrapped June 2012). In 1977, Iran placed an order for ten E-3s, but this

The new and the old! The nose of 8 Squadron's Sentry AEW.1 XH107 'Bashful' with XW664, a 51 Squadron R.1P Nimrod behind taken during a series of severe snowstorms that hit RAF Waddington on 26 January 1996. The E-3 wears the city of Lincoln crest below the captain's window. (author)

An RAF Sentry waddles out to the end of Coningsby's main runway to take off on another sortie. At the time 8 Squadron were away from their normal base of RAF Waddington which was undergoing runway work. (author)

order was cancelled following the 1979 revolution.

The United Kingdom and France are not part of the NATO E-3A Component, instead procuring E-3 aircraft through a joint project. The UK and France operate their E-3 aircraft independently of each other and of NATO. The UK operates six aircraft (with a seventh now retired) and France operates four aircraft, all fitted with the newer CFM56-2 engines. The British requirement came about following the cancellation of the British Aerospace Nimrod AEW3 project to replace the Avro Shackleton AEW2 during the 1980s. The UK E-3 order was placed in February 1987, with deliveries starting in 1990.

The Royal Air Force operates the Sentries in the airborne surveillance and command-and-control role. The aircraft are based at RAF Waddington, where they are operated by 8 Squadron as the UK's contribution to the NATO Airborne Early Warning and Control Force. The E-3D also forms one arm of the UK Intelligence, Surveillance, Target Acquisition and Reconnaissance (ISTAR) triad of Sentinel R1, E-3D and Shadow R1 aircraft. Whilst primarily procured as an airborne early warning aircraft, the E-3D has been extensively employed in the Airborne Warning and Control System (AWACS) role. The E-3D Sentry, known to the RAF as the AEW1, has been extensively modified and updated to accommodate modern mission systems. Mission endurance is approximately eleven hours, although this can be extended by air-to-air refuelling. The E-3D is the only aircraft in the RAF's inventory capable of air-to-air refuelling by both the American 'flying-boom' system and the RAF's 'probe-and-drogue' method.

The normal crew complement of eighteen comprises four flight-deck crew, three technicians and an eleven-man mission crew. The mission crew comprises a tactical director (mission crew commander), a fighter allocator, three weapons controllers, a surveillance controller, two surveillance operators, a data-link manager, a communications operator and an electronic-support-measures operator. The Sentry's roles include air and sea surveillance, airborne command and control, weapons control and it can also operate as an extensive communications platform.

The aircraft cruises at 30,000 feet and 400 knots and its Northrop Grumman AN/APY-2 high-performance, multimode lookdown radar is able to separate airborne and maritime targets from ground and sea clutter. One E-3D flying at 30,000 feet can scan at distances of over 300 nautical miles; it can detect low-flying targets or maritime surface contacts within 215 nautical miles and it can detect medium-level airborne targets at ranges in excess of 280 nautical miles. The multi-mode radar provides lookdown surveillance to the radar horizon and an electronic vertical scan of the radar beam provides target elevation and beyond-the-horizon operation for long-range surveillance of medium and high-altitude aircraft. These attributes allow it to determine the location, altitude, course and speed of large numbers of airborne targets. The aircraft's mission systems can separate, manage and display targets individually on situation displays within the aircraft, or it can transmit the information to ground-based and ship-based units using a variety of digital data links

Almost immediately upon becoming operational on the Sentry in 1991, 8 Squadron was deployed on operations over the Balkans. The squadron, along with its sister 23 Squadron, assumed the Airborne Early Warning role upon reformation in April 1996, sharing the RAF's Sentry AEW1 fleet with 8 Squadron. Both squadrons operated the Sentry over Bosnia, Kosovo, Afghanistan, Iraq and Libya until 23 Squadron disbanded on 2 October 2009, when it amalgamated with 8 Squadron.

Just as 8 Squadron Shackletons used to carry

XH104 'Sleepy' seen surrounded by ground equipment during a temporary deployment from RAF Waddington to RAF Coningsby on 24 October 2014 while runway work was carried out at the former airfield. (author)

the names of *'Magic Roundabout'* and *'The Herbs'* characters, the Sentries are also named, after Walt Disney's *'Seven Dwarfs'*. The names on a plaque, along with a embroidered caricature is located on a bulkhead just to the right of the main crew entry door. For the record, ZH101 *Doc;* ZH102 *Dopey;* ZH103 *Happy;* ZH104 *Sleepy;* ZH105 *Sneezy;* ZH106 *Grumpy* and ZH107 *Bashful.*

While still operating the venerable Shackleton AEW aircraft from Lossiemouth in Scotland, 8 Squadron had been earmarked in 1987 to be the unit to fly the new Sentry AEW.1 aircraft from Waddington.

Some personnel were sent to the NATO air base at Geilenkirchen for training, the first qualifying in October 1988. Over the next year, the equivalent of two more crews were trained at Geilenkirchen, returning in 1990 to form elements of the STS and 8 Squadron crews. The aircraft for the RAF were, meanwhile, under construction at the Boeing plant at Seattle, where the first one, ZH101, took to the air on 5 January 1990. First to arrive at Waddington however, was ZH102, which flew in on 4 July 1990, followed by ZH101 on 26

March 1991.

Although not yet officially in existence as the Sentry squadron, 8 Squadron (Designate) began operating the Sentry on UK air defence duties on 8 May 1991, when Flt. Lt. David Buchanan captained ZH102 on a flight of almost nine hours during which the crew co-operated with the Sector Operations Centre at Neatishead, Norfolk.

On 1 July 1991 8 Squadron formally took up its first posting in England in seventy years, when on that day the 'old' squadron was disbanded, to be instantly reformed at Waddington. Previously the squadron had spent nineteen years in Scotland and before that had been stationed in the Middle East since October 1920, using a wide variety of aircraft over the years.

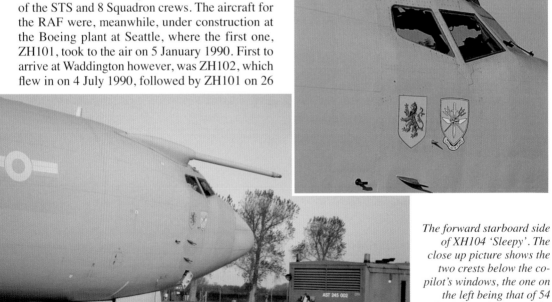

The forward starboard side of XH104 'Sleepy'. The close up picture shows the two crests below the co-pilot's windows, the one on the left being that of 54 Squadron, the one on the right being the NATO AEW emblem. (author)

To mark the new circumstances, the squadron paraded at Waddington, two Flights of personnel marching in review order behind a kilted pipe band. On the apron where the parade was held stood two Sentry aircraft flanking one venerable Shackleton, and at the right moment another Shackleton flew by at low level to symbolise the change of aircraft. The squadron standard was paraded and handed over by Wg Cdr C J Booth to the new CO, Wg Cdr R G Thompson, and those on parade were inspected by AM Sir Kenneth Hayr, a former member of 8 Squadron and now the Deputy Chief of Defence Staff.

8 Squadron's first operation after reformation took place on 4 July 1991 as part of an offensive support exercise involving control of Jaguars, Tornados and Harriers. The final Sentry, ZH107, was handed over to the RAF in March 1992, enabling 8 Squadron to reach full operational standard on 1 July, and two weeks later the squadron was tasked by NATO AEW Force Command at SHAPE to operate in support of UN sanctions in Bosnia. Since then, the RAF Sentries have worked closely with the similar NATO aircraft and with the USAF, Italian Air Force and l'Armee de l'Air, providing detachments at forward operating bases in Italy and Norway. During the Bosnian crisis 8 Squadron maintained regular surveillance of the Bosnia-Herzogovina 'no fly' zone under Operation 'Sky Monitor'. On 19 January 1993 one of the Sentries and a NATO E-3 visited Budapest in Hungary to show appreciation for the use of that country's airspace, in which orbits south of Budapest were flown to allow the radar coverage to be enhanced.

In addition, the squadron in its first eighteen months deployed aircraft to Alaska, Cyprus, Denmark, Holland, France, Germany and Canada to take part in NATO exercises. A notable milestone was reached on 3 March 1992, when a Sentry was air-refuelled twice during a five-and-three-quarter hour flight, once by the British 'probe and drogue' method and once by the USAF's rigid boom, the aircraft being fitted with both systems. The aircraft can be airborne for up to twelve hours without refuelling, and much longer after 'topping up', though in normal practice this is not necessary.

In RAF service the Sentry AEW.1 has a crew that can be divided into two sections: Flight Deck and Mission. On the flight deck the Captain (1st Pilot) is responsible for the safety of the aircraft and its occupants.

Co Pilot: Both pilots are fully qualified to operate the aircraft, which is generally 'operated' from the left-hand seat. Pilots, therefore, fly most sorties from the left-hand seat to ensure 'hands on' time is shared evenly. The pilot in the right-hand seat is responsible for radio communication and the monitoring of navigation radio aids.

Navigator: His duties, amongst others, include ensuring that the aircraft reaches and maintains its orbit position, often in airspace giving little margin for error.

This head on shot of XH104 'Sleepy' taken during the walkround shows the dual re-fuelling system fitted to the RAF E-3Ds, the aircraft being capable of taking fuel from both probe and drogue and flying boom systems.(author)

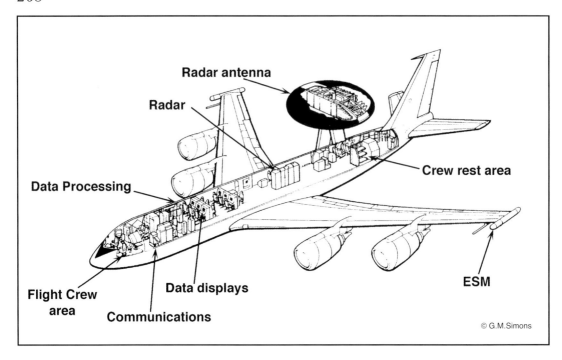

Above: the main cabin layout of a Royal Air Force E-3D Sentry, showing most of the crew positions.

Below: the Data Processing section, with display screens. The Communications and Encripto section is further forward. (author)

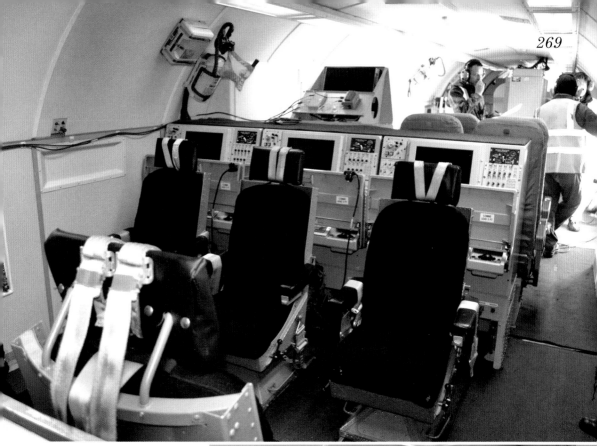

Above: the data processing area of XH104 'Sleepy' looking aft towards the radar and radar operator's area. At the time the aircraft was having maintenance done on the wing spoilers, so the over-wing escape hatches were open. Nevertheless, considering the interior has no real windows, just 'portholes' in the escape hatches, the light levels are good, and there is no sense of being inside a gloomy, claustrophobic tube.

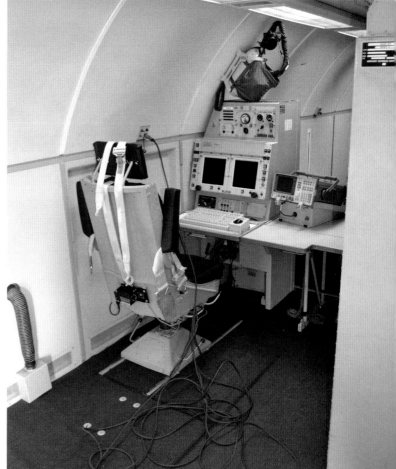

Right: the radar operator's position. All the chairs have full four-point harnesses, and rotate away from the work stations. (both author)

Although basically the Boeing 707, the RAF's E-3D are fitted with CFM-56 engines and the fuselage does not have the long row of windows on either side; they also carry 'low visibitity' markings. (author)

Flight Engineer: The flight engineer is responsible for monitoring the engine power and flight performance of the aircraft.

Head of the Mission Crew is the Tactical Director, responsible for the overall conduct of the mission, as tasked by the operating authorities. He is the senior member of the mission crew and liaises directly with the operating authorities.

The Surveillance Team is commanded by the Surveillance Controller, who provides the optimum radar picture with which to work. Working for him are the Links manager, who ensures the efficient employment of the digital data links, two or three Surveillance operators and an ESM operator who compile the recognised air and surface picture for onward transmission to the ground and other units.

The weapons team is headed by the Fighter Allocator who is responsible for the safe conduct of all aircraft which have been allocated to the E-3D to control. His two or three Weapons Controllers can control a wide variety of air missions including Offensive and Defensive Counter Air operations using fighters, Close Air Support and Battlefield Air Interdiction using bombers and a wide variety of operational support aircraft.

The Communications Operator is in charge of all the Sentry's on-board communications. He allocates access to radios and data links to those who need them.

Because of the complexity of the on-board systems the E-3D is unique in the Royal Air Force in carrying airborne technicians who initialise, monitor and provide basic maintenance of the highly sophisticated mission equipment:

The Communications Technician assists the Communications Operator in the running of all the on-board communications systems including the physical data links.

The Display Technician initialises, runs and maintains the on-board computer systems which are the heart of the mission equipment.

The Radar Technician runs the mission radar, without which there would be no mission. He liaises with the Surveillance Controller and the Display Technician to provide the best possible

radar picture for the surveillance and weapons teams to work with.

Formed on 1 January 1993, the Sentry Standards Unit was responsible for checking flying standards of all Sentry crews. It gradually expanded to the point where it had a crew of instructors which was virtually operational, covering all the special functions.

Over the years the SSU gradually evolved until on 5 September 2005, 54 (R) Squadron officially reformed with a new role, taking over operational training of three aircraft types at RAF Waddington as the Intelligence Surveillance, Target Acquisition and Reconnaissance (ISTAR) Operational Conversion Unit to train aircrews from the three ISTAR platform, E-3D Sentry, Nimrod R1 and Sentinel R1.

French Sentries

In the late 1990s France's E-3F fleet received upgrades such as electronic support measures that could detect and backtrack incoming radar beams and other electromagnetic emissions, a passive listening and detection system, and a radar system improvement programme, which enhanced the capability to detect and track aircraft and missiles. This brought them to roughly Block 30/35 equivalent.

Above: the low visibility marks including the 8 Squadron emblem and tiny fin flash on the tail of XH107 'Bashful'. Below: XH104 undergoes work on the wing spoilers. (both author)

E-3D Details

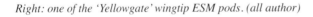

Above: the back end and (below) the front, both covered and uncovered CFM-56s that power the RAFs Sentries.

Right: one of the 'Yellowgate' wingtip ESM pods. (all author)

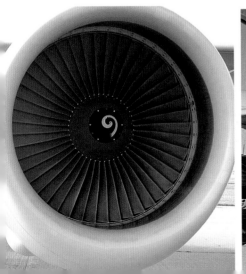

One for the modellers! Lumps, bumps, hatches and aerials. The rear fuselage of the last 707 airframe built, ZH107, shows an array of 'interesting things'. (author)

In 2004 France decided to look at upgrading their E-3Fs from Block 30/35. They contracted with Hanscom AFB's Electronic Systems Center to perform a feasibility study to identify what would be the new French AWACS mid-life upgrade for mission computing and air battle management.

The study was performed to compare the US Block 40/45 system and the NATO mid-term system. After the study, the French concluded they wanted to pursue the US Block 40/45, with French-specific requirements added or retained.

On 26 September 2008 the US Defense Security Co-operation Agency announced France's request to upgrade four E-3F AWACS with Block 40/45 Mission Computing, Electronic Support Measures and Radar System Improvement Program Interface, and Mode 5/S Identification Friend or Foe. In addition, this proposed sale was to include related spare and repair parts, support equipment, publications and technical documentation, integration, personnel training and equipment, contractor engineering and technical support services, and other related elements of programme support. The estimated cost was $400 million.

France used this upgrade to maintain full interoperability and interchangeability with US and other NATO coalition partners, and would have no difficulty absorbing the additional AWACS aircraft into its armed forces. Boeing Integrated Defense Systems in Seattle, WA would be the prime contractor, but implementation of this sale would not require the assignment of any US Government and contractor representatives to France.

On 7 January 2011 Air France Industries and KLM Engineering & Maintenance, which joined forces following the Air France/ KLM merger, announced a contract with Boeing Defense, Space & Security to install the E-3F's modification kits.

The work was begun in 2012 in the AFI facility at Le Bourget, outside Paris, and ended when the 4th and last aircraft was refitted. A team from Boeing was on-hand throughout the program to oversee operations.

Later that year, on 12 September, Air France and the French MdlD's SIMMAD Aircraft Through Life Support Organization announced the renewal of the through-life support contract for France's fleet of four E-3F AWACS. This five-year deal increment was to run through to 1 September 2016 and although Air France KLM would not disclose costs, a press release said:

"Through life support covers the complete array of AWACS engineering support services… technical and documentary support for the aircraft and its mission-specific systems, painting, and

702-CB is towed into the hangar for updates at Le Bourget. (AFI/KLM)

heavy maintenance concurrently with Mid-Life Upgrade work, maintaining the related engineering resources, and providing IT and logistics support services. Two related projects will also by continued under the terms of the contract, namely the digitization of all technical documentation, and the integration of airworthiness monitoring into the AWACS computer systems."

Then, on 24 September 2012, France had problems in upgrading its E-3F AWACS fleet became apparent, thanks to bureaucratic bungling on the American side of the table. The problem was that the Pentagon ordered Boeing to stop work on the upgrade, because they needed to hold a review regarding technologies that might be too sensitive for export. Boeing already had staff in

Paris, who needed to be kept but could not work. Overall costs: another $5 million.

The US government wanted France to pay the extra $5 million. France had already spent $10 million on a 2009 risk reduction study that looked at engineering and technologies, and the Pentagon didn't make an issue of anything at that time. France said, not unreasonably, that if the Pentagon's serial mistakes caused the problem, and they were the ones managing the programme under Foreign Military Sale rules, then the Pentagon could pay for the extra costs.

On 17 February 2014 Boeing's team successfully completed the first of the four Mid-Life Upgrades to France's E-3F fleet. All machines underwent ground and flight tests at Avord Air Base, following their upgrade rotation through AFI

36-CA, one of the four French E-3F fleet in flight. (Armee de L'Air)

The same aircraft is rolled out at Le Bouget on completion of the upgrades. (AFI/KLM)

KLM E&M's facility at Charles De Gaulle Airport in Paris.

The other operator of the type, delivered between June 1986 and September 1987, is Saudi Arabia which operated five aircraft, all fitted with CFM56-2 engines.

E-3 Sentry aircraft were among the first to deploy during Operation Desert Shield, where they immediately established an around-the-clock radar screen to defend against Iraqi forces. During Operation Desert Storm, E-3s flew 379 missions and logged 5,052 hours of on-station time. The data collection capability of the E-3 radar and computer sub-systems allowed an entire air war to be recorded for the first time in history. In addition to providing senior leadership with time-critical information on the actions of enemy forces, E-3 controllers assisted in 38 of the 41 air-to-air kills recorded during the conflict.

NATO E-3s joined their USAF colleagues for joint air defence as part of Operation Eagle Assist in the wake of the 11 September 2001 terrorist attacks on the World Trade Center towers and the Pentagon.

J-Stars

The Northrop Grumman E-8 Joint Surveillance Target Attack Radar System, known as Joint STARS, is a USAF Airborne ground surveillance, battle management and command and control aircraft. It tracks ground vehicles and some aircraft, collects imagery, and relays tactical pictures to ground and air theatre commanders. The aircraft is operated by both active duty Air Force and Air National Guard units and also carries specially trained US Army personnel as additional flight crew.

Joint STARS evolved from separate United States Army and Air Force programmes to develop, detect, locate and attack enemy armour at ranges beyond the forward area of troops. In 1982 the two programmes were merged and the USAF became the lead agent. The concept and sensor technology for the E-8 was developed and tested on the Tacit Blue experimental aircraft. The prime contract was awarded to Grumman Aerospace Corporation in September 1985 for two E-8A development systems.

The E-8C is an aircraft modified from the Boeing 707-300 series commercial airliner. It carries specialised radar, communications, operations and control sub-systems. The most prominent external feature is the 40 foot canoe-shaped radome under the forward fuselage that houses the 24 foot long side-looking APY-7 passive electronically scanned array antenna.

The E-8C can respond quickly and effectively to support worldwide military contingency operations. It is a jam-resistant system capable of operating while experiencing heavy electronic countermeasures. It can fly a mission profile for nine hours without refuelling. Its range and on-station time can be substantially increased through in-flight refuelling.

The AN/APY-7 radar can operate in wide area surveillance, ground moving target indicator (GMTI), fixed target indicator (FTI) target classification, and synthetic aperture radar (SAR) modes.

To pick up moving targets, the radar looks at the Doppler frequency shift of the returned signal. It can look from a long range, which the military refers to as a high standoff capability. The antenna can be tilted to either side of the aircraft for a 120-degree field of view covering nearly 20,000 square miles and can simultaneously track 600 targets at more than 150 miles. The GMTI modes cannot pick up objects that are too small, insufficiently dense, or stationary. Data processing allows the APY-7 to differentiate between armoured vehicles and trucks, allowing targeting personnel to better select the appropriate ordnance for various targets.

The system's SAR modes can produce images of stationary objects. Objects with many angles - for example, the interior of a truck bed - will give a much better radar signature, or specular return. In addition to being able to detect, locate and track large numbers of ground vehicles, the radar has a limited capability to detect helicopters, rotating antennas and low, slow-moving fixed-wing aircraft.

The radar and computer subsystems on the E-8C can gather and display broad and detailed battlefield information. Data is collected as events occur. This includes position and tracking information on enemy and friendly ground forces. The information is relayed in near-real time to the US Army's common ground stations via the secure jam-resistant surveillance and control data link and to other ground nodes beyond line-of-sight via ultra high frequency satellite communications.

Other major E-8C prime mission equipment are the communications/datalink and operations and control subsystems. Eighteen operator workstations display computer-processed data in graphic and tabular format on video screens. Operators and technicians perform battle management, surveillance, weapons, intelligence, communications and maintenance functions.

Northrop Grumman has tested the installation of a MS-177 camera on an E-8C to provide real time visual target confirmation.

In missions from peacekeeping operations to major theatre war, the E-8C can provide targeting data and intelligence for attack aviation, naval surface fire, field artillery and friendly manoeuvre forces. The information helps air and land commanders to control the battlespace.

The E-8's ground-moving radar can tell approximate number of vehicles, location, speed, and direction of travel. It cannot identify exactly what type of vehicle a target is, tell what equipment it has, or discern whether it is friendly, hostile, or a bystander, so commanders often crosscheck the JSTARS data against other sources. In the Army, JSTARS data is analyzed in and disseminated from a Ground Station Module.

Midway through the ratification testing, in 1991 Iraq invaded Kuwait, so the two E-8A development aircraft were rapidly deployed to participate in Operation Desert Storm under the direction of Albert J. Verderosa, even though they were still in development. Technicians still working on the aircraft, along with 770 tons of material, were flown to Riyadh in Saudi Arabia by C-141 Starlifter and C-5 Galaxy in support.

The joint programme accurately tracked mobile Iraqi forces, including tanks and Scud missiles.

Joint Stars E-8A 86-0416 was the former QANTAS 707-338C VH-AEF. (USAF)

The E-8C Joint Surveillance Target Attack Radar System is the only airborne platform in operation that can maintain realtime surveillance over a corps-sized area of the battlefield. A joint Air Force - Army programme, the Joint STARS uses a multi-mode side looking radar to detect, track, and classify moving ground vehicles in all conditions deep behind enemy lines. 92-3290 is the former N4115J and has an interesting history. This B707, named 'City of Tamworth' was delivered to QANTAS on 6 June 1967. It was sold to Zambia Airways as 9J-AEL on 20 May1977, and Trans Arabian as ST-ALP in March 1989. It was refurbished and converted to a E-8C J-Stars 92-3290 based at 93rd ACW, Robbins AFB Georgia. (US Air Force photo)

Crews flew developmental aircraft on 49 combat sorties, accumulating more than 500 combat hours and a 100% mission effectiveness rate.

Excellent results shown in combat led to a contract for the series production on 24 April 1992, revised in May 1993 for the addition of a further six units to those already planned.

The provision for the manufacture of two per year was delayed following Boeing's withdrawal from the project, alleviated by the intervention of Northrop, who continued production at their Melbourne, Florida plant. The third unit was ready in December 1993 and made its first flight on 25 March 1994, by which time three more units were ready in USAF hangers.The acquisition of three second-hand CC-137s - the designation given to five Boeing 707-347C which served with the Canadian Forces from 1970 to 1997, was also required, each costing 6.8 million dollars, and these started arriving in 1996.

That same year Variant C was declared operational of which thirteen were destined for Wing 93 of Airborne Control and Surveillance at Robins Air Base in Georgia.

At one time six units for NATO's Airborne Ground Surveillance programme were being considered. These Joint STARS developmental aircraft also participated in Operation Joint Endeavor, a NATO peacekeeping mission, in December 1995. While flying in friendly air space, the test-bed E-8A and pre-production E-8C aircraft

monitored ground movements to confirm compliance with the Dayton Peace Accords agreements. Crews flew ninety-five consecutive operational sorties and more than 1,000 flight hours with a 98% mission effectiveness rate.

The 93d Air Control Wing, which activated on 29 January 1996, accepted its first aircraft. On 11 June 1996, and deployed in support of Operation Joint Endeavor in October. The provisional 93d Air Expeditionary Group monitored treaty compliance while NATO rotated troops through Bosnia and Herzegovina. The first production E-8C and a pre-production E-8C flew thirty-six operational sorties and more than 470 flight hours with a 100% effectiveness rate. The Wing declared initial operational capability on 18 December 1997 after receiving the second production aircraft. Operation Allied Force saw Joint STARS in action again from February to June 1999, accumulating more than 1,000 flight hours and a 94.5% mission-effectiveness rate in support of the US led Kosovo War.

On 1 October 2002, the 93rd Air Control Wing (93 ACW) was amalgamated with the 116th Bomb Wing in a ceremony at Robins Air Force Base, Georgia. The 116th BW was an Air National Guard wing equipped with the B-1B Lancer bomber at Robins AFB. As a result of a USAF reorganization of the B-1B force, all B-1Bs were assigned to active duty wings, resulting in the 116 BW lacking a current mission. Extensive efforts

The Ground Moving Target Indicator display overlaid on a ground image. (USAF)

by Georgia's governor and congressional delegation led to the resulting amalgamation, with the newly created wing designated as the 116th Air Control Wing. The 93rd ACW was inactivated the same day. The 116th ACW constituted the first fully blended wing of active duty and Air National Guard airmen.

The 116th ACW has been heavily involved in both Operation Enduring Freedom and Operation Iraqi Freedom, earning high marks for operational effectiveness and recently completing 10,000 combat hours. The Wing took delivery of the 17th and final E-8C on 23 March 2005. E-8C Joint STARS routinely support various taskings of the Combined Force Command Korea during

the North Korean winter exercise cycle and for the United Nations, enforcing UN resolutions on Iraq. The twelfth production aircraft, outfitted with an upgraded operations and control subsystem, was delivered to the USAF on 5 November 2001.

On 13 March 2009, a Joint STARS aircraft was damaged beyond economical repair when a test plug was left on a fuel tank vent, subsequently causing the fuel tank to rupture during in-flight refuelling. There were no casualties but the aircraft allegedly sustained $25 million in damage.

On 3 September 2009, Dr Loren B Thompson of the Lexington Institute raised the question of why most of the Joint STARS fleet was sitting idle instead of being used to track insurgents in Afghanistan. Thompson stated that the JSTARS' radar has an inherent capacity to find what the Army calls 'dismounted' targets - insurgents walking around or placing roadside bombs. Thompson's neutrality has been questioned by some since Lexington Institute has been heavily funded by defense contractors, including Northrop Grumman.

Recent trials of JSTARS in Afghanistan are destined to develop tactics, techniques and procedures in tracking dismounted, moving groups of Taliban.

On 28 November 2010, amidst escalating danger of war breaking out between North and South Korea, the South Korean government requested the US to implement JSTARS in order to monitor and track North Korean military movements near the DMZ.

On 17 January 2011, Northrop Grumman's E-8C Joint STARS test bed aircraft completed the second of two deployments to Naval Air Station Point Mugu, California, in support of the US Navy Joint Surface Warfare Joint Capability Technology Demonstration to test its Network-Enabled Weapon architecture.

The Joint STARS aircraft executed three Operational Utility Assessment flights and demonstrated its ability to guide anti-ship weapons against surface combatants at a variety of standoff distances in the NEW architecture. The Joint STARS aircraft served as the network command-and-control node, as well as a node for transmitting in-flight target message updates to an AGM-154 C-1 Joint Standoff Weapon carried by US Navy F/A-18 Hornets using its advanced long range tracking and targeting capability.

From 2001 to January 2011 the Joint STARS fleet flew over 63,000 hours in 5,200 combat missions in support of Operations Iraqi Freedom, Enduring Freedom and New Dawn.

On 1 October 2011, the amalgamated construct of the 116th Air Control Wing combining Air National Guard and Regular Air Force personnel in a single unit was discontinued. On this date, the 461st Air Control Wing was established at Robins AFB as the Air Force's sole active duty E-8 JSTARS Wing while the 116th ACW reverted to a traditional Air National Guard Wing within the Georgia Air National Guard. Both units share the same E-8 aircraft and will often fly with mixed crews, but now function as separate units.

Four variants were allocated the E-8 designation: E-8A: original platform configuration TE-8A: Single aircraft with mission equipment removed, used for flight crew training. YE-8B: a single aircraft, was to be a US Navy E-6 but transferred to the US Air Force as a development aircraft before it was decided to convert second-

The forty-foot 'canoe' fitted under the front lower fuselage of the Joint STARS aircraft provided very little ground clearance. (USAF)

hand Boeing 707/CC-137 for the JSTARS role;
E-8C: Production Joint Stars platform configuration converted from second-hand Boeing 707/ CC-137.

E-6 Mercury

The Boeing E-6 Mercury - formerly E-6 *Hermes* is an airborne command post and communications relay based on the Boeing 707-320. The original E-6A manufactured by Boeing's defense division entered service with the United States Navy in July 1989, replacing the EC-130Q. It conveyed instructions from the National Command Authority to fleet ballistic missile submarines, a mission known as TACAMO (TAke Charge And Move Out). The E-6B model deployed in October 1998 kept this role, but added further command post capabilities and control of land-based missiles and nuclear-armed strategic bombers. The E-6B replaced Air Force EC-135Cs in the 'Looking Glass' role, providing command and control of US nuclear forces should ground-based control become inoperable. With production lasting until 1991, the E-6 was the final new derivative of the Boeing 707 to be built.

Like the E-3 Sentry AWACS aircraft, the E-6 is adapted from Boeing's 707-320 airliner. The first E-6 made its maiden flight from Boeing's Renton Factory on 19 February 1987, when it was flown to Boeing Field, Seattle, for fitting of mission avionics. The aircraft was delivered to the Navy for testing on 22 July 1988. The E-6A, which was initially named *Hermes,* entered service with VQ-3 on 3 August 1989, the second squadron, VQ-4, receiving its first E-6As in January 1991, allowing the EC-130Q to be phased out in June that year. The E-6A was renamed *Mercury* in autumn 1991 by request of the US Navy. Sixteen were delivered from 1988 to 1992.

The E-6B is an upgrade to the E-6A. It included a battlestaff area and updated mission equipment. The flight deck systems were later replaced with an off-the-shelf 737 Next Generation cockpit. This greatly increases the situational awareness of the pilot and saves significant cost over the previous custom avionics package. The first E-6B was accepted in December 1997. All sixteen E-6A aircraft were modified to the E-6B standard, with the final delivery taking place on 1 December 2006.

The E-6 fleet is based at Tinker Air Force Base, Oklahoma, and operated by Fleet Air Reconnaissance Squadron 3 (VQ-3) and VQ-4.

C-137

There seems to be something of a myth that the C-137 was a KC-135 variant - it was not. The Boeing C-137 Stratoliner was a USAF VIP transport aircraft based on and derived from the 707. A number of other nations also bought both new and used 707s for military service, primarily as VIP or tanker transports. As already seen, the 707 served as the basis for several specialised versions, such as the E-3 Sentry AWACS aircraft.

USAF procurement of the Boeing 707 was very limited, amounting to three Model 707-153s designated VC-137A. When delivered in 1959 these had four 13,500 pound dry thrust Pratt & Whitney J57 (JT3C6) turbojets; when subsequently re-engined with 18,000 pounds dry thrust TF33-P-5 (JT3D) turbofans they were redesignated VC-137B. Operated by the 89th Military Airlift Wing, they were further redesignated C-137B when downgraded from the VIP role.

Only one other variant served from new with the USAF: this was the VC-137C presidential transport, the two examples of which were Model 707-320B Intercontinentals with specialized interior furnishings and advanced communications equipment. They were internally configured to seat twenty-two in comfort with extra equipment to serve occupants as an Airborne Command Post. Two further non-presidential C-137C aircraft were later added. Contrary to popular legend these were not named 'Air Force One', which was the aircraft's call-sign only used when the US President was on board. This was a special designation established in 1953 when President Dwight D. Eisenhower was on a flight that used that call sign to avoid confusion with other aircraft.

At the request of President Kennedy, a new paint scheme was developed by First Lady Jacqueline Kennedy and famous industrial designer, Raymond Loewy. In addition to the vibrant blue and white coloors, the words 'United States of America' were emblazoned in tall letters along the fuselage and an American flag was placed on the tail. These distinctive markings reflect the stature of the Office of the President and serve as a highly visible symbol of American prestige.

One of the world's most historic aircraft, SAM 26000 carried eight American presidents: Kennedy, Johnson, Nixon, Ford, Carter, Reagan, George H.W. Bush and Clinton. The aircraft played an important role in American presidential, political and diplomatic history, and it remains an important national symbol from the Cold War period. In June 1963, SAM 26000 flew President Kennedy via RAF

Waddington in Lincolnshire UK, to West Berlin, Germany, where he declared to the world that 'Ich bin ein Berliner' (I am a Berliner), boldly assuring continued American support in the face of communist threats and the construction of the Berlin Wall.

SAM 26000 bears an intimate connection to one of the nation's greatest tragedies, a moment that forever altered the course of American history. On 22 November 1963, President Kennedy was assassinated while travelling in a motorcade through downtown Dallas, Texas.

Many long minutes later after the dramatic events in Dealey Plaza, a phone call finally came through to the terminal at Love Field from Brigadier General Godfrey McHugh, the President's military aide, at Parkland Hospital: Fuel up and file a flight plan for Washington.

The pilot of Air Force One, Colonel James Swindal had no knowledge of what had occurred, but he obeyed the order, rushing for the stairs and shouting to his flight engineer standing on the tarmac below: *'Get fuel onboard! Get ready to go!'*

Swindal only found out what had actually happened to Kennedy when he turned on the TV in the presidential compartment and heard that he'd been shot. As word spread, Love Field came alive. Military personnel streamed out of the terminal, returning to Air Force One and Air Force Two, the Vice President's aircraft, parked nearby. Swindal's copilot, Colonel Lewis 'Swede' Hanson, who had driven to his mother-in-law's house close by the airport for a visit, raced back.

Sergeant John Trimble, one of the Air Force signalmen on the airliner, was working his radio, talking to Andrews Air Force Base, when word passed through the VC-137 that President Kennedy was dead. *'All the chatter ceased. We were all numb and did our jobs automatically as we waited for the body to arrive.'*

Extra security began to surround the aircraft. Then came the first sign of what had gone so terribly wrong: Shortly after 1:15, the presidential limousine, its back seat covered in blood, arrived back at the airfield and headed for the military C-130 Hercules transport that had brought the motorcade to Dallas. From the limo, Secret Service agent Samuel Kinney,

Below: Boeing VC-137C SAM 62-6000 during its final flight on 20 May 1998, arriving at the National Museum of the United States Air Force, Dayton Ohio. The 'SAM' prefix stands for Special Air Missions, used to mark the carriage of eight sitting presidents and countless heads of state, diplomats, dignitaries and officials on many historic journeys. (US Air Force photo)

Right: The flight deck of 62-6000. (author)

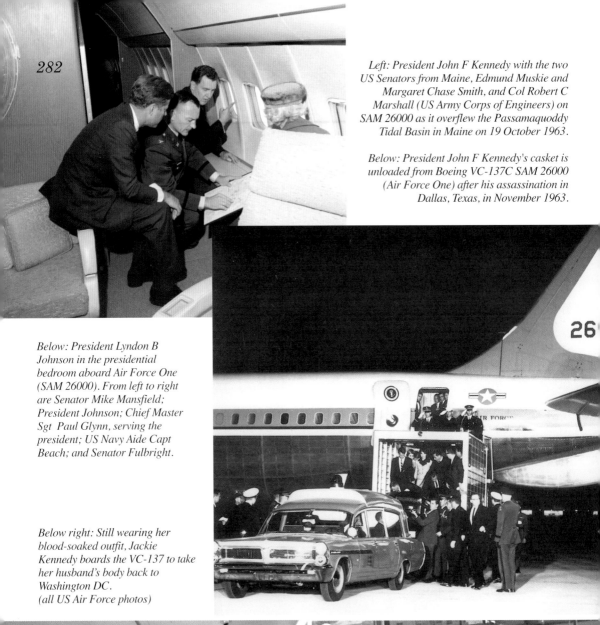

Left: President John F Kennedy with the two US Senators from Maine, Edmund Muskie and Margaret Chase Smith, and Col Robert C Marshall (US Army Corps of Engineers) on SAM 26000 as it overflew the Passamaquoddy Tidal Basin in Maine on 19 October 1963.

Below: President John F Kennedy's casket is unloaded from Boeing VC-137C SAM 26000 (Air Force One) after his assassination in Dallas, Texas, in November 1963.

Below: President Lyndon B Johnson in the presidential bedroom aboard Air Force One (SAM 26000). From left to right are Senator Mike Mansfield; President Johnson; Chief Master Sgt Paul Glynn, serving the president; US Navy Aide Capt Beach; and Senator Fulbright.

Below right: Still wearing her blood-soaked outfit, Jackie Kennedy boards the VC-137 to take her husband's body back to Washington DC.
(all US Air Force photos)

Colonel James Swindal and Colonel Lewis 'Swede' Hanson aboard one of the VC-137s at Andrews Air Force Base.
(USAF)

who had helped carry Kennedy into Parkland Hospital before reinstalling the car's bubble top for the drive back to the airport, radioed ahead to the Hercules: '...*Have the ramp down - we're driving right aboard.*'

Meanwhile, just outside the stateroom, the crew, Swindal, Hanson, flight engineer Joe Chappell, and steward Joe Ayres, began tearing apart the rear of the aircraft. As word arrived that Air Force One would be carrying the President's body home to Washington, everyone on the crew had had nearly the same thought: President Kennedy could not go into the baggage compartment.

They could get a casket through the rear door, but a partition would block the turn into the aisle, so the crew had taken a saw to the partition and unbolted four seats to make room. They carried the seats down the stairs and across the tarmac to the other Boeing that had been serving as Air Force Two. As Joe Chappell was later to recount: '...*we finished up just before the hearse arrived*'.

Disregarding the Dallas coroner's order that the President's corpse remain in the city, Kennedy aides had manhandled the casket through the crowded hallways of Parkland Hospital, past priests, medical workers, and security, and out into a hearse, racing as quickly for Love Field as they could, arriving there a little after 2pm.

Now Secret Service agents pulled open the hearse doors, as those aides gathered to carry their boss home. General Ted Clifton, who had run Kennedy's daily intelligence briefings, appraised the stairs nervously: '*Do you suppose we can get it up there?*. *It was too narrow to accomplish this without some difficulty,*' recalled O'Brien.

Activity on the tarmac fell eerily silent. Nearby, Air Force personnel saluted.

Many hands wrestled the casket, a solid-bronze Elgin Britannia, the very best at Vernon Oneal's Dallas mortuary, into the fuselage and around the partition cut open by the crew, then lowered it to the floor.

Generals Clifton and McHugh, the two highest-ranking military men on the aircraft, their pristine uniforms now soaked with sweat from carrying the casket in the heat knew their duty; both stood stiffly at attention beside the coffin, the lone honour guard observing a military custom since time immemorial: A fallen commander-in-chief is never left alone.

By all accounts there was confusion about the VC-137: McHugh turned to O'Donnell: '*Should we get airborne?*' McHugh ran for the cockpit, breezing past the closed door of the presidential stateroom, where LBJ was once again on the phone to Washington, not realising that the new President was aboard.

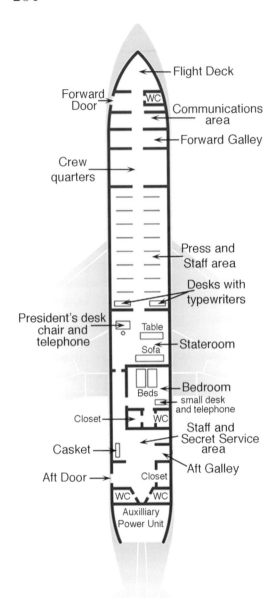

- Flight Deck
- Forward Door
- WC
- Communications area
- Forward Galley
- Crew quarters
- Press and Staff area
- Desks with typewriters
- President's desk chair and telephone
- Table
- Sofa
- Stateroom
- Beds
- Bedroom
- small desk and telephone
- Closet
- WC
- Staff and Secret Service area
- Casket
- Aft Galley
- Aft Door
- Closet
- WC   WC
- Auxilliary Power Unit

The interior layout of SAM 26000 as it was during the flight from Love Field to Washington DC with the body of President John Fitzgerald Kennedy.
(via USAFM)

'You leave right now,' O'Donnell commanded General McHugh when he returned to the rear and Air Force One still wasn't moving. 'Please, let's leave,...' Jackie pleaded to McHugh a second time.

Doubling back to the cockpit after a few minutes had passed without the engines starting up, McHugh couldn't understand why Swindal wasn't acting

immediately on his command to take off. He ordered Swindal a second time, now angrily: 'Take off! The President is aboard!'

'Mr. Kilduff says we can't.'Swindal flatly replied.

Johnson had quickly seized on Mac Kilduff, President Kennedy's Assistant Press Secretary as a key liaison - and the only press aide available. He had charged Kilduff with setting up the swearing-in.

After checking with Johnson, Kilduff ended up pulling aboard three reporters to witness the swearing-in: *Newsweek's* Charles Roberts, UPI's Merriman Smith, and Sid Davis of Westinghouse Broadcasting Company.

At Swindal's reply, McHugh's anger boiled over: he could not understand why some civilian press guy doing countermanding the order of an Air Force general.

'Not until Johnson has taken the oath,' Kilduff tried to explain, when McHugh confronted him outside the cockpit. 'Johnson isn't here...' McHugh argued. 'He's on the backup plane.'

'Then you go back and tell that six-foot Texan he isn't Lyndon Johnson,' Kilduff retorted. 'We're not going to Andrews until the President has been sworn.'

A detail view of the presidential seal on 26000.
(author)

McHugh's unwitting reply captured the entire day's confusion and sadness and, for all intents and purposes, ended his military career: *'I have only one President and he's lying back in that cabin.'*

As O'Donnell recalled. *'I was flabbergasted. Johnson could have waited until he got to Washington and spared all of us on Air Force One that day, especially Jackie, a lot of discomfort and anxiety.'* But the aircraft's schedule revolved around Lyndon Johnson's wishes. There may have been two Presidents on board, but only one of them counted for official purposes. JFK was no longer Passenger Number One.

While waiting for Judge Hughes to arrive to swear the new President in, Jackie Kennedy decided that while she wouldn't change her clothes, she could clean herself up. She took a step from the aft compartment toward the presidential bedroom and opened the door - only to find LBJ sprawled on the bed, her bed, dictating to Marie Fehmer. Johnson had realised that as uncomfortable as the room made him, it was the one space on the aircraft where he could have privacy.

He and Jackie looked at each other for a moment, and Johnson stood to exit, squeezing by her in the tight passageway. *'We scurried out of that bedroom,'* Fehmer was later to say: *'It was really embarrassing.'*

Jackie was left in the room where she'd last been alone with her husband that morning. She moved to the bathroom, looking at herself in the mirror, and proceeded to wipe the blood and hair from her face with a Kleenex. She immediately regretted it: *'History! Why did I wash the blood*

Air Force One Passenger Manifest

A complete list of passengers and crew aboard Air Force One's flight back from Dallas on 22 November 1963, does not appear to exist, possibly due to the confusion of the day. This manifest is the most comprehensive available based on eyewitnesses and written records.

1   President John F. Kennedy
2   Jacqueline Kennedy
3   President Lyndon B. Johnson
4   Lady Bird Johnson
5   Kenneth P. O'Donnell, special assistant to the President
6   Larry O'Brien, special assistant to the President for congressional relations
7   David F. Powers, special assistant to the President
8   Bill Moyers, associate director of the Peace Corps
9   Congressman Homer Thornberry (Texas)
10 Congressman Al Thomas (Texas)
11 Congressman Jack Brooks (Texas)
12 Malcolm 'Mac' Kilduff, White House assistant press secretary
13 General Chester 'Ted' V. Clifton Jr., senior military aide
14 General Godfrey T. McHugh, Air Force aide
15 Admiral Dr. George Burkley, President's physician
16 Evelyn Lincoln, personal secretary to the President
17 Mary Gallagher, personal secretary to Mrs. Kennedy
18 Pamela Turnure, press secretary to Mrs. Kennedy
19 Sergeant George "Boots" Miller, Air Force One crew
20 Master Sergeant Joseph Giordano, Air Force One crew
21 Staff Sergeant Paul J. Glynn, Vice President's valet
22 Chief Warrant Officer Ira D. Gearhart, military aide
23 Elizabeth 'Liz' Carpenter, executive assistant to the Vice President
24 Jack Valenti, partner, Weekley & Valenti advertising and political-consulting agency
25 Marie Fehmer, secretary to the Vice President
26 Cliff Carter, aide to the Vice President
27 George Thomas, President's valet
28 Roy Kellerman, assistant special agent in charge, presidential Secret Service detail
29 Clint Hill, First Lady's Secret Service detail

30 John J. 'Muggsy' O'Leary, presidential Secret Service detail
31 Warren Taylor, vice-presidential Secret Service detail
32 Henry Rybka, presidential Secret Service detail
33 William Greer, limousine driver, presidential Secret Service detail
34 Stewart 'Stu'" Stout, presidential Secret Service detail
35 Sam Sulliman, presidential Secret Service detail
36 Richard E. Johnsen, presidential Secret Service detail
37 Ernest E. Olsson, presidential Secret Service detail
38 Rufus Youngblood, special agent in charge, vice-presidential Secret Service detail
39 Lem Johns, assistant special agent in charge, vice-presidential Secret Service detail
40 Jerry Kivett, vice-presidential Secret Service detail
41 Paul Landis, presidential Secret Service detail
42 Merriman Smith, reporter, UPI
43 Charles Roberts, reporter, Newsweek

Secret Service records show the crew for the flight to Texas was as follows. It is assumed they also returned with the aircraft to Andrews Air Force Base.

1   Colonel James B. Swindal, pilot
2   Lieutenant Colonel Lewis G. 'Swede' Hanson, copilot
3   Senior Master Sergeant William J. 'Joe' Chappell
4   Major David D. Odor, flight engineer
5   Chief Warrant Officer John R. McLane
6   Master Sergeant John C. Trimble, flight engineer
7   Senior Master Sergeant Joseph C. Ayres, radioman
8   Master Sergeant Vernon J. 'Red' Shell, flight steward
9   Technical Sergeant R.M. McMillan, flight steward
10 Staff Sergeant John T. Hames
11 Master Sergeant Wyatt A. Broom, flight steward
12 Staff Sergeant Eulogio Gomez
13 Technical Sergeant Charles R. Ruberg, security aide

off? I should have left it there, let them see what they've done'.

Judge Sarah Hughes raced to the airport in her red sports car around 2:10 pm. The Dallas police chief spotted her car as she approached Love Field and cleared a path.

Police Chief Jesse Curry escorted her to the aircraft. A flight steward who had been assigned to wait for the judge saw a big Texan in his Stetson hat approach and stepped forward to greet the man he assumed was the jurist: *'Judge, will you come with me?'*

'Oh, just a minute,"' the chief said, gesturing to the small, 67-year-old woman behind him.

As they gathered for the swearing in aboard the VC-137, Kilduff realized they should record the oath, but no one had a tape recorder. *'There's a Dictaphone thing on the President's desk,'* Stoughton volunteered, and after some scrambling Kilduff had his arm outstretched with the microphone, holding on tightly to the five-inch reel recorder.

Just as Hughes, in her brown-and-white polka-dot dress, began, a military aide handed O'Brien a white box containing a Bible found in the presidential quarters. O'Brien interrupted the judge, handing her the book and saying, *'This is a Catholic Bible.'* It was a small book, with a black leather cover emblazoned with a cross. Handmade out of calfskin, it had the initials JFK embossed on the inside cover. No one noticed in the moment that it wasn't actually a Bible - it was a St. Joseph Sunday Missal, a prayer book the Catholic Church uses to lead the faithful through the annual cycle of Masses.

LBJ rested one hand on the book, raising his other one. Hughes began to recite the famous words *'I do solemnly swear . . .*

After the swearing in, the judge de-planed, the door closed and the VC-137 began to move.

The Love Field tower radioed Swindal: *'Air Force One, you are cleared for takeoff, runway 31L.'*

President and Mrs. Nixon are met by People's Republic of China Premier Zhou Enlai. For a short period, President Nixon renamed SAM 26000 as The Spirit of 76 in honour of the nation's bicentennial. (via USAFM)

Spectators watch one of two C-137B Stratoliner aircraft returning freed hostages to the USA after their release from Iran in 1981. (via USAFM)

The four turbofans began to scream as Swindal raised them to maximum throttle.

The President's casket rattled next to Jackie as she sat in the aft breakfast nook. The new President in his cabin, already on the phone again, was pushed into his seat by the acceleration.

President John F Kennedy was going home.

At 2:47, as the engines pushed the airliner past 150 knots, takeoff speed, Swede Hanson called V-1, and Colonel Swindal eased his yoke back,tilting the aircraft's nose upward, and Air Force One's wheels left the Texas soil.

Air Force One banked toward the northeast as news of its takeoff passed through the military radio channels, using the aircraft's longstanding Secret Service code name: *'Angel is airborne.'*

The aircraft then carried Kennedy's body and President Johnson back to Washington, DC, and a grieving nation.

During the Southeast Asia War, SAM 26000 transported President Johnson to visit US troops in South Vietnam. In 1970 President Nixon's national security advisor, Dr. Henry Kissinger, travelled aboard the aircraft on thirteen separate trips to secret peace talks with the North Vietnamese in Paris, France. In February 1972 SAM 26000 flew President Nixon to the People's Republic of China on his famous 'Journey for Peace,' the first visit by an American president to China. Three months later, it carried President Nixon on an unprecedented visit to the Soviet Union, where he signed two historic nuclear arms control agreements.

In December 1972 SAM 26000 became the president's backup aircraft when the Air Force acquired another Boeing VC-137C (serial number 72-7000). However, SAM 26000 continued flying presidents, vice-presidents and other high-ranking government officials on important missions. In October 1981, it carried former Presidents Nixon, Ford and Carter to the funeral of the slain Egyptian president Anwar Sadat. In March 1983 Queen Elizabeth II of the United Kingdom flew on SAM 26000 during her visit to the United States. When SAM 26000 left the presidential fleet in 1990, it continued to fly prominent government officials. Secretary of State James Baker flew aboard the aircraft prior to the 1991 Gulf War for talks with Iraqi leaders regarding their invasion of Kuwait.

The two 707-353Bs, termed VC-137Cs, were purchased by the USAF (one in 1961 and one in 1972) for service as presidential transports with call signs SAM 26000 and SAM 27000 and were later redesignated C-137C when downgraded from presidential use. Two further C-137Cs were acquired by the USAF, one 707-396C (a seized aircraft formerly used for arms smuggling acquired in 1985) and one 707-382B bought second-hand in 1987.

The C-18 is the US military designation for the conversions of the 707-320B series.

C-18A

Eight second-hand (former American Airlines) 707-323Cs bought as crew trainers for the EC-18Bs, four of which were later converted to EC-18B, two converted to EC-18D, one to C-18B; one was not taken into service and was used for spares.

288

Former Presidents Gerald Ford, Richard Nixon and Jimmy Carter on the steps of Boeing VC-137C SAM 26000 (US Air Force photo)

C-18B
One C-18A modified with instrumentation and equipment to support the Military Strategic and Tactical Relay System (MILSTAR).

EC-18B
Four C-18As modified alongside examples of the C-135 for Advanced Range Instrumentation Aircraft (ARIA) missions in support of the Apollo space program. The designation E-7 was originally applied to modified Boeing 707s before being replaced by the EC-18 designation.

EC-18C
Original designation for two prototype J-STAR aircraft, later redesignated E-8A.

EC-18D
Two C-18As modified as a Cruise Missile Mission Control Aircraft (CMMCA).

TC-18E
Two second-hand (former Trans World Airlines) 707-331 aircraft modified for E-3 pilot and crew training.

TC-18F
Two second-hand (former TAP Portugal) 707-382 aircraft modified for E-6 pilot training.

EC-137D
Two aircraft built as Early Warning and Control System prototypes. Later re-engined and re-designated E-3A. A further second-hand 707-355C aircraft was acquired and configured as an airborne special operations command post.

CT-49A
NATO Trainer-Cargo Aircraft (TCA) operated to support E-3A AWACS training and air transport/cargo for NATO (NAEW&CF) based on Boeing 707-320B.

Harvesting For Spares - or use.
The longer the USAF used the KC-135 and its derivatives, the harder to find and more expensive replacement parts became, especially after Boeing ceased manufacturing items for the type.

It was not surprising therefore that in 1984 Congress instructed the USAF to start buying commerical 707s for spare parts or for further use, the C-18 programme being a purpose in point.

Another reason for harvesting from civilian 707s was to use engines and spare parts in a re engineering programme for Boeing KC-135A Stratotanker aircraft. The modifications to the KC-135E entailed changing the J57 engine for the TF33-PW-102 engines, improved brakes, avionics upgrades and new horizontal stabilizers. The KC-135E was fourteen percent more fuel efficient than the KC-135A and could offload twenty percent more fuel.

Buying second, third or fourth-hand aircraft could be questionable, and it was not long before potential pitfalls for Air Force purchasers of used aircraft involving the condition and acceptability verification of used airframes started to appear. Used aircraft are very much like used cars, in that two identical models may be sitting on the ramp in very different conditions. Inspections of B-707 aircraft during the C-18 selection process showed an extreme variation in aircraft condition, even among aircraft operated by the same carrier. Variations in aircraft condition were even greater between carriers even though the airlines maintain aircraft to the same FAA requirements. According

to William Yri, C-18 programme manager at the time of the inspections , the maintenance philosophy of the individual carrier bore heavily on the actual condition of the aircraft. '*Some carriers appear to make maintenance decisions based solely on near term cost considerations. Their aircraft were best suited for scrap. Other carriers had obviously tried more to maintain a quality asset*'

The task of accurately evaluating condition and acceptability of commercial used aircraft was made more complex by differences in the ways the Air Force and the airlines measure aircraft age and need for service/overhaul. In the commercial environment aircraft are tracked by both flight hours and by ground-air-ground cycles. These were the primary means of establishing aircraft fatigue life, and are used by the aircraft manufacturer to develop service bulletins that correct maintenance or fatigue problems. Of particular significance to a potential buyer are the life extension and corrosion control bulletins that have been issued against the aircraft series being considered. Knowledge of the bulletins which

Retired 707s from the airlines were acquired by the USAF, flown or transported to the the high desert at Davis-Monthan in Arizona and 'harvested' for any spare parts that could be used on either the military 707s or KC-135 upgrades. (AMARC via USAF)

A technician checks the last pin for damage while a crane hold the fin at a 45 degree angle prior to proceeding in the operation of lowering the vertical stabilizer of a civil Boeing 707 aircraft on 6 December 1984. The Military Aircraft Disposition and Storage Center at Davis-Monthan Air Force Base, Arizona, was reclaiming commercial Boeing 707 aircraft, using engines and spare parts in a re-engineering program for Boeing KC-135A Stratotanker aircraft.

The low rainfall with resulting low humidity of the high desert meant that airframes and engines could be stored with little risk of corrosion as long as other environmental considerations - like dust - were protected against.(USAF)

have been issued and when installation is required or recommended gives the potential buyer the ability to decide which of the bulletins should be applied and to plan for the costs involved. In the case of engine condition verification the standard airline practice is acceptable, but must be understood by those responsible for inspections during the selection process. The commercial practice is to specify a minimum number of hours remaining before overhaul 'across the wing' with a minimum for wing with not less than 1000 hours on any one engine was typical.

The Air Force buyer had to keep in mind that commercial maintenance practices reflect the commercial concern for bottom line profit. Wheel wells, flap, and slat areas in particular, tend to have a great deal of surface corrosion. The airlines consider such corrosion to be a cosmetic rather than a safety problem, and the military customer may need to invest 1,000 or more manhours per aircraft with an allowance for miscellaneous parts to bring the aircraft up to acceptable military standards. Once again, anticipation is the key to developing an acquisition strategy flexible enough to discriminate quality used aircraft from the 'lemons'

Closely related to the many difficulties involved with condition verification are the potential problems presented by required modifications to the used aircraft. Again, both time and dollar costs are involved, so early planning was the key to remaining on track after the aircraft is in Air Force hands.

The most obvious modifications are those required to take the basic commercial aircraft and outfit it to perform its military mission. Depending on the nature of the programme this could take a few weeks or many months. It is the programme manager's task early on in the acquisition cycle to carefully outline and plan for every detail of modification that will be required on the aircraft.

Most of the acquired aircraft were initally stored at the Aerospace Maintenance and Regeneration Center (AMARC), based at Davis-Monthan AFB near Tucson, AZ. The current site was originally the Tucson municipal airport and is named after two local military aviators who were killed in accidents in the early 1920s. Expansion followed, and in 1945 the airfield began its role as a storage depot when the first aircraft were retired there after the second world war. The original plan was to both store aircraft for potential return to service and remove spare parts that could be re-used and scrap the remainder. During the late 1950s the facilities were unable to cope with the quantity and this led to the number of scrap yards like National Aircraft Inc., Bob's Air Park and Southwest Alloys that developed around the base. In 1963, to show the role was being expanded to address all US Air Forces, the name of the incumbent unit, the 2704th AF Storage and Disposition Group (AFSDG), part of Air Materiel Command, was changed to the Military Aircraft Storage and Disposition Center MASDC) but this was changed again in October 1985 to AMARC to put more emphasis on the regeneration of aircraft as well as storage.

The primary roles of AMARC are to provide a storage facility for aircraft that are currently not needed; provide a source of spare parts from aircraft that have been permanently withdrawn from service; prepare aircraft for return to service or for sale to overseas military forces.

The reasons for using this edge of the Sanora desert for storage are the low local annual rainfall coupled with the low humidity and the hard alkaline soil which make it possible to park aircraft without the need for concrete or steel aprons Because of the weather there is minimum deterioration or corrosion to the airframe, which undergoes a preservation process on arrival. Firstly all 'live' equipment such as guns and ejector seats are removed along with any classified equipment, then all fuel is drained from the aircraft and replaced by a lubricating oil which is itself then drained to leave a film protecting the fuel system. Aircraft are cleaned and any visible corrosion treated before being towed to an allocated parking area. All engine intakes, exhausts and other cracks and gaps are taped to prevent damage during the dust storms that occur in the area and then they are covered with a vinyl plastic covering called 'Spraylat', along with delicate parts like canopies, windows and radomes. The Spraylat is made up of two parts; the first layer is black and keeps out dust and water while the second coat, which is white, acts as a temperature controller. As can be imagined, the temperature in stored aircraft parked in the Arizona desert can cause damage to sensitive equipment but the Spraylat maintains a temperature only slightly above the ambient.

Undersides of aircraft are not sealed to allow circulation of air and prevent condensation build-up. The condition of the coating is usually checked every six months and replaced every four years, latterly some aircraft have been placed in large plastic 'bags' as a cheaper alternative.

Aircraft stored at AMARC fall in various categories as follows:

Type 1000 Long-term storage. These are the long term storage aircraft that undergo the four yearly renewing of the Spraylat; they are usually stored examples of types still current in the US Forces,making a return to service a possibility.

Type 2000 Storage for Reclamation. These are

N897WA was originally N764PA of Pan American. Behind is N6598W, originally a 707-344B of South African Airways. Like most 707s and 720s that were spares reclaimed, their vertical fins and rudders were put to immediate use. (Dr Harry Friedman)

N7158Z in African Express Airways colours aways the axeman. (Dr Harry Friedman)

aircraft that are being used for spares recovery.

Type 3000 Storage. After arrival aircraft are held in a flyable condition for ninety days (which can be extended) while awaiting a decision on their disposal; also held under this category are the aircraft for Foreign Military Sales.

Type 4000 - for Disposal. These are aircraft where all useable parts have been removed and basically only the hulk remains. They are usually sold to the local scrap-yards and are towed to the exit gates, where some scrapping takes place before being taken to the 'melting' pots.

Besides providing a storage environment, the staff at AMARC provide a valuable source of spare parts to keep other examples of a type still flying. They are also responsible for conducting some low level maintenance on aircraft removed from storage prior to Foreign Military Sales and preparing them, as in the case of the KC-135s for flights to McConnell and Tinker AFBs for depot level maintenance and painting.

On arrival an aircraft is allocated a unique identifier known as the AMARC inventory number which describes both the type of aircraft and its sequential number. All USAF C-135s had the prefix CA, while ex-civilian 707s for KC-135E spares were allocated CZ and ex USN aircraft are identified with a number and letter (e.g. 6G for NKC-135 and 3G for C-137s). Up to October 1994 these codes were followed by a three digit number but the impending arrival of the 1000th Phantom led to a fourth digit being added plus an extra two letters at the beginning to show which service flew the aircraft, thus a KC-135 with the code CA101 became AACAO101 (AA being the code for ex-USAF aircraft).

Each aircraft is allocated a unique storage code consisting of six digits and these refer to its location within the complex - the first two digits refer to the storage area (there are twenty-nine areas within AMARC with seventeen and nineteen being the Processing in and out as well as maintenance areas) followed by four numbers representing the position of an aircraft in a row in these numbered areas.

Chapter Nine

'Come Fly With me'

composed by Jimmy Van Heusen, with lyrics by Sammy Cahn; written for Frank Sinatra.

With so many aircraft built in the production run, even with a book this size, it is impossible to detail each and every airframe constructed - and even it was was, it is by no means certain that those histories would be described with any degree of certainty! Let me explain what I mean using an interesting machine with what is, a fairly simple history.

Not everyone can own their own 707; but American actor, producer, dancer, author and singer John Travolta is one such person.

His film, dancing and singing career is well documented elsewhere, and he is on record as saying that his acting funded his passion for aviation. He earned his private pilot's license at age 22 and today owns several aircraft, including a Boeing 707-138 that was previously part of Qantas Airways' fleet. His home is in Jumbolair Aviation Estates, a fly-in community at north central Florida's private Greystone Airport. He has a taxiway right to his door, where he parks the 707.

The airliner has been updated over the years, and is now fitted with hush-kits and upgraded avionics that include GPS and TCAS; It now has the tail number N707JT, and is the last of its kind in service.

Its luxurious interior features wide leather seats, sofas and rich wood panelling and it was serendipity that brought the actor and the 707 together: '*I was promoting a film called Get Shorty at the time and in the promotion of that movie, they wanted me to go to Berlin for just the weekend. I said: 'I'm not going to be able to go to Berlin for the weekend and be ready for work on Monday if I don't have a plane that at least has a bedroom.'*

"So they found one - they found this plane. That was the deal, so they rented it for me. I fell in love with it, because on departure I went into the bedroom, I fell asleep and arrived in Berlin so rested it was as though I had never travelled at all'.

Travolta knew he wanted the airliner but it was too expensive at the time. He was forced to wait three years until it hit the right price in 1998.

"I was told to put a certain kind of offer in and I would get the plane if I did and they were right on. I did and I never looked back."

His love of aviation went back to childhood when he lived under the flight path of New York's LaGuardia Airport.

'By the time planes were about 2000 feet after

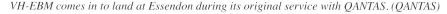

VH-EBM comes in to land at Essendon during its original service with QANTAS. (QANTAS)

departure, they were over my house. Constellations, DC-6s, DC-7s - I fell in love. I watched them all day long.

Then I started collecting books on aviation and that's where I learnt about Qantas and how they had a distinct personality with long-distance, over-water flights, their safety record - they were just kind of untouchable - and I always kept my eye on them, just to see what they were up to."

When Travolta was about six, his show-business sisters started to travel and the family would take them to the airport. Close-up views of the aircraft further fanned the young John's enthusiasm and at eight he took his first flight - a 30-minute trip from Newark Airport to Philadelphia. He still remembers that the outbound leg was on National Airlines DC-6 and the return trip on a United Airlines Caravelle.

Attesting to his early charisma, he persuaded the girls in his neighborhood to don their Brownie uniforms to play flight attendants as he 'captained' his backyard airliner. Every six months from then he was allowed to fly somewhere to visit his sisters.

"So twice a year I got to fly in an airliner and, finally, at 15, I start studying aviation. At 16, I started taking lessons and then at 19 I got my solo. At 23 I got my licence and at 25 I got my jet licence."

Was he tempted to become a pilot? *"I was at some point, but I realised that the routing for that would have taken a level of scholarships and finances that we didn't have in our upbringing. It just would have been too expensive and the military wouldn't have even supported me, because I wouldn't have the college behind me to be a pilot. So I really had no choice but to self-finance being a pilot. And I did it through theatre and television earlier, and then through movies. So my whole aviation career has been financed by my other profession."*

His first aircraft was an ERCO Aircoupe, that flew like a car and was advertised for doctors and lawyers, which he bought for $2500 instead of a car.

"I had a little motorcycle and I had the plane, That's all I needed. So I had a plane before I had a car."

An ambitious jump saw Travolta buy a legendary Douglas DC-3 before moving into a range of high-performance and jet aircraft as well as another legendary airliner, the four-engine Lockheed Constellation. Of all the aircraft he has owned, the 707 takes pride of place.

"This is majestic, and when I grew up I was dreaming about flying, so this is kind of a dream come true."

Travolta paid for maintenance of the 707 for the first four years, before striking a deal with then QANTAS chief executive Geoff Dixon to paint the aircraft in QANTAS colours and come on board as the airline's ambassador, a job he clearly relishes.

"The quid pro quo was that Qantas took over the aircraft's expensive maintenance. "Any plane this size is too pricey. I did it for four years on my own and it was much easier to do a barter system and promote the airline.

But more importantly, I really wanted to be part of the airline. So it was gorgeous, because I couldn't have dreamed of a better fit - owning a big plane like this without it looking like an airline seems odd to me."

VH-EBM was delivered to the airline in 1964 and flew with it until it was sold to Braniff International Airways in 1969. It was converted to a VIP jet in 1973 and had a number of owners, including singer Frank Sinatra and billionaire Kirk Kirkorian. **So just who HAD owned it?**

QANTAS re-painted VH-EBM in full Braniff blue and white livery before delivery as N108BN. (QANTAS)

Most pilots know that with aircraft - especially airliners - ownership is often not all that it seems, a fact that many enthusiasts completely fail to understand. The words 'Owned by' and 'Operated by' are two totally different things. As William 'Bill' Armstrong, owner and founder of Autair Airways and many other airlines once told me years ago; '...*unless you were actually there to see the suitcases full of cash change hands, never say that such-and-such aircraft was owned by xxxxx!*'

Often the only proof of who actually owns an aircraft can be gained from a visit to the flight deck, where a small, usually stainless steel plaque carries the legend '*Aircraft XXXXX, Construction Number YYYYYY is owned by ZZZZZZZ*'. The situation can be made even more complex when a machine enters the murky world of aircraft financing, leasing and asset management, often owned by a mortgage to a bank, trust group or insurance company. So it was for much of the life of John Travolta's 707-138B.

John's aircraft was built in 1964, constructed at Boeing Seattle and has Boeing construction number 18740 Line No.388, being delivered to QANTAS as VH-EBM '*City of Launceston*'. After that point, everything is open to discussion, doubt myth and legend.

The aircraft was primary used by QANTAS for routes from Sydney to Asia and North/South America until on 1 November 1968 it was withdrawn from use and stored engineless at Sydney Airport.

According to some sources, on 7 June 1969 its new owner became Braniff International Airways. It's registration number changed to N108BNanf it remained with the airline until 24 February 1972.

Here the first of a number of mysteries sets in: some sources say that it was then owned by singer Frank Sinatra until 1975, although he only operated it until 20 October 1973, when it was withdrawn from use and stored.

Enquiries with the Frank Sinatra Foundation and his daughter Nancy brought forth a list of aircraft her father owned - and there is no trace of a 707 on it. Of course, there is the possibility that the aircraft was chartered from Braniff.

Another source states that the aircraft was withdrawn from service and retired to Regency Income and registered to a Mr John M King, who passed it to Boeing in a trade-in deal in June 1975.

Other records suggest that it remained on the books of Braniff International until sometime in 1975, when it was sold to Boeing.

Whatever happened from 1972 to 1975, it is known that not long after it was sold to Boeing, it was registered in September to Kirk Kerkorian, an American billionaire.

Kerkor 'Kirk' Kerkorian (*b*. 6 June 1917 – *d*. 15 June 2015) was a businessman, investor, and philanthropist. Of Armenian American origin, Kerkorian was the president and CEO of Tracinda Corporation, his private holding company based in Beverly Hills, California. Kerkorian was known for having been one of the important figures in the shaping of Las Vegas and, with architect Martin Stern Jr has been described as the 'father of the mega-resort'. He, along with that other aviation entrepreneur and billionare Howard Hughes, played a large part in the development of Las Vegas. Kerkorian built the world's largest hotel in Las Vegas

Tucked away in a corner of the flightdeck - and remarkably difficult to photograph - is the aircraft data plate. Although in this case it is for Boeing 757 G-OOOU of Air 2000, it would be the same for many a 707. The plate states '**Serial No. 25240. This aircraft is owned by Abbey National June Leasing (2) Limited and is leased to Air 2000 Limited and may not be operated by any other person without the prior written consent of Rolls Royce and Partners Finance Limited.**' *(author)*

With that hillside covered with parked Vauxhalls it could only be Luton Airport in the late 1970s. Here N108BN is seen parked on the McAlpine executive jet port of the airport. 108BN wears the TIC livery, the full name being the Tracinda Corporation, but often reported as the 'Tracy Corp'. (DGR Photo Library)

three times: the International Hotel (opened in 1969), the MGM Grand Hotel (1973) and the MGM Grand (1993). He purchased the Metro-Goldwyn-Mayer movie studio in 1969.

Of immigrant origin and living in Los Angeles, he sensed the onset of World War Two, and not wanting to join the infantry, Kerkorian learned to fly at the Happy Bottom Riding Club in the Mojave Desert - adjacent to the United States Army Air Corps's Muroc Field, now Edwards Air Force Base. In exchange for flying lessons from pioneer aviator Pancho Barnes, he agreed to milk and look after her cattle.

On gaining his commercial pilot's certificate in six months, Kerkorian learned that the British RAF was ferrying Canadian-built de Havilland Mosquitos over the North Atlantic to Scotland. The Mosquito's

fuel tank carried enough fuel for 1,400 miles, while the trip directly was 2,200 miles. Rather than take the safer Montreal - Labrador - Greenland - Iceland - Scotland route, Kerkorian preferred the direct 'Iceland Wave' route, which blew the planes at jet-speed to Europe. Legend has it that the fee was $1,000 per flight. In May 1944, Kerkorian and Wing Commander John de Lacy Wooldridge rode the wave and broke the old crossing record. Wooldridge reached Scotland in six hours, 46 minutes; Kerkorian in seven hours, nine minutes. In two and a half years with RAF Ferry Command, Kerkorian delivered 33 aircraft, logged thousands of hours, travelled to four continents and flew his first four-engine aircraft.

After the war, having saved most of his wages, Kerkorian spent $5,000 on a Cessna. He worked as a general aviation pilot, and made his first visit to Las

N108BN seen in full TAG livery at Le Bourget, France. (DGR Photo Library)

Vegas in 1944. After spending much time there during the 1940s, Kerkorian gave up gambling and in 1947 paid $60,000 for Trans International Airlines, a small air-charter service that flew gamblers from Los Angeles to Las Vegas. He then bid on some war surplus bombers, using money on loan from the Seagram family. Gasoline, and especially airplane fuel, was in short supply at the time, so he sold the fuel from the aircrafts' tanks, paid off his loan, and still had the airpcraft. In 1962, Kerkorian bought 80 acres in Las Vegas, across the Las Vegas Strip from the Flamingo, for $960,000. This purchase led to the building of Caesars Palace, which rented the land from Kerkorian; the rent and eventual sale of the land to Caesars in 1968 made Kerkorian $9 million. He operated the airline until 1968 when he sold it for $104 million to the Transamerica Corporation.

Kerkoran's holding company retained ownership of the 707 until 26 September 1977, when it passed to TAG Aviation, a company based in Luxembourg.

The parent company, TAG (Techniques d'Avant Garde), was an investment company focused on advanced technologies. It had been formed in 1977 by Akram Ojjeh (1923 -1991), a Syria-born Saudi businessman. He was an intermediary in deals between Saudi Arabia and France, particularly for arms sales. Ojjeh brokered the sale of tanks, aircraft and electronic equipment to Saudi Arabia and large French purchases of oil.

During this time the 707 had the registration HK-KA1 allocated to it, supposedly for a lease to Saudi Arabian Sheikh Akram, for short time but the registration was never taken up.

The aircraft remained in service with TAG Aviation until 25 August 1981, when the 707 was again withdrawn from use, stored at Newark, New Jersey. Records suggest that the registration was cancelled in August 1982, but the aircraft was back in service that October. It was ferried to Le Bourget for further storage in August 1983. In September 1983 it returned to the American register as N108BN, again for TAG Aviation, remaining with them until 18 March 1985, when it passed to TAG Group USA, then back to TAG Aviation that October.

In November 1987 the records suggest it had been sold to what appears to be a somewhat shadowy organisation: Trans Oceanic Aviation. Very little is known about this organisation, apart from that they seem to have also leased another 707 - this time a -309C with a tail number N707ZS, for cargo flights.

During 1988 and 1989 it was out of service again. Sometime during this period a VIP interior was installed and the aircraft was modified with hush kits which converted it to a 707-138B(Q).

THE HISTORY OF BOEING 707-138, MANUFACTURERS SERIAL NUMBER 18740.
Line No: 388

First Flight: 1 September 1964.

VH-EBM: Delivered to QANTAS 10 September 1964. Withdrawn from serice and placed in storage at Sydney, Australia 1 November 1968.

N108BN: Purchased by Braniff International Airways 9 June 1969.

Purchased by Regency Income Corporation of Denver Colorado and leased to Braniff International on 24 June 1969. Wore blue 'jellybean' colours.

Withdrawn from service by Braniff on 10 October 1973 and registration transferred to John M King of Regency Income Corp.

To Boeing Commercial Airplane Co. June 1975

Purchased by Kerkor 'Kirk' Kerkorian on 1 September November 1975.

To the Tracinda Corporation 28 March 1977. This was a holding company of which Kerkorian was the CEO.

Sold to TAG Aviation, 26 September 1977. Based in Geneva, Switzerland, TAG Aviation is a provider of business aviation services, aircraft management, aircraft charter, maintenance, sales and acquisitions.

HZ-KA1 (registration allocated but not taken up): Leased to Sheikh Akram on 26 September 1977

N108BN: Withdrawn from use and placed in storage at Newark on 25 August 1981 and listed as for sale. Registration cancelled August 1982. Restored to register

Ferried to Le Bourget and place in storage in August 1983. Reentered service in December 1983.

Purchased by Trans Oceanic Aviation in November 1987.

New VIP interior installed while out of service 1988.

Recorded as being modified with hush kits which converted it to a 707-138B(Q) in 1989.

N707XX: Returned to service in July 1990

To Aviation Methods, Seattle in 1995.

Ferried to Istanbul and placed in storage on October 29, 1995

Offered for sale with a low TAT of 27,682hrs in September 1996

N707JT: Purchased by John Travolta on 20 May 1998.

'Captain John' during his world tour with N707JT, painted in the full QANTAS 'V-Jet livery. (QANTAS)

In July 1990, its registration number changed to N707XX it returned to service for an undetermined time. What records are available suggest that it was stored at Las Vegas until 2 March 1994, when according to some sources it was flown to London Heathrow on 3 May. In 1995 it changed hands again, this time to Aviation Methods Inc, an airline support and management company with a mailing address in Seattle. We then need to delve into the world of aircraft loggers, who record that N707XX flew from Washinton-Dulles to Shannon in Eire and then on to Istanbul on 29 October 1995. It was logged at London Heathrow again during November 1996 still in TAG colours. Previously, in September 1996, with only 27,682 of total flying hours, it was offered for sale.

On 20 May 1998 the airliner was registered to Jet Clipper Johnny LLC (John Travolta), sold on May 25, and changed registration on 13 December 1998 to N707JT *'707 Jett Clipper Ella'*. It was named after his children Jett and Ella, along with 'Clipper' in homage to legendary airline Pan Am, which used the term in all their aircraft names.

As previously described, in June 2002, the 707 finally returned home to QANTAS, since Travolta participated in the QANTAS 'Spirit of Friendship'tour, because it was always his dream to be involved with a major airline in some way. He was piloting his own Boeing 707 on a thirteen city, 35,000 mile tour. He continues as Ambassador-at-Large for QANTAS. For this campaign the plane was repainted in full classical Qantas 'V-Jet' livery. The same livery that was used for the 707's first flights, back in the old days.

At the time of writing (2017) the aircraft is kept at Travolta's house in Florida that has its own eight thousand foot runway.

As can be seen, there are huge sections of this single aircraft's history that is open to wide speculation as to what actually happened to it, and who was operating it, let alone who actually owned it! Multiply that by the simple fact that over one thousand airframes were built, and it becomes, in my opinion, impossible to research with any degree of accuracy!

Appendix I

Summary of new build aircraft.

707 Model New Build Summary Through January 2017

Model-Series	Orders	Deliveries
707-320B	174	174
707-120	56	56
707-E3A	61	61
707-138	7	7
707-E3D	7	7
707-KE3	8	8
707-E6A	17	17
720-000	65	65
707-120B	72	72
707-220	5	5
707-420	37	37
707-138B	6	6
720-000B	89	89
707-320C	337	337
707-320	69	69
707 Total	1010	1010

Model	Eng	Ordered	Quantity	Delivered	First Del
Aer Lingus (Ireland)					
707-320C	P&W	15/3/63	4	4	10/6/64
720-000	P&W	11/3/59	3	3	24/10/60
Subtotal			7	7	
Aerolineas Argentinas (Argentina)					
707-320B	P&W	21/9/65	4	4	20-11/66
707-320C	P&W	29/5/68	2	2	04/11/68
Subtotal			6	6	
Air France (France)					
707-320	P&W	28/12/55	21	21	21/10/59
707-320B	P&W	10/10/61	8	8	14/11/62
707-320C	P&W	15/4/64	9	9	05/8/65
Subtotal			38	38	
Air India (India)					
707-320B	P&W	15/5/63	3	3	25/5/64
707-320C	P&W	15/12/65	2	2	10/2/67
707-420	RR	31/8/56	6	6	18/2/60
Subtotal			11	11	
Airlift International (USA)					
707-320C	P&W	16/2/67	3	3	14/4/67
Subtotal			3	3	

Model	Eng	Ordered	Quantity	Delivered	First Del
Airline of the Islamic Republic (Iran (Islamic Republic of))					
707-320C	P&W	13/12/68	3	3	31/12/69
Subtotal			3	3	
American Airlines (USA)					
707-120	P&W	09/11/55	25	25	23/10/58
707-120B	P&W	07/7/59	31	31	25/5/61
707-320B	P&W	03/4/68	10	10	09/4/69
707-320C	P&W	24/10/62	37	37	19/11/63
720-000	P&W	30/7/58	10	10	24/7/60
720-000B	P&W	30/7/58	15	15	03/2/61
Subtotal			128	128	
Avianca (Colombia)					
707-320B	P&W	18/1/67	2	2	07/3/68
720-000B	P&W	30/6/60	3	3	08/11/61
Subtotal			5	5	
Aviation Service & Support (USA)					
707-320B	P&W	08/1/75	1	1	08/1/75
707-320C	P&W	09/6/75	1	1	09/6/75
Subtotal			2	2	
Braniff Airlines (USA)					
707-220	P&W	01/12/55	5	5	03/12/59
707-320C	P&W	15/5/65	9	9	26/5/66
720-000	P&W	09/3/60	5	5	11/2/61
Subtotal			19	19	
British Airways (United Kingdom)					
707-320B	P&W	16/1/70	2	2	18/2/71
707-320C	P&W	15/1/65	8	8	19/12/65
707-420	RR	24/10/56	19	19	27/4/60
Subtotal			29	29	
British Caledonian Airways (United Kingdom)					
707-320C	P&W	15/11/65	2	2	13/7/67
Subtotal			2	2	
British Eagle International (United Kingdom)					
707-320C	P&W	06/1/67	1	1	21/12/67
707-420	RR	25/5/61	1	1	27/2/62
Subtotal			2	2	
British Royal Air Force (United Kingdom)					
707-E3D	CF	25/2/87	7	7	01/3/91
Subtotal			7	7	

The stunning red and white scheme on Air Bahama's 707C N525EJ. (author)

CAAC-Civil Aviation of China (China)

707-320B	P&W	12/9/72	4	4	24/8/73
707-320C	P&W	12/9/72	6	6	12/11/73
Subtotal			10	10	

Cameroon Airlines (Cameroon)

707-320C	P&W	31/5/72	1	1	20/11/72
Subtotal			1	1	

Canadian Air Force (Canada)

707-320C	P&W	28/2/70	5	5	28/2/70
Subtotal			5	5	

China Airlines (Taiwan)

707-320C	P&W	18/10/68	2	2	07/11/69
Subtotal			2	2	

Eastern Air Lines (USA)

720-000	P&W	03/8/60	15	15	11/8/61
Subtotal			15	15	

Egyptair (Egypt)

707-320C	P&W	20/6/66	9	9	18/9/68
Subtotal			9	9	

EL AL Israel Airlines (Israel)

707-320B	P&W	15/9/64	3	3	07/1/66
707-320C	P&W	05/12/67	2	2	15/5/69
707-420	RR	25/3/60	3	3	24/4/61
720-000B	P&W	03/5/61	2	2	23/3/62
Subtotal			10	10	

Estado Nacional Argentino ENA (Argentina)

707-320B	P&W	11/6/75	1	1	11/6/75
Subtotal			1	1	

Ethiopian Airlines (Ethiopia)

707-320C	P&W	11/11/66	2	2	08/4/68
720-000B	P&W	16/7/60	3	3	02/11/62
Subtotal			5	5	

Executive Jet Aviation (USA)

707-320C	P&W	17/11/66	2	2	19/5/67
Subtotal			2	2	

FAA (USA)

720-000	P&W	26/1/61	1	1	12/5/61
Subtotal			1	1	

Flying Tiger (USA)

707-320C	P&W	15/1/65	4	4	28/9/65
Subtotal			4	4	

German Air Force (Germany)

707-320C	P&W	08/11/67	4	4	28/9/68
Subtotal			4	4	

Government of Egypt (Egypt)

707-320C	P&W	26/9/73	1	1	21/8/74
Subtotal			1	1	

Iraqi Airways (Iraq)

707-320C	P&W	01/10/73	3	3	27/8/74
Subtotal			3	3	

Islamic Republic of Iran Air Force

707-320C	P&W	10/5/74	15	15	10/5/74
Subtotal			15	15	

Kingdom of Saudi Arabia (Saudi Arabia)

707-320C	P&W	25/9/75	1	1	25/9/75
707-E3A	CF	16/6/83	5	5	29/6/86
707-KE3	CF	16/6/83	8	8	12/2/87
Subtotal			14	14	

Korean Air (South Korea)

707-320C	P&W	02/4/71	1	1	06/8/71
Subtotal			1	1	

Kuwait Airways (Kuwait)

707-320C	P&W	29/11/67	5	5	04/11/68
Subtotal			5	5	

LATAM Airlines Group (Chile)

707-320C	P&W	20/12/69	1	1	20/12/69
Subtotal			1	1	

Libyan Airlines (State of Libya)

707-320C	P&W	19/7/76	1	1	19/7/76
Subtotal			1	1	

Lufthansa Group (Germany)

707-320B	P&W	18/12/61	12	12	28/2/63
707-320C	P&W	15/9/64	6	6	10/11/65
707-420	RR	24/4/56	5	5	25/2/60
720-000B	P&W	01/2/60	8	8	08/3/61
Subtotal			31	31	

Middle East Airlines (Lebanon)

707-320C	P&W	03/8/68	4	4	18/11/68
Subtotal			4	4	

MSA-Malaysia/Singapore A/L (Singapore)

707-320B	P&W	16/5/67	3	3	28/5/68
Subtotal			3	3	

NATO (Belgium)

707-E3A	P&W	30/5/80	18	18	01/1/82
Subtotal			18	18	

Nigeria Airways (Nigeria)

707-320C	P&W	07/5/71	3	3	07/5/71
Subtotal			3	3	

Northwest Airlines (USA)

707-320B	P&W	11/6/62	10	10	05/6/63
707-320C	P&W	15/11/63	26	26	10/4/64
720-000B	P&W	16/3/61	13	13	26/5/61
Subtotal			49	49	

Olympic Airlines (Greece)

707-320B	P&W	11/1/68	2	2	19/12/68
707-320C	P&W	15/4/65	4	4	11/5/66
Subtotal			6	6	

Pacific Northern (USA)

720-000	P&W	06/4/61	2	2	23/3/62
Subtotal			2	2	

Pakistan International Airline (Pakistan)

707-320C	P&W	15/7/65	7	7	19/7/66
720-000B	P&W	17/4/61	4	4	26/12/61
Subtotal			11	11	

Pan Am World Airways (USA)

707-120	P&W	13/10/55	6	6	15/8/58
707-320	P&W	13/10/55	26	26	19/7/59
707-320B	P&W	13/2/61	60	60	12/4/62
707-320C	P&W	25/4/62	34	34	02/5/63
Subtotal			126	126	

Pelita Air Service (Indonesia)

707-320C	P&W	05/12/74	1	1	25/4/75
Subtotal			1	1	

QANTAS (Australia)

707-138	P&W	06/9/56	7	7	26/6/59
707-138B	P&W	01/3/60	6	6	29/7/61
707-320C	P&W	15/12/63	21	21	10/2/65
Subtotal			34	34	

Transavia Holland's 707-335 PH-TRF served for a short time with the Executive Jet fleet. It is seen at Schipol Airport during October 1968. (author)

Qatar Airways (Qatar)

707-320C	P&W	30/6/76	1	1	28/7/77
Subtotal			1	1	

Republic of France (France)

707-E3A	CF	25/2/87	4	4	01/5/91
Subtotal			4	4	

Republic of Portugal (Portugal)

707-320C	P&W	05/1/71	2	2	23/9/71
Subtotal			2	2	

Royal Jordanian (Jordan)

707-320C	P&W	15/7/70	2	2	26/1/71
Subtotal			2	2	

Royal Moroccan Air Force (Morocco)

707-320C	P&W	10/3/82	1	1	10/3/82
Subtotal			1	1	

SABENA (Belgium)

707-320	P&W	28/12/55	7	7	04/12/59
707-320C	P&W	15/5/64	7	7	15/4/65
Subtotal			14	14	

Saudi Arabian Airlines (Saudi Arabia)

707-320C	P&W	03/5/67	7	7	08/1/68
720-000B	P&W	01/9/61	2	2	20/12/61
Subtotal			9	9	

Seaboard World Airlines (USA)

707-320C	P&W	05/6/67	2	2	27/2/68
Subtotal			2	2	

Socialist Republic of Romania (Romania)

707-320C	P&W	12/3/73	2	2	03/6/74
Subtotal			2	2	

South African Airways (South Africa)

707-320	P&W	21/2/58	3	3	01/7/60
707-320B	P&W	15/3/64	2	2	01/9/65
707-320C	P&W	11/8/66	5	5	23/2/68
Subtotal			10	10	

Sudan Airways (Sudan)

707-320C	P&W	30/5/73	2	2	17/6/74
Subtotal			2	2	

TAP Portugal (Portugal)

707-320B	P&W	15/12/64	7	7	17/12/65
Subtotal			7	7	

TAROM S.A. (Romania)

707-320C	P&W	12/3/73	2	2	21/2/74
Subtotal			2	2	

Trans World Airlines (USA)

707-120	P&W	07/2/56	15	15	29/1/59
707-120B	P&W	01/5/61	41	41	29/3/62
707-320	P&W	19/3/56	12	12	10/11/59
707-320B	P&W	01/5/61	38	38	01/11/62
707-320C	P&W	15/4/63	17	17	18/11/63
720-000B	P&W	01/5/61	4	4	22/7/61
Subtotal			127	127	

United Airlines (USA)

707-120	P&W	12/12/55	5	5	19/4/59
707-320C	P&W	15/6/64	13	13	21/8/64
720-000	P&W	22/11/57	29	29	30/4/60
720-000B	P&W	13/6/61	8	8	28/4/62
Subtotal			55	55	

United States Navy (USA)

707-E6A	CF	12/2/86	17	17	01/8/89
Subtotal			17	17	

US Air Force (USA)

707-120	P&W	14/5/58	3	3	19/5/59
707-320B	P&W	09/2/62	2	2	01/10/62
707-E3A	P&W	31/12/71	34	34	01/3/77
Subtotal			39	39	

Varig Airlines (Brazil)

707-320C	P&W	15/8/65	6	6	28/12/66
707-420	RR	06/9/57	3	3	07/6/60
Subtotal			9	9	

Wardair (Canada)

707-320C	P&W	12/1/68	2	2	17/4/68
Subtotal			2	2	

Western Airlines (USA)

707-120	P&W	01/1/60	2	2	04/5/60
707-320C	P&W	22/5/67	5	5	22/6/68
720-000B	P&W	15/2/60	27	27	07/4/61
Subtotal			34	34	

World Airways, Inc. (USA)

707-320C	P&W	16/5/62	9	9	16/7/63
Subotal			9	9	

707 Total	1010	1010
	Orders Deliveries Unfilled	

Appendix II
Specifications

Model 367-80

Type:	transport prototype.
Accommodation:	3 crew and specialist personnel as required.
Powerplant:	four 10,000 pounds thrust Pratt & Whitney JT3C turbojets.
Maximum Speed:	582 mph at 25,000 ft.
Cruising Speed:	550 mph.
Initial Climb Rate:	2,500 feet per minute.
Service Ceiling:	43,000 ft.
Range:	3,530 miles.

Weights

Empty Equipped wt:	892,120 pounds.
Normal Take-Off wt:	—
Maximum Take-Off wt:	190,000 pounds.
Maximum Payload:	—
Span:	129 feet 8 inches.
Length:	127 feet 10 inches
Height:	38 feet.
Wing Area:	2,400 square feet.
Max. Fuselage Width:	132 inches
Max. Fuselage Height:	164 inches

KC-135A Stratotanker

Type:	inflight-refuelling tanker with airlift capability.
Accommodation:	flightcrew of 5, plus up to 145 passengers.
Powerplant:	four 13,750 pounds thrust Pratt & Whitney J57-P-59W turbojets.
Maximum speed:	630 mph.
Cruising speed:	532 mph at 35,000 ft,
Initial climb rate:	1,290 feet per minute.
Service ceiling:	45,000 feet.
Range:	1,150 miles with 120,000 pounds of transfer fuel.
Empty equipped wt:	106,305 pounds
Normal take-off wt:	301,600 pounds
Maximum take-off wt:	316,000 pounds
Payload:	120,000 pounds of transfer fuel 50,000 pounds of freight
Span:	130 feet 10 inches.
Length:	134 feet 6 inches.
Height:	41 feet 8 inches.
Wing area	2,433 square feet.
Max. Fuselage Width:	144 inches
Max. Fuselage Height:	166 inches

C-135B Stratolifter

Type:	transport
Accommodation:	flightcrew of 4, plus up to 126 passengers
Powerplant:	four 13,750 pounds thrust Pratt & Whitney J57-P-59W turbojets.
Maximum speed	600 mph.
Cruising speed	530 mph at 35,000 ft.
Initial climb rate:	—
Service ceiling:	—
Range	4,000 miles with a 55,000-pounds payload
empty equipped wt:	—
normal take-off wt:	—
maximum take-off wt:	272,000 pounds.
payload	89,000 pounds.
Span:	130 feet 10 inches.
Length:	134 feet 6 inches.
Height:	41 feet 8 inches.
Wing area	2,433 square feet.
Max. Fuselage Width:	144 inches
Max. Fuselage Height:	166 inches

KC-135R

Type:	inflight-refuelling tanker with airlift capability
Accommodation:	flightcrew of 4
Powerplant:	four 22,000 pounds thrust GE/SNECMA CFM56 turbofans
Maximum speed:	600 mph.
Cruising speed:	530 mph at 35,000 feet.
Initial climb rate:	—
Service ceiling:	—
Range:	4,000 miles with a 55,000 pounds payload
Empty equipped wt:	—
Normal take-off wt:	—
Maximum take-off wt:	325,000 pounds
Span:	130 feet 10 inches.
Length:	134 feet 6 inches.
Height:	41 feet 8 inches.
Wing area:	2,433 square feet
Max. Fuselage Width:	144 inches
Max. Fuselage Height:	166 inches

Model 707-100

Type:	transcontinental transport.
Accommodation:	3 crew on flightdeck, up to

179 passengers, and variable cabin staff.

Powerplant:	four 12,500 pounds thrust Pratt & Whitney JT3C-6 turbojets.
Maximum speed:	623 mph.
Cruising speed:	592 mph at 40,000 feet .
Initial climb rate:	1,400 feet per minute.
Service ceiling:	40,000 feet .
Range:	3,915 miles with maximum payload.
Empty equipped wt:	114,500 pounds .
Normal take-off wt:	247,000 pounds .
Maximum take-off wt:	257,000 pounds .
Maximum payload:	42,433 pounds.
Span:	130 feet 10 inches.
Length:	144 feet 6 inches.
Height (short fin):	38 feet 7 inches.
Wing area:	2,433 square feet.
Max. Fuselage Width:	148 inches
Max. Fuselage Height:	170.5 inches

Model 707-100B

Type:	transcontinental transport
Accommodation:	3 crew on flightdeck, up to 179 passengers, and variable cabin staff.
Powerplant:	four 18,000 pounds thrust Pratt & Whitney JT3D-38 turbofans

Maximum speed:	623 mph
Cruising speed:	612 mph at 40,000 feet.
Initial climb rate:	—
Service ceiling	40,000 feet
Max Payload Range:	4,900 miles
Empty equipped wt:	118,500 pounds
Normal take-off wt:	—
Maximum take-off wt:	258,000 pounds
Maximum payload:	44,000 pounds
Span:	130 feet 10 inches.
Length:	144 feet 6 inches.
Height (short fin):	38 feet 7 inches.
Wing area:	2,433 square feet.
Max. Fuselage Width:	148 inches.
Max. Fuselage Height:	170.5 inches

Model 707-200

Type:	transcontinental transport
Accommodation:	3 crew on flightdeck, up to 179 passengers, and variable cabin staff.
Powerplant:	four 15,800 pounds thrust Pratt & Whitney JT4A-3 turbojets.
Maximum speed:	623 mph.
Cruising speed:	592 mph at 40,000 feet.
Initial climb rate:	1,400 feet per minute.
Service ceiling:	40,000 feet.
Range:	3,915 miles with maximum payload.

The Condor was modification of the Boeing 707 for the Airborne Early Warning role (AEW) designed by Isreali Aircraft Industries and Elta, of Israel. The aircraft started its development in 1990 and the prototype, built for Chile's Air Force, made its first public showing at the Paris Air Show in 1993. IAI named it Phalcon, but in Chile it is known as the Condor and FACH has asigned to it the serial N° 904. (author's collection)

Olympic Airways' 720-051B SX-DBH was withdrawn from use at Athens in 1980. It was scrapped in 1982.

Empty equipped wt:	—
Normal take-off wt:	—
Maximum take-off wt:	257,000 pounds
Maximum payload	—
Span:	130 feet 10 inches.
Length:	144 feet 6 inches.
Height (short fin):	38 feet 7 inches.
Wing area:	2,433 square feet.
Max. Fuselage Width:	148 inches
Max. Fuselage Height:	170.5 inches

Model 707-300 Intercontinental

Type:	intercontinental transport
Accommodation:	4 crew on flightdeck, up to 189 passengers, and variable cabin staff
Powerplant:	four 17,500 pounds thrust Pratt & Whitney JT4A-11 turbojets
Maximum speed:	623 mph
Cruising speed:	602 mph at 25,000 ft.
Initial climb rate:	2,890 feet per minute
Service ceiling:	37,200 feet
Max Payload Range:	4,784 miles.
Empty equipped wt:	135,000 pounds.
Normal take-off wt:	—
Maximum take-off wt:	312,000 pounds.
Payload:	55,000 pounds.
Span:	142 feet 5 inches
Length:	152 feet 11 inches
Height:	41 feet 8 inches
Wing area:	2,892 square feet
Max. Fuselage Width:	148 inches
Max. Fuselage Height:	170.5 inches

Model 707-300B lntercontinental

Type:	intercontinental transport
Accommodation:	4 crew on flightdeck, up to 189 passengers, and variable cabin staff

Powerplant:	four 19,000 pounds thrust Pratt & Whitney JT3D-7 turbofans (typical)
Maximum speed:	627 mph
Cruising speed:	600 mph at 25,000 feet
Initial climb rate:	2,370 feet per minute
Service ceiling:	6,000 feet
Max Payload Range:	6,160 miles
Empty equipped wt:	140,525 pounds.
normal take-off wt:	—
maximum take off wt:	335,000 pounds.
Payload:	54,475 pounds.
Span:	145 feet 9 inches
Length:	152 feet 11 inches
Height:	42 feet 5 inches
Wing area:	3,010 square feet
Max. Fuselage Width:	148 inches
Max. Fuselage Height:	170.5 inches

Model 707-300C Convertible

Type:	intercontinental convertible freight - passenger transport.
Accommodation:	4 crew on flightdeck, up to 219 passengers, and variable cabin staff.
Powerplant:	four 18,000 pounds thrust Pratt & Whitney JT3D-3B turbofans (typical installation)
Maximum speed:	627 mph
cruising speed:	600 mph at 25,000
Initial climb rate:	4,000 feet per minute
Service ceiling	39,000 feet
Max Payload ange	4,300 miles
Empty equipped wt:	133,875 pounds for cargo
Normal take-off wt:	-
Maximum take-off wt:	333,600 pounds
Payload:	84,000 pounds for passenger, 91,390 pounds

	for cargo
Span:	145 feet 9 inches
Length:	152 feet 11 inches
Height:	42 feet 5 inches
Wing area:	3,010 square feet
Max. Fuselage Width:	148 inches
Max. Fuselage Height:	170.5 inches

Model 707-400

Type:	intercontinental transport
Accommodation:	4 crew on flightdeck, up to 189 passengers, and variable cabin staff
Powerplant:	four 18,000 pounds thrust Rolls-Royce Conway 508A turbofans
Maximum speed:	627 mph
Cruising speed:	600 mph at 25,000 ft
Initial climb rate:	2,370 feet per minute
Service ceiling:	36,000 feet
Max Payload Range:	4,865 miles
Empty equipped wt:	133,000 pounds
Normal take-off wt:	-
Maximum take-off wt:	335,000 pounds
Payload:	57,000 pounds
Span:	145 feet 9 inches
Length:	152 feet 11 inches
Height:	42 feet 5 inches

Wing area:	3,010 sq feet
Max. Fuselage Width:	148 inches
Max. Fuselage Height:	170.5 inches

Model 720 (Model 707-000)

Type:	medium-range transport
Accommodation:	4 crew on flightdeck, up to 165 passengers, and variable cabin staff
Powerplant:	four 12,000 pound thrust Pratt &Whitney JT3C-12 turbojets
Maximum speed:	627 mph
Cruising speed	601 mph at 25,000 feet
Initial climb rate	2,100 feet per minute
Service ceiling	38,500 feet range 3,005 miles with maximum payload
Empty equipped wt:	99,920 pounds
Normal take-off wt:	203,000 pounds
Maximum take-off wt	229,000 pounds
Payload;	37,000 pounds
Span:	130 feet 10 inches
Length:	136 feet 9 inches
Height:	37 feet 11 inches
Wing areaL	2,521 sq feet
Max. Fuselage Width:	148 inches
Max. Fuselage Height:	170 inches

Braniff International's advertsing was decidedly risqué for the time, and just as colourful as their fleet of 707s.

Model 720B

Type:	medium-range transport
Accommodation:	4 crew on fiightdeck, up to 181 1 passengers, and variable cabin staff
Powerplant:	four 18,000 pounds thrust Pratt & Whitney JT3D-3 turbofans
Maximum speed:	627 mph
Cruising speed:	608 mph at 25,000 feet
Initial climb rate:	3,700 feet per minute
Service ceiling:	40,500 feet
Max Payload range:	4,110 miles
Empty equipped wt:	11500010 pounds
Normal take-off wt:	-
Maximum take-off wt:	234,000 pounds
Payload:	41,000 pounds
Span:	130 feet 10 inches
Length:	136 feet 9 inches
height	41 feet 7 inches
wing area	2,521 sq feet
Max. Fuselage Width:	148 inches
Max. Fuselage Height:	170.5 inches

VC-137C

Type:	VIP and special freight transport
Accommodation:	flightcrew of 4, plus passengers
Powerplant:	four 18,000 pounds thrust Pratt & Whitney JT3D-3 turbofans
Maximum speed:	627 mph
Cruising speed:	600 mph at 25,000 ft
Initial climb rate:	-
Service ceiling:	about 40,000 feet
Range	7,610 miles, no reserves
Empty equipped wt:	-
Normal take-off wt:	-
maximum take-off	327,000 pounds
Span	145 feet 9 inches
Length	152 feet 11 inches
Height	42 feet 5 inches
Wing area	3,010 square feet
Max. Fuselage Width:	148 inches
Max. Fuselage Height:	170.5 inches

E-3A Sentry

Type:	airborne warning and control system aircraft
Accommodation:	flightcrew of 4 and 13 AWACS specialists
Powerplant:	four 21,000 pounds thrust Pratt & Whitney TF33-P-100A turbofans
maximum speed	530 mph
cruising speed	-
initial climb rate	-
service ceiling	39,370 feet
range	6 hours on station at 1,000 mile radius
Empty equipped wt:	about 172,000 pounds
Normal take-off wt:	-
Maximum take-off wt:	325,000 pounds
Span:	145 feet 9 inches
Length:	152 feet 11 inches
Height:	42 feet 5 inches
Wing area:	3,010 square feet
Max. Fuselage Width:	148 inches
Max. Fuselage Height:	170.5 inches

Bibliography

'*Air Force Posts Request for Proposals for Tankers*' (Press
    release). US Department of Defense. January 30, 2007.
'*BAE SYSTEMS delivers final Pacer CRAG KC-135*'.
    Aerotech News and Review. Lancaster, California:
    September 20, 2002.
'*Boeing 707 Accident Statistics.*' Aviation-Safety.net,
    February 9, 2014.
'*Boeing 707 Accident summary.*' Aviation-Safety.net,
    February 9, 2014.
'*Boeing 707-820: First details of the longer, faster, heavier
    and more*' (Press release). Flight International. June 3,
    1965.
'*Boeing KC-135 - Rockwell Collins Pacer CRAG Avionics
    Upgrade*'. Jane's Aircraft Upgrades. London, England
'*Boeing Protests US Air Force Tanker Contract Award*'
    (Press release). St Louis, Missouri: Boeing. March 11,
    2008.
'*Boeing's Jet Stratoliner.*' Popular Science, July 1954.
'*Farewell Flight.*' Time, November 14, 1983.
'*Gamble in the Sky.*' Time, July 19, 1954.
'*Jets Across the U.S.*' Time, November 17, 1958.
'*KC-135E.*' Global Security. Retrieved December 30, 2009.
'*KC-X Tanker Modernization Program, Solicitation Number:
    FA8625-10-R-6600*' (Press release). US Department of
    Defense. February 8, 2010.
'*Tanker Contract Award Announced*'. Air Force News.
    February 29, 2008.
'*Towards 200-seat Boeings*' (Press release). Flight
    International. March 25, 1965.
'*World Airliner Census*'. Flightglobal Insight, August 16–22,
    2013.
Baugher, Joe '*1957 USAF Serial Numbers*'.
    JoeBaugher.com. (28 July 2016).
Boeing Magazine Vol XVI-No.1: January 1946.
Boeing Magazine Vol XVI-No.9: September 1946.
Boeing MagazineVol XVI-No.10: October 1946.
Boeing MagazineVol XVI-No.12: December 1946.
Boeing Magazine Vol XVII-No.1: January 1947.
Boeing Magazine Vol XVII-No.11: November 1947.
Boeing Magazine Vol XX-No.1: January 1950.
Boeing Magazine Vol XX-No.2: February 1950.
Boeing Magazine Vol XX-No.3: March 1950.
Boeing Magazine Vol XX-No.4: April 1950.
Boeing Magazine Vol XX-No.5: May 1950.
Boeing Magazine Vol XXI-No.2: February 1951.
Boeing Magazine Vol XXI-No.6: June 1951.
Boeing Magazine Vol XXII-No.3: March 1952.
Boeing Magazine Vol XXII-No.8: August 1952.
Boeing Magazine Vol XXII-No.10: October 1952.
Boeing Magazine Vol XXIII-No.1: January 1953.
Boeing Magazine *Vol XXIII-No.3*: March 1953.
Boeing Magazine Vol XXIII-No.4: April 1953.
Boeing Magazine Vol XXIII-No.5: May 1953.
Boeing Magazine Vol XXIII-No.6: June 1953.
Boeing Magazine Vol XXIII-No.7: July 1953.
Boeing Magazine Vol XXIII-No.8 August 1953.
Boeing Magazine Vol XXIII-No.9: September 1953.
Boeing Magazine Vol XXIII-No.10: October 1953.
Boeing Magazine Vol XXIII-No.11: November 1953.
Boeing Magazine Vol XXIII-No.12: December 1953.
Boeing Magazine Vol XXIV-No.1: January 1954.
Boeing Magazine Vol XXIV-No.2: February 1954.
Boeing Magazine Vol XXIV-No.3-4: March/April 1954.
Boeing Magazine Vol XXIV-No.5: May 1954.
Boeing Magazine Vol XXIV-No.6: June 1954.
Boeing Magazine Vol XXIV-No.7: July 1954.
Boeing Magazine Vol XXIV-No.8: August 1954.
Boeing Magazine Vol XXIV-No.9: September 1954.
Boeing Magazine Vol XXIV-No.10: October 1954.
Boeing Magazine Vol XXIV-No.11: November 1954.
Boeing Magazine Vol XXIV-No.12: December 1954.
Boeing Magazine Vol XXV-No.1: January 1955.
Boeing Magazine Vol XXV-No.2: February 1955.
Boeing Magazine Vol XXV-No.3: March 1955.
Boeing Magazine Vol XXV-No.4: April 1955.
Boeing Magazine Vol XXV-No.5: May 1955.
Boeing Magazine Vol XXV-No.6: June 1955.
Boeing Magazine Vol XXV-No.7: July 1955.
Boeing Magazine Vol XXV-No.8: August 1955.
Boeing Magazine Vol XXV-No.9: September 1955.
Boeing Magazine Vol XXV-No.10: October 1955.
Boeing Magazine Vol XXV-No.11: November 1955.
Boeing Magazine Vol XXV-No.12: December 1955.
Boeing Magazine Vol XXVI-No.1: January 1956.
Boeing Magazine Vol XXVI-No.2: February 1956.
Boeing Magazine Vol XXVI-No.3: March 1956.
Boeing Mazagine Vol XXVI-No.4: April 1956.
Boeing MagazineVol XXVI-No.5: May 1956.
Boeing Magazine Vol XXVI-No.6: June 1956.
Boeing Magazine Vol XXVI-No.7: July 1956.
Boeing Magazine Vol XXVI-No.8: August 1956.
Boeing Magazine Vol XXVI-No.9: September 1956.
Boeing MagazineVol XXVI-No. 10: October 1956.
Boeing Magazine Vol XXVI-No.11: November 1956.
Boeing Magazine Vol XXVI-No.12: December 1956.
Boeing Magazine Vol XXVII-No.1: January 1957.
Boeing Magazine Vol XXVII-No.2: February 1957.
Boeing Magazine Vol XXVII-No.3: March 1957.
Boeing Magazine Vol XXVII-No.4: April 1957.
Boeing Magazine Vol XXVII-No.5: May 1957.
Boeing Magazine Vol XXVII-No.6: June 1957.
Boeing Magazine Vol XXVII-No.7 : June 1957.
Boeing Magazine Vol XXVII-No.8: August 1957.
Boeing Magazine Vol XXVII-No.9: September 1957.
Boeing Magazine Vol XXVII-No.10: October 1957.
Boeing Magazine Vol XXVII-No.11: November/December 1957.
Boeing Magazine Vol XXVIII-No.1: January/February 1958.
Boeing Magazine Vol XXVIII-No.2: March/April 1958.
Boeing Magazine Vol XXVIII-No.3: May/June 1958.
Boeing Magazine Vol XXVIII-No.4: July 1958.
Boeing Magazine Vol XXVIII-No.5: August 1958.
Boeing Magazine Vol XXVIII-No.6: September 1958.
Boeing Magazine Vol XXVIII-No.7: October 1958.
Boeing Magazine Vol XXVIII-No.8: November 1958.
Boeing Magazine Vol XXVIII-No.9: December 1958.
Boeing Magazine Vol XXVIX-No.1: January 1959.
Boeing Magazine Vol XXVIX-No.2: February 1959.
Boeing Magazine Vol XXVIX-No.3: March 1959.
Boeing Magazine Vol XXVIX-No.4: April 1959.
Boeing Magazine Vol XXVIX-No.5: May 1959.
Boeing Magazine Vol XXVIX-No.6: June 1959.
Boeing Magazine Vol XXVIX-No.7: July 1959.

Boeing Magazine Vol XXVIX-No.8: August 1959
Boeing Magazine Vol XXVIX-No.9: September 1959
Boeing Magazine Vol XXVIX-No.10: October 1959
Boeing Magazine Vol XXVIX-No.11: November 1959
Boeing Magazine Vol XXVIX-No.12: December 1959
Boeing Magazine *Vol XXX-No.1*: January 1960.
Boeing Magazine *Vol XXX-No.2*: February 1960.
Boeing Magazine *Vol XXX-No.3*: March 1960.
Boeing Magazine *Vol XXX-No.4*: April 1960.
Boeing Magazine *Vol XXX-No.5*: May 1960.
Boeing Magazine: *Vol XXXII-No. 1:* January 1962.
Boeing Magazine: *Vol XXXII-No. 2:* February 1962
Boeing Magazine: *Vol XXXII-No. 3:* March 1962.
Boeing Magazine: *Vol XXXII-No. 4:*April 1962.
Boeing Magazine: *Vol XXXII-No. 5:* May 1962.
Boeing Magazine: *Vol XXXII-No. 6:* June 1962.
Boeing Magazine: *Vol XXXII-No. 7:* July 1962.
Boeing Magazine: *Vol XXXII-No. 8:* August 1962
Boeing Magazine: *Vol XXXII-No. 9:* September 1962.
Boeing Magazine: *Vol XXXII-No. 10:* October 1962.
Boeing Magazine: *Vol XXXII-No. 11:* November 1962.
Boeing Magazine: *Vol XXXII-No. 12:* December 1962.
Boeing Magazine: *Vol XXXIII-No.1:* January 1963.
Boeing Magazine: *Vol XXXIII- No.2:* February 1963.
Boeing Magazine: *Vol XXXIII-No.3:* March 1963.
Boeing Magazine: *Vol XXXIII-No. 4:* April 1963.
Boeing Magazine: *Vol XXXIII-No.5:* May 1963.
Boeing Magazine: *Vol XXXIII-No.6:* June 1963.
Boeing Magazine: *Vol XXXIII-No.7:*July 1963.
Boeing Magazine: *Vol XXXIII-No.8:* August 1963.
Boeing Magazine: *Vol XXXIII-No.9:* September 1963.
Boeing Magazine: *Vol XXXIII-No.10:* October 1963.
Boeing Magazine: *Vol XXXIII-No.11:* November 1963.
Boeing Magazine: *Vol XXXIII-No.12:* December 1963.
Boeing Magazine: *Vol XXXIV-No.1:* January 1964.
Boeing Magazine: *Vol XXXIV-No.2:* February 1964.
Boeing Magazine: *Vol XXXIV-No.3:*March 1964.
Boeing Magazine: *Vol XXXIV-No.5:*May 1964.
Boeing Magazine: *Vol XXXIV-No.6:*June 1964.
Boeing Magazine: *Vol XXXIV-No.7:*July 1964.
Boeing Magazine: *Vol XXXIV-No.8:*August 1964.
Boeing Magazine: *Vol XXXIV-No.9:*September1964.
Boeing Magazine: *Vol XXXIV-No.10:* October1964.
Boeing Magazine: *Vol XXXIV-No.11:*November 1964.
Boeing Magazine: *Vol XXXIV-No.12:*December 1964.
Boeing Magazine: *Vol XXXV-No.1:* January 1965.
Boeing Magazine: *Vol XXXV-No.2:* February 1965.
Boeing Magazine: *Vol XXXV-No.3:*March 1965.
Boeing Magazine: *Vol XXXV-No.5:*May 1965.
Boeing Magazine: *Vol XXXV-No.6:*June 1965.
*Boeing Magazine: Vol XXXV-No.7:*July 1965.
*Boeing Magazine: Vol XXXV-No.8:*August 1965.
*Boeing Magazine: Vol XXXV-No.9:*September1965.
Boeing Magazine: Vol XXXV-No.10: October1965.
*Boeing Magazine: Vol XXXV-No.11:*November 1965.
*Boeing Magazine: Vol XXXV-No.12:*December 1965.
Bowers, Peter M. *Boeing Aircraft since 1916*. Putnam
    Aeronautical Books, 1989 London. ISBN 0-85177-804-
    6.
Bradley, Catherine. *'Boeing 707 Super Profile'*. Haynes
    Publishing, Yeovil, Somerset UK: 1983. ISBN 0-85429-
    356-6.
Breffort, Dominique. *Boeing 707, KC-135 and Civilian and
    Military Versions*. Paris: Histoire & Collections, 2008.
    ISBN 978-2-35250-075-9.
Bright, Charles *'VII - The Heartbreak Market: Airliners'*.

The Jet Makers: The Aerospace Industry from 1945-
    1972. Lawrence, Kansas: University Press of Kansas.
    ISBN 978-0700601721. (January 1986).
Caidin, Martin. *Boeing 707*. New York: Bantam Books,
    1959.
Cearley, George Walker. *Boeing 707 & 720: A Pictorial
    History*. Dallas, TX: G.W. Cearley Jr, 1993. No ISBN.
Cook, William H. *Road to the 707: The Inside Story of
    Designing the 707*. Bellevue, WA: TYC Publishing
    Company, 1991. ISBN 0-9629605-0-0.
Curtin, Neal P. Testimony Before the Subcommittee on
    Projection Forces, Committee on Armed Services, House
    of Representatives; MILITARY AIRCRAFT:
    Information on Air Force Aerial Refueling Tankers
    (Report). General Accounting Office. (June 24, 2003).
Donald, David. *'Boeing Model 717 (C/KC-135
    Stratoliner/Stratotanker).' The Complete Encyclopedia of
    World Aircraft*. Barnes & Noble Books, 1997. ISBN 0-
    7607-0592-5.
FAA Type Certificate Data Sheet
    http://rgl.faa.gov/Regulatory_and_Guidance_Library/rg
    MakeModel.nsf/0/8b6ebaa7513ba29a852567240060420
    c/$FILE/4a21.PDF
Federal Aviation Administration issued Supplemental Type
    Certificate SA2699NM to SHANNON engineering
    March 6, 1985.
Finlan, Alastair. *The Royal Navy in the Falklands Conflict
    and the Gulf War: Culture and Strategy* (British Politics
    and Society). London: Rutelage, 2004. ISBN 978-0-
    7146-8569-4.
Francillon, René. *Boeing 707: Pioneer Jetliner*. Shrewsbury,
    Shropshire, UK: Motor Books International, 1999. ISBN
    0-7603-0675-3.
Freeman, Roger. *'The Strategic Bomber'* Macdonalnds and
    Janes, London 1975
Gilmore, Gerry J. 'Air Force Awards Tanker Contract to
    Northrop Grumman'. American Forces Press Service.
    (February 29, 2008).
Gunston, Bill. 'Diamond Flight. British Midland 1938-1988.'
    Henry Melland, London 1989.
Haenggi, Michael *Boeing Widebodies*. Saint Paul,
    Minnesota: Zenith Press. ISBN 0-7603-0842-X. (2003).
Hebert, Adam J. *'When Aircraft Get Old'*. Air Force
    Magazine. Arlington, Virginia: Air Force Association.
    (January 2003).
Hopkins, III, Robert S. Boeing KC-135 Stratotanker: More
    Than Just a Tanker. Leicester, England: Midland
    Publishing Limited. ISBN 1-85780-069-9. (1997).
*HQ USSTRATCOM/CSH History of the United States
    Strategic Air Command, June 1, 1992 — October 1,
    2002* (Report). United States Strategic Command.
    (January 2004).
Johnston, A.M., Tex Johnston: *Jet-Age Test Pilot*,
    Smithsonian Books, December 2000, p. 247. ISBN 978-
    1-56098-931-8.
Lloyd, Alwyn T. *Boeing 707 & AWACS in Detail and Scale*.
    Falbrook, CA: Aero Publishers, 1987. ISBN 0-8306-
    8533-2.
Lombardi, Michael *'Historical Perspective, Start of a Proud
    Mission' Boeing Frontiers*. Chicago, Illinois: Boeing.
    (July 2006).
May, Mike *'Gas Stations in the Sky'*. Invention &
    Technology. American Heritage Society. (Spring 2004).
MILITARY AIRCRAFT: DOD Needs to Determine its
    Aerial Refueling Aircraft Requirements (Report). US
    General Accounting Office. June 4, 2004.

Air Force reservists help the 97th Air Mobility Wing train crew members on KC-135 Stratotankers (above) and C-17 Globemasters (below). An Air Force Reserve Command associate unit is slated to stand up at Altus Air Force Base, Okla., in 2010. (U.S. Air Force photo/Airman 1st Class Marianne E. Lane)

Miller, Kent; Putrich, Gayle S.; Tran, Pierre 'Tanker Contract Decision Announced'. Army Times. Springfield, Virginia. (February 29, 2008).

Opall-Rome, Barbara 'Israelis Slam US-Hyped Arms Package'. Defense News. Gannett Government Media Corporation. (29 April 2013).

Pellerin, Cheryl 'Hagel, Yaalon Finalize New Israel Military Capabilities'. American Forces Press Service. Pentagon. (22 April 2013).

Pither, Tony. *The Boeing 707, 720 and C-135*. Tonbridge, Kent, UK: Air-Britain (Historians) Ltd., 1998. ISBN 0-85130-236-X.

Price, Alfred. The Boeing 707. Leatherhead, Surrey, UK: Profile Publications, 1967.

Proctor, Jon (2001). Boeing 720. Miami, FL: World Transport Press. ISBN 1-892437-03-1.

Proctor, Jon; Mike Machat; Craig Kodera (2010). From Props to Jets: Commercial Aviation's Transition to the Jet Age 1952–1962. North Branch, MN: Specialty Press. ISBN 978-1-58007-146-8.

Proctor, Jon. Boeing 720. Miami, FL: World Transport Press, 2001. ISBN 1-892437-03-1.

Reed, John (February 25, 2010). 'USAF Sets KC-X First Flight, IOC Dates'. Defense News. Springfield, Virginia.

Riley, Charles 'Air Force awards Boeing $35 billion contract'. CNN. (24 February 2011).

Ruffin, Steven A. *Aviation's Most Wanted: The Top 10 book of Winged Wonders, Lucky Landings and Other Aerial Oddities*. Washington D.C.: Potomac Books. p. 320. ISBN 1574886746. (2005)

Rummel, Robert W. *'Howard Hughes and TWA'*.

Smithsonian Aviation Series, Washington, DC. 1991.

Schiff, Barry J. *The Boeing 707*. Blue Ridge Summit, PA: Tab Books, 1982, First edition 1967. ISBN 0-8168-5653-2.

Smallpeice, Sir Basil. *'Of Comets and Kings'*. Airlife Publishing, London. 1981.

Smith Jr, Myron J. *'The Airline Encyclopedia 1909-2000 Vol. 1'*. Scarecrow Press Inc. (2002)

Smith Jr, Myron J. *'The Airline Encyclopedia 1909-2000 Vol. 2'*. Scarecrow Press Inc. (2002)

Smith Jr, Myron J. *'The Airline Encyclopedia 1909-2000 Vol. 3'*. Scarecrow Press Inc. (2002)

Smith, Paul Raymond. *Boeing 707 – Airline Markings No. 3*. Shrewsbury, Shropshire, UK: Swan Hill Press, 1993. ISBN 1-85310-087-0.

Stachiw, Anthony L. and Andrew Tattersall. *Boeing CC137 (Boeing 347C) in Canadian Service*. St. Catherines, ON: Vanwell Publishing Ltd., 2004. ISBN 1-55125-079-9.

Tirpak, John A. (February 2004). *'Tanker Twilight Zone'*. Air Force Magazine. Arlington, Virginia: Air Force Association. Archived from the original on February 6, 2004. Retrieved October 23, 2014.

Whittle, John A. *The Boeing 707 and 720*. Tonbridge, Kent: Air Britain (Historians), 1972. ISBN 0-85130-025-1.

Wilson, Stewart. *Airliners of the World*. Fyshwick, Australia: Aerospace Publications, 1999. ISBN 1-875671-44-7.

Wilson, Stewart. *Boeing 707, Douglas DC-8, and Vickers VC-10*. Fyshwick, Australia: Aerospace Publications, 1998. ISBN 1-875671-36-6.

Winchester, Jim. *Boeing 707*. Shrewsbury, Shropshire, UK: Airlife, 2002. ISBN 1-84037-311-3.

Index

A KC-135 Stratotanker from Fairchild AFB, Wash., refuels a C-5 Galaxy from Travis Air Force Base, California, during a refueling mission 13 March 2014. The flight was an all-female mission held to honour and commemorate Women's History Month. (US Air Force photo by Staff Sgt. Veronica Montes)

A B-1B Lancer assigned to the 9th Expeditionary Bomb Squadron, deployed to Andersen Air Force Base, Guam, receives fuel from a KC-135 Stratotanker over the Pacific Ocean 10 March 2017. The B-1B's are deployed to Andersen AFB as part of U.S. Pacific Command's continuous bomber presence operations. This forward deployed presence demonstrates continuing U.S. commitment to stability and security in the Indo-Asia-Pacific region. (U.S. Air Force photo/ Airman 1st Class Christopher F. Quail)

Airmen from the 92nd Aircraft Maintenance Squadron work together to deice a KC-135 Stratotanker 29 January 2014, at Fairchild Air Force Base, Wash. Aircraft deicing is a process in which liquid solutions are sprayed onto an aircraft during the winter to both defrost and prevent future precipitation from freezing. Snow and ice on the wings and rear tail component change their shape and disrupt the airflow making it difficult to fly and diminishes fuel economy. (U.S. Air Force photo/Staff Sgt. Alexandre Montes)

A KC-135 Stratotanker connects with a B-52H Stratofortress from Minot Air Force Base, N.D., during an aerial refueling mission over the Alaskan coastline as part of exercise Amalgam Dart 15-28 May 2015. The annual North American Aerospace Defense Command exercise afforded American and Canadian forces field training aimed at improving NORAD's operational capability in a binational environment. The exercise spanned two forward operating locations in Canada's Northwest Territories, two US Air Force bases in Alaska, and a mobile radar site in Resolute, Nunavut, as well as the sky over much of NORAD's area of responsibility. (U.S. Air Force photo/Staff Sgt. Benjamin W. Stratton)

A Luftwaffe Tornado disconnects from the boom of a KC-135 Stratotanker 14 October 2014, over Germany. (US Air Force photo/Airman 1st Class Dillon Johnston)

A B-2 Spirit moves into position for refueling from a KC-135 Stratotanker over the Pacific Ocean on Tuesday, 30 May 2006. The B-2 is from the 509th Bomb Wing at Whiteman Air Force Base, Mo., and the KC-135 is from the Pennsylvania Air National Guard's 171st Air Refueling Wing at the Pittsburgh International Airport. The bomber is part of Pacific Command's continuous bomber presence in the Asia-Pacific region. (U.S. Air Force photo/Staff Sgt. Bennie J. Davis III)

Maj. Christopher Marriott and Capt. Alexandra Trana, both KC-135 Stratotanker pilots from the 909th Air Refueling Squadron, taxi behind several KC-135s during an elephant walk as part of the Forceful Tiger exercise on Kadena Air Base, Japan, 1 April 2015. During the aerial exercise, the Stratotankers delivered 800,000 pounds of fuel to approximately 50 aircraft. (U.S. Air Force photo/Staff Sgt. Maeson L. Elleman)

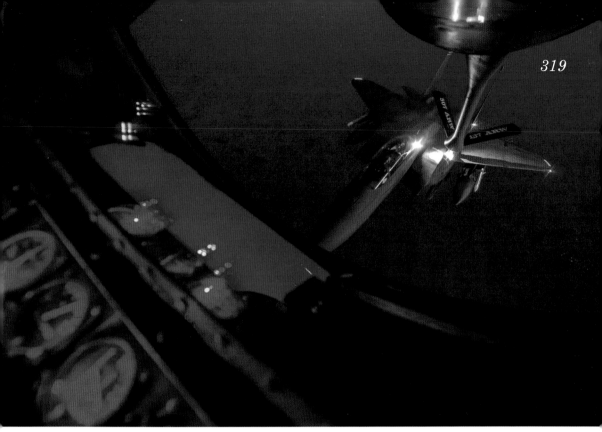

An F-15E Strike Eagle receives fuel from a KC-135 Stratotanker 23 September 2014, over northern Iraq after conducting airstrikes in Syria. These aircraft were part of a large coalition strike package that was the first to strike Islamic State of Iraq and the Levant targets in Syria. (US Air Force photo/Senior Airman Matthew Bruch)

Finished with engines! Senior Airman Clarissa Banks, a 340th Aircraft Maintenance Unit crew chief, controls the movement of a KC-135 Stratotanker on Al Udeid Air Base, Qatar, 8 April 2015. Al Udeid is a strategic coalition air base in Qatar that supports over 90 combat and support aircraft and houses more than 5,000 military personnel. (U.S. Air Force photo/Senior Airman James Richardson)